A FORTRESS IN BROOKLYN

A FORTRESS
IN BROOKLYN

Race, Real Estate, and the Making of

Hasidic Williamsburg

NATHANIEL DEUTSCH
AND MICHAEL CASPER

Yale

UNIVERSITY PRESS

New Haven and London

Published with assistance from the Louis Stern Memorial Fund.

Yale University Press books may be purchased in quantity for
educational, business, or promotional use. For information,
please e-mail sales.press@yale.edu (U.S. office) or sales@yaleup.
co.uk (U.K. office).

Designed by Sonia L. Shannon

Set in Janson type by IDS Infotech Ltd.
Printed in the United States of America.

ISBN 978-0-300-23109-0 (hardcover : alk. paper)
Library of Congress Control Number: 2020947091
A catalogue record for this book is available from the British
Library.

This paper meets the requirements of ANSI/NISO Z39.48-1992
(Permanence of Paper).

10 9 8 7 6 5 4 3 2 1

In memory of Moshe Yida Leibowitz

I want a fortress to remain here.

—THE SATMAR REBBE, YOEL TEITELBAUM

Contents

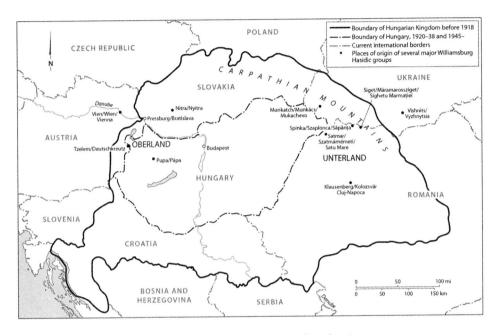

Greater Hungary (Map by Bill Nelson)

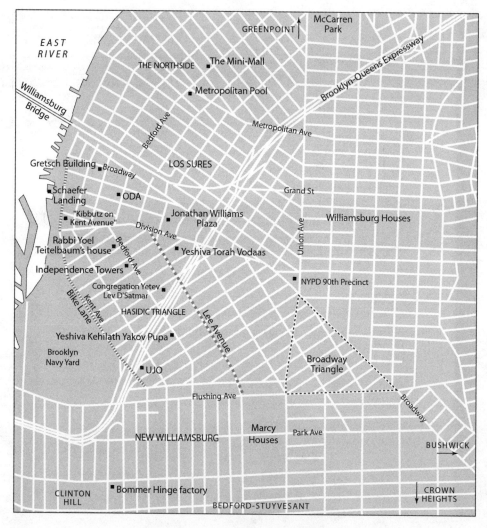

Hasidic Williamsburg (Map by Bill Nelson)

A FORTRESS IN BROOKLYN

Introduction

An American Epic

T HE STREETS OF WILLIAMSBURG were not paved with gold, as early waves of immigrants had dreamed, nor did they contaminate those who walked upon them, as the Hasidim had feared before they arrived as refugees from war-torn Europe. Instead, their names evoked a different mythology, one more redolent of that other place called Williamsburg, located a world away in Virginia rather than Brooklyn. George Taylor, James Wilson, Caesar Rodney, Edward Rutledge, John Penn, William Hooper, and more— all signers of the Declaration of Independence—were the men whose names formed the street map of South Williamsburg. When these members of the Second Continental Congress met in 1776, they could never have imagined that a community of Yiddish-speaking Hasidic Jews from the hinterlands of eastern Europe would one day turn the streets honoring them into their own "Jerusalem of America." Or that these Hasidim would share the same streets, as well as a public housing project named after the Declaration of Independence, with one of the largest Puerto Rican communities in New York City. Members of these two communities, as well as other working-class residents, weathered the city's infamous decline only to grapple later with the dramatic changes wrought by yet another wave of newcomers, who would transform Williamsburg into a global symbol of gentrification. This book explores how a neighborhood named in honor of Jonathan Williams, the grandnephew of Benjamin Franklin who first surveyed its territory in the early 1800s, became the site for a uniquely American epic of religion, race, class, and, above all, reinvention.

Like the Puritans who founded New England three hundred years earlier, the Hungarian Hasidim who settled in Williamsburg in the 1940s were members of pietistic religious communities whose charismatic leaders railed against the corruption of the world and, especially, against their insufficiently pious co-religionists. The goal of both was to create biblically grounded utopian settlements that would serve to inspire—and chasten—those around them. In 1630, while en route to North America from England, the Puritan leader John Winthrop delivered a now-famous sermon about what he considered to be the divinely ordained role of the Massachusetts Bay Colony: "We shall find that the God of Israel is among us, when ten of us shall be able to resist a thousand of our enemies. . . . For we must consider that we shall be as a city upon a hill. The eyes of all people are upon us."[1] More than three centuries later, in a working-class corner of Brooklyn far removed from the idyll of colonial New England, Rabbi Yoel Teitelbaum, one of the founding fathers of Hasidic Williamsburg, sought to create a holy community that would serve as a model for the rest of the Jewish world and, perhaps, beyond. Looking back on the early days of Hasidic settlement in Williamsburg, Sender Deutsch, one of Teitelbaum's chief lieutenants, recalled: "Our rabbi emphasized that the mission to repair the entire country was a difficult task but that it was our duty to try by all measures to protect our camp. . . . And so the first matter at hand was to guard our own vineyard and then the Holy One would help us to influence near and far."[2]

In the post–World War II era, when liberal Jews in the United States were reinventing the kabbalistic concept *tikkun* to mean the "repair of the world" through social justice, civil rights, environmental activism, and so on, Hasidim in Williamsburg employed the same term in a dramatically different sense: to repair their own small corner of Brooklyn and make it a "vineyard," free from the corrupting influences of the outside world, albeit one that would ideally spur a much wider spiritual renaissance. They would accomplish this not by stressing what they had in common with their fellow Americans, or even their fellow Jews, but by doubling down on their differences—large and, especially, small. As David, a non-Hasidic employee of a large Hasidic-run real estate firm in Brooklyn, put it to us when describing his co-workers, "They are like the Puritans in New England. Some [Puritans] said you can't eat nuts on Sunday, others said you can't eat apples on Sunday, and that's why people went and founded Rhode Island."[3]

From the late 1940s on, in Williamsburg, elsewhere in Brooklyn, and eventually in satellite communities in upstate New York and New Jersey, Hasidic groups went on to found their own versions of Rhode Island, where they venerated their religious leaders, maintained distinctive customs, and sometimes came into conflict with one another. From the perspective of Hasidic history, this efflorescence represents the second major expansion of the movement, following its earlier spread across the breadth of eastern Europe, and is part of the globalization of Hasidism that took place in the wake of the Holocaust, with other large communities now located in Los Angeles, Montreal, Buenos Aires, London, Antwerp, and Melbourne as well as Israel, where Hasidic communities have existed since the eighteenth century. From the perspective of American Jewish history, the revolution that began in Williamsburg represents a key turning point whose historical impacts have yet to be fully documented or understood and whose potentially enormous implications for the future of Jews in the United States are only beginning to be appreciated.[4]

A Counter-History of American Jewry

Histories of Jews in the United States have tended to focus on the waves of eastern European immigrants who settled in poor urban neighborhoods at the turn of the twentieth century before moving on to more middle-class areas of the city and, eventually, the suburbs beyond. Without a doubt, the classic work of this genre was *World of Our Fathers*, published by Irving Howe in 1976.[5] Howe told the story of largely working-class Jews from eastern Europe, many of whom arrived in New York City with a dual passion for socialist politics and secular Yiddish culture that they enthusiastically transplanted to the proverbial *goldene medine* ("golden land") of America. Though some of these Jews had grown up in Hasidic families in the old country, most had long since abandoned meticulous observance of the commandments and devotion to a rebbe, even if the synagogues they established upon arrival—and then, typically, chose not to attend except for a few occasions a year—remained Orthodox. By World War II, most of the children of these immigrants had embarked on a path of Americanization that would create a gulf between them and the now-lost world of their immigrant fathers and mothers. Like the Great Migration of African Americans from the rural South to northern cities, the subject of *World of Our Fathers* constituted one of the iconic American historical narratives of the twentieth century, and it was not surprising when Howe's book received the National Book Award in 1977.

Yet in the late 1940s and 1950s, at precisely the moment when so many Jews in New York City and elsewhere were beginning their exodus to the suburbs, another, much less storied wave of Jewish immigrants arrived in Brooklyn. In direct contrast with their more secularized predecessors, most of the Jewish immigrants who settled in Brooklyn neighborhoods such as Williamsburg, Borough Park, and Crown Heights still belonged to Hasidic groups that had refused to come to the United States before the war because they believed that "in America even the water is not kosher, and the air can defile a religious man."[6] Rather than the largely secular Jewish "world of our fathers," this postwar wave of Hasidic immigrants went on to establish religious enclaves in Brooklyn that by the end of the twentieth century had become by far the fastest-growing segment of the Jewish population in New York City, and the vanguard of a much broader demographic trend that promises to radically transform the face of American Jewry by the end of the twenty-first century.

Of all the neighborhoods that became home to large numbers of Hasidim in the postwar period, Williamsburg achieved iconic status in the popular imagination as the Hasidic enclave par excellence. This identification occurred because of the neighborhood's proximity to Manhattan and the numerous profiles of the neighborhood that began to appear as early as the 1950s in *Life*, *Time*, and *Commentary* magazines as well as, most famously, in Chaim Potok's best-selling novel *The Chosen*, from 1967. Perhaps most importantly, Williamsburg's Hasidic residents pursued a "life apart," with unparalleled rigor, thereby transforming the community into a seemingly impenetrable "island in the city"—as Israel Rubin called the enclave in a 1972 book—located just across the East River from the nation's financial and media capital.[7] In short, the Hasidim of Williamsburg were hard-core even by the standards of the broader Hasidic movement.[8]

It was far from given that Hasidim would settle in America at all, let alone establish enclaves in Brooklyn—Hasidic Williamsburg foremost among them. The Hasidic movement was founded in the eighteenth century by the Baal Shem Tov, a Jewish holy man who wandered the Carpathian borderlands between Poland and the Ottoman Empire before settling in the town of Medzibozh (now in western Ukraine), where he attracted a circle of disciples.[9] Over time, the first few generations of Hasidic holy men, or *tsadikkim*, gave way to dynasties whose leaders, known by the title "Rebbe," inherited their positions and were associated with the towns where they held court. By the nineteenth century, the Hasidic movement had spread among Jews throughout eastern Europe, including Transylvania and Maramureş, those remote parts of Hungary—now Romania—where most of the Hasidim who eventually settled in Williamsburg originated.

In striking contrast with their fellow eastern European Jews, who immigrated by the millions between 1880 and the passage of the Immigration Act of 1924, most Hasidim—or "pious ones," in Hebrew—adamantly refused to come to the United States, condemning it as a *treyfene medine*, an impure land so contaminating that it would spiritually destroy those who set foot on its soil, transforming even the most religious Jews into secular Americans. For this reason, most Hasidim refused to leave Europe before the Holocaust, and were subsequently murdered in large numbers. Those who survived the ghettos, camps, and death marches became refugees or, as they called themselves in a phrase taken from the biblical book of Ezra, the "surviving remnant."

After the war, unable or unwilling to return to their homes, many Hasidic survivors instead decided to immigrate to the United States, with those from Hungary and Romania settling in Williamsburg in particular. What happened next represented the first in the series of extraordinary reversals and reinventions that mark the history of Hasidic Williamsburg. Rabbi Yoel Teitelbaum, the leader of Satmar, which would become the largest and, ultimately, the most politically and economically powerful of the neighborhood's Hasidic groups, radically revised his view of America. Rather than denouncing it as a land that pious Jews had to avoid at all costs, Teitelbaum reimagined America as the very center of an epic theological drama that would lead to the arrival of the messiah and the redemption of the Jewish people, a redemption that would begin on American soil before culminating in the Land of Israel. Teitelbaum and, perhaps even more importantly, his followers now believed that it was his personal destiny to settle in America following the catastrophe of the Holocaust and, once there, to establish a holy "camp in the desert" (Numbers 10:31) in Williamsburg that would elevate the country's lowly spiritual level, turning it from a "land that devours its inhabitants" (Numbers 13:32) into a *malkhus shel hesed*, or "kingdom of grace."

The messianic redemption has yet to arrive—at least as of this writing. But in the following decades, Williamsburg became the site of an amazing renaissance that not only transformed the neighborhood itself, but also served as the launching ground for a wider spiritual and social "revolution," as an Israeli newspaper put it in the 1950s, whose impact continues to be felt far beyond its borders.[10] At the center of this revolution was Satmar, which went from being a relatively small, newly established Hasidic court before the Holocaust to becoming by far the largest Hasidic group in the world.[11] Satmar succeeded because of a potent—though, at times, seemingly paradoxical—commitment to extreme ideological purity, on one hand, and a remarkably flexible pragmatism on the other. Maintaining this dynamic enabled the famously conservative Satmar community to "change without changing," as one member put it to us; to adopt sometimes significant innovations in a wide variety of areas, including technology, economics, housing, politics, and even religious practice, without undermining its core identity as a holy community modeled on earlier generations of pious Jews, or what Teitelbaum liked to call Yisroel Saba ("Grandfather Israel").

The extreme insularity of the Hasidic enclave in Williamsburg, combined with the political savvy of its leaders, inspired some observers to label it a kind of state within a state or a "kingdom," an appellation that was also embraced by some within Satmar.[12] Yet Yoel Teitelbaum insisted that members of his community needed to be loyal to their newly adopted country.[13] As he put it in a 1961 letter: "Being faithful to the government of one's country of residence is one of the basic principles of Jewish religion."[14] The result was a distinctly Hasidic version of citizenship that combined an enthusiastic embrace of American values regarding the importance of voting, civic engagement, and freedom of religion with a commitment to Hasidic values regarding self-segregation, cultural distinctiveness, and communal unity that often translated politically into bloc voting.

At a time when conformity of all kinds was expected in American society, Hasidim in Williamsburg challenged the status quo in ways large and small. In the 1950s, precisely when most American Jews were abandoning Yiddish, Satmar Hasidim in Williamsburg purchased *Der Yid* (The Jew), and eventually transformed it into the most widely read Yiddish newspaper in the world. They insisted on teaching the language to their children in the network of private schools they quickly established in Williamsburg and spoke it both at home and, most shockingly for the time, in the streets of the neighborhood. Hasidic men and women wore clothes, head coverings, and hairstyles that distinguished them not only from non-Jews but also from their own co-religionists, including those American Jews who identified as Orthodox yet embraced contemporary fashions. When the postwar economic boom helped turn consumerism into a kind of religion in the United States, the Satmar Rebbe declared a war on luxury. At the height of the golden age of television, when the new technology helped create a common national culture that bridged regional differences and introduced viewers to a host of new ideas and, just as importantly, consumer goods, Hasidic leaders in Williamsburg banned the device. In a further attempt to prevent cultural assimilation, they prohibited Hasidic schoolchildren from playing or watching baseball in the late 1940s and 1950s, when the local Brooklyn Dodgers of Jackie Robinson and, for a few years, a young Jewish pitcher named Sandy Koufax, later known as the "left hand of God," were at the height of their glory.

Of all the ways that Williamsburg's Hasidim diverged from the American Jewish mainstream, however, the one that generated the most tension with their fellow Jews was undoubtedly their stance on Zionism. Yoel Teitelbaum and his followers excoriated the Zionist movement as a form of idol worship that sought to replace religious Judaism with secular nationalism. In their eyes, Zionists were guilty of seeking to establish a Jewish state in the Land of Israel by human means instead of waiting for the arrival of the messiah to usher in the final redemption. Whereas most American Jews either enthusiastically supported the creation of the state of Israel in 1948 or at least came to accept its existence, Yoel Teitelbaum published two book-length jeremiads against Zionism, took out ads against Israel in the *New York Times*, and encouraged his followers to hold anti-Zionist demonstrations in front of the White House. Some of his Hasidim went even further by engaging in violent confrontations with members of other Hasidic groups who failed to demonstrate sufficient opposition to Israel. That these actions made Satmar anathema was actually welcomed by its leaders, who viewed the vast majority of American Jews as having abandoned the path of "Torah-true Judaism" in favor of false idols.[15] Within the community's Manichean worldview, opposition from other Jews confirmed that Satmar was the legitimate "righteous remnant" and that its Brooklyn neighborhood, rather than the state of Israel, was the true center of world Jewry.[16] Indeed, Teitelbaum initiated his own "ingathering of the exiles," bringing Jews from Hungary, Romania, Morocco, Yemen, and elsewhere to Williamsburg, rather than to the state of Israel, where he feared they would be transformed into secular Israelis.[17]

What was happening in Williamsburg was unprecedented in American Jewish history. To many casual observers, the Hasidic community was as exotic and anachronistic as an uncontacted tribe in the Amazon, its members, in the words of *Life* magazine, "carryovers from an archaic way of life."[18] For contemporary Jewish critics, by contrast, Hasidim were not merely a benign curiosity: they were the return of the repressed. As an Orthodox rabbi observed to the *New York Times*, "Nothing is so revolting to the third-generation American Jew as the sight of his Hasidic brethren on the street. With their Yiddish accents and East European clothing . . . they remind him of something he had a nose job to forget."[19] Yet Hasidic Williamsburg represented something very different for the small and embattled Orthodox Jewish community in the United States during the 1950s—hope that at least some American Jews would resist the temptation to assimilate and instead establish in Brooklyn what had been destroyed in Vilna, Warsaw, and many other European Jewish centers during the Holocaust. "Thanks to its specific way of life, Williamsburg has become a place of Torah," Rabbi Simcha Elberg, a prominent Orthodox activist, wrote in 1954. "America has had Torah for a long time but it has not had a place of Torah."[20]

In the following decades, as more and more young Jews in particular became dissatisfied with the sterile Judaism of the suburbs, a small number decided to become Hasidim. Many more would find inspiration in Hasidism as they searched for an authentically Jewish source of spirituality, helping create the Jewish Renewal movement in the 1960s and 1970s.[21] These same Jews continued to have little or no contact with flesh-and-blood Hasidim. Indeed, the vast majority of American Jews, including those who found some spiritual inspiration in Hasidism, differed dramatically from the separatist, religiously conservative, and anti-Zionist Hasidic community of Williamsburg. And all the while, this "island in the city," and the other enclaves in and around Brooklyn that formed a kind of Hasidic archipelago, continued to grow.

A New York Story

Hasidim steadfastly remained in Williamsburg when other Jews and white ethnics were abandoning it and the rest of the city by the millions. Between 1957 and 1970, the Jewish population of New York City declined by more than 40 percent, or nearly 900,000 people.[22] Had the Hasidim of Williamsburg joined their fellow Jews in this mass exodus, the history of Brooklyn and New York City as a whole would have been dramatically different. Instead, how Hasidic Williamsburg survived and even thrived in a Brooklyn neighborhood that became notorious for poverty, crime, and environmental degradation, at a time when the city's overall decline was commonly depicted in apocalyptic terms, is one of the great New York stories of the past century.

To remain in Williamsburg, Hasidim systematically and stubbornly engaged in behaviors that went against the prevailing practices of both Jewish and white residents of the city, but that were pragmatically suited to conditions in what was then one of Brooklyn's poorest neighborhoods. Indeed, it would be hard to imagine a group of people more suited to face the challenges of New York City from the 1960s through the 1980s than the Hungarian Hasidim who settled in Williamsburg. Already toughened by their experiences in ghettos and concentration camps, united by a common sense of purpose, and guided by politically sophisticated leaders, the neighborhood's Hasidim were more than ready to survive whatever came their way, including the divestment of city services from poor areas and the subsequent struggle over remaining resources that characterized New York in this period.

At a time when whites were leaving public housing in droves because it had become synonymous with racialized poverty, Hasidim moved heaven and earth to get units in newly built high-rise projects in Williamsburg, where they lived alongside Puerto Rican and African American residents. After the federal government launched its Great Society poverty programs, Hasidim in Williamsburg, unlike other Jews or white ethnics in the city, immediately and successfully lobbied to be included, transforming their enclave into one of the largest recipients of certain kinds of federal and state aid to the poor in New York. This was made possible because, as with African American and Puerto Rican communities during the same period, a robust activist culture developed in Hasidic Williamsburg. Ultimately, some of these Hasidic activists succeeded in having Hasidim—but not other Jews—added to an official list of "disadvantaged minority groups" that were eligible for federal assistance programs.[23]

As crime rates skyrocketed in New York City, and as Williamsburg became the neighborhood with the largest concentration of street gangs in Brooklyn, Hasidim bucked long-standing stereotypes regarding Jewish passivity and so forcefully—at times, violently—responded to threats that they were accused of vigilantism and of acting like a gang in their own right. In a city that was home to competing racial- and ethnic-pride organizations such as the Black Panthers, the Young Lords, the Italian-American Civil Rights League, and the Jewish Defense League, Williamsburg's Hasidim proudly positioned themselves—sometimes explicitly over and against these other groups—as representing the "Torah true" Jews of New York. And when city leaders decided to place an enormous waste incinerator plant on the Williamsburg waterfront, members of the local Hasidic community joined forces with the same Hispanic and African American residents whom they regularly fought over housing and crime to protest and ultimately defeat the plan, in a stunning example of grassroots activism and local alliance building.

Hasidim shared something else with blacks and Hispanics in Williamsburg: they were frequently dismissed by critics—including other Jews—as belonging to the "undeserving poor" and accused of abusing governmental aid programs, because their large number of children and lack of secular education contributed to high poverty rates within the community.[24] In all these ways and more, Hasidim in Williamsburg came to resemble their Hispanic and African American neighbors far more than their fellow Jews in the suburbs.[25] Williamsburg's Hasidim were among the only Jews in the country who retained the urban sensibility and swagger that had characterized Jews since the dawn of the modern period, when cities as disparate as Oran in Algeria, Baghdad in Iraq, Salonika in Greece, Budapest in Hungary, Warsaw in Poland, and New York became home to large and dynamic Jewish populations.

Some have argued that Jews of European origin in the United States underwent a racial reclassification in the post–World War II period, a phenomenon that Karen Brodkin has called "how Jews became white folks."[26] Whether this transformation was ever complete for American Jews in general remains debated, but the degree to which Hasidim in Williamsburg "became white folks" is even more complicated. During the 1960s and 1970s, Hasidim in Williamsburg rejected key socioeconomic markers typically associated with whiteness—unlike most Jews in the United States—and instead moved into public housing, lived in the inner city alongside African Americans and Puerto Rican residents, and participated in government antipoverty programs that were almost universally identified with "disadvantaged minority" communities. Hasidic Jews were officially designated as nonwhite by the federal government, which included them in a Minority Business Development Agency program that excluded "Caucasians." Some of their neighbors also viewed Hasidim as racially ambiguous, including the rapper Jay-Z, who remarked in his memoir of growing up in the Marcy Projects across Flushing Avenue from Hasidic Williamsburg, "There are no white people in

Marcy Projects ... strictly blacks and Puerto Ricans, maybe some Dominicans, rough Arabs ... [and] pockets of Hasidim."[27]

In those decades, Hasidim in Williamsburg preferred to live among poor blacks and Puerto Ricans rather than among assimilated Jews, who "acted like goyim" and thereby confused the otherwise clear-cut taxonomic distinction that was supposed to exist between "the people of Israel" and the "the nations of the world." Indeed, to the degree that the racial difference between Hasidim and blacks and Puerto Ricans was seen as unbridgeable, this could only help reinforce the more fundamental difference between Jews and non-Jews. And insofar as the Hasidim in Williamsburg sought to separate themselves as much as possible from corrupting influences, this racial difference could be seen as beneficial rather than threatening to the well-being of the community.[28]

The divide between Hasidim, Puerto Ricans, and African Americans helped the Hasidim strengthen their community in Williamsburg even as the same divide encouraged other Jewish residents—along with white ethnics in general—to abandon the neighborhood in droves beginning in the 1950s. At the same time, the subsequent decades of living together in Williamsburg, including in the neighborhood's public housing projects, and even just remaining in New York when the city was seen as irrevocably in decline, meant that in certain important respects, including speech patterns and their relationship to space, Hasidim in Williamsburg came to resemble their Puerto Rican and black neighbors more than their fellow Jews in the suburbs.

Although Hasidim and other longtime residents of Williamsburg had much in common, they generally led parallel lives. Some worked together, served on community boards together, or interacted in other ways besides the battles over limited resources, street crime, and vigilantism that rocked the neighborhood over the years. But most of the time, they tried to stay out of one another's way. As Rabbi Bernard Weinberger, a longtime Orthodox activist in Williamsburg, put it in 1969, "I believe that Jews have succeeded in avoiding racial flare-ups simply because we have been uninvolved. We live side-by-side with Puerto Ricans and Blacks but, they can readily appreciate that Hasidic Jews are only interested in preserving their own life-style and institutions and are not in their way."[29] As in other working-class neighborhoods in New York City, most of Williamsburg's residents were members of discrete communities, each possessing its own sense of collective identity and history, religious institutions, and leaders, as well as an informal but critically important "map" of which blocks, playgrounds, buildings, and other local sites belonged to them, which belonged to other communities, and which were shared by everyone. And so things remained until the arrival of gentrification.

Gentrification

In addition to telling the remarkable story of how Hasidim thrived in their rough-and-tumble corner of Brooklyn in the decades following World War II, this is the first book to explore what happened next when gentrification jumped the East River and encountered in Williamsburg one of the most fiercely separatist, intensely religious, and politically savvy urban communities in the United States. It details the crucial role played by Hasidim in the gentrification of the neighborhood via their involvement in the burgeoning real estate industry, the significant effects of gentrification on the Hasidic community, and the organized efforts of some Hasidim to resist the upscaling of their neighborhood, even launching what they called "The War Against the Artists," which they likened to other catastrophes, including the Babylonian and Roman destructions of the First and Second Temples in Jerusalem, the Holocaust, and the 9/11 terrorist attacks on the World Trade Center buildings, which were located across the East River from Williamsburg.[30] This grassroots anti-gentrification movement, which singled out "artists" and the businesses that served them, was a harbinger of the kind of resistance that would later emerge in places such as the Bronx and Boyle Heights, Los Angeles.

The period before gentrification is commonly referred to as the decline of New York, but it was also an era of tremendous cultural vibrancy in which hip-hop, disco, salsa, and other art forms flowered in the city.[31] For its boosters, gentrification helped bring about New York's remarkable rebirth, while to critics, it was a key element in the "revenge" that elites took on the working class and the liberal state by reclaiming urban spaces for themselves.[32] The first wave of gentrifiers in Williamsburg consisted primarily of young, single white artists and musicians who were attracted by the neighborhood's low rents, available loft spaces, proximity to Manhattan, public transportation, and gritty authenticity. Arriving at the tail end of the punk rock movement, they constituted the bohemian vanguard of what Richard Florida has called the "creative class."[33] At least some had been driven out of SoHo and the East Village by the recent gentrification of those areas, and like the Jews of the Lower

East Side a century before, they had decided to make the quick trip over the Williamsburg Bridge in search of greener pastures.

By the late 1980s, real estate prices on the Manhattan side of the bridge had climbed significantly, while those on the Brooklyn side were undervalued relative to their potential levels.[34] This rent gap attracted the interest of investors and developers seeking to exploit the difference between current and future values; they provided financing for the broader infrastructural, social, and cultural shifts associated with gentrification. Indeed, as real estate prices rose dramatically on the North Side of Williamsburg in the 1990s, rent gaps were created in the adjoining areas of South Side, Greenpoint, East Williamsburg, and, ultimately, Bushwick, thereby driving gentrification in those neighborhoods as well. By then, the hipsters, as they were commonly called in Williamsburg, were themselves being displaced by more moneyed professionals, and the gentrification "frontier" shifted again.

Hasidim were both pioneers in residential and commercial real estate development in Williamsburg and victims of the rapidly rising housing costs that this development triggered. As a result of gentrification, some Hasidim became fabulously wealthy as developers, while others found blue-collar work alongside Latinos and African Americans in the construction trade and its adjunct businesses. Still others were forced to live in cramped apartments or to leave Williamsburg entirely because they could no longer afford to remain. Like their Puerto Rican neighbors in particular, Hasidim were decades-long residents of Williamsburg, but they were often rendered invisible in racial statistics for the neighborhood and lumped together with white residents, most of whom were newcomers in the early 2000s.

The gentrification of Williamsburg came at a critical time for the neighborhood's Hasidic community. By the 1990s, the Hasidic population of Williamsburg had grown from a few hundred families in the late 1940s to tens of thousands of people, and further growth was ensured by the community's extraordinarily high birthrate. At the same time, two of the main industries that had traditionally employed Hasidic residents were in steep decline. Hasidic involvement in the diamond trade took a hit because of a global glut of stones; the rise of new, far less expensive centers for diamond cutting and polishing; and changing retail habits, especially among younger people.[35] The garment industry also experienced a dramatic citywide decline, decreasing from 100,000 jobs in 1987 to 26,000 in 2012.[36] In Brooklyn alone, apparel- and textile-manufacturing jobs declined by 12.2 percent between 1993 and 1998.[37]

When gentrifiers first started moving into the neighborhood, Hasidim who owned property on the North Side of Williamsburg or on its waterfront were well positioned to transform their warehouses and factories into residential lofts and commercial spaces and to buy up undervalued properties throughout the area for future development. Local Hasidim soon became involved in all aspects of the booming construction and real estate industries, with wealthier ones providing investment capital; others serving as mortgage brokers, contractors, and builders; others selling building supplies; and still others working in the construction trades.[38] A key impact of gentrification on Hasidic Williamsburg, therefore, was to transform real estate from an important sector of the community's economy, as it had historically been for decades, into the most powerful engine for creating new wealth and jobs. That transformation also made the Hasidic community in Williamsburg particularly vulnerable to the ups and downs of the real estate market, something that became clear when the mortgage-industry bubble burst in 2008.[39] Yet the Great Recession also created many new opportunities for Hasidic investors and developers in heavily hit areas adjoining Williamsburg, where they would eventually expand the Hasidic enclave beyond its traditional southern border of Flushing Avenue into neighboring Bedford-Stuyvesant and Clinton Hill, thereby creating what came to be called "New Williamsburg."[40]

Within a few decades after the arrival of the first artists, no neighborhood in the United States or, arguably, the world, had become more identified with gentrification than Williamsburg. As the *Guardian* explained in 2010: "The neighbourhood . . . has been transformed from a sleepy, poor, residential area of Jewish, eastern European and Hispanic working-class immigrants to one where most denizens appear to have beards, piercings, lots of tattoos and belong to at least one band."[41] A few years later, the transformation was so complete that *Business Insider* could state matter-of-factly, "Williamsburg, Brooklyn is pretty much synonymous with 'gentrification.' "[42] Some Hasidic residents viewed the presence of thousands of hip and moneyed white people as posing a greater existential threat—particularly to younger members of their community—than the largely working-class Hispanic and African American residents of the neighborhood ever had. Others were ambivalent about the newcomers, and still others welcomed the opportunity to experiment with or even adopt a different lifestyle, especially one that seemed to represent a kind of upward mobility. Beyond the tremendous economic impact on Hasidic Williamsburg, therefore, gentrification affected the community culturally and, Hasidic critics bitterly lamented, spiritually. In turn, the presence of Hasidim, like the neighborhood's dwindling Latino population, helped make Williamsburg seem authentically urban and, consequently, even more appealing to many newcomers.[43]

Despite the obvious dynamism of Hasidic Williamsburg since the first Holocaust refugees arrived in the 1940s, the most enduring stereotype of the community has been that its members merely transplanted their way of life intact from the shtetls of eastern Europe to the streets of Brooklyn. As gentrification drew new attention to Williamsburg a half century later, numerous media accounts persisted in depicting the Hasidic enclave as if it were a community suspended in amber, one that not only arrived unchanged from eastern Europe but also had remained unaltered in the intervening years.[44] Why did so many observers want to see Hasidic Williamsburg as unchanging despite ample evidence to the contrary?

In a deep, even unconscious way, the iconic image of the bearded Hasid may have triggered associations with the proverbial "eternal Jew," that atavistic survivor whose presence haunted the European imaginary for centuries. Seen within this light, media references to Hasidic Williamsburg as unchanging likely reflected the much longer tradition of viewing Jews in general as fundamentally timeless and therefore outside history. Some Jewish observers, in turn, may have possessed a wistful desire to see Hasidim as the last survivors of the destroyed world of eastern European Jewry and believed that they, at least, had preserved Jewish tradition intact. Finally, beyond these specifically Jewish associations lies a broader tendency to see the longtime residents of neighborhoods affected by gentrification as akin to precontact natives living outside history, whom gentrifiers have "discovered" and will then, of course, inevitably displace.

Yet it must also be pointed out that the common misperception of Hasidic Williamsburg as unchanging would not have displeased the architects of the community, though they knew better than anyone else that things in Brooklyn were significantly different from what they had been in Satmar, Sighet, Klausenberg, or any of the other towns in Europe from which they originally hailed. These men—and they were all men—embraced the statement "the new is forbidden by the Torah," which Rabbi Moses Sofer (1762–1839), the leader of traditional Hungarian Jewry and founding father of the Haredi movement, had turned into a battle cry against Jewish reformers in the nineteenth century.[45] Taking to heart Sofer's deathbed admonition that Jews should not change their traditional names, language, or dress, the founders of the Hasidic community in Williamsburg insisted that their followers speak Yiddish, wear Hasidic garb, and maintain numerous customs that other Jews, including many Orthodox Jews in the United States, had long since abandoned. As Sender Deutsch, one of the leaders of the Satmar community in Williamsburg, explained, "When we dress in the same way as our ancestors did in previous generations, we are always reminded to strengthen our resolve to follow in the paths of our ancestors and not to turn aside from their ways and their customs even a bit. And this is because [the Torah states] 'Listen my son to the rebuke of your father and do not forsake the Torah of your mother.' "[46]

The result was that to outside observers, the Hasidim of Williamsburg looked, sounded, and acted as they imagined Jews in eastern Europe must have. Yet even in the realm of language, dress, and customs, many members of the Hasidic community of Williamsburg underwent substantial changes after arriving in the United States. Far from being timeless or unchanging, Hasidic Williamsburg was shaped from its very beginnings by a series of internal transformations and a dynamic set of historical forces at the center of urban change in New York City during the postwar period. Members of the Hasidic community did not merely transmit Jewish tradition while passively—and disapprovingly—observing the many changes taking place in the city around them; instead, they actively struggled over the fate of Williamsburg, together with the other communities in the neighborhood, reinventing themselves in the process. Rather than an eastern European shtetl miraculously transported to Brooklyn, the Hasidic enclave in Williamsburg is a distinctly American creation, and its journey from the 1940s to the present a classic New York City story.

CHAPTER ONE

A Land Not Sown

I N HIS AUTOBIOGRAPHICAL NOVEL *The Tropic of Capricorn*, Henry
Miller bitterly recalled how his idyllic childhood was shattered
when the Williamsburg Bridge opened in 1903: "There followed
the invasion of the Jews from Delancey Street, New York. This
brought about the disintegration of our little world."[1] The bridge,
known colloquially as the "Jews' highway," meant something very different for the Jews of the Lower East Side, then the most densely
populated place on earth: an avenue of escape to the greener pastures
of Brooklyn. Not quite the Promised Land, Brooklyn in the early decades of the twentieth century nevertheless promised more space and
better living conditions than the dilapidated tenements of Manhattan.
Between 1905 and 1930, the number of Jews in the borough went
from 100,000 to 800,000, representing nearly half the Jewish population of New York City.[2] The Jewish population of Williamsburg alone
had reached 100,000 residents as early as 1918. The neighborhood of
Miller's youth was so transformed that the future theater impresario
Joseph Papp—born Yosl Papirofsky in a Williamsburg walk-up in
1921—simply assumed its name was Yiddish, since he always heard it
pronounced "Vilyamsburg."[3]

Most significantly for what was to come, Williamsburg emerged
during the interwar period as the most important center for Orthodox
Jewish life not only in Brooklyn but also in New York City as a whole.
At a time when most Jews in New York sent their children to public

schools, and young Jews were more likely to set foot in Yankee Stadium or Ebbets Field than a synagogue, the Jewish community in Williamsburg supported an abundance of religious schools, synagogues, mikvehs (ritual baths), kosher butchers, and other businesses.[4] The neighborhood was also home to a sprinkling of *shtiblekh*, or small houses of worship, which were led by Polish Hasidic rabbis whose congregants continued to pray in the Old World Hasidic style even while, almost to a man, they adopted typically American styles of dress and comportment.

The Orthodox institution that anchored the neighborhood was Yeshiva Torah Vodaath. Originally located on South 3rd Street off Bedford Avenue—demonstrating how far north the Jewish presence in Williamsburg once extended—the yeshiva was founded in 1918. For the next several decades, before it decamped for Kensington, Brooklyn, Torah Vodaath was, in the words of Jeffrey Gurock, "a pillar of separatistic education."[5] Under the leadership of Rabbi Shraga Feivel Mendlowitz, who became *rosh yeshiva*, or principal, in 1922, the school became increasingly conservative and served as an anchor for the postwar efflorescence of Haredi Judaism in the United States. Yet it still was not up to the exacting standards held by the Hungarian Hasidim who would soon arrive in the neighborhood.

Another important precedent for the postwar Hungarian Hasidic community in Williamsburg was the "Malokhim" (literally, "Angels"), a group of especially pious students at Torah Vodaath. In the 1920s and 1930s, these students became followers of Rabbi Chaim Avrohom Dov Ber Levine HaCohen, known popularly as the "Malakh," or "Angel," a Hasidic holy man then living in the Bronx. Although Shraga Feivel Mendlowitz had originally invited the Malakh to study Hasidic texts with the students at his yeshiva, Mendlowitz and his fellow administrators became concerned when the students began to reject the religious norms of the school as being too lax and ditched their "American" clothes for the garb, long beards, and *payes* (sidelocks) that were traditionally worn by Hasidim in eastern Europe but were then almost unknown among even the most pious American-born Orthodox Jews. At that point, the Malokhim either left Torah Vodaath voluntarily or were kicked out—there are different versions of their departure—and founded a breakaway yeshiva in the neighborhood. People who grew up in Williamsburg at this time still remember this colorful group of religious zealots. Frida, who spent her childhood in the neighborhood, recalled that her parents and other working-class Jews would provide the

Malokhim and their families with free milk and bread, although it was the height of the Great Depression and they barely had enough for themselves, out of respect for their religious devotion.[6]

Of all the Jewish neighborhoods in New York City, therefore, Williamsburg would have struck Hasidic refugees from Europe as a receptive place to put down roots in the 1940s. Yet there was still a great gulf between the religious approach of the prewar Orthodox community in Williamsburg and that of the Holocaust refugees whose arrival quickly transformed the neighborhood into a Hasidic enclave. Indeed, Philip Fishman, who grew up in Williamsburg during the 1940s and 1950s, recalled that "in 1939, the neighborhood's Jewish culture was religiously heterogeneous, with little of the ultra-Orthodox attributes that dominate it today."[7] Furthermore, while Williamsburg was an Orthodox stronghold in the period before World War II, many of its Jewish residents did not adhere to Orthodox prescriptions and considered themselves "just Jews."

Another crucial factor that drew Hasidic refugees to Williamsburg after World War II was the neighborhood's economic character. Whereas Crown Heights and Borough Park, the two other Brooklyn neighborhoods that attracted large numbers of Hasidic refugees in this period, were largely middle-class areas with leafy streets lined with well-maintained private homes and apartment buildings, Williamsburg was overwhelmingly working class, and its housing stock consisted of numerous cold-water tenements, along with a core of brownstones on Bedford Avenue and its side streets. While the ongoing economic decline of Williamsburg made it less desirable to most Jewish immigrants, it had the opposite effect on the intensely pietistic Hungarian Hasidic leaders, who were profoundly opposed to the *luksus* (Yiddish, "luxury") of bourgeois American culture.[8] These Hasidic newcomers saw Williamsburg not as a poor ethnic ghetto to be avoided but as a place of spiritual opportunity where they could establish their own *kehile kedosha*, or "holy community," in an environment that was separated from the material and cultural temptations of middle-class Jewish neighborhoods. Williamsburg offered the poor refugees ample affordable housing, small-business opportunities, and relatively inexpensive buildings in which to establish new religious institutions. As one former resident of Williamsburg recalled: "[The neighborhood] was almost moribund at that time; buildings were boarded up on Bedford Avenue; some of the apartment buildings were closed and tenantless. But, with the influx of the Satmar Chassidim, Williamsburg had a revival."[9]

The Satmar Rebbe

Rabbi Yoel Teitelbaum (1887–1979) did more than any other person to
transform Williamsburg into a Hasidic enclave and Satmar into the biggest Hasidic group in the world. He was born in Sighet, a Transylvanian
town—later the home of Elie Wiesel—that was then in Hungary but became part of Romania following the Treaty of Trianon in 1920. A scion
of one of the most important Hasidic dynasties in Greater Hungary, Teitelbaum attracted attention as a young man for his extreme personal
piety, prodigious learning, opposition to compromise with ideological
opponents, and unwavering antipathy to Zionism, which he condemned
as nothing less than the work of Satan because it substituted secular Jewish nationalism for Judaism and sought to establish a Jewish state before
the arrival of the messiah.

Along with Rabbi Menachem Mendel Schneerson (1902–1994), the
Lubavitcher Rebbe, Teitelbaum emerged as one of the two most influential Hasidic leaders in the United States following World War II.
Whereas Schneerson distinguished himself by encouraging his followers
in Crown Heights, Brooklyn, to become *shluchim* (emissaries) to secular
Jews around the world, Teitelbaum exhorted his Hasidim to establish an
insular community in Williamsburg, one set apart from non-Jews as well
as fellow Jews who did not adhere to his strict religious standards. Indeed, Teitelbaum frequently condemned such Jews as heretics, and in the
streets of Williamsburg, his followers would sometimes dismiss their
non-Hasidic Jewish neighbors as *shkutsim*, a derogatory Yiddish term for
gentiles. Despite their differences, Teitelbaum and Schneerson both believed that they were living in the final days before the coming of the
messiah. Although Chabad Hasidism (another name for the Lubavitcher
movement) became famous for its messianic character, much less appreciated is how much the Satmar community saw itself in eschatological
terms during the lifetime of Yoel Teitelbaum.[10]

To understand the rapid growth and aggressively insular character of
the Hasidic community in Williamsburg under Teitelbaum's leadership, it
is necessary to appreciate the historical and ideological roots of his
worldview. Despite comporting himself as a Hasidic rebbe, Teitelbaum
expressed skepticism about many of the wonder tales told about Hasidic
holy men and also stressed that no one, not even other rebbes, still knew
the real teachings of the Baal Shem Tov.[11] Beginning in the eighteenth
century, when the Baal Shem Tov and his disciples founded the move-

ment, Hasidism was dominated by charismatic leaders and, over time, dynasties, centered in Poland and Ukraine. But Greater Hungary was home to a number of important Hasidic figures, including Moshe Teitelbaum of Ujhel (1759–1841), who first brought Hasidism to the region and established the dynasty to which his descendant Yoel Teitelbaum belonged. Nevertheless, in comparison with the movement's centers in Poland and Ukraine, Hungary remained something of a Hasidic backwater, with pockets of strength concentrated in the northeastern territories of Transylvania, Transcarpathia, and Maramureş, known collectively as "Unterland" in Yiddish.

In a number of ways, Yoel Teitelbaum was more influenced by the ideological orientation of the non-Hasidic Hungarian rabbi Moses Sofer (1762–1839) than by the Polish and Ukrainian figures who had historically dominated the Hasidic movement. Teitelbaum frequently emphasized his great respect for Sofer, stating that he studied the latter's teachings every day, and liberally cited his legal rulings in support of his own positions.[12] Popularly known as the "Hasam Sofer," after the title of one of his books, Moses Sofer headed a famous yeshiva and was also the town rabbi in Pressburg (today Bratislava, the capital of Slovakia) in what was then a Hungarian region called "Oberland" by its Jewish residents. During the first decades of the nineteenth century, Pressburg stood at the geographical and cultural crossroads between the German-speaking lands, where both the Jewish Enlightenment and the Reform movement had taken root, and the more traditional territories of eastern Europe. In this contentious frontier zone, Moses Sofer emerged as the most strident opponent of the Jewish reformers, and his descendants and disciples played a key role in the creation of the Haredi movement. Consciously or not, Teitelbaum shifted the focus away from Poland or Ukraine and instead created an alternative genealogy for his community that was anchored by Moses Sofer. By stressing the influence of Sofer, Teitelbaum also asserted a common heritage with the non-Hasidic Haredi Jews from Hungary, whom he wanted to draw into his community and "convert" to his distinctively Hungarian brand of Hasidism, especially following World War II.

During the nineteenth century, Jewish traditionalists took different approaches to the pressing question of how to interact with the increasing number of Jews who did not conform to their exacting standards of practice. In the eastern Unterland region of Hungary where Yoel Teitelbaum was born and raised, the traditionalists adopted a radically separatist approach whose goal was twofold: to make clear that nontraditionalist Jews were sinners (or even heretics) who should be condemned and ostracized; and to protect their own communities from ideological contamination by limiting contact with these other, less observant Jews as much as possible. This Hungarian Haredi tradition of separatism and self-segregation—especially from other Jews— would have a profound impact on the creation of the Hasidic enclave in Williamsburg after Teitelbaum and other like-minded refugees settled in the neighborhood during the 1940s and 1950s.

Like Moses Sofer, Yoel Teitelbaum distinguished himself as a charismatic and sophisticated ideologue, one who railed against innovation while nevertheless selectively accommodating some changes, and who positioned himself and his followers as a bulwark against the corrosive effects of assimilation and modernization. Despite an almost otherworldly piety that at least one critic would later attribute to obsessive-compulsive disorder, Teitelbaum demonstrated a keen talent for political maneuvering, a skill that enabled him and his loyal lieutenants to build a thriving community in the Democratic-machine-dominated precincts of 1950s and 1960s Brooklyn.[13] Long before he established his community in Williamsburg, Teitelbaum had emerged victorious in a contentious power struggle over who would be elected town rabbi of Satmar, which extended for more than a decade before; he assumed the position in 1934. Ironically, given its emphasis on tradition, Satmar was not a Hasidic dynasty with deep roots in the town that provided its name—unlike, for example, Lubavitch—but a new group whose members had gathered around the charismatic and learned Teitelbaum in the decades before the war. Even then, Teitelbaum's following was still relatively small in Europe, though his Hasidim tended to be very devoted.

Before World War II, the town of Satmar, known in Romanian as Satu Mare, or "big village," was a far cry from the idealized shtetls made popular in fictional portraits like *Fiddler on the Roof.* Despite the town's seeming isolation, Satmar was a regional center for commerce and industry whose multiethnic population was exposed to the wider cultural and political trends then transforming Europe. Satmar's Jewish community was similarly diverse, with large numbers of Yiddish- and Hungarian-speaking Hasidim, non-Hasidic Orthodox, and Neologs, who were essentially the Hungarian version of Reform Judaism. In a harbinger of his future strategy in Williamsburg, once Teitelbaum became rabbi of Satmar, he set about trying to enforce ideological and behavioral conformity among the town's Orthodox Jewish residents while stridently condemning its non-Orthodox Jews for what he considered their heretical ways.

The Satmar Rebbe, Yoel Teitelbaum, in Satu Mare, Romania
(Photograph in the public domain)

Hungary was occupied by the Nazis in March 1944, and over the course of only a few months, more than 400,000 Hungarian Jews were sent to Auschwitz, where most were murdered on arrival. After hiding in Satmar and then fleeing the town, Teitelbaum was interred in a ghetto in Klausenberg (Romanian, Cluj-Napoca). There, because of his status as one of Hungary's most prominent rabbis, Teitelbaum and his immediate family were placed on a special train along with approximately 1,600 other Jews whose rescue had been negotiated by Rudolf Kastner, a Hungarian Jewish lawyer, journalist, and prominent Zionist, who paid Adolf Eichmann a large ransom to spare their lives. After the Kastner transport, as it became known, was unexpectedly diverted to the Bergen-Belsen concentration camp by the Nazis in July 1944, Teitelbaum and his family remained there until December 1944, when they were put on a train to Switzerland. From there, Teitelbaum made his way to Palestine, where he stayed for a year before boarding a ship for the United States. In September 1946, on the Jewish holiday of Rosh Ha-Shanah, Teitelbaum arrived in New York City, and following a brief sojourn on the Lower East Side, he and a small group of followers settled in Williamsburg, where they promptly established the Yetev Lev Congregation in 1948.

"This Land That Devours Its Inhabitants"

It was not a given that such refugees would settle in the United States. This was especially the case for Yoel Teitelbaum, who frequently stressed his great love for the land—though decidedly not the state—of Israel, and who had spent a year in Palestine before immigrating to New York City. Teitelbaum even made it clear after arriving in the United States that he hoped to return to the Land of Israel to settle there permanently. Satmar sources describe four interrelated factors that inspired Teitelbaum to settle in Williamsburg, thereby changing the course of the neighborhood's history. The first factor was Teitelbaum's abiding hatred for the Zionist movement and, once it was established in 1948, for the new State of Israel. The second was his belief that there was a positive purpose to God's exile of the Jews and that it was therefore spiritually necessary for some Jews to remain outside the Land of Israel until the final redemption.[14] The third was his belief that despite, or perhaps because of, its lowly spiritual state, America was fated to play a key role in the redemption, serving as the final stop of the portable "camp of Israel" in a long chain of exiles extending all the way back to Babylon. And finally, Teitelbaum believed that Divine Providence had brought him personally to America because he alone could cleanse the land of its spiritual impurity, a necessary stage before the coming of the messiah. Taken together, these factors, along with the Hungarian Haredi tradition of separatism, combined to form a potent ideology that gave meaning to the Hasidic refugees who rallied around the Satmar Rebbe and inspired them to create an enclave in Williamsburg despite conditions that would have been daunting to almost any other community.

Of all these factors, the glue that held together the different strands of Satmar ideology was also the aspect of the community that was most enraging to many observers, even today: its strident and uncompromising anti-Zionism. Before the creation of the State of Israel, most Haredi leaders were opposed to Zionism, which they viewed as a form of idol worship that substituted secular nationalism for traditional Judaism.[15] Yet even

among contemporary Haredi leaders, Teitelbaum was widely known before World War II for being especially critical of the Zionist movement.[16]
Teitelbaum condemned Zionists in demonological terms for attempting
to establish a Jewish state in the Land of Israel before the coming of the
messiah. In so doing, he claimed, the Zionists had broken the first of the
"three oaths" (*shalosh shavuot*) that the Babylonian Talmud stated were incumbent upon the Jewish people and the nations among whom they were
exiled, that Jews should not "storm the wall"—that is, establish a state in
the Land of Israel by force before the final redemption.

Two events ultimately inspired most other Haredi leaders to accept a
modus vivendi with Zionism. First, many of them interpreted the Holocaust as an abrogation of the third of the "three oaths"—that the "nations of the world should not oppress Israel [i.e., the Jewish people] too
much"—and therefore, they argued, Jews were no longer bound by the
prohibition against "storming the wall." Second, the subsequent creation
of the State of Israel was viewed as miraculous by many religious Jews.
These Haredi leaders remained formally opposed to Zionism on religious grounds, but in practice they accepted financial aid from the new
state for their institutions and eventually established Haredi political
parties that ran for elections and participated in the Knesset (the Israeli
parliament).

By contrast, Yoel Teitelbaum emerged after the war as the leader of
the Haredi faction in Israel and abroad that remained unremittingly opposed to any compromise with the Zionists, refusing to take financial aid
from the state and even blaming Zionism for bringing down God's wrath
in the form of the Holocaust.[17] Teitelbaum's opposition to Zionism was
one of the chief reasons that he ultimately decided to remain in the
United States. Nevertheless, he maintained close connections with his
followers in Israel, visited the country on four occasions, and served as
the leader of the Edah Ha-Haredis, the main anti-Zionist Haredi organization in Israel, until his death in 1979.

In postwar America, Teitelbaum's unbending anti-Zionism put him
and his followers at odds with the majority of their fellow Jews, including
members of other Orthodox and Haredi communities. In Williamsburg,
before the Hasidic transformation of the neighborhood, most congregations were both Orthodox and pro-Zionist. As a former resident named
Philip Fishman recalled, "The three largest synagogues—the Clymer
Street Shul, the Hewes Street Shul and the Young Israel—were Orthodox
but with strong Zionist orientation. . . . I am told that on the day in 1947

that the UN voted for the establishment of the State of Israel, all of the many synagogues lining Bedford Avenue joyfully displayed the blue and white Israeli flag outside their window, with the notable exception of the small anti-Zionist Agudah synagogue."[18] For Teitelbaum and his Hasidim, the fact that they were outliers in Williamsburg and pariahs in some Jewish circles because of their anti-Zionism merely strengthened their conviction that only they were the true *mahane yisrael*, or "camp of Israel."

Despite his antipathy toward Zionism, Teitelbaum did not portray his decision to remain in the United States simply in negative terms—that is, merely as a refusal to live in a country controlled by Zionists. Rather, one of the Satmar Rebbe's chief motivations in establishing a holy community in Williamsburg was so that it could serve as a counterpoint and even a rebuke to Zionists and their supporters in the global Jewish community, who argued that an authentic Jewish life was possible only in a Jewish state established in the Land of Israel. Thus, the Satmar community's anti-Zionism cannot be separated from the subsequent transformation of Williamsburg into a Hasidic enclave.

In 1958, Teitelbaum published *VaYoel Moshe*, the most detailed and influential exposition of his distinctive worldview. While the anti-Zionist character of the book has been well noted, it is less appreciated that in crucial ways *VaYoel Moshe* may also be described as pro-exile. Drawing on earlier kabbalistic sources, Teitelbaum compared the current exile of the Jews to the expulsion of Adam from the Garden of Eden: "He (Adam) was exiled due to his sin but he also came to this world on a mission from God in order to repair the world. . . . We are also emissaries from the Holy One blessed be He to every place that we arrive outside of the Land of Israel to repair these places according to the knowledge of the Creator."[19] Elsewhere in the book, Teitelbaum added, "The decree was ordained upon Israel that they be exiled among the nations, so that by means of Israel being exiled among the nations, the Glory of God should fill the entire planet so that belief in Him and His Torah will be made known to the entire world."[20] In these and other passages, Teitelbaum gave positive meaning to the Jewish experience of exile, or *golus*, religiously justifying his own decision to live outside the Land of Israel and transforming the Satmar community in Williamsburg into a vehicle for repairing a broken world in preparation for the coming of the messiah.[21] Thus, Teitelbaum viewed the creation of Hasidic Williamsburg as nothing less than a divinely ordained mission to help bring about the *geulah*, or final redemption of the entire world.

Drawing on Hasidic traditions, Teitelbaum's followers interpreted his so-journ in America as a kind of *yerida le-zorekh aliya* ("descent in order to ascend"), the belief that the tsaddik, or holy man, must sometimes descend into a lowly realm in order to help others perform a spiritual ascent. It was precisely by establishing a holy community in such an impure land that God's glory could be truly revealed, or as the Hasidic author Yonah Landau described the founding of the Satmar community in Williamsburg: "Who would have even imagined in those years, in their wildest dreams, that the land of Columbus would later be turned around into a place of Torah? A place that has no equal in the whole *golus*."[22] Shlomo Yaakov Gelbman, a Satmar Hasid and historian once described as an "encyclopedia" of the community, was even more explicit about the special significance of America: "The final exile before the redemption will be in the country of America. . . . The people of Israel have already suffered many exiles, and now the exile of America has arrived and from there they will receive the face of the messiah."[23]

In a letter to a follower, Yoel Teitelbaum drew on the Lurianic Kabbalah to explain that in the days preceding the final redemption, each Jew was required to settle in the place connected to his particular soul root: "I have already written to many people what is explained in the writings of the Ari [Rabbi Isaac Luria], may his memory be for a blessing, and in other holy texts, that in the period of the exile before the arrival of the messiah, each individual member of Israel must come to the place which is connected to the spark of his soul root."[24] Regarding the place connected to his own soul root, Teitelbaum stressed that even as a young boy in Hungary, he saw the United States as his destiny. "When I was a small child," Teitelbaum recalled, "only a small child, I dreamed I was in America."[25] Later, while serving as rabbi in the town of Kroly, Teitelbaum had a dream in which his dead father, the Sigheter Rebbe, told him that "the time will come that you will need to travel to America."[26]

In 1946, Teitelbaum wrote in a letter while en route from Palestine to New York: "Here I am on the ship in the heart of the sea on my journey to America. . . . And I hope, God willing, that in a short while I will return to the Land of Israel."[27] Sender Deutsch, a member of Teitelbaum's inner circle who would become the publisher of the Satmar newspaper *Der Yid* in the 1950s, later confirmed Teitelbaum's initial desire to remain in America only temporarily, but explained the benefit of his staying: "For all the reasons that would unfold, our rabbi remained here: to erect a fence and stand in the breach and establish [true] religion. And by virtue of his merit America was transformed into a remnant."[28] The term "remnant,"

or *she'arit* in Hebrew, refers to the biblical concept of the "remnant of Israel," that portion of the Jewish people that in every generation remains
faithful to God and will eventually be redeemed.[29] In the wake of the Holocaust, the related phrase *she'arit hapleta*, or "surviving remnant," was applied to Jewish survivors, like those who founded Hasidic Williamsburg.
In a seeming paradox, therefore, America, derided for years before World
War II by Hasidic leaders in eastern Europe as a *treyfene medine*, or impure land, became destined to play a starring role in the redemption of
the Jewish people and, by extension, the world.

Leading his flock in this final, American exile before the *geulah* would
be the Satmar Rebbe, now based in Williamsburg, Brooklyn. According to
his followers, Teitelbaum would accomplish what earlier generations of Jewish holy men had achieved for previous places of exile. As Gelbman put it:

> After the decree of exile and the children of Israel were com-
> pelled to be scattered among the lands of the gentiles, the Holy
> One Blessed Be He seeded *tsadikim* in every generation and due
> to their great holiness they succeeded in purifying the atmo-
> sphere of the places to which they had been exiled, and so they
> [the Jewish people] wandered from Babylonia, to Spain, to
> France, to Germany, to Poland, until the days of the holy Besht
> [the founder of Hasidism] and his disciples.

Extraordinarily, according to Gelbman, the global, millennia-long epic of
the Jewish people had finally culminated on the rundown streets of
1940s Williamsburg: "Now God ... sent to America the Satmarer
Rebbe, may his memory be for a blessing, and placed in his hands, thank
God, the responsibility to purify the atmosphere, something that no one
was able to do until now."[30]

Elsewhere, Gelbman explicitly described America before the arrival of
the Satmar Rebbe as a kind of spiritual wasteland, a place whose hard soil
presented both a challenge and an opportunity to one who sought to sow
the seeds of a holy community: "In our lowly generation, the Holy One
Blessed be He planted our rabbi, may his memory be for a blessing, to purify spiritually this hard place, the soil of America, and prepare it as an ap-
propriate place for tens of thousands of Jews in the final exile. And thus
divine providence brought our holy rabbi to America so that through the
might of his holiness he would make known His blessed divinity in this
'land not sown.' "[31] The phrase "a land not sown" comes from Jeremiah 2:2,

in which God exhorts his prophet, "Go proclaim to Jerusalem: Thus said the Lord, 'I accounted to your favor the devotion of your youth, your love as a bride. How you followed Me in the *midbar* ['desert' or 'wilderness'] in a land not sown."[32] In the original biblical text, the "land not sown" is the desert that the Israelites traversed when they left bondage in Egypt and followed God to the Promised Land. In the Hasidic reformulation of this biblical image, the United States was the desert where the movable "Camp of Israel"—reimagined as the Satmar community—was destined to wander until the arrival of the messiah, or as Gelbman put it, "When the Torah was exiled from Europe to the United States, our rabbi established his holy tabernacle in the neighborhood of Williamsburg in the city of Brooklyn."[33]

In striking contrast to Satmar's own sources, which consistently portray Yoel Teitelbaum's departure from Palestine and settlement in the United States as divinely preordained elements in a spiritual mission of the highest order, the historian Menachem Keren-Kratz offers a dramatically different interpretation of the same events. Keren-Kratz argues from a range of Haredi sources of the era that Teitelbaum's sojourn in Palestine and departure for the United States was not a mythical journey but, instead, an abject failure. As Keren-Kratz puts it, Teitelbaum's attempt to establish a Hasidic community in Jerusalem "ended in failure owing to his political mistakes, as well as to his dubious conduct during the Holocaust"; the journey to America was motivated less by spiritual concerns than monetary ones: "Eventually, after the institutes he established [in Palestine] accumulated tremendous debts, Teitelbaum, persecuted by his creditors, was forced to flee penniless on a ship that sailed a few days before the holy days of Rosh Ha-Shanah—a ship that lacked a proper minyan [quorum of ten men] for the festival's prayers."[34] It is unclear whether or to what degree Satmar sources engaged in a conscious hagiographical project to rehabilitate Teitelbaum's time in Palestine and subsequent immigration to the United States. What is clear is that the version of events articulated by Teitelbaum and his disciples played a key role in shaping the heroic self-conception of the Satmar community in Williamsburg.

In the Satmar imagination, the United States became Yoel Teitelbaum's personal destiny and a place of refuge where his Hasidim could practice their religion freely and prepare for the redemption. Teitelbaum frequently enjoined his followers to demonstrate loyalty to their adopted country and to its leaders. Nevertheless, he roundly criticized American culture, cynically calling the United States "a crazy country" where the "best profession" was to be a painter, since "in America . . . everything is a lie, and people gloss over everything."[35] Yet Teitelbaum saved his sharp-est criticism—as he had done in the town of Satmar before the war—for Jews whom he felt had strayed from the proper path, often employing his sardonic sense of humor to condemn what he dismissed as the *Ameri-kaner yidishe gas*, or "American Jewish street."

Soon after arriving in Williamsburg, for example, Teitelbaum is said to have declared, "People often say that the American Jews have, God forbid, no *emunah* [belief or faith]. I don't know how people can suspect them. We see in fact that they are great believers, because when the mer-chant tells them that the product is kosher, they have great *emunah* in him and blindly believe in his word."[36] On another occasion, Teitelbaum was being driven to a bris (circumcision) in Crown Heights, then home to a large population of non-Orthodox Jews as well as several Hasidic groups. When the car stopped at a red light, Teitelbaum asked where they were. Pointing to the Christmas trees visible in the windows, the driver responded that they were in a non-Jewish area, to which Teitel-baum retorted: "How do you know that we're in a gentile neighbor-hood? Because there are beautiful trees here? I think that the beauty of the trees actually indicates that Jews live here, for when a Jew puts out a Christmas tree he takes special care to make it beautiful."[37]

While Teitelbaum liked to joke about what he considered to be the absurdities of American Jewish life, he took the threats posed to his vul-nerable community of war refugees very seriously. As he looked around at the assimilated children and grandchildren of pious Jewish immigrants from eastern Europe, he shuddered at the thought that the same Hasidim who had only recently survived ghettos, concentration camps, and death marches might end up straying from the path of "Torah-true Judaism" in the United States, not because of oppression but because of opportunity and temptation. "Where are the descendants of these Jews?" he asked. "Did not almost all of them disappear and assimilate completely into their surroundings? . . . And there is a great fear upon us who now find ourselves in this hard country, this land that devours its inhabitants. We need to take counsel so that we, too, will not be lost, God forbid."[38]

The "Haredization" of Williamsburg

From the moment that Yoel Teitelbaum set foot in Williamsburg, he was determined that his then-small community would not succumb to the temptations that had, in his mind, dragged down their pious Jewish predecessors on American soil. And so he and his trusted circle of disciples methodically set about doing in Williamsburg what they could only dream about while still in Satmar—creating a true *kehile kedosha*, a "holy community," in a land not sown. The radical transformation of South Williamsburg into New York City's most densely populated Hasidic enclave took roughly two decades to complete. From the vantage point of the twenty-first century, the creation of Hasidic Williamsburg, beginning in the 1940s, should be seen as the first and still, in certain respects, most dramatic case of what has come to be called "Haredization," or *hithardut* in Hebrew, to take place anywhere in the world.[39]

The process of neighborhood change pioneered in Williamsburg was repeated in other neighborhoods around the globe, from Buenos Aires to Montreal, Antwerp to London and Beit Shemesh. The stages of Haredization include the explosive growth of the local Hasidic community because of large family sizes; the creation of independent, self-segregating Hasidic institutions and businesses; the adoption of Hasidic practices and even identity by some members of the "native" Jewish community; and the eventual outmigration of the remaining native Jews. Together, these factors combined to transform much of South Williamsburg from what had been a multidenominational Jewish neighborhood with the largest Orthodox population in New York City before World War II into an almost exclusively Hasidic stronghold by the late 1960s.

For Hasidim to succeed in their campaign to refashion Williamsburg in their own image, certain claims about the preexisting Jewish community in the neighborhood had to be advanced. Most fundamentally, the neighborhood's Orthodox Jewish institutions and modes of religious observance had to be undermined and delegitimized. Whereas Reform, Conservative, and secular Jewish residents were completely beyond the pale in the eyes of the Hasidic newcomers, Williamsburg's large Orthodox community posed a far greater existential threat to their separatist vision of what it meant to be Jewish. In the middle of the twentieth century, Orthodox Jews in the United States continued to follow the legal requirements of the Halakhah (Jewish law), but they also made a variety of accommodations to modern secular culture, including when it came to education, language, and appearance. Orthodox Jews in Williamsburg represented the possibility of affirming Jewish tradition, on one hand, while integrating into American society, on the other. This was precisely the kind of accommodation that was anathema to Rabbi Yoel Teitelbaum and his followers. As Aviezer Ravitzky noted, "Under his [Teitelbaum's] guidance, the time-honored call for the establishment of separate 'holy communities' turned into an insistence on total self-segregation by the new 'remnant of Israel' and the delegitimation of all those who continued to falsely consider themselves part of the Jewish people."[40]

One of the biggest potential obstacles to creating a separate Hasidic community in Williamsburg was a Halakhic concept known as *minhag ha-makom*, or "the custom of the place." Rooted in centuries of Jewish legal tradition, this principle required that local Jewish customs be respected and, depending on the circumstances, adopted by Jews settling from elsewhere. By virtue of their own interpretation of Jewish law, therefore, the Hasidim who settled in Williamsburg might have felt compelled to accommodate themselves to at least some of the practices of the local Orthodox Jews, thereby undermining their broader goal of creating a separatist community in the neighborhood. Rather than feel stymied, however, Satmar leaders formulated legal arguments justifying why the requirements of *minhag ha-makom* did not apply to the United States and stressed that Hasidim should continue to follow the customs of the communities they had hailed from in Greater Hungary. Thus, Yoel Teitelbaum stated in one of his legal responsa: "It is certain that in America there is no custom [of the land], for something cannot be called a custom if it was not established in a place of giants in Torah and fear of God. . . . And from the beginning in America, the country was not settled by giants of Torah and with the fear of God, as is known, and everything was a custom of ignorance from the very beginning and it continued to worsen over time."[41] For Teitelbaum, there was an obligation to follow the customs of the place from which immigrants came, "and woe unto him who changes them!"

In the eyes of the Satmar Rebbe, then, America was a kind of legal *terra nullius*. This meant that Teitelbaum could establish a new community without having to make any concessions to existing religious authorities or communal norms. On the contrary, after years of struggling in Hungary against well-entrenched Orthodox opponents who did not share his outlook in key respects, Teitelbaum finally found himself free to create a "camp in the desert" according to his highly exacting specifications. In this way, the Hasidim joined a long series of religious communities, beginning with the Puritans, that have understood America as an unsettled wilderness, a place of refuge and reinvention. For the Hungarian Hasidim who settled in Williamsburg, reinvention involved embracing not the new—at least openly—but what they considered authentic Jewish tradition.

Rather than integrate into the existing network of Orthodox institutions, businesses, and ritual sites in Williamsburg, the newly arrived Hasidim immediately sought to invalidate their legitimacy. Especially harsh criticism was reserved for Jewish educational institutions in which girls and boys learned together and also for those that were gender segregated but combined secular and Jewish studies in the curriculum. With financial contributions from nearly all male householders, Teitelbaum founded the Yetev Lev D'Satmar Congregation (named in honor of his grandfather), the Torah VeYirah yeshiva, and the Beis Rochel school for girls.[42] The establishment of these schools meant that Satmar children would be segregated from the other Orthodox Jewish children in Williamsburg, who attended the Torah Vodaath yeshiva and Bais Yaakov school for girls in the neighborhood—that is, before these institutions departed for other parts of Brooklyn, along with most of the native Orthodox Jewish population.

In addition to creating new religious and educational institutions, Yoel Teitelbaum declared that the mikvehs (ritual baths), mezuzahs (biblical verses affixed to doorposts), matzah (unleavened bread for use on Passover), kosher meat, phylacteries, tsitsis (ritual fringes), and Torah scrolls in Williamsburg did not measure up to his ritual standards. In short order, Teitelbaum designated trusted lieutenants to establish Satmar butcher shops, a matzah bakery, and their own system of *hashgacha* (rabbinic certification). Hasidim were exhorted to purchase all their needs from Satmar stores in order to support them economically and for more esoteric, perhaps even mystical reasons, as Sender Deutsch noted: "Our rabbi stated that there were . . . secret reasons why each and every member had to buy meat only from the community."[43] Moshe Karona, writing for the Israeli newspaper *Ha-Tsofe*, noted the transformation of the neighborhood as early as 1953. "In a short time," Karona wrote, "Williamsburg has managed to gain fame for itself throughout America. . . . The rabbis who came from Hungary succeeded in imposing their spirit on the secular life. . . . Here Jews make a living from one another more than in another place in America."[44] Writing a few years later in the Israeli newspaper *Davar*, Yemimah Tchernovits put it succinctly by describing Williamsburg as a "fortress of Judaism in the heart of the city."[45] Less than a decade after arriving, therefore, Satmar had successfully established a parallel Jewish universe within Williamsburg, one that initially competed with and ultimately displaced the native Orthodox community.

Interviews with longtime Orthodox Jewish residents of Williamsburg conducted by the sociologists Solomon Poll and George Kranzler during this period reveal a complex set of emotions and attitudes toward the Hasidic newcomers as they came to dominate the neighborhood. Local Orthodox Jews respected the Hasidim for their strict adherence to Jewish tradition, especially at a time of widespread assimilation, but they also increasingly felt that, despite their own dedication to Jewish law and practice, especially compared with most Jews in New York City, the Hasidim nevertheless viewed them as not pious enough to be considered part of a single Jewish community in Williamsburg. As one resident of the neighborhood put it to Kranzler about what happened when the "Hungarian elements began to gain the upper hand" after the war:

> There was no need to change everything to suit their own tastes and customs. No doubt, whatever they did was for a sincere motive and well-founded in their tradition ... I just don't like the feeling one gets in their company that they are the ones who represent Orthodoxy, and everyone who looks or acts different just isn't as good a Jew. They made themselves independent in most aspects of the community life, and thus created a differentiation that had not existed before, and that forces us who have not yet left Williamsburg to change the style of our living in quite a few respects.[46]

Ironically, despite stressing their adherence to tradition, many of the newcomers underwent substantial changes after settling in Williamsburg. Some arrived in the United States primarily speaking Hungarian or German rather than Yiddish; some men did not wear Hasidic hats or clothing, and some women did not cover their hair or covered it in ways deemed unacceptable by religious authorities; some of them were not even Hasidic originally but had belonged to other communities and essentially became Hasidim in Williamsburg.[47] Indeed, the children and grandchildren of the Hungarian Jewish refugees in Williamsburg frequently spoke Yiddish more fluently and dressed and acted more *khsidish* (Hasidic) than their Old World forebears ever did. As Phyllis Franck observed of the community in the 1960s, "It is not unusual to hear the remark, 'He is more Hasidic than his father.'"[48]

Not only did many of the children of the Hungarian immigrants become "more Hasidic" than their parents over the course of the 1950s, but some Jewish youths in Williamsburg also decided to join the Hasidic community. In 1956, the sociologist Jacob Leschinsky described, in an Israeli newspaper, what was happening in the neighborhood as "The Revolution in Williamsburg."[49] Leschinsky noted that "13–14-year-old youths [in Williamsburg] are becoming Hasidim in opposition to the desire of their parents." They did so out of a rejection of normative American society and an attraction to the radical character of the Hasidic community. He concluded, "Williamsburg is the maximal response to the maximal assimilation that has devoured almost the entirety of American Jewry— and this provides the reason for why the zealous Hasidim succeed in attracting numerous children from the most irreligious families."

While many outside observers assumed that Hasidic Williamsburg had merely transplanted its ways unchanged from Europe, those within the community realized that at least some things were different. As George Kranzler observed, "A holiday in Williamsburg became a sensation for strangers, and an experience unparalleled even for those who had known Chassidic life in Europe. 'I have never seen or heard anything like this at home,' remarked an old timer critically, as he viewed an all-night spectacle of the *Simchath Torah* holiday on Bedford Avenue. He thought of his home town which had never seen busy streets like Bedford Avenue blocked off for hours, while thousands of Jews . . . joined in dancing."[50] Nevertheless, the importance of resisting change was one of Yoel Teitelbaum's favorite topics, as Chaim Moshe Stauber, his former *hoyz-bokher*, or live-in helper, recalled: "The main message that the Rebbe repeated endlessly, in all of his *drashos* [sermons] and in public appearances as well as in private conversations, was that nothing had changed because of the Holocaust. 'We must not stray from the ways of our parents,' was the Rebbe's constant refrain."[51] If there were to be any changes, they should always be in the direction of greater stringency, or *khumre*, as Teitelbaum stated: "In theory, we have to be even more stringent than in previous generations, due to the challenges we now face, but at the very least, we must insist upon the standards of the previous generation. If we let go of the previous generation's standards, we may *chas v'shalom* [God forbid] end up looking like the rest of society."[52]

In Hungary, it had not been the custom of non-Hasidic Orthodox Jews to wear a *shtreyml* (fur hat) or *bekishe* (long black coat). As one Hasidic source put it, "The Ashkenazi [non-Hasidic] Jews [in Hungary] were God fearing and whole despite the fact that they didn't wear shtreymels on their heads."[53] But in Williamsburg it was necessary for all those who sought to join the nascent community, even those who had dressed differently in Europe, to adopt the same Hasidic clothing. The goal of wearing such clothing, like the use of Yiddish, was twofold: to create unity within the emerging Hasidic community in Williamsburg and to generate as much difference as possible from the local population, including those Jews who had already assimilated sartorially and linguistically into the wider American society. Rather than be ashamed of these visible and audible markers of Jewish difference, Hasidim in Williamsburg were encouraged to embrace them as symbols of "a people that dwells alone and shall not be reckoned among the nations" (Numbers 23:9).

In the 1950s, the pressure to conform to narrow social norms regarding personal appearance and dress was intense. For American Jews, in particular, there was the added element of the Holocaust, when Jewish difference had been used to justify genocide; widely viewed photographs of bearded Hasidic Jews being taunted or worse by the Nazis became iconic images of Jewish victimization. Within this climate, the Hasidic insistence on wearing distinguishing clothing, beards, and sidelocks was particularly vexing to local Jews in Williamsburg, including those who identified as Orthodox.[54] Until the arrival of the Hungarian Hasidim, it was rare for any Orthodox Jew in the United States except for elderly rabbis from the Old Country to wear a long beard and sidelocks. By contrast, all Hasidic men in Williamsburg were expected to maintain what had previously been a uniquely rabbinic mien in America, including the considerable number of Hasidim involved in manual labor. When a bearded Zero Mostel premiered on Broadway in 1964 as the Jewish everyman Tevye the milkman, he provoked feelings of nostalgia among Jewish audience members. By contrast, when flesh-and-blood Hasidim engaged in manual labor in Williamsburg, they often inspired embarrassment among the striving middle-class children of the immigrant generation. As an Orthodox resident of Williamsburg explained to Solomon Poll:

> I think these Hungarian Hasidic Jews have lowered the prestige of the "Jew with a beard." . . . I mean that a Jew with a beard does not have the great status that he used to have before the Hasidim of Hungary came to the United States. . . . The reason is that the American Jew, and also the non-Jew, associates a Jew with a beard with a rabbi. Today the picture has changed. A Jew with a beard doesn't mean a rabbi at all, especially when one sees Hasidic Jews engaged in all kinds of menial labor.[55]

This interview attests to one of the most enduring characteristics of Hasidic Williamsburg since its founding: the community has always

Textile factory, Williamsburg, 1993 (Photograph by Maud B. Weiss; copyright Maud B. Weiss/Gina Kehayoff Verlag)

included a significant working-class element engaged in a variety of trades. As Poll noted, "The Hasidim themselves . . . are not surprised at all that 'Jews with beards' work at menial labor. Some of the Hasidim of Hungary come from sections of the country [particularly Maramureş] where menial labor on the part of Hasidic Jews was common practice."[56] In fact, Yoel Teitelbaum was adamant that his Hasidim work for a living, including as manual laborers if necessary, and that they wear beards and sidelocks no matter what their station in life. With his typical sardonic sense of humor, Teitelbaum turned the tables on those who saw the Hasidic "uniform" as making it difficult to distinguish one Hasid from another. "A man came before our rabbi without a beard and *payes*," one Hasidic source recalled, "He had previously had an audience and was certain that our rabbi would beckon him. However, to his surprise, our rabbi asked him who he was. The man responded, I am so and so; why is it that you don't recognize me? And our rabbi replied: 'All Jews without a beard look the same to me.' "[57]

This was a powerful, even defiant message of Jewish pride, especially for a community that had been decimated in the Holocaust and had arrived in

the United States during a postwar period when assimilation was expected
from all immigrants. As a Hasidic source emphasized, "Here in America the
shtreyml and *bekishe* are not just for honor and splendor alone, but are also a
fence around the Torah so that we will not mix with the gentiles, God forbid,
and so that we will not be embarrassed before the mocking American Jews
who were already corrupted. . . . Everyone in our community must seek to
acquire Hasidic garb as soon as he is financially able, in order to walk the
streets of the neighborhood in a *shtreyml* on his head without any shame at
all, rather, it 'will strengthen his heart in the ways of the Lord.' "[58] The
founders of Hasidic Williamsburg thus consciously and methodically sought
to establish modes of speech, dress, and practice that *signified* tradition while
ostracizing those who refused to accept these norms.

By the early 1960s, many Hasidic groups from Greater Hungary had
set down roots in Williamsburg, including Klausenberg, Pupa, Spinka,
Kasho, Krasna, and Vishnitz, yet no community would come close to rivaling the numerical, religious, economic, or political strength of Satmar.
Nor would any other Hasidic leader approach the extraordinary influence of Yoel Teitelbaum, not only in the neighborhood, but also wherever Hungarian Hasidim established centers in the postwar period,
including Israel, London, Antwerp, Montreal, and Buenos Aires. Within
Williamsburg, other Hasidic groups quickly fell within the orbit of Satmar, and in the coming years, they almost always followed its lead when
it came to important decisions affecting the neighborhood. When tensions sometimes occurred, for example, between Satmar and Pupa, which
was Williamsburg's second-largest Hasidic group and was led by Rabbi
Yosef Greenwald (1903–1984), another charismatic leader, Satmar asserted its hegemony.[59] Over time, Haredi groups that were not originally
Hasidic, such as Vien and Tselem, essentially became so by adopting Hasidic customs and other markers of identity.[60]

Collectively, these fiercely determined Hungarian Holocaust survivors and refugees turned their small triangle of South Williamsburg into
a Hasidic enclave during the 1950s and 1960s just as another wave of arrivals, this time from Puerto Rico, was also beginning to transform parts
of the neighborhood—and others throughout New York City—in its
own distinctive ways. As neighbors, rivals, and, on rare occasion, allies,
these two vibrant communities shaped the character of South Williamsburg from the 1960s until the arrival of gentrification in the 1980s while
trying to survive in the rough-and-tumble political, racial, and economic
climate of New York City.

CHAPTER TWO

Paths of Heaven

"ENTRIFICATION HAS REVERSED 'white flight,'" *New York* magazine breathlessly declared in a July 2010 article titled "A Racial U-Turn."[1] Yet the situation on the ground was much more complicated than the attention-grabbing headline suggested. While the white—and Asian—populations of New York City's most gentrifying neighborhoods, including Williamsburg, had increased dramatically since the 1990s, the number of white residents had decreased in many more neighborhoods throughout the city, particularly in the outer boroughs, from a combination of natural decline and outmigration. Nevertheless, gentrification had clearly played a decisive role in racially transforming those parts of New York City—most of Manhattan and a large swath of North Brooklyn—where the mainstream media tended to look when seeking to portray the city as a whole. Moreover, by the beginning of the twenty-first century, gentrification had replaced white flight as the dominant model for understanding the intersection of race and real estate in the city.

The history of Williamsburg would have been dramatically different had the neighborhood's Hasidim joined so many other Jews and abandoned New York City during the late 1950s and 1960s, when white flight was at its height. Even as nearly a million Jews left New York City during those years, the ones who were most likely to remain at the height of this transition were Haredim, especially Hasidim, while more centrist Orthodox Jews increasingly joined their co-religionists in fleeing to the suburbs.[2] As a result, by the late 1960s, Hasidim had gone from being a tiny presence in Brooklyn to one of the most demographically significant segments of the Jewish population of the borough, and in Williamsburg and Crown Heights, practically the only Jewish residents. These Hasidim were largely dismissed—when outsiders paid attention to them at all—as remnants of a bygone era, stubbornly refusing to abandon what seemed to many like a rapidly sinking ship. And yet, through the lens of time, they now appear as the vanguard of the Hasidic demographic expansion that later transformed parts of Brooklyn as well as communities in upstate New York and New Jersey.

The first Haredi leader to take a public stand against "Jewish flight," in the 1960s, was Rabbi Menachem Mendel Schneerson, the seventh Lubavitcher Rebbe and leader of the Chabad Hasidic community headquartered in Crown Heights.[3] Located a few miles away from Williamsburg down Bedford Avenue, the historically middle-class central Brooklyn neighborhood had leafy streets lined with well-maintained brownstones and good subway service, amenities that would make it attractive to gentrifiers decades later. Since the early twentieth century, Crown Heights had been home to a large and diverse Jewish community. By 1950, the neighborhood was 89 percent white, and around 50–60 percent of its population (approximately 75,000 people) were working- and middle-class Jews whose religious orientation ranged from completely secular to Reform, Conservative, and mainstream Orthodox, with a small but rapidly growing Hasidic community. Between 1940 and 1957, the African American and Afro-Caribbean population in the neighborhood expanded fourfold to nearly 25 percent of the overall population (37,000 people), a dramatic rate of growth that proved to be a harbinger of things to come.[4]

Indeed, even by the standards of New York City, Crown Heights experienced an extraordinary demographic transformation in the 1960s as the neighborhood went from 70 percent white in 1960 to 70 percent black in 1970.[5] During this period, almost all non-Hasidic Jews left Crown Heights. In 1968, the Bobover Hasidim decamped from their base on Brooklyn Avenue and relocated southwest to Borough Park, which by then had become home to the largest Orthodox Jewish population in the city, including many transplants from neighborhoods such as Williamsburg and Crown Heights.[6]

A transition of this scale, in which tens of thousands of Jews departed Crown Heights and a roughly equal number of African American and Afro-Caribbean residents arrived, would not have been possible without

blockbusting, which was especially common in central Brooklyn neighborhoods like Crown Heights in the 1960s.[7] In this widespread practice,
which was made illegal by the federal Fair Housing Act of 1968, real estate agents played on the fear, racism, and economic anxiety of white residents to encourage them to sell their homes at below-market prices lest
they lose their investment entirely if African Americans moved into the
neighborhood in large numbers. The same agents then resold the homes
at higher prices to African American buyers who were unable to get market rate mortgages because of discriminatory lending practices and therefore had to accept artificially high financing, with the agents profiting on
the arbitrage (or price difference) between white sellers and black buyers.

By the late 1960s, the remaining Jews in Crown Heights, almost all of
them members of the Chabad-Lubavitch Hasidic group, felt that they
were under siege, abandoned by other Jewish residents, vulnerable to
predatory real estate brokers, and increasingly subject to property crimes
and physical assaults. To what degree these incidents reflected crimes of
opportunity, or what would later be called "hate crimes" (legislation
against hate crimes was not passed by New York State until 2000, although
the Civil Rights Act of 1968 made it a federal offense), was intensely debated at the time. Regardless of the reality on the ground, however, the
widespread perception within the Hasidic community was that Crown
Heights had become a dangerous place for Jews to live. This perception
was reinforced by widespread black-Jewish tensions in New York City in
the late 1960s, which came to a head in the Ocean Hill–Brownsville school
conflict, which pitted African American and Puerto Rican parents against
the largely Jewish leadership and rank and file of the United Federation of
Teachers in 1968.[8]

Given the proximity of Crown Heights to Brownsville, as well as the
Chabad-Lubavitch movement's long history of activism, stretching back
to the Russian Empire, it is not surprising that the Lubavitcher Rebbe
was at the vanguard of Haredi efforts to stanch the outflow of Jews from
the city. On April 10, 1969, Schneerson delivered a public talk, or *sicha*,
on the subject at the community's headquarters, 770 Eastern Parkway in
the heart of Crown Heights.[9] Before a crowd of nearly three thousand
followers who had gathered to celebrate the last day of Passover,
Schneerson decried what was "spreading among our brothers, the children of Israel, like a 'plague,' mercy upon us, the phenomenon of flight
from Jewish neighborhoods, and as a result of that—the sale of homes in
those neighborhoods to non-Jews."[10]

In his remarks that day, and in related statements in the coming weeks, Schneerson cited Halakhic (Jewish legal) sources to argue that Jews were absolutely prohibited from abandoning their neighborhoods.[11] He listed numerous reasons for such a prohibition, including the economic damage done to Jews who sold their property at below-market prices; the negative spiritual impact of leaving a neighborhood in which synagogues, schools, and other institutions were within walking distance for ones where such institutions were either absent, inconveniently located, or employed different customs; and perhaps most fundamentally, the weakening of the Jewish people, and the strengthening of their enemies, by such an exodus, creating a snowball effect in cities around the country. According to Schneerson, there were wider implications as well: "The heart of the matter is that the sale and transfer of houses and neighborhoods from Jews to non-Jews, weakens, heaven help us, the power of Israel and adds strength to the haters of Israel, whose intention in buying houses in a Jewish neighborhood is to separate Jews, God forbid, from their inheritance [*nahalah*]. And clearly, each and every house that is sold to them strengthens their power and aids them in achieving their goal."[12] Schneerson further elaborated that when a whole neighborhood fell, it created a domino effect in surrounding Jewish neighborhoods. Perhaps referring to the practice of blockbusting, he added, "And the rumor that this has occurred in one city—immediately arrives in other cities and inspires there the haters of Israel ... the damage spreads by means of this from city to city, heaven help us, as we have already seen."

According to Schneerson, the widespread fear and panic that accompanied such flight increased the incidence of theft and violence against the remaining Jewish community by creating an impression of weakness: "There are some who claim that these neighborhoods are dangerous places. ... But it is clear that selling more and more houses to non-Jews weakens the power of Jews in the neighborhood and strengthens the power of the haters of Jews and thus the seller plays a part in the creation of the danger."[13] Instead of running, Schneerson emphasized that Jews should view any attempt to intimidate them as "just a test," one that they could withstand as long as they trusted in God and demonstrated to others that they were determined to stay put and even expand their presence: "As we have seen in practice in several neighborhoods, because the Jews came out in force against budging from their neighborhoods— because they sought to have the city authorities put in place security and so on, they reside securely in their neighborhoods, and they have even increased the number of synagogues and houses of study, in addition to private homes and institutions."[14]

Schneerson exhorted his followers to follow the example of two Jewish communities in New York City: Washington Heights, in Upper Manhattan, where a small but tenacious community of Orthodox Jewish refugees from Germany had remained despite changing neighborhood demographics, and Williamsburg, where the Hasidic community had not only stayed but also grown in size. "We see that there are two neighborhoods that made it known to all that they would remain intact," Schneerson observed. "And they succeeded. Take action so that we can achieve here [in Crown Heights] what they accomplished in Williamsburg and Washington Heights. They built new buildings, more Jews moved in, and they succeeded!"[15]

The Miracle of Williamsburg

The new buildings that had enabled Hasidim to remain in Williamsburg were not single-family homes, brownstones, or co-op apartments. Instead, they were high-rise low-income public housing projects—precisely the kind of buildings that by the 1960s had widely come to symbolize urban decay, crime, and racialized poverty for many Americans. Indeed, white flight in general had dramatically transformed the racial makeup of cities across the United States in the postwar period, and white flight from public housing projects in these cities had been even more profound. As Lawrence Friedman observed in 1966, "The whites streamed out. . . . The attention of the public was now directed to public housing not as a hopeful program of reform but as the site of public folly and private decay—vandalism, crime, and unrest. . . . Who wanted such places in their neighborhood?"[16] In New York City in particular, the city employed a variety of means to retain white residents throughout the 1950s, but its public housing came to represent what Nicholas Dagen Bloom, a scholar of urban planning, has called, "something of a 'second ghetto': new communities now segregated by income, mostly by race, built atop the old slums."[17]

The segregation of public housing in the postwar period did not happen by accident.[18] Not only were working-class whites encouraged to move out of urban areas by real estate agents, bankers, developers, auto manufacturers, and other private-sector actors who would benefit economically from white flight, but the federal government, including the Federal Housing Administration, created financial incentives for them to do so while prohibiting African Americans from participating in the same programs. For example, the monthly payments for veterans in new, postwar developments such as Levittown, Long Island, which expressly prohibited sales to blacks, were *lower* than rents in comparable units in nearby public housing projects, thereby creating a financial incentive for whites to abandon them. As Richard Rothstein wrote, "As more whites took advantage of FHA and VA subsidies to move, earlier residents were gradually replaced by much-lower income minorities. . . . Public housing nationwide became racially identifiable and associated solely with poverty."[19] Whereas in 1950 public housing residents earned 57 percent of the national median income, by 1970 they were earning only 29 percent.[20] The result of these shifts was that during the 1960s, urban public housing became overwhelmingly black (and in New York City, Puerto Rican as well), and its residents came to occupy a uniquely stigmatized position in the popular imagination.

This is the wider historical context for understanding one of the most important and contentious aspects of the second phase of the Hasidic settlement in Williamsburg, and one that would have profound implications for the community in the decades leading up to the gentrification of the neighborhood. In dramatic contrast to the nationwide trend of white residents abandoning housing projects, from the early 1960s on Hasidim in Williamsburg did whatever they could to occupy as many units as possible in public housing projects in the neighborhood, including participating in set-asides that were later deemed racially discriminatory by the courts. In this regard, the Hasidim of Williamsburg were striking outliers compared with not only other whites, but also other Jews, who were rapidly suburbanizing during the same period, and even other Hasidic groups elsewhere in Brooklyn, whose neighborhoods did not have a significant concentration of housing projects. Why, then, did the Hasidim in Williamsburg decide to move into public housing precisely when so many whites in New York City and around the country were doing whatever they could to get out? Asked from a different perspective, why weren't Hasidim deterred from living in public housing projects at a time when so many whites were either ashamed or afraid to live in them?

Although Hasidim in Williamsburg began to move into public housing projects in the mid-1960s, the roots of their decision may be traced to the very beginnings of the ongoing housing crisis in the neighborhood. Long before World War II, Williamsburg suffered from inadequate affordable housing for its largely working-class and poor population. For this reason, a decade before Hungarian Hasidim arrived in the neighborhood in large numbers, Williamsburg was already at the vanguard of public housing in the United States. In the mid-1930s, the newly established Housing Division of the Public Works Administration (PWA) and the New York City Housing Authority (NYCHA) identified the impoverished neighborhood as an ideal candidate for slum clearance and the construction of one of the earliest public housing projects in the nation. Starrett Brothers, the contractor that completed the Empire State Building in 1931—and would go on to build Stuyvesant Town, a massive private residential development on Manhattan's East Side—was chosen to develop the $12,500,000 project in Williamsburg. As William Starrett put it at the time, "It is the hope of people who are discussing this (slum) problem that those same brains that put together the great skyscrapers . . . will turn toward this."[21]

Beginning in 1935, 568 buildings were demolished and 5,400 people relocated to make room for the new housing project in Williamsburg. As the massive construction project proceeded, the need for it became apparent: "From every dank basement and crumbling wall rats fled in droves. Backyards disgorged an assortment of rusted cans, trash, filth and litter that would have discouraged the most voracious goat."[22] In April 1936, New York City mayor Fiorello La Guardia shoveled the first concrete for the development, officially called the Ten Eyck Houses but later known as the Williamsburg Houses, located one mile east of the Williamsburg Bridge and two blocks south of Grand Street. Reflecting the great need for decent affordable housing in the city, 20,000 applications were submitted for 1,622 units.[23] By September 1937, the buildings, lavishly praised by the *Brooklyn Eagle* as "an eagerly sought spot to live," were ready for occupancy by the first tenants, a Jewish couple named Louis and Bessie Grabkowitz, who, like most of their new neighbors, were working-class whites of immigrant or first-generation backgrounds.[24]

World War II interrupted significant new construction, but the postwar period witnessed an unprecedented surge of new public housing projects around the country, and New York City was no exception.[25] This remarkable boom was made possible by the Housing Act of 1949, a cornerstone of President Harry S. Truman's legislative Fair Deal, and in New York City by Robert Moses's program for slum clearance and urban renewal.[26] In his State of the Union address in 1949, Truman argued that low-income housing was a crucial part of his vision for the country. "The

American people have decided that poverty is just as wasteful and just as unnecessary as preventable disease," the president declared. "The housing shortage continues to be acute. As an immediate step, the Congress should enact the provisions for low-rent public housing, slum clearance, farm housing, and housing research which I have repeatedly recommended. The number of low-rent public housing units provided for in the legislation should be increased to 1 million units in the next 7 years."[27] Later that year, the NYCHA spent $50,000 to conduct a survey of South Williamsburg, where Hungarian Hasidim had only recently begun putting down roots, to identify blocks eligible for the slum clearance funded by Title I of the Housing Act.[28]

By 1955, city, state, and federal programs had combined to fund 87,963 new NYCHA apartments in New York City, housing 335,000 residents and, in the words of Nicholas Dagen Bloom, "effecting the kind of rapid, dramatic change only imagined by reformers of other eras, before and since."[29] In 1955, *Der Tog-Morgn Zhurnal*, a New York Yiddish newspaper with a large Orthodox readership, reported that the city was committed to building 15,000 more low- and middle-income apartments, including thousands of units in Brownsville, East New York, and Coney Island—that is, "in neighborhoods densely inhabited by Jews."[30] Noticeably absent from the article was any mention of Williamsburg.

Plans for the neighborhood had been put on hold while the city planner Robert Moses pushed through his controversial construction of the Brooklyn–Queens Expressway (BQE), which cut through the heart of residential Williamsburg. Like the other highways built by Moses in New York City during this period, the BQE was a conduit for white flight and suburbanization. To many longtime Jewish residents of Williamsburg, the expressway seemed like the last nail in the coffin of the community, and a veritable flood of Jews abandoned the neighborhood in the 1950s for Crown Heights, Borough Park, Long Island, and elsewhere. As Rabbi Bernard Weinberger, who became the leader of Williamsburg's Young Israel of Brooklyn congregation in this period, later put it, "Because of the massive dislocation involved, Williamsburg was then regarded as doomed. . . . With the heavy flow of traffic through a major thoroughfare within the community, the pollution, debris, and vacant lots parallel to the highway that were left without landscaping, slum conditions set in. . . . This once glorious neighborhood was headed for extinction due to the mass exodus of Orthodox Jews to other urban and suburban areas of New York City."[31] And yet rather than end up like

Brownsville, another Brooklyn neighborhood once known as the "Jerusa-lem of America," whose massive Jewish population almost completely de-camped during this period, Williamsburg retained a large Jewish community, albeit one that was almost exclusively Hasidic.

Given the prevailing trends in New York City, what happened in the neighborhood seemed so improbable, even impossible, that Weinberger described it as the "Miracle of Williamsburg" in a 1965 article that ap-peared in the *Jewish Observer*, a publication of Agudath Israel of America.[32] Rather than a miracle, however, an examination of sources from the late 1950s and early 1960s reveals that the large-scale settlement of Hasidim in Williamsburg's high-rise public housing projects resulted from a com-plicated and, at times, highly contentious set of debates and negotiations between factions within the Jewish community, city housing officials, ma-chine politicians, and representatives of the growing Puerto Rican popu-lation in the neighborhood. Nor was it a story of unambiguous triumph for the entire Jewish community of Williamsburg, as Weinberg suggested in the article's subtitle, "How a Community Managed to Halt a Popula-tion Shift." First, many of Williamsburg's Orthodox Jewish leaders had opposed the construction of the public housing projects from the begin-ning, though that opposition did not prevent the Orthodox establishment from claiming credit after the fact. And second, the only Jews who ended up reaping the benefits of the "Miracle of Williamsburg" were the Ha-sidim. For by the time the public housing projects were completed, in the mid-1960s, it was clear that they alone would represent the future of Jewish Williamsburg.

Looking back in 1965 from the pages of the *Jewish Observer*, Wein-berger stressed his pivotal role and that of other like-minded Orthodox rabbis in bringing the housing projects to Williamsburg. "The rabbis of the community were determined to keep Williamsburg alive and they set out to do something about it," he wrote. "With some local political assis-tance, they managed to gain the interest of the New York City Housing Authority. On a Spring afternoon in 1956 this writer rode the streets of Williamsburg with the chairman of the Housing Authority, to select a site for a project that the Authority would erect. Discussions took place on a daily basis as to the type of projects, the suitable sites, the importance of keeping relocation down to a minimum and all related subjects."[33] The rabbis referred to by Weinberger were, like himself, leaders of non-Hasidic Orthodox synagogues who supported the effort to bring public housing to the neighborhood because they thought it would benefit the members of their own congregations. They allied themselves with what Weinberger called "influential Jewish leaders in the city" who hoped that slum clearance and the construction of public housing would revive South Williamsburg. They were opposed, in turn, by other members of the neighborhood's Orthodox Jewish establishment, "particularly the heads of schools ... [who] felt that the *status quo* was desirable since any housing development would destroy rather than preserve the homogeneity of the community. Heated discussions took place, but planning went on."[34]

In November 1957, a group of local Jewish leaders publicly launched a drive for "middle-income housing" in the "Lower Williamsburg Area" (that is, South Williamsburg).[35] Supported by the Williamsburg Chamber of Commerce, the campaign was announced at the Williamsburg Young Men's and Young Women's Hebrew Association (YM & YWHA), the central cultural institution for the neighborhood's once large but now rapidly dwindling assimilated Jewish community. The *Williamsburg News*, a weekly newspaper that served as a mouthpiece for this community, reported on the event. Middle-class, clean-shaven, proudly Jewish, and fully integrated into American culture, the men who made up the Housing Committee represented a constituency that was getting smaller in Williamsburg with every passing year. They hoped to stanch the outflow of Jewish residents similar to themselves by working with the city and private developers to build middle-income housing such as Lindsay Park, a giant development being planned for another part of Williamsburg; that would become the largest Mitchell-Lama co-op in Brooklyn when its 2,702 units were completed in 1965.[36] In the late 1950s, it was still possible to imagine that the outflow of non-Hasidic Jews from South Williamsburg could be stopped or at least significantly reduced. For this reason, the Housing Committee had called for the city to build middle-income housing in the neighborhood, both because low-income public housing was already becoming associated with racialized poverty and crime and because many of their constituents earned too much money to qualify for low-income units.

But the New York City Housing Authority had other plans for South Williamsburg. Instead of middle-income housing, the NYCHA began, in the winter of 1958, to lay the groundwork for the construction of two high-rise low-income public housing projects in blocks that were densely inhabited by Jewish residents. NYCHA's proposal for South Williamsburg made it clear that it viewed the area as a prime location for the development being carried out in New York City during the 1950s by

Residential street in Hasidic Williamsburg with the construction of high-rise
public housing projects in the background, early 1960s (Irving I. Herzberg
Photograph Collection, Brooklyn Public Library, Brooklyn Collection)

Robert Moses, who served as the head of the Mayor's Committee on Slum Clearance.[37] The proposal stressed that officials were responding to the great citywide demand for low-income housing, as indicated by the 70,000-plus applications submitted in 1957 alone.[38] The NYCHA plan called for demolishing numerous substandard tenements in South Williamsburg and erecting "in their stead, decent, safe and sanitary dwellings for persons and families of low-income."[39] In a nod to the many streets in the neighborhood named after signers of the Declaration of Independence, one of the two proposed projects would be called Independence Towers, and the other, Jonathan Williams Houses (later "Plaza"), after the grandnephew of Benjamin Franklin who first surveyed the land in Brooklyn that was later designated "Williamsburg" in his honor. Unlike the massive Williamsburg Houses, which occupied twelve city blocks, the footprint of the proposed projects in South Williamsburg would be much smaller and better integrated into the existing neighborhood, reflecting the so-called vest-pocket projects that the NYCHA had begun developing in 1957.[40]

The city's decision to build two high-rise low-income public housing projects in the heart of Jewish Williamsburg ignited a firestorm of debate that embroiled different factions of the community for several years. On February 25, 1958, the City Planning Commission held a public hearing on the proposed housing projects.[41] The next day, the *New York Daily News* reported in an article headlined "Williamsburg in Donnybrook over Housing" that a "violent argument between Williamsburg Jewish leaders erupted."[42] Opposing the construction of the buildings were members of a newly organized group calling itself the United Synagogues and Yeshivas of Williamsburg, which claimed to represent the neighborhood's Orthodox institutions. The spokesman for the group, Rabbi Abraham Newhouse, cofounder of the Bais Yaakov School for Girls, decried the dispersal of residents that would occur if the projects were built. "To uproot all these families who have specific ties to the Williamsburg community, who have through great sacrifices built their own schools and cultural institutions and houses of worship," he argued, "would not be in the true interest of a planned city." This view was echoed by another neighborhood resident, Eliezer "Mike" Tress, then the national president of Agudath Israel of America, who invoked the memory of the Holocaust in condemning the potential impact of the buildings: "Nowhere outside of Israel will you find an area so dedicated to religious living and beliefs. I know these men who are here before you. They have lost everything and now they have found a haven. Don't uproot them again."[43]

Speaking on behalf of the local Jewish supporters of the housing projects was Jack Garrell of the YM & YWHA, who angrily declared, "If I have ever heard an argument in favor of creating a ghetto, I have heard it today."[44] For Garrell and his allies, the housing projects, even if they comprised low-income rather than middle-income units, represented an opportunity to demolish the rundown tenements and cold-water flats of South Williamsburg and replace them with new buildings that could attract young families from the local Jewish community who would otherwise move out. Among Garrell's allies at the meeting was Rabbi Chaim Pincus, who lamented, "There is not a young person married today who would want to take up residence in Williamsburg."[45] Even though it put him at odds with many of his Orthodox colleagues, Pincus had a personal interest in finding a way to retain young Jewish families in the neighborhood. In the early 1950s, his Orthodox synagogue, Congregation Beth Sholom, was demolished to make room for the Brooklyn–Queens Expressway. After merging with another Orthodox congregation in the same situation, the synagogue erected a new building in 1957 on Rodney Street. Having invested heavily in the future of the neighborhood, Pincus was willing to take a strong position in support of public housing.

For Orthodox opponents of the projects, "ghetto" was not a dirty word but a badge of honor, and the potential destruction of the Orthodox community in South Williamsburg was a looming catastrophe that would send shock waves far beyond its borders. As Rabbi Moshe Sherer, who became the national president of Agudath Israel of America after Mike Tress passed away, wrote in March 1958, "The danger that threatens Williamsburg is far beyond a local matter . . . Williamsburg has long ago ceased to be a mere geographic concept. When one says Williamsburg, it does not only signify a neighborhood within greater New York. Williamsburg means a uniquely Jewish way of life which few thought was possible in America."[46] Yet according to Sherer, it was not the NYCHA that was ultimately responsible for creating this existential threat to "a corner in America which is close to the heart of every Torah-Jew in the land," but the more assimilated Jews of Williamsburg, such as Jack Garrell. In Sherer's interpretation, "It is perhaps also not a surprise that it is precisely alienated Jews who are simultaneously doing everything possible to liquidate it. Williamsburg reminds them of something that they would rather forget. It is for them a symbol of the Jewish spirit which they have suppressed in themselves."[47]

On March 5, 1958, the City Planning Commission sided with what the *New York Daily News* described as the "more progressive Jewish leaders [who] backed the housing plan," and approved the two housing projects in the neighborhood "despite opposition from orthodox Jewish leaders in Williamsburg."[48] Nevertheless, to assuage the concerns of Orthodox opponents, the commission's report noted that preference would be given to "eligible families in the neighborhood" when it came time to rent units in the buildings, a decision based on a 1957 state law that gave priority to residents living within one mile of a new project.[49] In a concession that was unique to Williamsburg, the commission added that the NYCHA would provide "families, who may not use elevators on the Sabbath because of their religious beliefs . . . preference for apartments on the lower stories of the project buildings." The commission was clearly trying hard to balance the concerns of Orthodox Jewish leaders with the city's broader goals of slum clearance and urban renewal.

Rather than accept the housing projects as a fait accompli, however, Orthodox opponents in Williamsburg doubled down on their efforts to halt development. They agreed to eliminate the split that had emerged within the Orthodox camp and present a united front when the city's Board of Estimate met next to evaluate the project. On March 7, 1958, the *New York Daily News* reported that the two Orthodox camps had achieved a rapprochement and would, as a headline put it, "Join Forces to War on CHA Plans" and "storm the Board of Estimate meeting next Thursday."[50] In stating why he now opposed the projects, Rabbi Chaim Pincus echoed the negative views regarding low-income public housing that had by then become commonplace throughout the city: "[We were] misled into believing that they would be for middle-income families. When we learned they were low-income developments we became incensed. We believe low-income housing would make the neighborhood worse than it is." Whereas in the 1930s the construction of the Williamsburg Houses was greeted with great fanfare, the possibility of a low-income project in the neighborhood now prompted fear and anxiety among many longtime Jewish residents. What had changed in the intervening two decades was not the need for new public housing, especially in a chronically poor neighborhood such as Williamsburg, but the emerging perception of what such projects signified: a last resort for growing numbers of poor blacks and Puerto Ricans and for those poor, typically elderly whites who were left behind as others took advantage of governmental programs and favorable mortgage rates to leave the city for the suburbs.

In mid-March 1958, the Board of Estimate met to consider the construction of the public housing projects in what the *New York Daily News* described as "a section of Williamsburg, Brooklyn, that is considered by some to be the center of Jewish culture in this country."[51] Twelve people spoke in favor of the proposal and eighteen against, including Rabbi Pinchas Teitz, president of the Union of Orthodox Rabbis of the United States and Canada, the oldest organization of its kind in the country, who declared, "It will be a sad day in Jewish history if this section is destroyed."[52] Over the next few months, the city contemplated what to do in South Williamsburg, finally reaching a Solomonic compromise at the end of the summer that it hoped would satisfy all sides.[53] In September, the same day that it covered the twentieth-anniversary celebration of the construction of the Williamsburg Houses, the *New York Daily News* reported that the NYCHA had decided to go forward with Jonathan Williams Plaza as a low-income project, but to accept proposals from local residents to transform Independence Towers into a private, middle-income co-op.[54]

As these negotiations unfolded, Satmar, by far the largest and most powerful Hasidic group in Williamsburg, watched from the sidelines. Their every move was anxiously monitored by local Jewish leaders, who feared that if Satmar abandoned the neighborhood, it would trigger an exodus of the entire Hasidic community, which would cause the complete collapse of Jewish Williamsburg. On December 26, 1958, *Der Yid*, the newspaper of record for the Satmar community, published an article that summarized the "vigorous campaign" that "the leaders of the Orthodox congregations in Williamsburg, along with the administrators of the yeshivas and Bais Yaakov," had waged in the previous year against city officials, "on the grounds that the planned projects were liable to destroy the entrenched institutions of Torah and the entire gigantic edifice of the renowned Hasidic congregations that were established over the past ten years with such great effort."[55] Rather than defend or attack any of the parties involved, however, *Der Yid* merely stated that the Board of Estimate had arrived at a "compromise" in which the city would construct half the buildings at six stories so that Jews who kept the Sabbath would not have to climb too many flights of stairs, and "the other half would be 14 stories, though the representative of the Board of Estimate promised that in these taller buildings those who keep the Sabbath would also be given units on the lower floors."

A Shtetl in New Jersey?

What explains the calm tone of Satmar's press coverage, especially when *Der Yid* was typically happy to excoriate the community's enemies in the purplest of prose? Satmar was reluctant to come out publicly against city officials, whose favor they generally tried to cultivate, nor did they want to hitch their wagon fully to the Orthodox establishment of Williamsburg, with whom they had a profoundly ambivalent relationship. Like the Orthodox establishment, Hasidic leaders had initially opposed the construction of high-rise buildings because of the problem of using elevators on the Sabbath, yet they were happy to have Orthodox representatives wage a public campaign while they stayed in the background and waited to see how things unfolded. This did not mean, however, that Satmar was passively placing the future of its community in the hands of others. On the contrary, the debate over public housing in South Williamsburg during the late 1950s and early 1960s coincided with Satmar's early efforts to purchase land outside the city and begin construction of their own village, or shtetl, as they put it, where community members could live apart from the negative moral influences of New York City.

In support of this dream, Rabbi Yoel Teitelbaum cited Maimonides, the great medieval Jewish philosopher and jurist who taught that if there is a country in which the inhabitants are sinners, then God-fearing Jews "should not mix with them and follow their evil ways but instead should go to dwell in caves and deserts and not conduct themselves according to the way of the sinners."[56] As Teitelbaum looked around at what he considered the corrupt state of contemporary American society, he asked, "If this Halakhah was not spoken concerning our age, then of which age was it spoken?" Given these circumstances, how did Teitelbaum justify remaining in Williamsburg at all, rather than immediately going to dwell in the contemporary equivalent of caves and deserts? The answer was that the greatest threat to his community, namely, non-Orthodox Jews in New York City, wanted to avoid Satmar as much as Satmar wanted to avoid them. Or as Teitelbaum put it, "The reason that we do not flee to the deserts [right now] is that the *apikorsim* [Jewish heretics] in their hatred, do not want to have anything to do with us, and they separate themselves from us and therefore it is as if we were living in a desert [in Williamsburg]."[57] In a profound irony, therefore, the leader of the group that the Lubavitcher Rebbe hailed in 1968 as an inspiration for other Jewish communities to remain in New York City had not only sought to relocate his followers to the countryside in the 1950s but also fantasized about separating completely from other Jews.

Devoted as Teitelbaum was to realizing his dream of a shtetl in the countryside, he was remarkably pragmatic when it came to what steps had to be taken for his community to survive in Williamsburg while they waited for the opportunity to move their portable camp in the desert. At a gathering to celebrate the dedication of a new Satmar school on the corner of Bedford Avenue and Hewes Street, Teitelbaum indicated that all present were expected to contribute one hundred dollars and explained, in eschatological terms, why it was still important to strengthen communal institutions in the neighborhood:

> Every place that we settle is merely a temporary waystation for we do not know at any given moment when the redemption will take place. . . . And especially our sojourn here in "Williamsburg" is always like a time of transit for we are expecting to move away from here and travel to another place at any moment. If this is the case, then why are we continually making new investments here? The necessity of this for the current moment becomes evident when we look at the example of the desert, when the Israelites did not know whether they would be setting up camp for a single day or even just for one night. Nevertheless, they erected the tabernacle . . . as if they had come there to settle permanently. . . . Similarly, we can say the same thing about Williamsburg.[58]

In these efforts, Teitelbaum was aided by his lieutenants, at least some of whom were profoundly skeptical about leaving the neighborhood because they viewed the prospective sites in the countryside as too far from the city and its economic opportunities, and were personally concerned about losing the power and prestige they had accrued in Williamsburg.[59] By the late 1950s, these men had come to realize that Satmar's position—and therefore their own—within the neighborhood's political landscape was becoming stronger with every passing year as other Jewish residents continued to abandon Williamsburg.

Despite being on the receiving end of Satmar's scorn, the non-Hasidic Jewish leaders of Williamsburg, including the most Americanized among them, desperately lobbied for the Hasidim to remain in the neighborhood. In April 1959, Sol Levy informed readers of the *Williamsburg News* that "thousands of Chassidic Jews are contemplating a mass exodus from Williamsburg."[60] The prospect of such an outmigration terrified Levy and, he assumed, many of his readers. "Can you imagine what an exodus of 10,000 would mean to the Burg," Levy wondered. "It's a menacing thought. But, even with the project, there are steps that could halt and even bring about the reversal of the trend of Chusids leaving." The solution proposed by a spokesman for the Hasidic community was for the NYCHA to set aside apartments "for exclusive use of the Chusids and they will be happy." In Levy's view, "This seems like a reasonable request. After all, the circumstances here are vastly different from that in other communities. Williamsburg is the world capital for the Chusids. It would be most unfortunate because a simple adjustment was not made by the Housing Authority that the entire community is destroyed. . . . It can be stopped." Levy saw an easy solution to the predicament: "The Authority, which is partially responsible for the unrest, can help merely by setting aside the apartments. We hope they cooperate."[61]

While Sol Levy brought news of a potential Hasidic exodus to the attention of his readers, representatives of the neighborhood's Orthodox establishment worked behind the scenes to intervene directly with Rabbi Yoel Teitelbaum. As Bernard Weinberger recalled, rumors circulated that Satmar planned to relocate to Mount Olive Township, New Jersey: "It was agreed that all efforts would be abortive if so large a segment of the community left *en masse*. A rabbinic delegation met with the *Satmar Rebbe* at 1:00 A.M. one Sunday morning to discuss with him mutual problems and the group left with the feeling that the *Rebbe* appreciated all the ramifications of relocating and that he would not undertake it unless forced by external factors."[62]

Over the next few years, as the city made progress on the construction of the housing projects in Williamsburg, the Satmar Rebbe continued to pursue his goal of establishing a settlement in the countryside, and the neighborhood's non-Hasidic Jews continued to leave the neighborhood. In June 1962, *Time* published an article titled "Exodus from Brooklyn," which suggested that after World War II, Hasidim had transformed Williamsburg into a veritable stairway to heaven but were now on the verge of abandoning their urban enclave for a suburban idyll of "ranch-style and split-level houses," in part because they refused to move into high-rise public housing projects whose elevators they could not use on the Sabbath. "For nearly 40 years, the majority of Hasidic Jews in the U.S. have sought to make paths of heaven out of the streets of a grimy corner of New York City: the Williamsburg section of Brooklyn. Now this colorful way of life is coming to an end."[63] Most readers of *Time* must have found the Hasidic prohibition against riding elevators on the Sabbath exotic or quaint, like the Amish avoidance of electricity. (The two groups were often lumped together in media accounts as black-clad long-bearded Luddites, despite their complex relationships to technology.)[64] But it may have been an even greater curiosity that Hasidim seemed to care more about potentially violating the Sabbath than about the typical, sometimes unspoken reasons why whites in New York City chose to abandon their neighborhoods for the suburbs rather than move into public housing—namely, fear of crime, an aversion to living with blacks and Latinos, and a desire to avoid the stigma of living in "the projects."

In 1963, the Mount Olive Township deal fell through because of local opposition in New Jersey, prompting Satmar to file a complaint in court charging " 'arbitrary, unreasonable and discriminatory' acts."[65] The community had to wait another decade before it could break ground on its self-styled shtetl. When that happened, in the mid-1970s, the long-anticipated founding of Kiryas Joel in Monroe County, New York, did not spur the mass exodus of the Hasidic community from Williamsburg that many had predicted in the late 1950s. Whether such a migration would have occurred earlier is impossible to know in retrospect. What is certain is that in 1963, in the absence of a new settlement outside the city where the community's rapidly growing population could find less expensive housing, the Hasidim of Williamsburg committed themselves to moving into the neighborhood's nearly completed public housing projects in large numbers and on their own terms.

Moving In

The first of the two public housing projects to be completed in South Williamsburg was Jonathan Williams Plaza, which began renting its 575 units in the summer of 1963—that is, in the same period that Satmar learned that it would not be able to move to New Jersey. While the projects were still in the planning stages in the late 1950s, the city had taken several steps to help encourage Jews to move into the buildings. First, housing officials informed potential applicants that based on a 1957 state law, preference in tenanting would be given to displaced residents who lived within one mile of the project. Since Jews constituted a majority of the residents in the area that had been cleared for the housing project sites, they possessed a significant advantage in obtaining units in the new buildings from the outset,

Jewish family moving into a public housing project
(Photograph by Nancy Rudolph, from *New Neighborhoods,*
New Lives [New York: NYCHA, 1964])

even though the citywide NYCHA waiting list at the time was overwhelmingly African American and Puerto Rican.[66] Second, as the NYCHA had
promised—in a concession that was unique to the Williamsburg projects—
Orthodox Jewish tenants would receive units on lower floors in order to
avoid the problem of riding elevators on the Sabbath.

These efforts echoed a broader NYCHA policy to attract and retain
white residents at a time when the number of blacks and Puerto Ricans
in public housing was skyrocketing. As Nicholas Dagen Bloom noted,
"William Reid [chairman of the NYCHA] welcomed a 1957 state law
that gave priority to residents already living within one mile of a new
project because it might attract more white tenants."[67] In explaining his
support of the law, Reid stated, "We don't try to create too sharp or too
sudden a difference between our projects and the neighborhoods around

them. It is our aim to stimulate integration, not to force it."[68] Under
Reid, the NYCHA created a division called Intergroup Relations; it was
initially headed by Madison Jones, formerly the youth director and special assistant in housing for the NAACP, who declared, "We're trying to
kill the idea that public housing is minority housing."[69] In parts of the
city where whites were particularly opposed to minority residents, Jones
conceded that "as little as 10 percent Negro or Puerto Rican tenancy
would be regarded as satisfactory."[70]

To meet its policy goals, the NYCHA developed the "Phase Program," which categorized housing projects based on the degree of preference that white applicants would receive in tenanting: "whites first,"
"whites only," and "non-whites first, half the time."[71] While the Phase
Program succeeded in increasing the number of new white tenants in
some of the city's projects in the early 1960s, it did nothing to stop the
broader outflow of white residents from public housing. It also attracted
the attention of the State Commission Against Discrimination, which
determined in 1962 that the program, which included identifying all
applicants by race, was discriminatory.[72] In response, the NYCHA eliminated racial coding of applicants, but as Bloom noted, "Intergroup
worked doubly hard to sell projects to whites. Efforts in 1964 brought
forth new success stories, including Williams Houses [Jonathan Williams
Plaza] tenanted at 70 percent white, Chelsea at 68 percent white, Clare-
mont at 33 percent white, and McKinley at 27 percent white."[73]

Seen within this broader context, the fact that roughly 70 percent of
the units in Jonathan Williams Plaza were rented to whites reflected the
NYCHA's long-standing policy goals as much as it did the lobbying efforts of local Jewish boosters in Williamsburg. That these whites were almost exclusively Hasidic reflected the very particular demographics of
South Williamsburg. The figure for Jonathan Williams was the highest
of any new housing project in the city, indicating the unusual degree to
which Hasidim were willing to live in public housing at a time when only
3.5 percent of the city's white population lived in the projects and those
who did were increasingly moving out.[74] Indeed, the overall percentage of
whites in New York's public housing declined from 42.7 percent in 1962,
to 27.9 percent in 1969, to 14.1 percent in 1974, eventually reaching 5.0
percent in 2006.[75] Yet throughout the 1960s and into the 1970s, when the
construction of new public housing in Williamsburg, as in the rest of the
city, basically came to a halt, Hasidim continued to move into the neighborhood's projects in large numbers. Thus, while the high percentage of

whites (that is, Hasidim) in Jonathan Williams may be viewed as a sign of the success of NYCHA policies, the outcome owed more to the anomalous nature of the local Hasidic community and the housing authority's willingness to accommodate its distinctive concerns.

The first of these concerns involved the issue of elevators on the Sabbath, which had prompted members of the Orthodox Jewish community to criticize the high-rise design of the projects from the very beginning. Yet as Bernard Weinberger recalled in "The Miracle of Williamsburg," NYCHA officials were determined to find a solution, even hiring an engineer who was a member of the Association of Orthodox Jewish Scientists to design a special "Shabbos elevator" that would not contravene Sabbath laws by automatically stopping on each floor. The engineer consulted with both the Satmar Rebbe and Rabbi Moshe Feinstein, the preeminent legal authority for non-Hasidic Haredi Jews in the United States. According to Weinberger, neither rabbi "would formally approve the proposed arrangements for the elevator system," yet they also did not issue a formal prohibition, or *issur*.[76] This account was later confirmed by a NYCHA official who explained in detail: "The Pupa and Tselem Hasidim agreed on the Shabbos elevators. Viener hesitated. I went to the Satmarer Rebbe. I explained to him that there was no increase in the flow of electricity when someone stepped in. The Rebbe felt that using the elevators on Shabbos would look like one was doing a job on a weekday."[77] Yoel Teitelbaum worried that people would see Hasidim riding the special elevators on the Sabbath and wrongly assume it was permissible in general, thereby contravening the Jewish legal principle known as *maris ayin*, or "appearance to the eye." But according to the NYCHA official, "He agreed not to give out an issur (ban or edict) prohibiting use of the elevator."

In the absence of a definitive legal ruling from the Satmar Rebbe, his Hasidim were now free to decide for themselves which of several approaches to take. Although some were willing to use the Sabbath elevators, many continued to reject the idea outright. At this critical juncture, NYCHA decided to prime the pump, in several ways: "The Housing Authority assigned to this project a manager who was a former Williamsburg resident, known to many old-timers, and as his assistant they sent a former rabbi of Chasidic background. Both of these extremely able men helped foster confidence in the development and rendered invaluable service in the renting of the apartments."[78] Stephen Price, who lived in Williamsburg from 1967 to 1975 and worked for the Williamsburg Community Corporation, the local antipoverty program, from 1966 to 1967, interviewed one of these NYCHA officials in 1978 about what happened next. "The rentals weren't going well," the official told Price. "I went directly to the Satmarer Rebbe. I wanted to get a 'star tenant' to move in. [Yosef] Ashkenazi said he might be interested. I took out an application and made sure he would get the best apartment in the best building of Jonathan Williams. He signed it right away. The Rebbe was silent, which the Gemora [the Aramaic section of the Talmud] interprets as a consent."[79]

NYCHA realized that to convince Hasidim to move into the buildings, it needed to get the imprimatur of the Hasidic elite. It accomplished this by giving "the best apartment in the best building" to Yosef Ashkenazi, the Satmar Rebbe's *gabbai*, or assistant, and one of the most powerful people in the community. Half a century later, a Hasidic resident of Williamsburg confirmed this approach in an interview with the authors, telling us, "Some of the best families moved into public housing in the 1960s," adding that Hasidim were attracted by the units' new construction and modern appliances; plus, renting made sense financially because real estate in the neighborhood was considered a poor investment.[80] Since a cross-section of the Hasidic community, including members of the elite, moved into public housing during the 1960s, living in the buildings did not carry the social stigma that it did for many other New Yorkers, and was even viewed as a step up from the neighborhood's decrepit tenements.

Once the Hasidim decided to move into the projects in large numbers, intense jockeying erupted over who would get units on the more desirable, lower floors. At this point, according to the former NYCHA employee interviewed by Price, some of the Hasidic applicants lobbied local politicians to intervene on their behalf, invented medical conditions that supposedly prevented them from walking up and down stairs, or offered bribes in an effort to secure one of the prized low-floor apartments:

> The Hasidim went to [George] Swetnick to get the lower floors.
> . . . When I designated a high floor for a Satmarer family, I called
> the Rebbe, and he gave his blessing to the apartment. The Ha-
> sidim wanted the lower floors because they wouldn't use the ele-
> vators on Shabbos. They all came in with doctors' notes. All the
> husbands had hernias and the wives had varicose veins. I called
> [Lipa] Friedman and told him not to give out doctors' notes in-
> discriminately. . . . I decided to rent the lower floors first so that I
> could be honest with the Hasidim who wanted lower floors by

telling them none were available. . . . A few of the Orthodox Jews and Hasidim offered bribes. I told [Bernard] Weinberger and Friedman to announce in shul [synagogue] that anyone who offered a bribe would be sent to jail. There was also pressure from the politicians.[81]

These behaviors point to an enduring cynicism about civil authority among Hasidim in Williamsburg who had grown up in the corrupt environment of eastern Europe and then survived the depredations of the Holocaust. As one Hasidic leader in Williamsburg succinctly put it to Price, "If you can bribe the Nazis, you can bribe anyone."[82] Having survived concentration camps like Auschwitz in part by successfully "organizing"—camp slang for using one's wits to get more food, a better bunk, and so on—some Hasidim evidently viewed it as natural that they would apply the same approach to getting an apartment on a lower floor in the projects.

The local politician to whom Hasidim turned when they needed something in Williamsburg during the 1960s was George Swetnick, the son of Russian Jewish immigrants. He had succeeded Joe Sharkey as district leader and, in 1966, as city councilman for the neighborhood. When Swetnick passed away, in 1968, the *New York Times* described him as "a thoroughly political man who savored the intrigues, battles, and friendships of the old-style Brooklyn Democratic organization." He worked "from behind his rolltop desk at the Seneca Democratic Club . . . held office hours on Monday and Thursday evenings, and found jobs, apartments, health and legal services for 100 constituents a week."[83] By then, the Seneca Club, whose building Swetnick had purchased—he transferred ownership to the club in his will—was already legendary as a "colorful conglomerate of his polyglot district, where Negroes and Puerto Ricans mingled with Hasidic Jews in fur-brimmed hats and long black coats."

The Seneca Club was located on Lee Avenue, right in the heart of what had become the Hasidic enclave. Like any good machine politician, Swetnick doled out favors to all his constituents, but he was especially solicitous to the Hasidic community.[84] Swetnick had thrown in his lot with the Hasidim because they now represented the biggest bloc of white—or at least white enough—voters in a district that was rapidly becoming majority Puerto Rican and African American. As Stephen Price noted, "The Jews fleeing the Southside had decided to leave Williamsburg and move to Long Island or the suburbs. This posed a dilemma for the politicians, and they resolved it by making direct appeals to the Hasidim."[85] In this regard, Hasidim were the ironic inheritors of the political capital built up by generations of non-Hasidic Jews in Williamsburg—ironic because the Hasidim had assiduously separated themselves from, and even sought to displace, other Jews living in the neighborhood for more than a decade.

For their part, Hasidim were happy to support the local Democratic machine as long as their particular needs were addressed. Stephen Price observed, "Many of the Hasidic and other Jewish informants stressed that the Democratic leader, George Swetnick, needed the Hasidim more than they needed him. This is probably true. With the older Jewish community leaving the area in large numbers, Swetnick needed to solidify his base in the white community to offset the large numbers of Puerto Ricans moving in."[86] The result was that machine politicians like Swetnick cultivated the Hasidim assiduously, including helping them get apartments in the new housing projects. As one Hasidic community leader later recalled to Price, "The Hasidim liked the politicians. It was easy to get in [to public housing]."[87]

Besides the problem posed by elevators, the other main concern Hasidim had about the housing projects was their reputation for crime. As one community leader put it, "At first Hasidim didn't want to get in [the projects]. They were afraid of the high-rises, they were afraid of being mugged, the girls were afraid of getting into the elevators alone."[88] In 1958, the journalist Harrison Salisbury had published an influential exposé of juvenile delinquency in New York City's housing projects in the *New York Times*. Referring to the projects as "new-style ghettos," "housing jungles," and "slums . . . shut up within new brick and steel," Salisbury informed his readers that "chaos, conflict, confusion have inevitably resulted."[89]

Crime had become a flashpoint for Williamsburg's Hasidic community when, on October 15, 1962, Rabbi Bernard Eisdorfer, a Holocaust survivor and close disciple of Yoel Teitelbaum, was fatally assaulted two blocks from his home. Although crime had been increasing in the neighborhood for several years, the murder shocked the Hasidic community. A day after Eisdorfer's burial, Lipa Friedman, a local Hasidic powerbroker, told the *Brooklyn Eagle*, "The people are afraid. Parents do not let their children out in the evening. The murder has made a very bad impression on all of us."[90] That week, the *Williamsburg News* weighed in on what it called the "Williamsburg Crime Crisis," lamenting, "There have been strong suggestions that the Satmar group will uproot itself from our community because of the killing. We sympathize with them. There is little solace that we can offer other than our sincere hopes that leaders of the Satmar group will reconsider such decision, if such a decision has been made. ... We urge the Chassidic community—one which has brought Williamsburg untold credit—to remain where it belongs—IN WILLIAMSBURG."[91]

A year later, in 1963, with the option of moving to their own settlement off the table because of the collapse of the Mount Olive deal, Hasidic leaders worked to ensure the safety of community members moving into Jonathan Williams Plaza. As the NYCHA official interviewed by Stephen Price recalled:

> The [Satmar] Rebbe questioned me closely. He asked about security, and who would get apartments. He was determined that there be a strict screening of tenants. I told him that there would be integration on every floor. The Hasidim are concerned with the class of people they are living near. They don't mind Puerto Ricans or blacks if they're middle class. ... I told the Puerto Ricans that they might hear singing from the Hasidim on Friday nights. I told the Jewish families that they should tolerate singing on Christmas, I selected nice Puerto Rican families.[92]

The Satmar Rebbe's desire for a "strict screening of tenants" jibed with the housing authority's standard practices in that era. Ruben Franco, the head of the NYCHA under Mayor Rudolph Giuliani in the late 1980s, observed, "In the early years ... Housing Authority managers could apply rigorous, and sometimes subjective or even discriminatory screening criteria to new applicants. As admission rules changed ... the screening of new applicants was essentially eliminated."[93] In 1953, the NYCHA had introduced twenty-one criteria for assessing the "desirability" of potential tenants, including "narcotic addiction, single parenthood, out-of-wedlock children, teen parenthood, 'highly irregular work history,' 'lack of parental control,' mental illness, poor housekeeping, and 'lack of furniture.' "[94] Despite these rigorous—or to critics, invasive and discriminatory—screening criteria, William Reid, the chairman of the NYCHA, still dreamed in 1959 about a "new invention—something akin to a Geiger counter that would enable us to reject unerringly the potential troublemakers, when they apply for an apartment."[95]

As long as black and Puerto Rican applicants were screened to filter out "potential troublemakers," Hasidim, unlike the many whites who continued to abandon public housing in the early 1960s, were happy to move into Jonathan Williams Plaza and, a year later, Independence Towers. While they worried about crime, there is no evidence that Hasidim were concerned about the social stigma then commonly associated with living in public housing or the corrosive moral and social effects that dwelling in the buildings might have on their children, which so bothered contemporary critics. Nor did they express any general aversion to living with blacks or Puerto Ricans. On the contrary, Hasidim preferred to live with members of these communities rather than with the non-Hasidic Jews who had once formed a majority in South Williamsburg. The reason for this was simple: Hasidic leaders were unconcerned that community members would seek to emulate the neighborhood's Puerto Ricans and blacks, since they were widely perceived to be at the bottom of New York City's socioeconomic and racial hierarchy. By contrast, non-Hasidic Jews posed a much greater threat, since their lifestyle represented a possible path of assimilation and upward mobility for members of the Hasidic community. What troubled Hasidim in the renting process, therefore, was the potential physical danger posed by the Puerto Ricans and blacks with whom they would be sharing the projects, not any moral threat they might have posed.

There was a striking contrast between the extraordinary solicitousness with which the housing authority treated potential Hasidic tenants throughout the renting process at Jonathan Williams Plaza and the rigorous screening applied to black and Puerto Rican applicants to ensure that they were "nice," as the NYCHA official put it. This unequal treatment eventually inspired a successful lawsuit filed in 1976 by the Williamsburg Fair Housing Committee on behalf of Puerto Rican and African American applicants who claimed that they had been systematically discriminated against in the renting of the neighborhood's public housing projects since the early 1960s. During the planning and construction of Jonathan Williams Plaza and Independence Towers, the concerns of South Williamsburg's already large and rapidly growing Puerto Rican population and its much smaller African American community had not been taken into consideration. There were several reasons for this omission. First, as the housing authority admitted in the course of the 1976 lawsuit, "The NYCHA decided prior to, and at initial tenanting to rent apartments at Jonathan Williams [and Independence Towers] in order to achieve an ethno-racial distribution of 75% white, 20% Puerto Rican, and 5% black."[96] In short, the housing authority did not see the need to consult with Puerto Ricans or African Americans because they had determined in advance that their numbers would be strictly limited by quotas.

The second reason why the NYCHA had ignored the concerns of the area's blacks and Puerto Ricans regarding public housing was that the local Democratic machine viewed their growing presence as a threat to its hegemony in the neighborhood. As a Puerto Rican community leader bluntly recalled, "The Seneca Club had no interest in the Puerto Ricans."[97] By 1960, Puerto Ricans (divided between South and East Williamsburg) constituted around 45 percent of Williamsburg's total population of 165,000 people, with Jews an estimated 25 percent, African Americans (concentrated on the border with Bedford-Stuyvesant) 15 percent, and others (mainly Italians in East Williamsburg, Poles and Lithuanians in North Williamsburg, etc.) 15 percent. In South Williamsburg, however, Hasidim and other Jewish residents represented a much higher percentage than in the neighborhood overall, and they constituted a majority in the blocks where the new public housing projects were located.[98]

In the late 1950s, when decisions regarding the housing projects were initially being made, the leaders of the Puerto Rican community in Williamsburg were not yet able to compete effectively with the well-organized Jewish community and its supporters in the local political machine. African Americans, though they represented an especially significant segment of the applicants for public housing citywide, were largely excluded from the political jockeying over its construction in South Williamsburg, since they lacked a strong activist presence in the neighborhood—unlike their clout in the adjoining areas of Bedford-Stuyvesant and Clinton Hill. Instead, their interests were typically represented by organizations dominated by Puerto Ricans or by white clergymen. The gross imbalance of political power in Williamsburg changed over the course of the late 1960s and early 1970s as local Puerto Rican leaders came into their own and began to challenge the waning Democratic machine in Williamsburg. During this period, a new generation of Puerto Rican activists in Williamsburg emerged out of the intercommunal competition for Great Society poverty funds in the neighborhood, and out of the ethnic pride movement of the late 1960s, which led to the creation of the Young Lords, among other groups.

In the early 1960s, as Jonathan Williams Plaza reached completion, a new cohort of leaders emerged to represent the interests of local Puerto Ricans and African Americans in what became a highly contentious tenanting process. The struggle over apartments in the project served as a crucible for these leaders, many of whom would go on to fight future battles with representatives of the Hasidic community in Williamsburg over housing, poverty program funds, and crime. The first to speak out on the issue were young white progressive Christian clergymen whose congregations had once been populated by white ethnics but were now almost entirely Puerto Rican or African American.[99] Perhaps more than any other neighborhood in New York City during this period, Williamsburg became a place where Jewish and Christian religious leaders competed with one another to shape the built environment.[100]

Foremost among the local clergymen was Father (later Monsignor) Bryan Karvelis, a half-Lithuanian, half-Irish priest who arrived in Williamsburg straight out of seminary in 1956 and remained for the following four decades at Transfiguration Roman Catholic Church on Marcy Avenue.[101] Inspired by the *Catholic Worker* founder Dorothy Day, with whom he had volunteered as a young seminarian, Father Karvelis played a key role as a spokesperson and political broker on behalf of the Puerto Rican community in the 1960s and early 1970s. Initially, Karvelis, whose parish borders included the new housing projects, opposed their construction, telling the *New York Sunday News* in September 1962 that the city should invest its resources in improving existing housing stock. "A lot of housing in Williamsburg neighborhoods could be repaired and made more livable at less of a cost than the monstrous projects," he said.[102] Karvelis lamented what he saw as the devastating social and psychological impact of the projects: "Such huge housing developments produce problems in an exaggerated form almost overnight. . . . People who move into them soon begin to suffer a sense of inferiority because of the impersonality and regimentation in the low-income projects. The youngsters feel it too, and seek membership in street gangs to find some sense of status and belonging."[103]

These remarks reflected the growing chorus of voices in the late 1950s and early 1960s that rejected the slum clearance and public housing construction mandated by the Housing Act of 1949. Indeed, they clearly echoed—and were probably directly influenced by—the stinging critique leveled by the urbanist Jane Jacobs in her now classic work, *The Death and Life of Great American Cities*, published in 1961. Jacobs wrote, "Low-income projects that become worse centers of delinquency, vandalism, and general social hopelessness than the slums they were supposed to replace. . . . This is not the rebuilding of cities. This is the sacking of cities."[104]

In 1963, a year after publicly opposing the projects, Karvelis reversed himself and joined forces with another young white clergyman, the Reverend Richard J. Neuhaus, to establish the Williamsburg Area Renewal

Effort, or WARE, an organization whose stated purpose was "to deal with matters of housing, particularly those problems and opportunities arising from urban renewal programs."[105] Neuhaus had become the pastor of St. John the Evangelist Church in Williamsburg in 1961 when he was only twenty-five years old, taking over a Lutheran congregation that was once German but was now primarily African American. Although he later converted to Catholicism, took priestly vows, and, famously, embraced conservatism (serving as an adviser to President George W. Bush and founding the conservative journal *First Things*), Neuhaus spent the 1960s fighting for affordable housing in Williamsburg, protesting the war in Vietnam, and getting arrested while demonstrating at the Democratic National Convention in Chicago in 1968.

On October 25, 1963, Neuhaus wrote a letter, in his capacity as chairman of WARE, to the housing authority regarding tenanting at Jonathan Williams Plaza. He noted that in August community leaders had informed WARE of a "discriminatory pattern in the renting of Jonathan Williams Houses [*sic*] ... with particular reference to the treatment of Spanish-speaking applicants."[106] Throughout September and October, a series of meetings on the issue had been held between these community leaders, WARE, and housing authority officials, including two senior Intergroup Relations officers for the NYCHA, Alfred Waxman and Blanca Cedeno, who had started her career as a housing assistant in 1952 and would eventually work her way up to vice chair of the authority in 1978.[107] Cedeno was an advocate for the Puerto Rican community, later serving, for example, as the chair of the board of trustees for Boriqua College, a pioneering Puerto Rican educational institution that opened a branch on North 6th Street in Williamsburg during the 1970s.[108] Presiding over one of the meetings was Milton Mollen, the powerful chairman of the Housing and Redevelopment Board.

The city was finally taking the local Puerto Rican community's interests into consideration. The question was whether it was too late to affect the tenanting at Jonathan Williams Plaza. Neuhaus acknowledged that "decisions made long ago" precluded significant change. Consequences of those decisions included the construction of Jonathan Williams as a vest-pocket project, which meant that it was too small to satisfy the enormous demand for public housing in the local Puerto Rican community; the lack of "welfare assistance for rents"; and the rents in the project being higher than if it had been federally funded, rather than state sponsored, resulting in a "dangerous pattern of de facto segregation's being created by the concentration of new housing in Williamsburg which can be afforded only by families of at least middle income." Neuhaus summarized the situation: "It is obvious, of course, that whatever discrimination exists in connection with Jonathan Williams is a result of the planning of the project." At the same time, striking a conciliatory tone, he commended the NYCHA, writing that Jonathan Williams was "being rented on a non-discriminatory basis and [WARE] has reason to expect that this will be true also in the renting of the remaining units."

Despite generally praising the housing authority staff, Neuhaus implicitly criticized Alfred Waxman, the Intergroup Relations officer assigned to Jonathan Williams Plaza, in his letter. On November 6, 1963, Waxman responded by sending an angry, exculpatory report with his version of events to his boss, William Valentine, the recently appointed African American director of Intergroup Relations for the NYCHA, who had previously served as the assistant housing director of the New York State Commission Against Discrimination (later renamed the State Commission for Human Rights). Valentine forwarded the report to William Reid, the chairman of NYCHA, explaining that Waxman "has made very deliberate and complete efforts to answer [WARE's] questions and to dispel any suspicions on their part that any discriminatory practices were employed in any phase of the renting process at Williams."[109]

Both men were clearly anxious to demonstrate that Intergroup Relations was not engaging in illegal discrimination against Puerto Rican and black applicants, even though it was under a mandate to attract and retain white residents. Caught between a proverbial rock and a hard place, Valentine and Waxman were undoubtedly aware that sentiment was shifting away from the NYCHA policies of the 1950s. Only a few months later, in January 1964, the *New York Times* reported, "The City Housing Authority has quietly given up a policy of holding apartments for tenants whose presence would further racial integration and is now simply 'encouraging' applicants to go to projects where they would provide better balance."[110] A separate article noted that a temporary state commission had "urged that the state repeal a [1957] law giving preference in housing projects to families within a one-mile radius of the project, saying this tended to promote racial segregation," and had recommended studying "the question of revising the 'rigid and inflexible formula' for determining the eligibility for admission to and continued occupancy of public housing."[111]

With these changes already in the air, Waxman began his report by bitterly observing, "The Williamsburg Area Renewal Effort organization operates in an area rife with antagonism and mistrust. They believe that secret commitments, secretly arrived at, made by persons they do not name, with persons in the Housing Authority, they do not name, are responsible for the high rents at Jonathan Williams, the high-priced cooperative at Independence, and the complete lack of low rent housing in the area, and that it all represents a concerted attempt to drive Puerto Ricans from the area."[112] The clear implication was that the local Jewish community was a party to these "secret commitments." Waxman also noted that members of WARE had "demanded to know why special groups were allowed to file applications in advance, what racial quotas we were setting, etc.," and stated that the organization would be happy with 30 percent minority tenancy, but "it really didn't matter because, regardless of what we did, the entire development would go minority in ten years." In response to WARE's allegations, Waxman "promised to cooperate with them in any way I could in reference to establishing a good racially balanced-tenancy at Jonathan Williams," but did not deny that there were racial quotas in place at the project.[113]

In his report, Waxman named the local "community leaders" whose complaints had inspired WARE to take up the issue of rentals at Jonathan Williams Plaza. Unlike the young white clergymen who had only recently arrived in the neighborhood to serve their congregations, these leaders were members of the local Puerto Rican community.[114] Celia Vice belonged to the early wave of Puerto Ricans who had settled along the Navy Yard adjoining Williamsburg in the 1920s. Vice became a pioneering businesswoman, a member of civil rights and community organizations, and, in 1960, the first woman to serve as grand marshal of the city's Puerto Rican Day Parade.[115] As the first Puerto Rican woman to work as a real estate broker in Brooklyn, Vice also had an intimate knowledge of housing issues, which would prove useful in her negotiations with the housing authority over Jonathan Williams Plaza. According to Waxman, Vice called or met with representatives of the NYCHA on several occasions in the fall of 1963, alleging that Puerto Ricans who had applied to Jonathan Williams Plaza were not being called in for interviews, or if they were, that the "all-white and Jewish" staff tried to dissuade them from renting units, charges that Waxman denied.

Another local Puerto Rican who joined the struggle over tenanting was Felix Cosme, who worked as a social worker at Epiphany Church, a Catholic congregation in Williamsburg led by another progressive priest, Matthew Foley. Epiphany and Catholic Charities had cofounded Arriba

Juntos (Upward Together), an organization dedicated to housing issues and family counseling among the neighborhood's rapidly growing Puerto Rican population. After getting his start with Arriba Juntos, Cosme later became involved in grassroots efforts to secure poverty-program funding in the mid-1960s for Williamsburg's Puerto Rican residents, eventually becoming deputy commissioner of the New York City Human Resources Administration.[116] Cosme provided WARE with the names of 125 Puerto Ricans who had applied for units in Jonathan Williams Plaza, of whom, Cosme claimed in a 1963 meeting with the housing authority, "only one Puerto Rican had been called in."[117] As with Celia Vice's allegations, however, Waxman dismissed these charges, writing to Valentine: "I questioned the accuracy of their figures, based solely on Cosme's work . . . and offered to prove my statements: Theirs were only vocal issuances based on nothing."[118]

The archives of the New York City Housing Authority do not preserve any record of how, or even whether, William Reid responded to Waxman's report. Nor did Vice, Cosme, Neuhaus, or any of the other activists representing the Puerto Rican community leave accounts of the negotiations and their outcome. In contrast to Jonathan Williams Plaza, there are no extant documents regarding any similar negotiations that may have occurred over the tenanting of Independence Towers, which took place the following year. It was no accident that the plans of local boosters to purchase Independence Towers and convert the buildings from low-income housing into a private, middle-income co-operative, a proposal previously endorsed by Reid, ended up being blocked by the state on the eve of the project's completion.[119] It was one more sign that popular sentiment was inexorably shifting away from the concerted efforts to attract and retain white residents at any cost that had characterized housing policy in the 1950s, and was moving instead toward providing as many affordable units as possible for the most financially needy.[120] And yet because many Hasidim in Williamsburg were poor, numerous members of the Hasidic community were able to satisfy the low-income requirement at Independence Towers, and as in Jonathan Williams Plaza, they would come to form a large majority of its residents once the project's 742 units were finally tenanted in 1965.

After many twists and turns, Hasidim remained in Williamsburg during the 1960s by anchoring themselves in what had originally seemed to many the unlikeliest of places—high-rise low-income public housing projects. As they had done in the 1950s with the neighborhood's tenements,

Hasidic man walking past the construction of the Independence
Towers public housing project, early 1960s (Irving I. Herzberg
Photograph Collection, Brooklyn Public Library,
Brooklyn Collection)

the Hasidim transformed the projects into "paths of heaven" where they
could continue to embrace their distinctive lifestyle in an environment
that was at once radically different from the towns they had come from in
Europe and yet, in its multiethnic character, more similar to them than the
virtually homogenous "shtetl" that they would soon establish in Kiryas
Joel. In retrospect, it is easy to criticize the zero-sum approach that Hasidim took when it came to public housing in Williamsburg. And yet the
simple fact that they were willing to live with Puerto Ricans and African
Americans in the 1960s, let alone in housing projects, strikingly distinguished them from the vast majority of whites, including many liberal critics of racism who nevertheless resided in highly segregated suburbs and
would never have dreamed of setting foot in public housing.

The Hasidim did not move into the projects out of a liberal desire to support racial integration. They did so because the housing was a step up from the tenements in which many of them had previously resided, because it was affordable, because they could not—yet—move out of the city to their own settlement, because they were not deterred by the widespread stigma associated with public housing, and because whatever fear of crime they had was outweighed by these other factors and by their confidence that they would be able to deal with any threats effectively. In short, they did so for the same reasons that hundreds of thousands of African American and Puerto Rican residents of New York City moved into public housing in the same period. Had Hasidim not moved into the public housing projects in such large numbers when they did, it is very unlikely that the community would have been able to remain in Williamsburg. So their decision was fateful, not only for the Hasidic community but for the future of the neighborhood as well.

CHAPTER THREE

The Politics of Poverty

O N APRIL 24, 1964, President Lyndon Johnson visited Inez, Kentucky, in the heart of coal country, to open the first front in the War on Poverty, which he had declared in his State of the Union address earlier in the year. The iconic photo of Johnson squatting on a porch with Tom Fletcher, an unemployed father of eight, belonged to a long tradition of representing poverty in the United States with images of rural and, especially, Appalachian whites. Two years later, on February 4, 1966, Senator Robert Kennedy took a walking tour of Bedford-Stuyvesant in Brooklyn to see up close what the recently published Moynihan Report had called the problems of the "urban Negro."[1] In December 1966, with Mayor John Lindsay and Senator Jacob Javits at his side, Kennedy announced the creation of his own antipoverty initiative, the Bedford-Stuyvesant Development and Service Corporation.[2] By then, the face of poverty in America, at least as promoted by the national media and federal policy makers, was no longer primarily rural or white. Instead, as Martin Gilens has written, "Although the true racial composition of the American poor remained stable the face of poverty in the news media became markedly darker [and more urban] between 1965 and 1967."[3]

It is safe to say that one group neither Johnson nor Kennedy had in mind when they launched the War on Poverty in the mid-1960s was the Hasidim of Williamsburg. During his campaign for the U.S. Senate

in 1964, Kennedy visited Congregation Yetev Lev D'Satmar on Bedford
Avenue in Williamsburg and met with Rabbi Yoel Teitelbaum before
speaking to a large crowd of Hasidim, so he was at least aware of the community.[4] But this was part of a whirlwind vote-getting tour of Brooklyn
that included "appearances before Negroes in Bedford-Stuyvesant, Italians in Williamsburg and Poles in Greenpoint," as the *New York Daily
News* put it, not part of his later "poverty tour," as it became known, of
hard-hit communities around the United States.[5]

Yet back in 1930, when Mike Gold published his best-selling novel
Jews Without Money, about hardscrabble immigrant life on the Lower East
Side, the existence of Jewish poverty had been a given. As Gold put it,
"The great mass of Jews in the world today are not millionaire bankers, but
paupers and workers. I have told in my book a tale of Jewish poverty in one
ghetto, that of New York. The same story can be told of a hundred other
ghettoes scattered over all the world."[6] By the time Mike Gold died, in
1967 in suburban Terra Linda, California, however, the idea of poor Jews
had become practically oxymoronic, as Naomi Levine and Martin Hochbaum lamented in their exposé *Poor Jews: An American Awakening* in 1974:
"To many people, the phrase 'the Jewish poor' is a contradiction in terms.
Jews are simply not regarded as poor."[7]

In the decades following World War II, Jewish poverty in the United
States became virtually invisible—but did not actually cease to exist—for
a variety of reasons, including the entry of most American Jews into the
middle and upper classes, their large-scale suburbanization, the emerging
focus on other impoverished urban communities, the widespread perception that Jews "take care of their own," and the stubborn persistence of
anti-Semitic stereotypes regarding hidden Jewish wealth.[8] In addition, as
Levine and Hochbaum noted, "traditional Jewish pride, which prevents
many poor Jews from seeking out the public and private services to
which they are entitled, is another reason why it is has been difficult to
identify poor Jews."[9]

In New York City, where roughly a third of the entire American Jewish population resided in the early 1970s, the sheer scale of the problem
made it particularly vexing. Despite stereotypes to the contrary, approximately 15 percent of the Jewish population of New York was poor or
nearly poor in 1970, constituting around 15 percent of the overall number of impoverished residents in the city.[10] And at a time when the federal poverty threshold for a nonfarm family of four was $3,968, 15.7
percent of foreign-born Jews in New York City were surviving on $3,000

a year or less, comparable to the rate of 16.3 percent among the city's Puerto Ricans, though poverty within the latter community received much more attention.[11]

The War on Poverty did not render New York's poor Jews more visible—with one notable exception. In fact, its programs tended to obscure the problem of Jewish poverty in the city, especially in comparison with those groups for whom the programs were originally designed. As Levine and Hochbaum put it, in New York and elsewhere, "the poverty program is frequently viewed as a program that 'belongs' to blacks and Puerto Ricans."[12] Poor Jews faced challenges that were distinctive, even compared with those confronting other white ethnics. As "one active participant in New York City's poverty program" observed to Levine and Hochbaum, "Jews are always perceived as having money hidden away, and that the poorest among them are viewed as having secret sources of income."[13]

Structural obstacles diminished Jewish participation in federal anti-poverty programs. The Economic Opportunity Act of 1964 called for the creation of a decentralized system of local poverty areas to which federal funds would be distributed and administered by community corporations run by locally elected boards of directors.[14] In New York City, twenty-six poverty areas were created, and federal funds were allocated according to three major indices: "welfare population; number of live births in city hospital wards per 100 population; and juvenile delinquency per 100 juveniles between the ages of seven and 20."[15] As Cassie Miller noted, "The criteria used to designate the city poverty areas tended to favor those inhabited by blacks and Puerto Ricans, and to discount the problems faced by white ethnic communities. Poor white senior citizens, in particular, tended to be overlooked."[16]

This had an especially deleterious impact on poor Jews in New York City. During the late 1960s and early 1970s, more than 60 percent of the Jewish poor in New York City were sixty years or older, in dramatic contrast to the general population, where 75 percent of the poor were younger than sixty years old.[17] In addition, many of the Jewish poor, especially the elderly, were ashamed to apply for welfare programs and believed that "poverty is simply a burden that one accepts."[18] The result, according to an investigation by the Office of Economic Opportunity (the federal agency created and originally headed by R. Sargent Shriver to administer much of the War on Poverty) was that "group characteristics (of the Jewish poor) do not relate to the indices originally used by the Poverty Council to determine target areas."[19]

And yet from the very beginning of the War on Poverty in New York City there was one group of Jews that insisted on making itself visible and on receiving its share of antipoverty services—the Hasidim of Brooklyn, especially the Hasidic community of Williamsburg. In a 1972 exposé, "The Invisible Jewish Poor," Ann Wolfe identified Hasidim as "the third largest poverty group in New York," after blacks and Puerto Ricans.[20] Demographically, poor Hasidim differed dramatically from the majority of impoverished Jews in the city and more closely resembled poor blacks and Puerto Ricans in that most were under sixty years of age and many had families with small children. (The median family size in Hasidic Williamsburg was 6.3 children in 1972.)[21] Moreover, Hasidim initially appeared on the radar screen of antipoverty programs because of their proximity to other affected communities. As Phyllis Franck noted in her study of Jewish poverty: "Because the community is so insulated . . . it was only when poor blacks and Puerto Ricans living in Williamsburg began to receive aid that the problems of the Hasidim came to light."[22] And once they became aware of the scale of the aid available, Hasidim in Williamsburg quickly understood that either they could literally get with the program or they would be frozen out of the significant antipoverty funds allocated to the neighborhood, then considered the sixth poorest in the city.[23]

The aggressive approach of Hasidim in Williamsburg toward the poverty program differentiated them from other Jews in New York City. Mayor John Lindsay assigned Eleanor Norton, the director of his Human Rights Commission, to address the growing concern among white ethnics that their communities were not receiving enough of the poverty funds allocated to the city. On the one hand, Norton, who had earlier served as an organizer for the Student Nonviolent Coordinating Committee and worked for the American Civil Liberties Union, advocated in a memo to Lindsay for the "strengthening of liaison efforts with emerging protest groups: emerging white ethnic groups (Italians, Jewish, etc.); homosexuals; the handicapped; women's rights organizations, etc."[24] Yet Norton also expressed concern that such efforts might lead to balkanization: "I believe we are courting disaster by handing out resources to each community on an ethnic basis and that the likely result will be Italians comparing the 'Italian' share to the 'Jewish' share and right on down the line for a dozen or so ethnic groups—so that it will all ultimately come back to haunt City Hall."[25] While Poles and Italians in the city generally supported "distributing services through ethnic channels," Miller wrote, "Jewish New Yorkers were fundamentally opposed to anything that resembled a quota system."[26] Indeed, leaders of a number of important Jewish organizations in the city wrote to Lindsay in 1973 regarding the matter: "The granting of benefits to persons on the basis of their race or ethnic origin would amount to discrimination against equally meritorious persons who are of a different grouping."[27]

By contrast, Hasidic leaders in Williamsburg supported the distribution of antipoverty resources to specific ethnic communities as long as they too received a piece of the pie. One of the factors contributing to this difference in outlook was that while most Jewish organizations in New York, such as the Jewish Federation, were citywide in scope, Hasidim focused exclusively on their own neighborhoods. This gave them an advantage in the decentralized, community-oriented structure of the poverty program, in which local organizing translated into influence, voting power, and access to services. As they had done a few years earlier with the public housing projects in the neighborhood, Hasidim in Williamsburg took quick and decisive action beginning in the mid-1960s to ensure that they would benefit from the antipoverty program.

Seen from this perspective, Hasidim in Williamsburg were in the vanguard of a wave of grassroots activism that transformed ethnic communities—and local politics—in New York City during the late 1960s. The result was what Douglas Yates has called "street fighting pluralism," the struggle between local groups over resources and power in a citywide atmosphere of decentralization.[28] As a Puerto Rican activist in Williamsburg later recalled of this period: "The poverty program helped the Puerto Rican community to organize itself. It was through politics that you got what you wanted. . . . The blacks took more advantage than the Puerto Ricans. They organized and demonstrated. The Hasidim used the poverty program a lot to organize themselves."[29] Indeed, the structure of the federal poverty program in New York City encouraged ethnic groups to compete with one another for resources.

Interviewed by Stephen Price in 1978, one Puerto Rican leader in Williamsburg highlighted the effects of the poverty program on local interethnic relations. "Before the poverty program," he said, "all the ethnic groups sat together at meetings. You didn't have to sit with your own people. . . . Now it's Puerto Ricans at one place, blacks at another. . . . The poverty program strengthened ethnic groups but helped segregate us."[30] Richard Neuhaus, who had served as the minister of St. John's Lutheran Church in Williamsburg during the 1960s and as a de facto representative of the neighborhood's African American community in this period, spoke bitterly to Price about the impact of the poverty program on Williamsburg's ethnic communities, with one exception: "The poverty program was a disaster. Voluntarism was ended, people were bought off. . . . Once the big money came in, the whole idealistic thrust of the Church became undercut. It became a matter of distributing jobs. . . . These communities have become 'governmentalized.' To a large extent this has happened to the Puerto Ricans, but not to the Hasids. The Hasidim have the best of both worlds. They have political clout but it is done in a way that doesn't mess up their infrastructure."[31]

As the competition for resources heated up in the late 1960s, Puerto Rican activists complained that African Americans were receiving a disproportionate share of funds in New York City because the latter had been the initial focus of the War on Poverty in urban areas and because they tended to control the elected boards that governed the community corporations in neighborhoods shared by the two groups. In 1968, the Council Against Poverty, which set city policy for the poverty program in New York City, determined that Central Harlem and Bedford-Stuyvesant, neighborhoods with the largest number of African Americans, had received more than twice their "fair share" of poverty funds, at the expense of other, more racially integrated, areas including Williamsburg, Bushwick, and Crown Heights. That same year, Model Cities, a Great Society program inaugurated in 1966, floundered in Harlem and East Harlem due to infighting between local blacks and Puerto Ricans over resources. The Puerto Rican activist Robert Anazagasti remembered, "That's the name of the game. They're [blacks] more politically sophisticated than the Puerto Ricans. They came in here and picked out puppets and ran roughshod over us."[32] A few years later, in 1971, when a Puerto Rican slate won a majority of seats on the governing board in Morrisania, in the South Bronx, Carmelo Saez, a Puerto Rican board member, told the *New York Times*, "The Puerto Ricans have been frozen out by the blacks until now," while Albert Goodman, a black member of the board retorted, "This is a Puerto Rican take-over."[33]

Like advocates for New York City's poor Jews, Italian American activists lamented the persistent invisibility of their community when it came to the poverty program. A study by the Congress of Italian-American Organizations (CIAO) revealed that 10 percent of Italian Americans in "heavily Italian neighborhoods" were living below the poverty line in 1970, yet very few benefited from federal antipoverty funds. In its report, CIAO lamented, "We were aware of the shocking absence of Italian-Americans as recipients of many government-funded programs, and of the lack of awareness on the part of the Italian-American communities that such programs exist."[34] In response, Mary Sansone, the executive director of the organization, told the *New York Times*, " 'We are going to fight for our share of the pie ... [and] our rightful share' of public money for minorities and disadvantaged people." Bayard Rustin, the African American civil rights leader, praised their efforts: "It is marvelous to see that the Italian community is learning a lesson the black community learned long ago. Very simply it is that the squeaky wheel gets greased."[35]

Within this context of interethnic competition, Hasidim in South Williamsburg quickly mobilized to become a "squeaky wheel" and involve themselves in all aspects of the antipoverty program. By contrast, the large Italian American community in East Williamsburg remained reluctant to participate or to challenge prevailing notions among antipoverty workers that its members did not need help. June Price, a poverty program director in the School Settlement Association in East Williamsburg, noted, "The Italian community did not identify or perceive itself as poor or working class, when that was the reality." Moreover, the "belief at School Settlement that Italians would not use their services," combined with "the absence of Italian employees and Board members [in the poverty program]," meant that poor Italian residents of East Williamsburg did not receive their share of poverty funds. According to Price, "You could see there's no programs in the Italian community, with people desperately trying to keep their houses going with inflation going up. Here the black and Hispanic communities were getting services. There was a war on poverty, and there was nothing here [in the Italian American community]."[36]

Working-class whites in New York City sometimes banded together in the early 1970s to increase their representation in the poverty program. By contrast, Hasidim in Williamsburg eschewed citywide alliances with Italians, Poles, the Irish, or other white ethnics.[37] Nor did they join with either the Puerto Rican or black residents of Williamsburg to form a neighborhood-based coalition. Instead, as members of those two communities sometimes did, Hasidim generally treated the interethnic competition for poverty program resources as a zero-sum game. The key figure in ensuring that Hasidim in Williamsburg received their share of the poverty-program funds was Leopold "Lipa" Friedman, a savvy and charismatic former bank director in Czechoslovakia and survivor of Auschwitz and Dachau who emerged in the 1950s and 1960s as the most powerful lay leader in the Satmar community. Friedman developed such a reputation as a local power broker that his funeral in 1972 was attended by Mayor John Lindsay and other New York City dignitaries.

Many contemporary observers referred to Friedman as the "foreign minister" of Satmar and as Rabbi Joel Teitelbaum's "right hand man." In this regard, Friedman appeared to be continuing the venerable European Jewish tradition of the *shtadlan*, or Jewish community intercessor with the outside world. Yet Friedman was also very much a man of his time and place, completely at home in the intensely local, interethnic competition that came to dominate the poverty program in Williamsburg during the 1960s and early 1970s.[38] Reflecting the quietist approach that Hasidic leaders had frequently taken in eastern Europe, the Satmar Rebbe was initially reluctant to have his lieutenants engage in politicking around the antipoverty program in Williamsburg. Yet according to a Satmar Hasid interviewed by Stephen Price in 1978, it was "Lipa Friedman [who] convinced the Rebbe to do it; the Rebbe didn't want to get involved because of the problems of dealing with the government."[39]

In 1966, the same year that Robert Kennedy announced the launch of his antipoverty program in neighboring Bedford-Stuyvesant to great fanfare, Friedman and a handful of local Hasidic and Orthodox leaders, including Sender Deutsch of Satmar, Joseph Zeitlin of Vien, Julius Templer of Pupa, Chaim Pincus, and Bernard Weinberger, established the United Jewish Organizations (UJO), which brought together a number of Jewish institutions in Williamsburg under a single umbrella with a mission to help needy members of the community. Although the UJO never received the widespread publicity given the Bedford-Stuyvesant Restoration Corporation (which was founded a year later), it would play a key role in South Williamsburg in the coming decades. Eventually, under the leadership of Rabbi David Niederman, who became the executive director in 1989, the UJO helped the Hasidic community navigate the challenges posed by the gentrification of Williamsburg.

In addition to helping establish the UJO, the Hasidic community in Williamsburg ran candidates in the local poverty board elections.[40] After winning seats on the board in 1966, twelve Jewish members resigned in February 1967 to protest "that other ethnic groups represented on the committee had refused to recognize that there were 'acute pockets of poverty' among the Hassidic Jews of Williamsburg," as Rabbi Bernard Weinberger put it in an interview at the time.[41] The gambit appears to have worked, for on October 13, 1967, *Der Yid* published an editorial encouraging community members to vote in the upcoming board election: "This year's election has special significance for the community in Williamsburg. A number of prominent Jews are running as candidates and it is important that they win so that the Jewish population be properly represented in, and benefit from, the antipoverty help program. Only a large turnout of Jewish voters can ensure that Jewish interests are defended."[42] In a harbinger of how the Hasidic community of Williamsburg would approach government aid programs in the coming years, *Der Yid* provided its readers with precise instructions—in an ever-evolving Yiddish that was peppered with bureaucratic terms drawn from the War on Poverty—for how, when, and where to vote in the local poverty board elections. *Fiddler on the Roof* this was not.

By 1971, as a result of these well-coordinated Hasidic efforts, Williamsburg, of the twenty-six poverty areas in New York City, had by far the best rate of Jewish participation, representing 33 percent of the total number of people receiving aid. In addition, its fifty-five Jewish staff members were also by far the most in any poverty area in the city (the next highest was fifteen on the Lower East Side), and its thirteen Jewish community corporation board members was second only to the figure for Crown Heights. Along with the creation of the United Jewish Organizations and the high Hasidic turnout in local antipoverty elections, the participation of Hasidim as both staff and board members in the Williamsburg community corporation served as an important milestone in the distinctive form of Americanization that the Hasidic community of Williamsburg underwent in the 1960s.

In eastern Europe, Jewish communities had supported a network of institutions to help needy members, including orphanages, almshouses, homes for the elderly, and other charities. After arriving in the United States, Satmar continued this tradition, achieving renown among other Hasidic Jews for the many philanthropic organizations that the community established to help poor brides, new mothers, hospital patients, poor students, and people in need of a loan. Significantly, Satmar required wealthy members of the community to support the less fortunate through substantial charitable donations. Satmar Hasidim told numerous anecdotes about the personal devotion of their rebbe, Yoel Teitelbaum, to philanthropy, while he declared of his followers in Williamsburg that they "have three good qualities: they have a lot of children, they give more *tzedaka* [charity] than they are able to, and they want their children to be better than they are."[43] At the same time, Teitelbaum refused on principle to accept aid from the Jewish Federation, the chief umbrella philanthropy for Jews in New York City; from wealthy donors whose religious practice he considered inadequate or who embraced Zionism; and from the State of Israel, which made his community an outlier even among most other Haredim, who benefitted significantly from support provided by the Israeli government.[44]

In contrast to these refusals, the Hasidic community of Williamsburg demonstrated remarkable openness when it came to the federal War on Poverty and its programs. A new class of savvy Hasidic activists, known as *askunim* in Yiddish, emerged to advocate for community interests, and rank-and-file Hasidim were encouraged to vote in poverty board elections, apply for government aid, and participate in programs. The result was that within a few short years, Hasidic Williamsburg was characterized as much by its robust participation in the Great Society envisioned by President Johnson and his successors as by its continuation of traditional Jewish norms and practices regarding charity. In this respect, Hasidim in Williamsburg came to resemble their Puerto Rican and African American neighbors far more than they did the majority of American Jews, who by then resided in the suburbs, or the significant population of poor non-Hasidic Jews who still lived in New York City but did not participate in the poverty program to nearly the same degree, as recipients of aid, elected representatives on local poverty committees, or community activists.[45]

Even as Hasidim in Williamsburg were becoming profoundly enmeshed in the antipoverty program, some outside observers refused to believe that members of the community were open to receiving "welfare," as means-tested assistance was popularly—and often pejoratively—called. Thus, for example, in a *New York Times* article on the 1972 presidential election, Rabbi Ronald Greenwald, identified as "the Nixon campaign's liaison to East Coast Jewish communities," confidently predicted that Hasidim would vote for his candidate, because, among other things, they were opposed to welfare: "Hasidic Jews see the liberal Establishment moving away from traditional moral and political values. . . . They don't care about the 'root causes' of crime—they care that their neighborhoods aren't safe. The Hasidic [*sic*] are little business men who work like dogs 80 hours a week to support families of seven or eight. They don't believe in welfare or in $1,000 hand-outs."[46] Greenwald was only half-right. Hasidic attitudes regarding crime and morality were more in line with those of Republican candidates, but their approach to governmental aid programs was decidedly not, a tension that persisted over the coming decades.

Textile factory, Williamsburg, 1993 (Photograph by Maud B. Weiss; copyright Maud B. Weiss/Gina Kehayoff Verlag)

Greenwald's characterization of Hasidim working "like dogs" to support their large families was accurate for many community members in Williamsburg. From the beginning of Satmar settlement in the neighborhood, Yoel Teitelbaum stressed that men in the community should work, at manual labor if necessary; as he put it, "To me, an *adam chashuv* [important person] is someone who works for a living and sets aside time to learn."[47] For this reason, unlike many Haredi leaders, Teitelbaum only reluctantly established a kollel, an institute where newly married men devoted themselves—sometimes for years—to learning Torah; he was concerned that it would discourage young men from entering the labor force, since kollel students received a living stipend. Even when he did authorize the creation of a kollel, Teitelbaum stressed that learning should not be a full-time vocation for the majority of Hasidim.[48] As in other Haredi communities, many Hasidic women in Williamsburg worked outside the home, though their employment opportunities were limited by family obligations, concerns about modesty, and a lack of higher education. In short, many Hasidim in Williamsburg—like a majority of poor people in the United States—were members of the "working poor."

In the early 1970s, both the mainstream media and Hasidic leaders downplayed or rejected the idea that community members in Williamsburg were "on welfare," even when a significant percentage of them were receiving some form of government aid. As Rabbi Sender Deutsch, the publisher of *Der Yid*, put it in a 1974 *New York Times* article on rising unemployment rates in Williamsburg during the global recession triggered by the oil crisis of 1973: "Our people don't go on welfare. . . . They are law-abiding, they work hard. But their very existence is now at stake."[49] Likewise, another article in the newspaper from 1974 simply stated, "The Hasidim [of Williamsburg] consider welfare subsidies a stigma and have their own social programs to care for the needy."[50]

In light of the growing public backlash to the War on Poverty and its beneficiaries, exemplified by the dubious figure of the "welfare queen," made infamous by Ronald Reagan during the 1976 presidential campaign, it is not surprising that Hasidic activists sought to distance their community from the term "welfare," even if not the programs associated with it. At the same time, the widespread assumption outside the community that Hasidim rejected welfare out of hand—despite much evidence to the contrary—reflected both the racialization of the image of the poor during the 1960s and 1970s as well as long-standing negative stereotypes regarding Jews and money.

Electoral Politics

Just as it did with African American and Puerto Rican communities throughout New York City, the federal antipoverty program helped inspire a new spirit of activism among the Hasidim of Williamsburg. This activism, combined with a growing reliance on governmental aid, encouraged Hasidim throughout Brooklyn to view electoral politics as an effective means of bringing much-needed resources to their communities. As the Hasidic chairman of the Crown Heights Jewish Community Council put it to the *New York Times* in 1972, "We are experiencing a political awakening. . . . We found that without political power we could not get anything. We want subsidized housing, aid to our schools and better Police protection. These are impossible without political power."[51] In certain respects, the political outlook of Hasidic voters throughout Brooklyn overlapped with those of white ethnics in the outer boroughs, as well as with those of working-class Jews who still resided in large numbers in Canarsie, Sheepshead Bay, and other parts of South Brooklyn. Yet insofar

Hasidic man walking past Puerto Rican youths in Williamsburg, 1962 or 1963 (Photograph © 2020 The Estate of Jan Yoors/Artists Rights Society [ARS], New York)

as they benefited significantly from a wide range of governmental poverty programs, the Hasidim in Williamsburg and Crown Heights, in particular, had political interests that intersected much more closely with those of their African American and Puerto Rican neighbors than with the priorities of white ethnics and even other Jews elsewhere in the city.

Since the 1950s, Hasidim in Williamsburg had cultivated local politicians associated with the neighborhood Democratic machine, headquartered in the Seneca Club. Even though they were relatively small in number at the time, Hasidim benefited from the political capital built up by generations of non-Hasidic Jews in Williamsburg, in marked contrast to the neighborhood's Puerto Rican residents. By the early 1970s, Jewish flight and the dramatic growth of the Hasidic population had transformed the demographic and political landscape in Brooklyn. Now, Hasidim represented a large voting bloc in their own right, and in some areas the only significant non–African American or non–Puerto Rican constituency. Moreover, their relative influence was magnified by an extremely high rate of voting, especially compared with their African American and Puerto Rican neighbors—one estimate was 80 percent compared with 15 percent—and by their unique willingness to vote as a bloc for candidates endorsed by community leaders.

A turning point in the political arrival of the Williamsburg Hasidic community occurred in the contentious 1969 mayoral election, which pitted John Lindsay, who ran on the Liberal Party line after losing the Republican primary, against the Democrat Mario Procaccino and the Republican John Marchi. A coalition of African Americans, Puerto Ricans, and white liberals—most of them Jews residing in Manhattan and parts of Queens—carried Lindsay to victory over the second-place Procaccino, who won primarily white working-class areas of Brooklyn and the Bronx while splitting the overall Jewish vote with Lindsay (each candidate received 44 percent). A month before the election, on October 1, 1969, the *New York Times* reported on the raucous reception that Hasidim in Williamsburg gave Procaccino, a law-and-order Italian American candidate from the Bronx, who vociferously defended the rights of "the people," against "the limousine liberals who live in penthouses": "Later he [Procaccino] was cheered by a crowd of several hundred young Hassidic Jews in the Williamsburg section of Brooklyn when he paid a visit to Grand Rabbi Jack [*sic*] Teitelbaum and about 15 other Hassidic Jewish leaders. The enthusiastic crowd outside the rabbi's house at 500 Bedford Avenue mobbed Mr. Procaccino until two helmeted policemen escorted him into the house."[52] The article then described an encounter that not only revealed the political gulf between Hasidic and Puerto Rican residents in Williamsburg, but also the combustibility between the two communities, a subject dealt with in the following chapter:

> The Hassidic Jews who greeted him [Procaccino] in Williamsburg later were there for the candidate and not for the cameras. At one point, when Mr. Procaccino got into his car after meeting with the rabbis, two young Puerto Rican boys came down the street holding hand-made signs that said, 'Lindsay will Beat Ya' and 'We want Lindsay.' Then, they raced away down Bedford Avenue and around the corner to Division Street as several hundred of the Hassidic Jews took off after them. Members of the crowd caught the boys, but they escaped, seemingly unhurt.

At a time when the mainstream media commonly portrayed black and Puerto Rican youth as predators preying on their fellow city dwellers, the image of a group of Orthodox Jews chasing Puerto Rican youths down a New York City street confounded stereotypes of both groups—and their relationship to each other—but it was only one of the ways that the Hasidim of Williamsburg were turning conventional wisdom on its head in this period.

Many contemporary observers assumed that Hasidim would reflexively support Jewish political candidates because "Jews stick together," a common refrain that paralleled assumptions about other groups with an immigrant past (Italians, Irish, Chinese, etc.), but that also reflected particular stereotypes concerning Jewish clannishness. In fact, however, Hasidim in Williamsburg did not support politicians simply because they were Jewish. On the contrary, they typically suspected the average Jewish politician in New York of harboring prejudice against Orthodox Jews, of being too soft on crime, and of having a heretical relationship to "Torah true Judaism."[53] In 1968, Fred Richmond, a Jewish businessman with liberal politics, challenged John Rooney, the old-school Irish Democratic congressman from the Fourteenth District, which included Williamsburg. Over the years, Rooney had earned the loyalty of Hasidic leaders for his help with immigration in particular. Despite giving substantial financial contributions to Satmar, Richmond was rejected by neighborhood Hasidim; a leader of the Klausenberger Hasidic community explained why: "Richmond approached the community in the worst possible way. He presented himself as Jewish, but he had a gentile wife. If he had just told us he would do something, it would be better. He was despised. He just happened to be born a Jew."[54]

In the 1970 New York gubernatorial race between Nelson Rockefeller and Arthur Goldberg, Hasidim overwhelmingly supported the non-Jewish candidate because of his support for state aid to parochial schools and his tough stance on crime.[55] Two years later, in 1972, the Hasidic community of Williamsburg endorsed the longtime incumbent John Rooney in his primary race against the liberal Jewish candidate Allard Lowenstein, who, among other things, opposed federal aid to parochial schools, a perennial campaign issue for Hasidim.[56] During the race, Lowenstein learned the hard way that being Jewish could actually be a liability with Hasidic voters when a Yiddish-language leaflet distributed in Williamsburg accused him of being "an assimilated Jew from Long Island," adding, "It is interesting to note that he has settled in Fort Greene among his friends. This goyish neighborhood is 100 per cent gentile. For those who know Lowenstein, this is not a surprise, for he has always danced at Goyish weddings."[57] After Rooney squeaked out a narrow victory, Lowenstein's campaign declared, "The Hasidic Jews killed us," acknowledging the decisive role played by the Hasidic community of Williamsburg as local kingmakers.[58]

For a variety of reasons, therefore, Hasidim usually endorsed non-Jewish candidates, whether Democrat or Republican, as long as they were seen as supporting issues important to the community. As one Hasidic activist put it in 1972 following local elections in Brooklyn, "If there is a man who is concerned with the needs of the Jewish community, we will support him. It doesn't mean a thing if he is black, Jewish or Spanish—as long he is sensitive to our needs. In Williamsburg we supported an Irishman; in Crown Heights we supported a black."[59] Hasidim differed from practically every other ethnic community in New York City during this period in that they did not run candidates of their own for city- or statewide office, nor did they see electing a Hasid to the city council or State Assembly as a litmus test of their political strength as a community—unlike other ethnic groups in the city.

There were a number of reasons for this. Hasidim in Brooklyn had inherited a long political tradition from their predecessors in eastern Europe of cultivating non-Jewish political leaders. In Brooklyn, Hasidim also assumed—probably correctly—that their gentile neighbors would not support Hasidic candidates. This was especially the case in Williamsburg and Crown Heights, where, despite their significant numbers, Hasidim were still a minority living among Puerto Rican and African American majorities, respectively. Instead of running their own candidates, therefore, Hasidim preferred to leverage their votes by serving as kingmakers or, just as importantly, by creating the impression among politicians that they had the ability to tip elections, a perception that in itself could bring resources to the community. Nor did Hasidic *askunim*, or activists, typically seek the kinds of benefits that flowed to political operatives in other communities, as *New York* magazine put it in 1977: "The thrust of the Hasidic [lay] leaders' political involvement is rarely for personal gain or patronage. They're zealous about job training, housing, day care, and other broad-based communal self-help programs tailored to the Hasidic community. Politicians experienced in bargaining with Hasidim know that the lure of an assistant commissionership will not do when a computer-training program is sought."[60]

The same article in *New York* noted another distinctive feature of the Hasidic approach to politics: "Almost never does the Lubavitcher *rebbe* of Crown Heights or the Satmar *rebbe* of Williamsburg—the other major

Hasidic leader—deign to give their personal seal of kosher to a candidate." Instead, as the author, Ronald Rubin, explained, influential *askunim*, such as Chaim Stauber, the editor of *Der Yid*, conducted their own research and recommended candidates to the United Jewish Organizations. Then, "On the Sabbath before election day, the sextons of Satmar synagogues in Williamsburg announce the UJO's endorsements from their pulpits to thousands of attentive worshippers."[61]

Just as they were coming into their own politically, however, the Hasidim of Williamsburg were dealt a major blow in 1974 when, in response to section 5 of the Voting Rights Act, the New York State Legislature decided to redraw the State Assembly and Senate districts in which the Hasidic community was located, in order to increase the voting strength of African Americans and Puerto Ricans in the redistricted areas. Under the new legislative map, Hasidim in Williamsburg would be divided into two districts rather than a single one as previously, effectively halving their voting strength. In response, the Hasidic community of Williamsburg, represented by the United Jewish Organizations, filed suit in federal district court to block the redistricting on the grounds that it illegally discriminated against them. Speaking to the *New York Times*, Rabbi Albert Friedman, a Satmar Hasidic spokesman, explained why the community in Williamsburg was taking action:

> We applaud efforts to help the Spanish-speaking minorities and all minorities who are at a disadvantage but we are also a disenfranchised minority in need of help. . . . Now we are afraid the democratic process is insensitive to us . . . that we are [also] socially dispossessed. The people are upset and discouraged. Our problems, aside from poverty and unemployment, involve discrimination on a broad and open basis. We do not ordinarily fight anti-Semitism in the courts. . . . We are philosophical about the attitudes that arise because of our need to be different.

Friedman concluded, "But we are shocked and frightened by what we see as an official sanction of prejudice and this time we intend to fight, all the way to the United States Supreme Court if we have to."[62]

It might be tempting to dismiss Hasidic claims of being a "disenfranchised minority" as a cynical or, at best, pragmatic ploy to compete with African Americans and Puerto Ricans for resources and political influence on a level playing field during an era of "street fighting pluralism."

Hasidic and African American neighbors in Williamsburg (Photograph
copyright Lucille Fornasieri Gold, Lucille Fornasieri Gold photographs,
Brooklyn Historical Society)

Yet the degree to which the Hasidic community of Williamsburg considered itself a disadvantaged minority group, especially in this period,
needs to be acknowledged. The Holocaust, when Jews were persecuted
precisely because of their supposed racial difference, was still a recent
memory during the 1970s. Hungarian Hasidim who founded the community in Williamsburg were Holocaust survivors who had experienced
discrimination as Jews before and after the war in Europe. The United
States in which these Hasidim settled was far more hospitable to Jews,
but various forms of anti-Semitism remained. In addition, Hasidim were
dramatically different from the majority of Americans—including other
Jews—when it came to language, dress, and behavior, and were sometimes discriminated against for these reasons in employment, housing,
and other areas of life. Finally, the Hasidic community of Williamsburg
lived in one of New York City's most notorious "slums," along with
Puerto Ricans and blacks, participated in the same poverty programs as
their neighbors, and suffered from the same lack of governmental services, high rates of environmental pollution, and other conditions that
diminished residents' quality of life.

Jerald Podair argued that the notorious 1968 conflict over local school control in Brooklyn's Ocean Hill–Brownsville district between African American and Puerto Rican parents and the largely Jewish teachers' union finalized the postwar transformation of New York City's Jews into "white folks," or as he put it: "Pushed by a black community that regarded them as 'whites, no more, no less,' and pulled by the promise of a race-based co-alition with white Catholics, they used the Ocean Hill–Brownsville crisis to complete their journey to unambiguous white identity, the last group of Caucasians in New York to do so."[63] Yet the Hasidic community of Williamsburg complicated this racial calculus, not because its members denied being white but because they asserted their Jewish difference in ways that enabled them to argue that, like African Americans and Puerto Ricans, they were "also a disenfranchised minority in need of help" and therefore that efforts to increase African American and Puerto Rican voting strength—however legitimate—should not come at their expense.

As cannily predicted by Friedman, the legal case brought by Hasidim to block the legislative redistricting in Brooklyn indeed made it all the way to the U.S. Supreme Court. Along the way, the U.S. Court of Appeals for the Second Circuit weighed in on the thorny question whether Hasidim should be considered a minority group with the same kind of legal status as African Americans and Puerto Ricans. In rendering its decision, the court acknowledged the basis of the plaintiffs' suit: "As representatives of the Hasidic community, appellants present a very appealing case. They properly point with pride to their closely-knit community as consisting of a 'substantially self-sustaining and totally law-abiding' group, which came to the Williamsburgh area as survivors of the Nazi Holocaust, lives scrupulously observant of distinctive religious practices, and—despite their initial skepticism of democracy—participates actively in civic affairs including the electoral process."[64] Nevertheless, the court argued that Hasidim were fundamentally a white "ethnic community" and that they thus should not receive any special protection under the law: "In contrast to the foregoing conclusion regarding Puerto Ricans ('that some Spanish-surnamed Americans are covered by federal statutes which protect the rights of non-white citizens'), there was nothing revealed by our review . . . which indicates that Hasidic Jews or persons of Irish, Polish or Italian descent are within the scope of the special protections defined by the Congress in the Voting Rights Act."

While the court ruled that Hasidim, like the Irish, Italians, and so on, had no legal standing as an "ethnic community"—even if they had historically experienced discrimination—they could nevertheless file suit as "whites"; in the words of the court: "A more difficult question is whether appellants have standing either as representing the Hasidic community or as white voters to seek relief against the State appellees. We hold that they do not as Hasidim but do as white voters." Under these circumstances, the relevant legal question was "whether appellants have standing to assert their claims as white voters that racial considerations cannot be used in drawing district lines in any manner, a claim which is grounded both upon the equal protection clause, i.e., that white voters are denied equal protection, and the fifteenth amendment, i.e., that white voters' rights are abridged on account of race or color." To which the court answered: "There is no reason, as we see it, that a white voter may not have standing, just as a nonwhite voter, to allege a denial of equal protection as well as an abridgement of his right to vote on account of race or color . . . regardless of the fact that the fourteenth and fifteenth amendments were adopted for the purpose of ensuring equal protection to the black person."[65]

In October 1976, the U.S. Supreme Court heard arguments in the case, now styled *United Jewish Organizations v. Carey*, after the newly elected governor of New York, Hugh Carey. On March 1, 1977, in what would become a landmark ruling in support of affirmative action, a majority of the justices, led by Byron White, affirmed the rulings of the lower district and appellate courts "that petitioners enjoyed no constitutional right in reapportionment to separate community recognition as Hasidic Jews; that the redistricting did not disenfranchise them; and that racial considerations were permissible to correct past discrimination."[66] Although they lost the case, the Hasidim had demonstrated a sophisticated and tenacious ability to navigate the legal system as well as a remarkable fluency in the language of contemporary racial politics. Far from being a timeless shtetl torn from the pages of a Sholem Aleichem story, the Hasidic community of Williamsburg had once again revealed its striking adaptability to changing circumstances. Nor were its efforts to be officially recognized as a disadvantaged minority group over.

Becoming a Minority

In 1974, the same year that they filed suit against the legislative redistricting of the neighborhood, Hasidim in Williamsburg, led by Zvi Kestenbaum, a Holocaust survivor from Hungary, established the Opportunity Development Association (ODA), with funding from the Minority Business

Development Agency (MBDA) of the U.S. Department of Commerce.[67] The primary purpose of the ODA, as Zvi Kestenbaum put it in an interview with *Minority Business Today* in 1985, was "to serve the Hasidic community in the New York metropolitan area, a community which had previously been overlooked in the implementation of federal social policy ... [and to provide] services to Hasidic entrepreneurs and other ethnic groups to compete effectively within the American economic mainstream."[68] In addition to helping Hasidim with loan applications, procurement bids for government contracts, and job training, the ODA received funds from federal, state, and local agencies (such as the U.S. Department of Health and Human Services) to run a community health clinic, provide home-health-care attendants, offer weatherization services, and implement New York State's largest women, infant, and children (WIC) supplemental food program.[69]

Over the next decade, Zvi Kestenbaum spearheaded an intensive lobbying campaign to have Hasidim officially recognized as a disadvantaged minority group by the federal government. In 1979, he submitted a petition to the Small Business Administration (SBA) to have Hasidim declared eligible for its 8(a) program, which granted preferential access to federal contracts to small businesses owned by members of officially designated disadvantaged groups, including African Americans, Latinos, Native Americans, Pacific Islanders, and a wide range of Asian American groups. As the *New York Daily News* put it in 1980, "Should Hasidic Jews have 'minority' status so they may qualify for special federal contracts? ... At stake is an estimated $20 million, or less than 2% of the SBA budget for minorities. But to the 100,000 Hasidic Jews in the United States ... that $20 million could mean the difference between making a decent living or going bankrupt."[70]

Opposition to the Hasidic petition was led by Representative Paren Mitchell of Maryland, the head of the Congressional Black Caucus and chair of the House Subcommittee on Housing, Minority Enterprise, and Economic Development, which controlled the budget for the SBA. Mitchell threatened to organize protests if Hasidim were granted disadvantaged status, and dismissed the fact that they lived in one of New York City's poorest, most resource-deprived neighborhoods. "They say they are in a poor area where there is high unemployment and all of this goes with being socially disadvantaged," Mitchell remarked. "But a person's location doesn't make him socially disadvantaged. If Howard Hughes had chosen to live in Harlem, would he have been socially disad-

vantaged?"[71] Along with the Congressional Black Caucus, other opponents of the Hasidim's petition included the NAACP, the National
Urban League, and the National Association of Black Manufacturers;
those groups expressed concern that the original purpose of the 8(a) program was in danger of being diluted, since, in their view, Hasidim did not
legitimately qualify for affirmative action. (They also opposed women
being included as a group, on the same grounds.)

According to the SBA, comments submitted in opposition to the Hasidim's petition focused on the "significant role" of Hasidim in the diamond trade, the claim that "Jews control great wealth and have succeeded
in business," and the fact that "in contrast to the Hasidim, Blacks and
other traditional minorities have no choice with respect to the color of
their skin and hence literally no control over the social disadvantage im-
posed on them by race."[72] This last point reflected a widespread criticism
of poor Hasidim, namely, that unlike impoverished blacks or Latinos,
who suffered from structural racism based on their phenotypes, Hasidim
essentially chose to be poor and therefore did not deserve to receive governmental aid. In short, in addition to circulating anti-Semitic tropes,
these critics argued that Hasidim constituted a kind of "undeserving
poor." Ironically, this was a label commonly applied to blacks and Latinos
by conservative opponents of welfare.

Hasidim and their allies vehemently rejected this view, arguing that
Jewish difference was equivalent to the racialized difference of blacks and
Latinos and therefore that poor members of the Hasidic community deserved to be granted the same disadvantaged status, along with the governmental aid that accompanied it. As the Williamsburg rabbi and activist
Bernard Weinberger put it, "Given the reality that anti-poverty programs
deal with blacks, Puerto Ricans, Mexican-Americans and Indians not only
as poor people but as members of their ethnic communities, we must insist
that poor Jews be included on the basis of very Jewish needs. . . . If we accept the premise that a poor black man is poor because he is black, we
must also recognize that many poor Jews are poor because they are
Jews."[73] Zvi Kestenbaum put it even more bluntly, "My father and grandfather were Hasidic Jews. Our life styles have never changed—even Hitler
could not change them. Just like a black man who is born black, we are
born this way and die this way."[74]

In responding to the African American–led opposition to the Hasidic
petition, the SBA noted that only a small minority of Hasidim were involved with diamonds and that "whatever the accuracy of this timeworn

stereotype [regarding Jewish wealth], there is little to suggest that the Hasidim, who are culturally distinct from most other American Jews, have
control over the levers of economic power in this country."[75] Regarding
whether Hasidim had a choice in being discriminated against, the SBA asserted: "From a literal standpoint, this argument is unassailable. The practice of the Hasidim which engender bias—their distinctive appearance for
example—are ultimately matters of choice. No matter how deep-rooted
the cultural convictions and religious beliefs which prompt behavior that
is objectionable to others, the decision to adhere to and act upon those
convictions is a voluntary one." It added that "from a legal standpoint,
however, this argument must be rejected," since "such a decision might
well abridge the right of Hasidic Jews to the free exercise of religion guaranteed them by the First Amendment."

Although the Hasidim's petition was supported by a number of U.S.
senators, congressional representatives, and the SBA's general counsel,
Edward Norton, it was ultimately rejected by the SBA, on the grounds
that it would contravene the First Amendment of the Constitution by establishing "an impermissible religious classification." In a kind of catch-
22, the Hasidic community's religious character had led the SBA to reject
its petition on constitutional grounds, yet the claim that Hasidim brought
discrimination upon themselves through their behavior could not be cited
as a reason to deny them disadvantaged status, because doing so might be
seen as challenging their constitutionally protected free exercise of religion. This was not the last time that Hasidim in Williamsburg became involved in a legal case that straddled both sides of the First Amendment.

Not to be deterred, Zvi Kestenbaum turned his full attention to lobbying the MBDA to have Hasidim added to that agency's official list of
"disadvantaged minority groups."[76] In due course, Kestenbaum invited
Malcolm Baldrige, the secretary of the U.S. Commerce Department, to
come to Williamsburg and see the Hasidic community and the challenges
it faced. The visit made a big impression on Baldrige, popularly known as
the "cowboy in Ronald Reagan's cabinet," and convinced him to grant official minority status to the Hasidim, albeit for reasons that members of
the community would not have appreciated:

Mac was impressed by the intellect of the children but was cha-
grined when he learned that no Hasidic children attended college
because they were expected to remain in their community. . . . After
his first visit, Mac told an aide traveling with him, "I'm going to

make sure these kids go to college. They are being held back by not being allowed to leave, and they and society lose." Mac had no qualms of taking on traditions that dated back centuries to achieve that goal. The visit convinced him that Hasidic Jews should be designated a minority group, and Commerce became the first federal agency to grant the designation to Hasidim.[77]

True to his word, in 1984 Baldrige added Hasidim to the list of "groups that are considered by the Government to have encountered severe economic problems because of discrimination."[78] According to the agency's website, "Neither Caucasians nor women are considered a minority and eligible for participation in MBDA programs. There is a specific test for social and/or economic disadvantage. One is assumed to be disadvantaged by virtue of his/her cultural or racial make-up." In addition, the agency determined that Hasidim met this criterion: "To be eligible for MBDA assistance, a concern must be BOTH a minority business enterprise, which is a business enterprise that is owned or controlled by one or more socially or economically disadvantaged persons AND a member of one of the following eligibility groups: Blacks, Puerto-Ricans, Spanish-speaking Americans, American Indians, Eskimos and Aleuts, *Hasidic Jews*, Asian Pacific Americans, and Asian Indians" (emphasis added).[79] From the perspective of the MBDA, Hasidim were now officially considered a "non-Caucasian" minority.

This extraordinary—and, at the time, highly controversial—decision represented the culmination of two parallel historical processes that had been unfolding for at least two decades: the self-segregation of the Hasidic community from the rest of American Jewry, and the integration of the Hasidic community of Williamsburg, in particular, into a governmentally sanctioned realm of disadvantaged minority groups eligible for special programs.[80] In the eyes of the U.S. Department of Commerce—though not, as we have seen, the U.S. Supreme Court—Hasidim were now legally distinct from the rest of the American Jewish community as well as from white ethnics such as Italians or Irish, and, instead, shared the same disadvantaged minority group status as their Latino and African American neighbors in Williamsburg. By lobbying for this identity, Hasidim demonstrated how much they had already diverged from the American Jewish mainstream and how much their own community had been shaped by the distinctive experience of living in Williamsburg. Now that difference was enshrined in the law of the land.

CHAPTER FOUR

Chaptsem!

If you snatched one of their hats in the wrong neighborhood,
you'd have a hell of a chase. If they caught you, you were going
to get an ass whuppin'. They weren't pussies. Hell no. They yell
one word in Yiddish, and everybody comes out the woodwork.

—PUERTO RICAN GANG MEMBER

BY THE MID-1960s, the Hasidic community had become too deeply
embedded in Williamsburg to abandon the neighborhood, despite
Rabbi Yoel Teitelbaum's ongoing dream of establishing a new settlement outside the city. "I want a fortress to remain here as well," the
Satmar Rebbe reassured his old friend, Rabbi Abraham Joshua Heshel,
the Kapishinitzer Rebbe, when the latter expressed concern about
what would happen to Williamsburg if Teitelbaum and his followers
were to decamp to his dreamed-of shtetl in the countryside.[1] The
image of a fortress—*festung*, in Yiddish—within the city reflected Teitelbaum's intense desire for his already insular community to remain
walled off from the outside world and its influences. It also reflected
the spirit of fierce resistance to external threats that Teitelbaum
sought to cultivate in his followers. This approach sometimes led to
conflict with others, but it also helped the Satmar community protect
its turf during a period of rising crime, reduced city services, and in-

98

tergroup strife not only with Puerto Ricans and African Americans in Williamsburg but also with Hasidim from other communities such as Belz and Lubavitch.

When gentrification arrived in Williamsburg in the 1980s and 1990s, the neighborhood quickly became a media darling for its vibrant art scene, renovated lofts, clubs, and cafés. In the 1970s, however, when Williamsburg appeared in the news—if it appeared at all—it was almost always for another, very different set of reasons: the street crime, drug dealers, and youth gangs that made Williamsburg notorious even within the rough-and-tumble urban landscape of 1960s and 1970s New York City. The neighborhood's pre-gentrification reputation for crime was cemented by highly publicized events such as the infamous shooting of Detective Frank Serpico in 1971 during an undercover drug bust on the South Side, which helped inspire the film about the police officer starring Al Pacino, and the so-called Williamsburg siege of 1973, when four gunmen robbed a sporting goods store on Broadway, took hostages, and killed a police officer before being arrested.[2]

For residents of Williamsburg in this period, life in the neighborhood was much more complex—and in some ways, positive—than the contemporary media coverage of crime suggested. Even as they struggled with poverty, environmental pollution, unemployment—the rate among residents of the neighborhood jumped from 5.8 percent in 1970 to 12.1 percent in 1978—a lack of governmental services, street crime, and a worsening housing shortage, Williamsburg's Puerto Rican and Hasidic communities thrived demographically and culturally in the 1970s, and began to flex their political muscles.[3] Crime, therefore, did not define life in pre-gentrification Williamsburg. Nevertheless, it emerged as a great source of mutual concern and, frequently, intercommunal conflict beginning in the mid-1960s, when both the crime rate and the public perception that New York City was in decline started to increase dramatically.

Hasidim policed the borders of their self-styled fortress in Brooklyn during the 1960s and 1970s by taking a forceful and at times violent approach to threats against their community. Rather than relying exclusively or even primarily on the New York City police—with whom they had an ambivalent relationship, to say the least, in this period—Hasidim in Williamsburg frequently took matters into their own hands, an approach that led to accusations of vigilantism by Puerto Ricans and African Americans in the neighborhood but that helped reinforce the Hasidic community's sense of pride and self-reliance. Just as the Hasidic attitude to public housing and poverty programs turned conventional wisdom on its head, this forceful response to crime confounded long-standing stereotypes concerning Jews in general and Hasidim in particular.

For centuries, anti-Semites had caricatured Jews as physically weak and passive in the face of danger. By the turn of the twentieth century, Zionists such as Max Nordau were critiquing diaspora Jews—exemplified by the figure of the bearded religious scholar—as hapless victims of anti-Semitism, and were instead promoting the ideal of the "muscular" or "new" Jew, whom, they fantasized, would build and defend a modern Jewish state. In post–World War II America, real estate agents and politicians tacitly assumed that Jews, unlike the Irish, Italians, and other white ethnics, would rather abandon their neighborhoods than engage in physical confrontations over racial integration. Finally, religious Jews traditionally contrasted their ideal of learning with the physical violence they associated with gentiles, exemplified by the classic rabbinic opposition between the "voice of Jacob" (learning Torah) and the "hands of Esau" (gentile violence), a distinction sometimes honored in the breach by Hasidim in Williamsburg.

Against this backdrop, the forceful, sometimes violent approach taken by the Hasidim of Williamsburg to street crime and other threats to the community may seem surprising at first. Seen from a different set of vantage points, however, the behavior of Satmar ceases to be anomalous. First is the historic role of intragroup violence within the Hasidic movement. In eastern Europe, Hasidic leaders sometimes employed physical intimidation to extend their territorial influence and compete for followers. Regarding Satmar, David Myers argued for "the centrality of a martial outlook—strategy, rhetoric, and temperament—in the rise of a 'Satmar kingdom,' " first in Hungary and Romania and then, after World War II, in the United States. Myers traced this "martial sensibility" and "combative tendency" to the beginnings of the dynasty that would later come to dominate Hasidic Williamsburg.[4]

After the war, Yoel Teitelbaum and his followers brought their militant approach to Brooklyn. There, in the same period when they were forcefully confronting crime on the streets of Brooklyn, Satmar Hasidim engaged in violent conflicts with other Hasidic communities too, especially those whom they considered soft on Zionism. In 1977, for example, the *New York Times* reported, "As many as 2,000 Lubavitch Hasidim took a three-mile walk on April 9 [from Crown Heights]. When they arrived at Bedford Avenue, they were met by at least as many Satmar Hasidim. The Lubavitch group contends that the Satmarer began striking elderly rabbis and hurling objects from apartment roofs."5 Similarly, in 1981 the newspaper reported, "Hundreds of [Satmar] Hasidic Jews hurled rocks, bottles and vehement curses at the synagogue of a rival group of Hasidim in Brooklyn last night and faced off with scores of police officers in a two-hour confrontation in which dozens of worshipers were trapped inside the temple. The incident was the latest involving followers of the two ultra-Orthodox groups, the Satmars and the Belzers."6

In addition to its long history of combativeness, Satmar was particularly sensitive to any perceived threats in Williamsburg, because of the lingering impact of the Holocaust. Most of the Hungarian Hasidim who had settled the neighborhood in the 1940s and 1950s and served as communal leaders during the next two decades were survivors of ghettos and concentration camps. These men and women had survived in part because they were physically and psychologically tough, and their experiences during the war—when many lost their first families—had hardened them further. When violent crime started to increase in Williamsburg during the 1960s, therefore, Hasidim were outraged, but not shocked or intimidated. After witnessing the cold-blooded murder of loved ones, toiling as slave laborers, and surviving selections and death marches in Europe, Hasidim were unwilling to give up without a fight the safe haven they had painstakingly created in Williamsburg. Indeed, it would be hard to imagine a community more prepared to face the challenges of New York City in decline than the Hungarian Hasidim who settled in Williamsburg during the postwar period.

The Waste Land

In August 1966, a few months after his much-publicized visit to Bedford-Stuyvesant, Robert Kennedy delivered a talk titled "Problems of the Cities" before a U.S. Senate subcommittee. In the aftermath of the Watts riots in Los Angeles, Kennedy warned his colleagues that in cities around the nation, "We confront an urban wilderness more formidable and resistant and in some ways more frightening than the wilderness faced by the pilgrims or the pioneers."7 Kennedy remained optimistic that this frontier could be tamed and civilized, though it would not be easy: "We will need more than poverty programs, housing programs, and employment programs, although we will need all of these. We will need an outpouring of imagination, ingenuity, discipline, and hard work unmatched

Hasidic man walking with his children past an abandoned lot, 1962 or
1963 (Photograph © 2020 The Estate of Jan Yoors/Artists
Rights Society [ARS], New York)

since the first adventurers set out to conquer the wilderness. For the
problem is the largest we have ever known." Later, the image of a frontier that needed to be tamed became a key trope in narratives of gentrification, including in Williamsburg, where the first gentrifiers were
described as colonizers settling an urban wilderness.

In the mid-1960s, however, the gentrification of Williamsburg would
have probably seemed less likely than the colonization of Mars to Hasidic residents of the neighborhood. For them, Williamsburg, like New
York City in general, was in the process of degenerating into a state of
chaos or, as they referred to it in Yiddish, a *hefker velt*, in a wordplay on
the Talmudic term for a neglected piece of land. A turning point in the
decline of the neighborhood came in October 1962 when Rabbi Bernard
Eisdorfer, a Hasidic Holocaust survivor from Czechoslovakia, was
mugged and beaten to death by two men in Williamsburg. The murder
galvanized members of the Hasidic community and inspired them to
take a public stand against crime for the first time since arriving in the
neighborhood. More than 10,000 mourners joined the funeral procession for Eisdorfer as it wound its way through the streets of South Wil-

liamsburg. "Many," a contemporary account noted, "were themselves survivors of the Nazi holocaust, and carried signs demanding police action to halt muggings in the section. Weeping mourners marched with the hearse to the police station in a protest against local police."[8]

In the wake of Eisdorfer's murder, a number of observers predicted an imminent exodus of Williamsburg's remaining Jewish residents, including its Hasidic community.[9] The journalist Samuel Schreig observed in the *B'nai B'rith Messenger*, "Once peaceful, 'Williamsburg' is now a changing area. . . . Thousands of pious and Chassidic Jews made Williamsburg their self-imposed ghetto. . . . Today these Jews are frightened. A rash of senseless beatings and robbers plagues the neighborhood. The victims are elderly bearded Jews, boys with 'Peios' [sidelocks] and women."[10] When Schreig asked a local rabbi what caused the change, the rabbi responded bitterly, "I know that this is the season for liberalism and equality but why is it that since the Negroes and the Puerto Ricans moved into Williamsburg they have made life impossible for us? All cases involving beatings, robberies, and murder were perpetrated either by Negroes or Puerto Ricans." In response to the crime wave, some Jewish residents of the neighborhood wanted to create a *zelbshuts* (self-defense) group that would be manned by members of the Jewish War Veterans—a proposal that was shot down by a leader of the veterans' organization in a subsequent letter to the editor. Schreig reported on other opposition to the idea: "Police warned that if carried out the plan could bring about chaos and bloodshed. They asked residents to be 'patient and reasonable' and leave law enforcement to the police." Most Jews, Schreig concluded, had decided that " 'Jewish Williamsburg' was doomed" and had moved to Crown Heights or Borough Park or were planning "to run away from their once beloved Williamsburg." Those who could not afford to move took a fatalistic approach, as one elderly *shamas* (synagogue beadle) informed Schreig: "The same God that protected men in Buchenwald will look after me in Williamsburg."[11]

Satmar leaders were in the middle of negotiations to build a settlement in Mount Olive Township, New Jersey, when Eisdorfer was murdered. Had the real estate deal gone through, Hasidim might have eventually abandoned Williamsburg en masse, since the community and its financial investments in the neighborhood were still small enough for such a mass relocation to be feasible. In 1963, however, the sale was blocked, and Satmar continued to set down ever-deeper roots in Williamsburg, building schools and other institutions for its rapidly growing community and moving into newly constructed public housing buildings.

By that point, Hasidim who wanted to escape the crime wave in Williamsburg could no longer turn to Crown Heights for a safe refuge. In 1964, just as the city was reeling from the shocking rape and murder of Kitty Genovese in Queens, a series of highly publicized attacks on Jews in Crown Heights—including the attempted rape of a Hasidic rabbi's wife, a violent assault by a gang of fifty teenagers on a group of Hasidic schoolchildren, and the brutal rape and fatal stabbing of a Jewish teacher named Charlotte Lipsik in the elevator of her building—transformed the once bucolic neighborhood into a symbol of New York City's descent into chaos.[12] While the citywide increase in crime affected members of all communities, many Jewish observers interpreted the events in neighborhoods such as Williamsburg and Crown Heights through the lens of their own long history of persecution—and intracommunal politics.

On June 1, the *New York Times* published an editorial titled "Violence in the City," highlighting the recent rape and murder of Charlotte Lipsik in Crown Heights. That same day, Aryeh Naor, then an up-and-coming member of the right-wing Israeli political party Herut, led by Menachem Begin, published a fiery article in the party's daily newspaper—also called *Herut*—titled "Kishinev in Brooklyn."[13] The site of an infamous 1903 pogrom in which scores of Jews were murdered, raped, and injured, Kishinev (present-day Chişinău, Moldova) had widely become shorthand for violence against Jews in general.[14] Soon after the pogrom, the Hebrew poet Hayim Nachman Bialik had visited the city and written "In the City of Slaughter," an elegy for the dead but also a stinging indictment of Jewish survivors, whom he accused of looking on silently as their fellow Jews were attacked. The poem quickly became a rallying cry for Zionists and helped inspire the emigration of thousands of Jews from the Russian Empire between 1904 and 1914, an exodus that became known as the Second Aliyah. Sixty years after Kishinev, Naor wrote to his readers in the State of Israel, "The rabbi's wife raped five times before the eyes of her own children; a group of children attacked, tormented on their way to school; blows rained down on the heads of teenage girls; a teacher murdered at dusk—No, this is not a description of a pogrom in Tsarist Russia. . . . This occurred in Brooklyn which is in New York, a part of the New World. And it did not happen decades in the past but only a few days ago."[15]

What Kishinev in 1903 and Brooklyn in 1964 had in common, according to Naor, was that both were part of the *galut*, or exile, and, therefore, despite their many other differences, they shared the same essence. "The exile has a single nature: pogroms," he argued. "The context, the manner, the reason, the methods—all of these change. But the essence, the foundation—they stand as firm as a rock. In every place and time under the heavens, they have persecuted Jews. Murdered, robbed, raped, and wounded. This is a law of history." Yet, Naor raged, just as when Bialik had written his poem in the aftermath of Kishinev, and just as during the Holocaust, some Jews still refused to accept the Zionist solution to the depredations of exile: "You are guilty . . . Guilty—because even as you went up in the smoke rising from the furnaces of Auschwitz, Treblinka, Ponary [a killing site outside Vilnius], Chelmno, Sobibor, Babi Yar, and Majdanek, you did not rise up to swing a punch or take up weapons to liberate your homeland [in Palestine] and live there. . . . They were silent at Kishinev and they are silent in Brooklyn."

It took little more than a month for the Satmar leadership in Williamsburg to take up the gauntlet thrown down by Naor. On July 17, 1964, Sender Deutsch, writing under his regular pseudonym, "Eliezer Epstein," published an article in *Der Yid* that began, sarcastically, "You sit here so calmly in America. You live in the greatest city in the world—New York. But you don't even realize that in truth you don't live in New York at all but rather in . . . Kishinev! Yes, you live in Kishinev!"[16] Turning the tables, Deutsch accused Naor of engaging in "Schadenfreude" and exploiting the suffering of his fellow Jews for political gain. "It is a field day for them," Deutsch wrote of the "hypernationalistic newspaper *Herut*," when they can bring up a "pogrom that has taken place outside of the Land of Israel." The truth, Deutsch countered, was that "such 'pogroms' only exist in their excited fantasies."

Despite the confident, even dismissive, tone of Deutsch's response, it was clear that Naor's article had struck a particularly sensitive nerve within the Satmar community of Williamsburg. Satmar, like all Hasidic groups, fundamentally accepted the view that the exile was a series of persecutions against the Jewish people, but nevertheless rejected the view that Zionism offered a solution. To make things even more complicated, Satmar leaders were outraged at the recent crime wave, though they sought to prevent a panicked exodus from Brooklyn by terrified community members. Thus, the Satmar leadership in Williamsburg found itself stuck between a rock and a hard place in the mid-1960s, determined to draw attention and resources to the neighborhood in order to prevent crime from worsening, yet also wary of inspiring "Jewish flight" from Williamsburg or providing further ammunition to Zionist critics already eager to attack a community famous for its anti-Zionism.

Over the rest of the decade, crime rates in New York City continued to climb higher and higher. As Joshua Zeitz noted, "In 1966 alone, the number of reported burglaries citywide increased by 96.4 percent, the number of robberies by 89.9 percent, and the number of rapes by 22.1 percent. Altogether, the felony rate jumped 59.9 percent. It became axiomatic that entire parts of the city were off-limits to law-abiding citizens."[17] Among the areas that many "law-abiding citizens" considered "off-limits" because of crime was Williamsburg. An important turning point for Hasidim in the neighborhood came on December 1, 1967, when a Hasid named Shimon (Shmaya) Friedman was shot to death in his slipcover store. According to *Der Yid*, Friedman's murder was symptomatic of a "national epidemic" of crime that had infected Williamsburg and was now the biggest threat facing the Hasidic community: "No other problem, whether it be the struggle against poverty, help for the private school system, better living conditions, etc., has any significance as long as we have not ensured the first and most important thing—protection and security for our lives."[18]

Der Yid stressed that the Hasidic community in Williamsburg could not rely on the criminal justice system, since even when "the police arrest—when they actually arrest—the criminals, the courts set them free." Instead, the newspaper exhorted the community to take action, quoting a famous teaching by Rabbi Hillel, "If I am not for myself, who will be?"[19] According to *Der Yid*, the Hasidic community had already taken positive steps, including a spontaneous demonstration of thousands at city hall following the murder of Friedman. "In the middle of the day, Jews abandoned their businesses, left work and came to express their bitterness and woe concerning this anarchy," *Der Yid* reported. "An especially strong impression was made by the march of over 700 students from the Satmar Yeshiva who walked on foot over the Brooklyn Bridge to City Hall to participate in this protest on behalf of the Jewish people." The newspaper called on the newly created United Jewish Organizations to organize another massive rally and for the city to set up a permanent commission to fight crime. "Meanwhile," it lamented, "once again the life of a fine Jew has been extinguished, a father of children has been cut down by murderers who stroll around clear and free in the jungle that is called New York."[20]

In the coming years, the image of New York City as an urban jungle became commonplace, fueled by rising crime, a deepening fiscal crisis, the divestment of city services from poor, outer-borough neighborhoods, or as it became known, "planned shrinkage." At the same time, nearly forty films, including *The Incident* (1967), *Hell Up in Harlem* (1973), *Taxi*

Driver (1976), *The Warriors* (1979), *Fort Apache, the Bronx* (1981), and *Escape from New York* (1981), shaped, and frequently distorted, the public's perception of the city.[21] The local press encouraged a sense of unfolding doom by publishing articles with headlines such as "South Bronx: A Jungle Stalked by Fear, Seized by Rage," whose author warned that "even for a native New Yorker, the voyage across the Willis Avenue Bridge is a journey to a foreign country where fear is the overriding emotion in a landscape of despair," and quoted a local health care provider as declaring bluntly, "The South Bronx is a necropolis—a city of death."[22] Like the South Bronx, Williamsburg became a synecdoche for everything that was wrong with New York City in the 1970s. The same article that elegized the South Bronx noted acerbically, "The Morrisania district of the South Bronx has 507 welfare recipients among every 1,000 residents, but that is not the highest rate in the city. That distinction goes to the Williamsburg section of Brooklyn, with 520 welfare recipients among every 1,000 residents."

For historians of New York City, the fall of Williamsburg was even more precipitous. One article described the neighborhood in its heyday: "[It] was once one of the elegant resort areas of the East Coast. The Vanderbilts, the Whitneys, the Morgans and others used to ferry over to enjoy the concerts, the beer gardens, the fine hotels."[23] In contrast to that golden era was the hellscape of 1973: "Most of the neighborhood has evolved into a festering urban canker—a rundown collection of hovel-like apartments into which blacks and Puerto Ricans and other Hispanics are crammed. Unemployment and underemployment are endemic. The schools, beset by massive problems of vandalism and discipline, are barely, if at all, teaching." Yet, the article claimed, there was one bright spot in Williamsburg, a kind of anachronistic island in a sea of misery: "In the midst of this depressing slumscape reposes what is essentially a small 18th century east European village. This part of Williamsburg has no crime, no drugs, no venereal disease, no graffiti. 'To us,' says one leader of this enclave, 'juvenile delinquency is a guy who gets caught watching a baseball game on a television set.'"

In reality, Hasidic Williamsburg was far from being an eighteenth-century shtetl, nor was it immune to the social problems besetting other neighborhood residents during this period, though its rates of certain kinds of crimes and drug abuse were certainly much lower. Perhaps most importantly for their survival in the embattled atmosphere of 1970s New York, many Hasidim in Williamsburg were willing to engage in behavior that they justified as self-defense but that critics, including many Puerto Rican and African American residents of the neighborhood, condemned as criminal. Thus, Hasidim joined a growing chorus of Jews in the city who believed that only forceful action—in some cases, involving violence—could ensure that Jews remained a strong presence in the city. As an article in the *New York Daily News* in 1973, titled "The Gentle People Get Tough," put it, employing the explicitly apocalyptic language that was common in coverage of New York City during that era, "The Hasidim are no longer frightened by threats. If this is to be their Armageddon, so be it."[24]

"Tough Jews"

While the Hasidic community of Williamsburg was uniquely prepared to survive in 1970s New York, its members were not the only Jews in the city to take a hard stance against crime and what they perceived as other signs of urban decay. The "tough Jew" of late-1960s New York was exemplified by a group of diverse, well-known figures: Norman Mailer, the famously pugnacious author who ran for mayor of New York City in 1969; Albert Shanker, the head of the United Federation of Teachers, who opposed community control in the Ocean Hill–Brownsville school district in 1968; Rabbi Mayer Kahane, who founded the militant Jewish Defense League (JDL) in 1968; and Rabbi Menachem Mendel Schneerson, the leader of the Lubavitcher Hasidim in Crown Heights, who prohibited his followers from abandoning their neighborhood in 1969.[25] The phenomenon was inspired, in part, by Israel's victory in the Six-Day War in 1967, but spread far beyond that point of origin. As Joshua Freeman noted, "[Albert] Shanker's rise ... marked the reemergence of the tough Jew in New York civic life. ... When in 1967 'little David slew Goliath,' many New York Jews concluded that they could and must fight like hell for themselves, and stop worrying if others saw them as pushy, rude, or unreasonable."[26]

In its own way, Satmar participated in this broader zeitgeist, but as was always the case, the community hewed to its own path, eschewing alliances with other Jewish groups, especially those that supported Zionism. The shunned groups included the Jewish Defense League, which had loudly positioned itself as the defender of the city's Jews, including those in Williamsburg, where it hoped to make inroads among the neighborhood's Hasidim. In June 1970, the *New York Times* reported that "Penn Street in the Williamsburg section of Brooklyn was the scene of street fighting ... as Hasidic Jews and blacks threw bottles and insults at one an-

other until the police took control."[27] Hasidic and black residents quoted
in the article described the street battle as nothing new, since something
like it "happens every summer"; members of both communities "insisted
that racial differences were not the issue . . . it was just a matter of young
people taunting each other." What was new in Williamsburg, according to
the newspaper, was that some Hasidic residents had supposedly invited
the JDL to help them defend their turf, an act that exacerbated the already volatile situation and led to "more violence than usual." Later, at a
press conference held outside the New York Board of Rabbis on the East
Side of Manhattan, Rabbi Kahane defended his group's actions: "If they
think Jewish blood is cheaper than anybody else's . . . let them know that
Jews can riot, too."

Even before this incident, the Hasidic leadership of Williamsburg
had come out unequivocally in the fall of 1969 against the JDL in the
pages of *Der Yid*.[28] Moreover, in an interview with the Jewish Telegraphic
Agency at the end of June 1970, the local rabbi Bernard Weinberger emphasized that "no responsible leader" of the Jewish community in Williamsburg had invited the JDL to the neighborhood and, on the contrary,
the United Jewish Organizations had sent Kahane a telegram stating that
he and his followers were not welcome.[29] It is unclear, therefore, whether
any Hasidim called the JDL in the summer of 1970 to participate in the
street battles then unfolding in the neighborhood or whether members of
the militant group showed up on their own accord and later claimed that
they had been invited.

Whatever the case, the leadership of the Satmar community responded by forcefully condemning the group. On September 27, 1970,
Der Yid published an editorial titled "And You Shall Expel the Wicked
from Among you" (a phrase from Deuteronomy 17:7), which stated,
"The 'Jewish Defense League' has turned to criminal ways from terrorism and hooliganism—and all under the name 'Jewish'—and this should
not be tolerated under any circumstances."[30] The editorial lamented that
"naïve young people" had "made the organization into a kind of cult,"
and it called on the "American Jewish public" to "once and for all place
this organization outside its camp." A few months later, the newspaper
published another critique, headlined "A Little Too Late," in which it laid
out its case against the JDL in damning detail.

> This militant group started with the ostensible program of pro-
> tecting the New York Jewish population against the hooligan

"Black Panthers," "Young Lords," and the like. However, the terror and hooliganism was not stopped. They merely added a "Jewish" hooliganism, "Jewish" terror, from a group that calls itself the
"Jewish" Defense League. ... They started ostensibly to defend
the rights of Jews, but soon it turned out that their entire aim is to
agitate and provoke, to act like hooligans and imitate the terroris-
tic shtik of the various contemporary lawless groups. ... However,
the world looks differently upon a Jewish terror group than a non-
Jewish one. The world will not say about all blacks that they are
terrorists and hooligans because there is a "Black Panthers." But
when it comes to the Jews, they will indeed apply a kind of "collective responsibility." If a group of Jews acts wantonly, all Jews are
accused of being hooligans and terrorists. The peoples of the
world understand the principle that "all of Israel are responsible
for one another." [Babylonian Talmud Shavuot 39a][31]

Among the things that bothered Satmar leaders most about the
Jewish Defense League—in addition to its "terrorism," a label they
applied over thirty years before the FBI classified the JDL as a terrorist
organization—was that the group claimed to be authentically Jewish and
to represent, and defend, the interests of all Jews, no matter their background. From the Satmar perspective, however, the Zionist ideology of
the JDL not only placed it beyond the pale of authentic Jewishness but
also encouraged anti-Semitism. Most disturbing to Satmar was that
their own community might be tarred by the actions of the JDL, since,
according to *Der Yid*, unlike blacks, all Jews were blamed even when
only a small minority was guilty of something. Of course, contrary to the
editorial's claim, many people did condemn blacks, in general, as "terrorists and hooligans" because of the actions of the Black Panthers, yet in
the eyes of the Satmar leadership, Jews carried a heavier burden than
other groups and anti-Semitism was more pernicious than other forms of
discrimination.

According to Satmar's leaders, the JDL's headline-grabbing stunts—
or shtik—made it no better than the Young Lords or the Black Panthers,
even though members of the JDL had violently clashed with the Black
Panthers at the group's headquarters in Harlem in May 1970 and Meir
Kahane had condemned the Panthers as "vicious anti-Semites" and "a
definite clear and present danger to Jews."[32] At the same time, however,
Kahane also acknowledged a grudging respect for the Panthers, and like

other radicals around the globe in this period, he was clearly influenced by them in a variety of ways, something that *Der Yid* had perceptively picked up on.

Despite strident efforts to distance members of their community from the JDL, Satmar had more in common with the militant group than its spokesmen were willing to admit. Both Satmar and the JDL shared a "never again" attitude to the Holocaust and both believed that "Jewish blood doesn't come cheap"—two of the JDL's slogans. Indeed, the ongoing campaign in the pages of *Der Yid* to delegitimize the JDL makes sense only if we appreciate that it was directed precisely to Hasidic readers who may have been receptive to the group's extremist message and tactics. After building their enclave in Williamsburg from the ground up, Satmar leaders were unwilling to cede any ground to another Jewish group, especially a pro-Zionist organization led by a charismatic rabbi like Meir Kahane.

One of Kahane's early followers, Alex "Sender" Sternberg, was a Williamsburg yeshiva student who trained in the legendary Tong Dojo, an African American–led karate studio on the border of Brownsville and Bedford-Stuyvesant.[33] There, as a star pupil of the dojo's sensei, George Cofield, Sternberg "participated in discussions with black martial arts leaders who trained the Panthers, the Fruit of Islam . . . and the young Rev. Al Sharpton." Sternberg recalled of this period, "Having recently graduated from the Yeshiva seminary, I was now attending college dressed in a dashiki with my hair combed in 'Afro style.' But on top of my head was a yarmulke."[34]

In retrospect, that trajectory might seem like an unusual one for the son of Hungarian Holocaust survivors who immigrated to Brooklyn in 1961 and graduated from Williamsburg's Yeshiva Torah Vodaath. Yet the climate in Brooklyn during this period was conducive to the emergence of Jewish pride, and the children of Holocaust survivors living in inner-city neighborhoods such as Williamsburg had much in common with the young African Americans who were drawn to the Black Panthers.[35] Alex Sternberg went on to serve as the JDL's director of defense and security. In 1972, not long after being indicted on federal gun charges along with other JDL members, Sternberg began to teach karate classes at the Young Men's and Young Women's Hebrew Association of Williamsburg. "The image of Jewish youth, especially the yeshiva student, must change," he told the *New York Times*. "They have been regarded too long as the 'patsy' on the street—someone to pick on, rob or mug."[36]

Chaptsem!

As early as October 1966, Hasidim had begun to employ violence to protect their turf in Williamsburg. In an incident that the *New York Times* described as "the first violence of this sort in the neighborhood," hundreds—some sources said thousands—of Hasidim were accompanying the Satmar Rebbe on his customary stroll home from the Yetev Lev synagogue following the end of Simhat Torah (a holiday celebrating the completion of the annual cycle of reading the Torah) when a car driven by a Puerto Rican man attempted to drive through the crowd gathered in the street.[37] Some Hasidim "responded by shattering its windshield and tail lights," leading the driver and his passenger to seek out the police and file a complaint. When the men later returned to their car and confronted the Hasidim, the latter "battered the car more and the men were chased three blocks into the precinct house." Following the melee, a sixteen-year-old Hasidic boy was charged with felonious assault of an officer. This was the first in a series of violent encounters between Hasidim, their neighbors, and the police in Williamsburg, many of which erupted around the Jewish holidays, when throngs of Hasidim took to the streets.

Two years later, in September 1968, the Spanish-language newspaper *El Diario–La Prensa* reported that on Rosh Hashanah, the Jewish New Year, around fifty people, most of whom were Puerto Ricans, engaged in a pitched street battle with members of Congregation Yetev Lev D'Satmar, in which people on both sides hurled bottles and rocks.[38] The conflict began, according to the paper, when Hasidim who were returning home from the synagogue blocked the passage of pedestrians and vehicles. At that point, "One of the members of said congregation hurled a bottle at the Boricuas [Puerto Ricans] and this incited the fight." Police, including fifty or sixty additional officers who were at hand because of the Jewish holiday, quickly broke up the brawl and arrested an African American teenager for assaulting an officer. Similarly, in March 1973, two Hasidim were arrested and one was charged with assault after they reportedly punched and kicked two police officers who were attempting to clear Lee Avenue of hundreds of Purim revelers, "wearing costumes of bears, tigers and clowns," so that cars could pass through.[39] It is unclear whether the fact that both officers were Jewish—Patrolmen Norman Horowitz and Joel Berkowitz—had anything to do with how the confrontation unfolded, though Jewish police in Williamsburg openly acknowledged the special challenges they faced in patrolling the Hasidic enclave.[40]

In the late 1960s and early 1970s, while the Satmar Rebbe focused on what he considered to be the existential threat of Zionism, he left lesser dangers, such as the rising crime rate in Williamsburg, to his savvy inner circle of lay leaders. This division of labor within Satmar, which was used on a wide range of issues, allowed Teitelbaum to retain his aura of otherworldly *kedusha,* or "holiness," while empowering his lieutenants to concentrate on more mundane matters. These activists, or *askunim,* took a multipronged approach to crime: advocating for political solutions in the pages of *Der Yid;* organizing public protests in which hundreds and sometimes thousands of Hasidim participated; and endorsing political candidates who presented themselves as tough on crime.[41]

They also put pressure on the New York City police, who responded in 1969 by unveiling Operation Hasidic Rabbi, in which undercover officers dressed as Hasidim stationed themselves in Williamsburg, Borough Park, Crown Heights, and the Lower East Side in a sting operation to arrest muggers.[42] Despite these efforts and the frequent accusations by Puerto Ricans and African Americans that Hasidim received preferential treatment from the force, the relationship between the Hasidic community in Williamsburg and the police during this period was far from cozy.[43] As an article in the *New York Daily News* put it in 1973, "Fate has placed the city's Hasidic neighborhoods, notably Williamsburg, in close proximity to minority poverty areas. As the drug explosion reached its zenith in the last few years, the Williamsburg crime rate has skyrocketed. The lack of adequate police protection has underlined the inborn Hasidic mistrust in police authority nurtured in centuries under the czar. Fighting back seems the only choice."[44]

As the article suggested, one of the chief reasons for the tension between Hasidim and police in Williamsburg was that while Hasidic lay leaders sought to address crime via official channels, community members sometimes—how often was a matter of debate—took matters into their own hands. In December 1971, for example, the *New York Times* reported that "an enraged band of students at a yeshiva in the Williamsburg section of Brooklyn mauled an apparent burglar last night after he allegedly set fire to a torah, or handwritten Biblical scroll, worth $10,000," that had been donated by a woman whose family had been murdered in the Holocaust. About twenty young men belonging to the Belzer Hasidic sect chased the Puerto Rican suspect "for several blocks and pummeled him," resulting in "a broken nose and wounds requiring nine stitches before he was rescued by police."[45]

It is worth contrasting this incident with another act of vandalism that took place in Williamsburg less than two years later, in September 1972. In that case, vandals struck Congregation Chevra Kadisha, a century-old synagogue whose elderly worshipers belonged to the old guard Orthodox Jewish community of Williamsburg, which by that point had almost completely disappeared from the neighborhood. The vandals stripped the building of its brass plumbing, caused a flood in the sanctuary, and desecrated the ark where the Torah scrolls were kept. The scrolls were "unrolled and draped throughout the synagogue" like toilet paper. The venerable house of worship, led by Rabbi Asher Katzman, who had also served as a *rosh yeshiva* (chief administrator) at Yeshiva Torah Vodaath, was forced to cancel the upcoming High Holiday services. One member, who requested anonymity "for fear of possible reprisals from the unidentified vandals" lamented that congregants had "resisted the massive Jewish exodus from Williamsburg," only to experience this final nail in the coffin of their community. "This is where they raised their families and spent most of their lives," he told the *New York Daily News*. "Their children have grown and moved away, but they're staying, trying to live out the rest of their years in peace and this has to happen and spoil it."[46]

Even if a growing penchant for dealing out vigilante-style justice sharply differentiated Hasidim from the remaining Orthodox Jews in Williamsburg—whose resigned approach more closely resembled that of their Jewish counterparts in Brownsville or the South Bronx—it did not make them unique in the neighborhood. On December 26, 1971, the *New York Times* reported that at the intersection of Lee and Flushing Avenues, only a few blocks from the Belzer yeshiva where the Torah scroll had been burned a year earlier, "a 40-year-old white Brooklyn motorist, whose auto struck and killed a 47-year-old Brooklyn Negro in Williamsburg shortly after midnight yesterday was attacked by a crowd of blacks and badly beaten shortly after the accident."[47] No charges were filed against the driver, who "suffered fractures of the nose and cheek bones, and a cerebral concussion," and was "rescued from the crowd by radio patrolmen of the Union Avenue station house." Other incidents from this period confirm the shared willingness of Hasidim, blacks, and Puerto Ricans in Williamsburg to respond to crime, car accidents, acts of perceived disrespect, and other provocations by taking the law into their own hands.[48]

By May 1973, cases of Hasidim apprehending and beating crime suspects in Williamsburg had become numerous enough that Father Bryan Karvelis held a news conference in the rectory of Transfiguration

Church to condemn the behavior. Karvelis still sometimes spoke on behalf of the neighborhood's Puerto Rican community, even though a new generation of local Puerto Rican activists was coming into its own. According to the *New York Times*, Karvelis claimed that Hasidim had engaged in an average of seven to nine "mob beatings" a month for the past few months, adding, "The Hasidic community comprises most of the political power in the area, and we feel that the police brass have been prejudiced in their favor. . . . We've met with the local police brass and urgently requested assailants be arrested, but nothing has been done."[49]

In an interview with the anthropologist Jerome Mintz for his book *Hasidic People*, Karvelis later acknowledged that street crime was commonplace in the neighborhood, but he downplayed its impact: "We don't keep poor boxes [in the church] any more. They were all robbed. I get robbed regularly but it's not the end of the world."[50] The real crime, in his view, was that the Hasidim refused to turn the other cheek, as it were, when they were robbed or assaulted. Within the Puerto Rican community, Karvelis had long sought to cultivate peaceful alternatives to violent confrontation. In the early 1960s, as the gang problem in Williamsburg began to reach crisis proportions, Karvelis had helped a group of young men from the neighborhood, at least some of whom were former gang members, create a youth group known as the Corinthians. Named after the New Testament book, the Corinthians were committed to nonviolence in the face of provocations by local gang members.[51]

Karvelis wanted Hasidim to respond similarly when attacked or threatened. Instead, he groused, "They blow whistles and shout *ganef*, thief, and in seconds there are two hundred people there. When they catch someone they act as judge and jury and beat the individual bloody. They are paranoid about being robbed. Their houses are like bird cages with bars on all the windows."[52] Yet many Hasidim in Williamsburg saw their current experience of crime through the lens of centuries of Jewish persecution in Europe at the hands of Christians who had long preached turning the other cheek while beating Jews, and worse. This stance was explained succinctly by Rabbi Marc Tannenbaum, a pioneer in Jewish-Christian relations who served as an official observer to the Second Vatican Council, which produced *Nostra Aetate* (*In Our Time*), a papal declaration that absolved Jews of deicide: "They [Hasidim] must react strongly, they believe, or face extinction. A mugger comes to symbolize much more than a mugger, he becomes another stormtrooper."[53]

Police officials from the 90th precinct denied both the scale of the problem in Williamsburg and their supposed inaction, asserting to the *New York Times* that in the three months before Karvelis's news conference, there were "no more than five such incidents. All were investigated and action was taken where warranted."[54] Yet they acknowledged that the Hasidim did not trust the police and preferred to handle many crimes themselves: "The Hasidim are a tightly knit community with a long distrust of the police in Europe and America. . . . Their tradition is not to report to authorities when they are victimized by a thief or assaulted, but to take matters in their own hands, administering a beating to the suspect and then releasing him." Speaking on behalf of the Hasidic community, Leopold "Leibush" Lefkowitz, then the president of the United Jewish Organizations of Williamsburg, emphasized that any actions taken by community members were done entirely in self-defense, but he added that Hasidim would not be scared away by crime: "We are a peaceful people . . . We do not attack anybody. But we will not be driven from our community by those who wield knives and come from elsewhere."

In its coverage of the same press conference, the *New York Daily News* reported: "[Karvelis] said he was beaten by a mob of several hundred Hasidim on Feb. 4 when he went to the aid of a youth whom, he said, they had spread-eagled over the hood of a car and were beating. The youth was reportedly accused by Hasidics of attempted robbery."[55] Leaders of the Hasidic community, in turn, expressed impatience with both their ongoing experience of crime in the neighborhood and with the response to their efforts to defend themselves. "Jews have gotten tired of being pushed around and are now learning to defend themselves," Chaim Stauber, the editor of *Der Yid*, stated. "Fear is rampant here. . . . It is very strange that we have to defend our record. We made the area stable." Nevertheless, Stauber admitted that even though Hasidim only sought to "apprehend the criminal," sometimes "things can get out of hand."

Increasingly, when Hasidim in Williamsburg experienced or witnessed a crime, they would yell, "*Chaptsem!*" (Yiddish, "Catch him!") at the top of their lungs, which prompted other community members in earshot to drop whatever they were doing to pursue the assailant. Gershon Kranzler, a former resident of the neighborhood who published several studies on the Hasidic community, described the phenomenon as follows: "Woe to the would-be attackers when the defense whistle sounds or there is a cry of '*Chaptzem.*' Crowds pour out of their homes all around and immediately overwhelm the attackers. Gangs of young toughs and even the occasionally contemptuous [police] officers have learned to respect the wrath and strength of this response of the *Chassidic* community to provocation and attack."[56]

The muscular approach of Williamsburg's Hasidic community to crime in the early 1970s not only distinguished it dramatically from Jewish communities in New York City that chose to run rather than fight, but also stood long-standing stereotypes on their heads, as a *Daily News* article in June 1973 headlined "The Gentle People Get Tough" made clear.[57] After recounting an incident in which a group of Hasidic men chased, apprehended, and, depending on the source, beat a knife-wielding mugger, the author noted, "Whatever else it may have done, the incident cracked the stereotype of the Hasidim as helpless milktoast mugger bait. In the weeks since then the cries of 'goniff' and 'chopsem' have rang repeatedly though the streets of Williamsburg with muggers chased, cornered, and collared by the Hasidim." Ironically, given Satmar's intense antipathy to the State of Israel, the article's explanation for why Hasidim in Williamsburg were embracing self-defense strongly echoed the motivation for what Max Nordau first called *Muskeljudentum* (muscular Judaism) at the Second Zionist Congress in 1898: "A new generation of Hasidic men—whose grandparents lived under the thumb of the Czar [albeit not in Hungary] and whose parents were led to Hitler's gas chambers—are asking, 'Why if we are now in the land of the free should we continue to be victimized?' As one elderly Williamsburg rabbi explained: 'We always took it. What was the choice? But the kids have shed the persecution complex. There's an old Yiddish expression that if a man picks up his hand, you pick up your feet. Now, our young men pick up their hands too.' "

Yet what seemed like justifiable self-defense to many Hasidim in Williamsburg "smacked of frontier justice" to many local Puerto Ricans, who, the article explained, "don't like muggers and junkies either, but contend that the Hasidim in their zeal are pursuing and beating up innocent persons. They predict retaliation if the attacks don't stop." Beginning in the early 1970s, Puerto Rican community activists and, in one case, a Latino officer from the 90th precinct, accused the police department of treating the Hasidic community in Williamsburg with kid gloves, even when its members engaged in vigilantism.[58] Hasidic activists, in turn, charged the police with showing preferential treatment to Puerto Rican and African American suspects accused of targeting Hasidic victims in the neighborhood. To make matters even more complicated, some Puerto Rican and black residents of Williamsburg acknowledged that the Hasidic approach to crime had made the neighborhood safer, even as they condemned what they considered to be excessive cases of vigilantism, and some Hasidim chastised fellow community members for taking the law into their own hands and alienating the police at a time when their help was most needed.

The following example illustrates how complex the issue of crime could be in Williamsburg during this period and how it was woven into the fabric of daily life in the neighborhood. In the summer of 1974, a year after the *New York Times* reported on Father Karvelis's press conference on Hasidic vigilantism in Williamsburg, Leibush Lefkowitz sent a dossier to the newly elected mayor, Abraham Beame, detailing the Hasidic community's complaints against the police department. The materials, preserved in the papers of Beame's deputy mayor, Judah Gribetz, included a "summary of criminal acts committed against Williamsburg Jews" in the month of May 1974, comprising 135 incidents "reported and recorded" by the police, which resulted in only 8 arrests.[59] Dismal as these statistics were in their own right, they did not convey the depth of the problem, Lefkowitz asserted: "Suffice it to say that most of the crimes perpetrated against the Jewish community go unreported. Many other incidents which are called in [to the police] go unrecorded."

In a letter dated June 12, 1974, Lefkowitz noted that Satmar students attending the community's yeshiva at 167 Sands Street in Vinegar Hill (another North Brooklyn neighborhood) had been attacked regularly, including eight times in the preceding week alone; at least five Hasidic women had been robbed, beaten, or slashed while leaving the mikveh between Lee and Marcy Avenues in Williamsburg over the past month; and Hasidic students at the Satmar school at 225 Patchen Avenue in the heart of Bedford-Stuyvesant were being "attacked daily during their travel from home to school and back . . . pelted with rocks, bottles and debris." The lion's share of the dossier, however, was devoted to a single incident in Williamsburg, one that had prompted Lefkowitz to petition the mayor with great urgency. The incident and its denouement reveal a great deal about the Hasidic community's response to street crime and its contentious relationship with the police during the pre-gentrification era, as well as the way in which crimes could frequently become flash points for intergroup conflict, as well as negotiation, between Hasidim and Puerto Ricans in Williamsburg.

Based on ten eyewitness testimonies from Hasidim, which were included in the dossier, Lefkowitz asserted that on the night of June 10,

1974, at approximately ten thirty, a group of "Hispanic youths," including one who was "brandishing a large knife," menaced and attacked a number of Hasidic pedestrians. A crowd of about twenty-five Hasidim quickly gathered and started to chase two of the youths down Lee Avenue, the community's main thoroughfare. At that point, a police car pulled up, and two officers hustled the youths into the backseat before turning to face the approaching crowd. Witnesses stated that several Hasidim, including at least one who had personally been threatened by the youth with the knife, requested that they be allowed to accompany the police to the station to ensure that the youths were arrested; in addition, they asked the police for their badge numbers. In response, the police officers concealed their badges and made "an anti-semitic slur" that was, according to one account, "get out of here you dirty Jew." The witnesses agreed that several Hasidim then "attempted to open the door of the police car and forcefully accompany them," which prompted the police to draw their weapons and threaten to shoot into the crowd. Soon after, the witnesses claimed, police reinforcements arrived on the scene, began to beat the assembled Hasidim with their nightsticks, and placed one person under arrest.

Not surprisingly, the official incident report filed by the officers at the 90th precinct described the events very differently. According to the police report, the responding officers "observed a group of Hasidic Jews chasing 2 male Hispanics" and "attempted to find out what had occurred without success." After placing the youths in their radio car, they were on their way to the precinct when a "private vehicle occupied by Hasidic Jews cut off the police car, and the occupants from car pulled the police officers and the 2 Hispanics and attacked them, the 2 Hispanics were severely beaten—Police reinforcements arrived and 1 arrest was made for assault. . . . Then about 400 Hasidic Jews gathered at Lee and Penn Street protesting the arrest."

As their testimonies made clear, what most upset Hasidim about the night's events was the behavior of the police, which several explicitly described as triggering personal memories of the Holocaust. One witness recalled, "I became very upset because to me as well as most likely many others it was a scene from my past when the German Nazis used to surround us and without any questions beat us, killed a couple of us and laughed into our faces. The scene was strikingly similar to what I endured this evening . . . because I wear a beard I will not be heard and will not be treated fairly. I will only be rediculed [sic], laughed at and abused."

Transcribe Det. all. Cappola.   Date June 11, 1974

Time	Caller	Pct	Incident
0100 hrs	P/o Santani	90	Lee Ave & Penn St.
			P/O's observered a Group of Hasidic
			Jews Chasing 2 Male Hispanics
			P/o's attempted to find out what
			had occurred, with out success
			P/o's Put the 2 Hispanics into their
			Radio Car And Proceeded to the 90th
			Pct. A Private vehicle occupied
			By Hasidic Jews cut off the Police
			Car, and 2 the occupants From Car
			Pulled the P/o's And the 2 Hispanics
			And attacked them. The 2 Hispanics
			were Severly Beaten - Police Reenforcements
			arrived and. 1 Arrest was made For
			Assault. 2 Hispanics were Treated at
			Greenpoint Hospital - 1 Police Sgt &
			3 P/o's were Slightly Injured.
			Then about 400 Hasidic Jews
			Gathered at lee & Penn St. Protesting
			the Arrest -
			At 0630 hrs I spoke to the Desk
			Officer of the 90th Pct who stated
			That. The District Attorney's Office
	OVER		was Investigating, And that things
			Had Quieted down.

Police report from New York City's 90th precinct recounting a *chaptsem* incident and its aftermath in the heart of Hasidic Williamsburg, June 11, 1974 (Mayor Abraham D. Beame Collection, Deputy Mayor Judah Gribetz Files; Courtesy NYC Municipal Archive)

Another witness stated, "The reaction of the Police Officers was imme-diate; wild and without regard to whom they are attacking. I was stand-ing innocently as a by stander [sic] and was also hurt by one of the Police Officers. I immediately fled the scene and returned home because the in-cident reproduced in my mind memories of Nazi Germany during the height of their anti-semitic campaign."

In the wee hours of the morning, community members informed Lefkowitz of the dangerous situation that was unfolding, and he rushed to the station house, where he "found a crowd assembled, consisting of the youth [accused of brandishing the knife], his family, as well as two or three representatives from the Puerto Rican community." A short while later, Inspector Ralph Cohen, the commander of the 90th precinct, ar-rived and began to negotiate with the Hasidic and Puerto Rican repre-sentatives. "We all came to the conclusion that this matter can be solved in an amicable fashion as we had been accustomed to in the past," Lefkowitz informed the mayor in his letter. "We were willing to forget and to forgive provided that the police department would do the same." Evidently, both sides had agreed that if no charges were filed against their respective community members, they would let bygones be bygones.

Ralph Cohen was in an unenviable position. On the one hand, his Jewish identity likely raised suspicion among some in the Puerto Rican community that he was prone to showing favoritism to the Hasidim, par-ticularly in a case like this. On the other hand, Hasidim in Williamsburg often complained that non-Hasidic Jews like Cohen were more likely to discriminate against them than non-Jews in order to avoid charges of fa-voritism or because they resented Hasidim for making Jews in general "look bad." Not long after this incident, in November 1975, Cohen ap-peared to confirm these Hasidic fears in a newspaper article on Jewish po-lice officers in which he argued that "Jewish cops simply don't work well there," in Williamsburg. "For some uncanny reason," he explained, "there's an identity problem for Jewish cops working in Chassidic areas, perhaps like a black working in Harlem. To a Jew who regards himself as an 'American,' there's something repulsive about these people who insist upon preserving anachronistic ways. The goyim are far more understand-ing in dealing with the Chassidim. A few years ago I noticed that two Jews working in the 90th Precinct were giving out far more summonses than anyone else [to Hasidim] and I had to pull them out of there."[60]

As the commander of a volatile precinct in which many Hasidic and Puerto Rican residents viewed the police—and one another—with profound suspicion or downright hostility, Cohen clearly sought to strike a balance between maintaining intergroup peace and enforcing the law. But when Cohen conveyed the informal agreement reached by Hasidic and Puerto Rican activists in the morning of June 11 to his superiors, they balked and sent an assistant district attorney to the station house to investigate whether any criminal charges should be brought. At that point, Lefkowitz met with a high-ranking police official who had been called to the scene; he stressed that he would "not advise anybody to assist in this one sided discriminatory investigation" if the Jewish community member accused of assault were arrested "even though we have witnesses to prove his innocence and even though the policemen [*sic*] initially admitted that he was not sure . . . who hit him, and also if these two Hispanics are not presently in police custody." In the conclusion of his letter, Lefkowitz stressed that "once again the attitude of many officers towards the Chassidic community is an extremely belligerent one with strong anti-semitic overtones and where nothing is thought of approaching a gathered crowd with drawn guns," and called on the mayor to order "an immediate investigation and reevaluation of June 10th's incident." The surviving records do not indicate whether Abraham Beame took a personal interest in the incident or whether anyone else in the city government took action.

In their communication with city officials, Hasidim in Williamsburg presented a unified front and laid the blame for the events of June 10 squarely on the criminals and the police department. Within the Hasidic community, however, the events exposed fault lines over how members dealt with street crime. Thus, on June 14, 1974, Chaim Moshe Stauber, the editor of *Der Yid* and an important Satmar lay leader, published a soul-searching article in the newspaper titled "*Chaptsem! Chaptsem!* But How?," in which he attempted to balance praise for what he considered to be community members' justified apprehension of criminal suspects with harsh criticism for the excesses that sometimes followed.[61] In essence, Stauber sought to draw a line between legitimate self-defense and illegal vigilantism. Regarding the confrontation of June 10, in particular, Stauber began by extolling the muscular response of the Hasidim on the scene:

> Two Puerto Rican *shkutsim* [plural of *shagetz*, a pejorative term for non-Jew] attacked several Jewish pedestrians and with the justifiable concern of one Jew for another, people started to yell: "*Chaptsem! Chaptsem!*" From one angle, this was moving and it was

extremely impressive how Jews started to run from all sides and pursue the hooligan criminals until they had, in fact, surrounded them with a human ring so that they would not be able to flee. This shows, may God be blessed, that in addition to the quality of mercy, Jews also have enough vigilance and firmness to not allow the criminals to escape as used to happen so often in the past.

Yet Stauber was also highly critical of how some of his fellow Hasidim had acted once they apprehended the suspects. Not only did they behave in a way that contravened American law, but they also went against the Torah by assuming the role of police, judge, and executioner. To make matters worse, their vigilantism risked provoking violent retaliation by non-Jews, who were supposedly already prone to such outbursts:

> We must once and for all stop the travesty of "young men" who want, as in the aforementioned case, to not only be the "rescuer" but also the "guard," "police," "judge," and "hangman." . . . This is unlawful, it is against the Torah and also extremely dangerous and harmful to the entire Jewish community, when we live encircled by so many more non-Jews, who will not stray from making use of their inheritance "And by the sword you shall live!" [Genesis 27:40] Don't we have enough lessons from the past with dangerous confrontations to know that we can, God forbid, ignite a conflagration if we seek to extinguish a fire with gasoline?

At a time when calling someone a Zionist was considered the insult ne plus ultra within the Satmar community, Stauber suggested that Hasidim who engaged in vigilantism were like those who participated in this worst of heresies: "Unfortunately, we must admit that in the last several years, among many American born young [Hasidic] men, a kind of 'sub-culture,' a new version of 'my might and the power of my hands' [i.e., hubristically relying on your own strength rather than on God] has emerged which is not very far from 'Zionism'—from defending oneself with one's own strength." Of particular concern to Stauber was that this behavior might alienate the police at precisely the moment when Hasidim most needed their help:

> Apprehending the criminal is a duty according to "the law of the land," and the police authorities greatly appreciate the help,

within the framework of the law, that citizens give them when they apprehend criminal suspects. However, we should not seek to play the role of the police, create a hindrance, or even confront the police when we Jews are always the ones who have the need for more police, even if it costs us some [parking and traffic] tickets. ... What happened last Monday night—and which incited the writer to compose these lines—is how the crowd conducted itself towards the police. As an eyewitness I must confess that although the public was in a certain sense provoked by the commotion and the yelling as well as by the unbelievable overreaction of the police, it was a frightful spectacle that did not bring any honor to heaven and certainly not any good for the entire community.

Rather than conduct themselves like the hated Zionists, Stauber exhorted his fellow Hasidim to remember that they were still living in *golus*, or exile, no matter how good things were in the United States: "If a policeman acts in a way that he is not supposed to according to the law, it is necessary, as civilized people, to bring charges against him. However, we should not think that it is *a hefker velt* [a state of anarchy]! After all, we must remember that we are in spite of everything in 'golus' [exile] even in the 'goldene amerike' [Golden America]."

In practice, proper conduct did not require the Hasidic community of Williamsburg to give up *chaptsem* but rather to ensure that it was done in a Jewish way. It meant acting according to the proverbial "voice of Jacob" instead of the "hands of Esau," even (or especially) when engaging in self-defense:

> *Chaptsem!*—is an expression of "the voice is the voice of Jacob" [Genesis 27:22]—in addition to our prayers and requests to the Master of the World. Of course, we must do that which is necessary to defend our Jewish neighborhoods. However, we must ensure that we do not employ "the hands are the hands of Esau," even when we must also use our "hands" [in self-defense]. We must appreciate that with such uncontrolled violence we achieve the opposite. The police district will also point a finger at honest Jews, as breakers of the law, and this can, God forbid, lead to very serious consequences. Let us once again emphasize ... that even when we must engage in self-protection in order to defend

one another, we do it within the framework of our inheritance as [a people who are] "merciful, with a sense of shame, and performing acts of kindness."

Despite Chaim Stauber's passionate plea for self-restraint and rapprochement, relations between Hasidim and the police, in Williamsburg and elsewhere in Brooklyn, remained volatile for years to come. Even as Hasidic leaders demanded more police protection in their neighborhoods and sought to cultivate good relations with the force, the Hasidic "street" sometimes erupted into open conflict with the police over what it believed was insufficient attention or outright mistreatment. Most infamously, in December 1978, hundreds of Hasidim in Borough Park—which was generally viewed as less combustible than Williamsburg—stormed the local police station following the murder of a community member during a mugging, resulting in violence that the *New York Times* described as "one of the worst clashes of civilians and police officers in New York since the riots of the 1960's."[62]

Gangs of New York

Perhaps the most racially charged and widely publicized symbol of New York City's decline during the 1970s was the street gang. To many critics, gangs came to signify the city's abdication of control over public spaces—parks, subways, schools, streets—and the supposed descent of its black and Puerto Rican youth, in particular, to a more primitive, tribal state. In the face of this threat to public order, police were seen as ineffectual, at best, or complicit, at worst. Under the Lindsay administration in the 1960s, the New York City Police Department was rocked by a series of corruption cases that prompted the mayor to create the Knapp Commission in 1970. While Abraham Beame's term in office during the mid-1970s did not witness any major police scandals, budget cuts led him to reduce the force by 6,000 officers even as the crime rate continued to rise.[63] With confidence in the police plummeting, fears that street gangs were filling the vacuum led to an apocalyptic mood in the city. And at the very heart of the gang crisis in New York City during the 1970s was Williamsburg.

In 1974, the *New York Times* identified the South Side area of Williamsburg as having the highest concentration of youth gangs in all of North Brooklyn. Among the gangs that called the neighborhood home

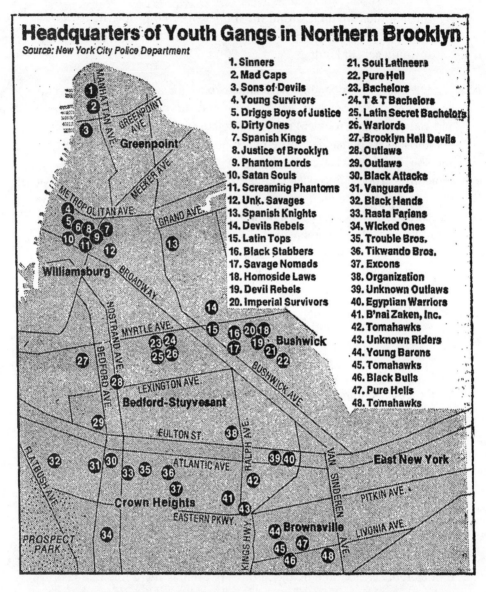

Headquarters of Youth Gangs in Northern Brooklyn
Source: New York City Police Department

1. Sinners
2. Mad Caps
3. Sons of Devils
4. Young Survivors
5. Driggs Boys of Justice
6. Dirty Ones
7. Spanish Kings
8. Justice of Brooklyn
9. Phantom Lords
10. Satan Souls
11. Screaming Phantoms
12. Unk. Savages
13. Spanish Knights
14. Devils Rebels
15. Latin Tops
16. Black Stabbers
17. Savage Nomads
18. Homoside Laws
19. Devil Rebels
20. Imperial Survivors

21. Soul Latineens
22. Pure Hell
23. Bachelors
24. T & T Bachelors
25. Latin Secret Bachelors
26. Warlords
27. Brooklyn Hell Devils
28. Outlaws
29. Outlaws
30. Black Attacks
31. Vanguards
32. Black Hands
33. Rasta Farians
34. Wicked Ones
35. Trouble Bros.
36. Tikwando Bros.
37. Excons
38. Organization
39. Unknown Outlaws
40. Egyptian Warriors
41. B'nai Zaken, Inc.
42. Tomahawks
43. Unknown Riders
44. Young Barons
45. Tomahawks
46. Black Bulls
47. Pure Hells
48. Tomahawks

"Headquarters of Youth Gangs in Northern Brooklyn": map published in the
New York Times, August 1, 1974 (© New York Times)

were the Young Survivors, the Driggs Boys of Justice, the Dirty Ones, the Spanish Kings, Justice of Brooklyn, the Phantom Lords, Satan Souls, the Screaming Phantoms, and the Unknown Savages.[64] A decade later, in 1983, the newspaper reported that "Williamsburg [was] the section of Brooklyn with the most gangs, 26," although by that point the largely Puerto Rican street gangs of the 1970s, which had helped transform the neighborhood into a center of the city's heroin sales, were giving way to the more loosely organized, heavily Dominican crews that came to dominate the crack trade in Williamsburg and neighboring Bushwick during the 1980s.[65]

The writer and anti-gentrification activist Dennis Farr (aka Dennis SinneD), who grew up in a Puerto Rican family on the South Side of Williamsburg during the 1970s and 1980s, has argued that the relationship between street gangs and the broader Puerto Rican community in Williamsburg was complex. On the one hand, gang members—including several of Farr's close relatives—belonged to the community and, in the eyes of some residents, performed functions in the neighborhood that were seen as valuable, especially at a time when the police—like other city services—were in short supply. "For residents," Farr writes, "the gangs were police, and there was no education and ideological gap between them, unlike the Young Lords' college education and Marxism, often incompatible with the community's socially-conservative quarters."[66] And yet the same gangs could make life miserable for Puerto Rican residents of Williamsburg.

In 1977, for example, the *New York Times* reported on two cases in which neighborhood youth gangs—the Love Brothers and the South Ninth Street Bikers—attempted to take over entire buildings on the South Side, robbing and assaulting Latino occupants before forcing them to vacate their apartments. The police were accused of ignoring residents' complaints until the press broke the story.[67] According to the newspaper, what was taking place in Williamsburg represented a new low point in the history of the city's gangs: "Gangs have troubled New York's slums in the past but they had generally limited themselves to warfare and competition with each other. The harassment of other slum residents seems to mark a new and more vicious turn in their activities. 'The gangs are messing up everybody's life,' said Israel Melendez, who grew up in Williamsburg and has since moved out."[68] Eventually, according to Farr, several gang-related murders of innocent bystanders in Williamsburg prompted other residents to act: "People had enough, a sharp and unprecedented separation formed between area gangs and community organizations, the latter marched on the 90th Precinct on Union Avenue and Broadway, led by Los Sures, and demanded changes."[69] (Los Sures, from the Spanish word for "south," is a community group named after the Hispanic section of Williamsburg.)

Even when they caused suffering for other Puerto Rican residents, however, gang members remained part of the broader community in the 1970s. After all, they were literally brothers, sons, and grandsons of the vast majority of Puerto Rican residents of Williamsburg who did not belong to one of the gangs. By contrast, the relationship of local Puerto Rican gangs to the Hasidic community in South Williamsburg was dramatically different. Lacking any familial or cultural ties, gang members viewed their Hasidic neighbors pragmatically and frequently targeted them for crimes of opportunity, or treated them like a kind of competing gang that possessed its own turf, specifically the area between Broadway and Flushing Avenues, known colloquially among local Puerto Rican and black residents as "Jew Town." Reminiscing about the 1970s, a member of the South Ninth Bikers placed the Hasidic enclave squarely within the gang landscape of South Williamsburg:

> The South 9th Bikers' turf was around Broadway, from like where the BQE starts at Havemeyer to what was called Jew Town, where the Hasidics start. The Unknowns used to be from Union to Rodney, Metropolitan to like South 4th. The Dukes were on Roebling and South 3rd, over to South 1st. Then you had the Satan's Souls for a while, who were on South 5th and Hoover. Then you had all these other little clubs in between. You had the Dirty Ones up by Graham Avenue. . . . We were fighting with everybody.[70]

A member of the Majestics during this period noted, "I never robbed anybody. It feels bad. Somebody else could come and rob your mother and you wouldn't like it. But I stole. I used to steal a lot from [Jewish-owned] factories. Every Friday and Saturday night I would go to factories on Bedford Avenue, Wythe Avenue, and Flushing Avenue. I would go anywhere Jews worked because on Fridays, they can't put on the light, the air conditioning, nothing. That was my opportunity. I would break into the sweater factory, the clothes factory, the pillow factory. . . . That's how I used to get my money."[71]

While Jewish-owned factories were easy targets, especially on the Sabbath, gang members had to be more cautious when confronting Hasidim on their own turf in "Jew Town." One of the chief reasons for venturing into the Hasidic enclave during this period was to nab a "Jew hat," which could then be modified with feathers, bandanas, and other accoutrements.[72] Like all New York City gangs during this period, those in Williamsburg had distinctive uniforms, including jackets, patches, and "colors," and the act of wearing another group's garb was not taken lightly. In this symbolic universe, Hasidim, with their long black coats, large hats, and full beards, were yet another group of men who projected their collective identity on the streets by means of masculine-coded clothing, facial hair, and so on. Indeed, this was not far from Rabbi Yoel Teitelbaum's original goal of cultivating pride and unity in his followers when he insisted that they all adopt traditional Hasidic garb after World War II, even if he probably would have rejected the term "gang," because of its negative associations.

The elements of the Hasidic uniform, the large number of young men in the community who congregated on the streets of the neighborhood, their aggressive, collective response to threats, their volatile relationship with the police, and their vehement opposition to snitching—or *mesire*, as it was known in Yiddish—support the view that Hasidim were gang-like in certain key respects. It is not surprising, therefore, that for Puerto Rican gang members in the 1970s, venturing into the Hasidic enclave and stealing a hat from someone's head was equivalent to stripping the colors from a rival gang member. It signified an act of disrespect as well as bravado, but only because real danger was involved. As one Puerto Rican gang member recalled of this period: "We never really had any problem with the Hasidics. Back in the early days, we used to have a habit of snatching their hats. We used to convert it to our style, with bandanas and patches and everything. The problem with that was, if you snatched one of their hats in the wrong neighborhood [i.e., 'Jew Town'], you'd have a hell of a chase."[73]

For Hasidim, meanwhile, the neighborhood's Puerto Rican gangs represented yet another group of violent goyim or *shkutsim*—the proverbial "hands of Esau"—who had sought to intimidate and attack Jews over the centuries. Some of these gangs wore jackets that included images of iron crosses or Nazi swastikas (not because they embraced Nazi ideology but because they were influenced sartorially by white biker gangs that had adopted these symbols), which strengthened the impression that Williamsburg's street gangs were only the latest in a long line of enemies that the Jewish people had endured—and overcome—in their long sojourn in exile. Having survived the Holocaust, the Hasidic community of

Williamsburg rejected a quietist approach to the threat posed by street gangs and other criminals. Instead, for many Hasidim, the proper response was an immediate show of force to mete out a kind of street justice that might serve as a deterrent in the future. Commonly stereotyped as a "gentle people"—at least by those who didn't live with them in Williamsburg—Hasidim in the neighborhood demonstrated a ready willingness to fight during the 1970s, which drew the surprised attention of outside observers. *Time* magazine, for example, published a profile of Isaac Abraham, a Hasidic resident of public housing who later became a prominent community activist in Williamsburg. "Abraham now lives in a subsidized housing project where 49% of tenants are white [almost all Hasidim] and 51% black or Hispanic, and race relations are often strained," the article noted. Abraham himself informed readers how Hasidim learned to "deal with demography," an apparent euphemism for physical force:

> When we got in (the housing project), there was a struggle to survive. It was the late 1970s, and the vibrations from both groups was very hostile, very, very hostile. There was almost every day a major crime—people getting mugged, robbed, chains snatched, children beaten. And not people of both groups: the victims were always somebody out of the 49%. A kid who was sent down to the grocery, an adult would escort him. Forget the playground. Only one kind of people used that, and that was the people who created the nuisance. My wife was mugged by a team. And at that time we decided we were just going to stand up and fight. Now if (someone tries a mugging) and we get him, you don't know what will happen.[74]

In 1972, Hasidim in Williamsburg created the Committee to Defend Against Thefts, probably inspired, in part, by the National Neighborhood Watch Program, which was established the same year with the support of the National Sheriffs' Association. In an announcement in *Der Yid*, the group—which claimed support from all the Hasidic sects in Williamsburg—proposed the creation of a "private police force" that would "hire private detectives with patrol cars who would patrol the entire Jewish neighborhood day and night."[75] Every Jewish family would be expected to contribute five dollars a month to a common fund and, in turn, would be given a sign to put in their window indicating their participation in the program. Ultimately, the plan to hire private detectives to patrol the Hasidic enclave's streets "twenty-four hours a day" never came to fruition. Yet in 1977, a year that many considered a low point in the city's steep descent, the Hasidic community came up with an alternative.

Concerning New York City during this period, Miriam Greenberg wrote, "The problems that began mounting in early 1977 became so horrific and all-encompassing that they seemed to many observers, and to the news media in particular, like a series of divine plagues, taking on the biblical proportions of apocalypse."[76] Of particular concern to many Hasidim in Williamsburg was the widespread looting that took place in the neighborhood during the citywide blackout of July 13–14, especially on Broadway, where seventeen stores were affected; further down the avenue in neighboring Bushwick, 134 stores were looted and, in many cases, set on fire.[77] In the midst of this annus horribilis, a sixty-six-year-old Holocaust survivor and Pupa Hasid named Moshe Hoffman founded the Shomrim (Guardians), an all-volunteer neighborhood patrol that was initially headquartered in his bookstore on Lee Avenue.

The creation of the Shomrim in Williamsburg did not occur in a vacuum. As early as 1964, a group of Lubavitcher Hasidim in Crown Heights led by Rabbi Samuel Schrage had created a volunteer security patrol called the Maccabees in response to a series of attacks on Jewish residents, including the attempted rape and slashing of a prominent rabbi's wife. In May 1964, the *New York Herald Tribune* described the origins of the group: "When Greeks and Syrians oppressed them in Pre-Christian days, the Jews struck back through the Maccabees, a vigilante-type group of warriors. Now, with the crime rate rising in the Crown Heights section of Brooklyn, the ultra-orthodox Hasidic Jewish community has formed a band of modern-day Maccabees, unarmed but equipped with roaming patrol cars and two-way radios."[78] By the 1970s, the Maccabees were defunct, but the spirit of self-defense—or, depending on whom you asked, vigilantism—was alive and well in New York City. Nor was it only embattled white ethnics who took up self-defense in this period. Not far from South Williamsburg, African American residents established the Fort Greene Youth Patrol in 1968. As the *New York Times* reported, members patrolled housing projects and other sites throughout the neighborhood. "When we first got into this," a member of the patrol recalled, "people bugged us—called us pigs." Yet after five years of patrolling, the paper reported, "the neighborhood's attitude has changed."[79]

Most famously, Curtis Sliwa, the Brooklyn-born night manager of a McDonald's restaurant in the Bronx, founded the Guardian Angels in

1979 after first establishing the Magnificent 13, a subway patrol group, in 1977. The Guardian Angels immediately garnered a tidal wave of fawning media coverage but were later criticized for faking many of their most famous crime-fighting exploits.[80] By contrast, the mainstream media paid little attention to the Shomrim even as they aggressively responded to crime in Williamsburg and helped inspire the creation of similar organizations in other Hasidic enclaves in Brooklyn. Many Latino residents and community activists in Williamsburg were far less sanguine about the group's impact, accusing its members of vigilantism and usurping the authority of the police. For example, David Pagan, then the executive director of Los Sures, condemned the Shomrim for being "a lynching mob more than it is a security patrol": "When there's a problem in the neighborhood, and you're not a Hasidic, they will jump you. . . . They take the law into their hands."[81] For their part, the Shomrim sought to cultivate close relations with the police department despite the lingering suspicions of many Hasidic residents regarding the force. As Joseph "Yossi" Pollack, a senior coordinator of the Williamsburg organization, later put it, "The Shomrim has always served as a kind of liaison between the community and the police. . . . The older generation is still afraid of police uniforms, and they pass this fear, phobia, whatever you want to call it, to their children. We have to explain that the NYPD is there to help."[82]

When Moshe Hoffman died in 2006, *Der Yid* lauded his creation of the Shomrim as a force that helped transform the neighborhood. "As a result of these efforts," his obituary stated, "people can now, with the help of God, walk even dimly-lit streets [of Williamsburg] at night, knowing that the volunteers from the Shomrim organization are on patrol, and the [criminal] elements also know it."[83] Violent crime had indeed declined dramatically in Williamsburg in the preceding decades, plummeting 71 percent from 1993 to 2010 in the 90th and 94th precincts. This drop, it should be noted, was part of a much broader one throughout the city from the record highs of the 1970s and 1980s. By the time of Hoffman's death, Hasidim in Williamsburg no longer viewed crime as the biggest threat to their community.[84] Instead, the dramatic gentrification of Williamsburg had intensified old challenges, most notably the lack of affordable housing, and created new ones, such as the moral dangers—and temptations—posed by the gentrifiers.

CHAPTER FIVE

The Gentrifier and the Gentrified

T HE GENTRIFICATION OF WILLIAMSBURG began in the late 1970s with an influx of artists attracted to the neighborhood's proximity to Manhattan, good public transportation, and numerous empty waterfront factories and warehouses. The repurposing of postindustrial buildings as live-work spaces was pioneered in Manhattan's SoHo district, just south of Greenwich Village, in the late 1960s by the Lithuanian conceptual artist George Maciunas. When Maciunas bought and renovated an old cardboard factory at 80 Wooster Street, in 1967, according to a history of the loft scene, "This single act would ultimately result in the redevelopment of SoHo and spur the conversion of industrial buildings to residential use throughout the world."[1] Maciunas, who headed the utopian Fluxus arts collective, went on to found dozens of similar artists' cooperatives in formerly industrial lofts throughout SoHo, thereby transforming that neighborhood into *the* symbol of gentrification in New York City—until Williamsburg.

The emergence of SoHo and, several decades later, Williamsburg, as iconic sites of gentrification was abetted by an amendment to New York's Multiple Dwelling Law in 1964 that allowed registered visual artists to live in commercial spaces. When the amendment, known as Article 7-B, was extended and revised in 1968 and again in 1971, it came to include artists working in other media, as well as a grandfather clause that legalized early loft conversions.[2] In the following years, the historic designation of multiple zones within SoHo, along with a set of tax incentives that the city offered to developers for residential conversions, caused rents and sale prices to rise dramatically in SoHo and adjacent downtown areas.[3] A 1982 amendment to the Multiple Dwelling Law, Article 7-C, also known as the Loft Law, further protected loft tenants from evictions and required landlords to maintain up-to-code buildings, and also permitted, and regulated, rent increases.

As downtown lofts, with their large square footage and hip cultural associations, became sought-after commodities, younger working artists and priced-out renters were forced to look elsewhere in the city for spaces that suited their needs. The Brooklyn waterfront, dotted with factories and warehouses, seemed to provide an ideal solution, so beginning in the late 1970s, a steady flow of artists decamped to northwestern Brooklyn neighborhoods such as Fulton Landing (later known as Dumbo) and Williamsburg. As early as 1980, a piece in the *Brooklyn Heights Press* claimed, "The only artists moving into SoHo and TriBeca these days are those who can afford the $100,000 mortgage; the real paintbrush pioneers are braving Williamsburg. Yes, Williamsburg."[4]

In the early 1980s, Williamsburg—long a major center of urban industry—still supported a significant number of working waterfront factories, such as the sprawling Domino Sugar Refinery and the Kedem kosher winery. But it was also heavily blighted by decrepit buildings, empty lots, abandoned cars, and crumbling piers. Just like SoHo's early factory dwellers, some of the first artists who moved to Williamsburg squatted illegally in abandoned or underused buildings. Much of the surrounding neighborhood was markedly unsafe, riven by gangs, open drug dealing, and decades of infrastructural neglect. "It was a desolate sad forgotten place on the riverfront then," remembered one artist. "Graffiti was everywhere you looked; at the river's edge floated sofas, TVs, tires, refrigerators, gutted cars, liquor bottles and crack vials. It was a surreal outdoor living room. Abandoned warehouses, abandoned storefronts, a giant abandoned brewery."[5] One prominent Latino community organizer, Luis Garden Acosta, in an oft-repeated statement, referred to his neighborhood circa 1981 as a "killing field" because of the large number of murders committed annually, particularly of young people.[6] Yet Williamsburg was also home to long-standing and proud communities of Latinos, Hasidim, Poles, Italians, and others who, while troubled by its

The Satmar Rebbe, Moshe Teitelbaum, after baking the matzot, Williamsburg, 1993 (Photograph by Maud B. Weiss; copyright Maud B. Weiss/Gina Kehayoff Verlag)

high crime rates and environmental problems, were also strongly attached to the neighborhood.

When gentrification arrived in Williamsburg, Hasidim and Latinos were still embroiled in what was by then a decades-long struggle over resources, including affordable housing, poverty-program funding, public spaces, and policing. In 1986, perhaps the most heated battle in this ongoing conflict erupted over PS 16, on Wilson Street between Lee and Bedford Avenues, right in the heart of the Hasidic section of the neighborhood. That a public school had become part of the contested turf in Williamsburg was not surprising. The 7,500 students in the Hasidic school system in Williamsburg in 1986 represented twice the total public school enrollment in Community District 14. PS 16, in particular, had lost more than one-fourth of its enrollment in the previous decade and a half as Latino families moved out of the blocks surrounding the school and had fewer children. By contrast, the number of Hasidic children continued to grow, and to serve their needs, the community built, purchased, or leased buildings throughout the neighborhood, including three that had once been public schools. Besides the need for space, the ever-increasing number of Hasidic children presented the community with yet another challenge, for as with any such demographic increase, there were now more students with special education needs.[7]

The roots of the controversy over PS 16 can be traced to 1965, when federal law mandated that remedial services be provided to all students who needed them, including those in parochial and private schools. From then until 1985, when the U.S. Supreme Court declared the practice an unconstitutional "entanglement" of religion and state, most eligible parochial- and private-school students were instructed in special classes by public school teachers who came to their schools. Following the court's decision, New York City, which had the nation's largest remedial program, serving 170,000 public and 21,000 private students, decided to deploy seventy mobile vans, where instruction could take place.[8] But in Williamsburg's Community District 14, local school officials decided to accommodate the 390 Hasidic girls from the Satmar community's Beis Rochel school who were eligible for remedial services by cordoning off nine classrooms in a wing of PS 16, where the Hasidic girls would be instructed by female Yiddish-speaking public school teachers.

The Parents' Association of PS 16 subsequently filed a lawsuit against Nathan Quinones, the New York City schools chancellor, charging that "the Plan invidiously discriminated against the public school students and so involved the City with the Hasidic religious sect as to constitute an establishment of religion in contravention of the First Amendment," and seeking a preliminary injunction against its implementation; for its part, "the city argued that its Plan was not intended to discriminate on a racial or religious basis."[9] As the case worked its way through the courts, on September 30, 1986, a group of primarily Latino parents occupied PS 16 for several hours until they were removed by the police. Meanwhile, hundreds of Latino and black students boycotted the school for a month in solidarity with the Parents' Association.

The long-embattled neighborhood, already volatile because of ongoing conflicts over housing and crime, seemed on the verge of explosion. An article in the *Washington Post* captured the mood in Williamsburg when it referred to Broadway as a "DMZ," or demilitarized zone, that divided Hasidic and Latino communities engaged in "block-to-block trench warfare": "This is no celebration of the melting pot. It is a story about the unreconciled passions of race and religion. Most of all, it is a story about turf."[10] In his criticism of the plan, Luis Garden Acosta, the leader of El

Puente, sought to portray the Hasidim as settler-colonial occupiers intent on displacing South Williamsburg's native inhabitants: "You get the feeling it's manifest destiny: You can't stop the Hasidim. . . . The Latinos feel like Arabs on the West Bank. This used to be our community. Now we are a minority in an area totally controlled by them."

Given the profound antipathy of Satmar to the State of Israel, Garden Acosta's choice of the Israeli occupation of the West Bank as a point of comparison was extremely ironic. Similarly, his efforts to paint the Hasidim as invaders in a community that had once belonged to Latinos ignored the fact that Jews in general, and Hasidim in particular, had lived in Williamsburg for many decades. Indeed, even the blocks between Grand and Broadway that constituted the heart of Latino South Williamsburg—Los Sures—had been home to numerous Jewish residents and institutions only a few decades earlier. Hasidim could not be accused of being settler-colonial occupiers who had dispossessed the area's indigenous inhabitants, one of the most popular models for understanding gentrification. No, what complicated the situation in Williamsburg was that despite their frequent antagonism, Hasidim and Latinos were equally at home in the neighborhood.

For their part, Hasidic leaders interviewed by the *Washington Post* also appeared to leave little room for compromise, let alone cooperation, with their Latino neighbors. Rabbi Naftali Frankel, an administrator in the Satmar school system, dismissed the concerns of Latino critics as little more than sour grapes at having lost out in a fair but harsh struggle over limited resources: "There's a competition. . . . Whoever gets it gets it. . . . This is the American system." Rabbi Albert Friedman, a Hasidic community leader and spokesman, was even more dismissive. "The Hispanics think we look down on them," he said. "It's not true. We don't even look at them. We keep to ourselves as much as possible."

From the perspective of the law, the problem was not that the Hasidim wanted to segregate themselves from others but that they wanted to do so in a public school employing public funds, thereby creating an unconstitutional entanglement of religion and state. After federal district judge Mark Constantino ruled against the plaintiffs, allowing the plan to educate the Hasidic girls in PS 16 to go forward, in October 1986 the U.S. Court of Appeals for the Second Circuit ruled against the city and issued an injunction, stating, "The City's Plan seems plainly to create a symbolic link between the state and the Hasidic sect that is likely to have a magnified negative impact on the minds of the youngsters attending P.S. 16."[11]

As the intercommunal struggle over PS 16 was being waged in the mid-1980s, another battle that was gaining steam in Williamsburg would ultimately have a much broader and longer lasting impact on the neighborhood and its residents. Instead of pitting Hasidim and Latinos against one another, this battle brought them together to face a common enemy: a massive, fifteen-story incinerator that the city sought to build in the Brooklyn Navy Yard in South Williamsburg. It was intended to process 3,000 tons of garbage a day and would generate enormous amounts of pollution, including numerous carcinogens.

From the time that it was first proposed, in 1979 during the Koch mayoral administration, until it was finally defeated, almost two decades later following a series of protests and court challenges, the incinerator project came to symbolize the city's utter disregard for Williamsburg's residents. An editorial published in *Der Yid* in September 1990 captured this sentiment: "When does Williamsburg figure into the city government's plans? When it needs to find a place to put something negative. If it wants, for example, to build a monstrous incinerator, which is harmful for the health of the community, then Williamsburg is the first place they look! ... Whenever there's something terrible, Williamsburg always comes to everyone's minds first."[12] A Yiddish-language pamphlet attacking the incinerator plans, and distributed through the mail by Congregation Yetev Lev D'Satmar, was titled "The Struggle for the Existence of Williamsburg."[13]

After initially opposing the incinerator separately, in the early 1990s Hasidim and Latinos in Williamsburg formed a coalition jointly led by Rabbi David Niederman of the UJO and Luis Garden Acosta of El Puente. Along with the New York Public Interest Research Group, a non-profit established in 1976, they created the Community Alliance for the Environment, which succeeded in delaying construction. In April 1992, more than one thousand residents of the neighborhood, representing both the Latino and Hasidic communities, gathered in the building of PS 16 to protest the incinerator.[14] In the coming months, activists brought hundreds of Hasidic, Latino, and African American children to city hall, where Rabbi David Niederman of the UJO declared, "Just because we are poor does not mean our children must breathe air made poisonous by garbage burning incinerators," and Garden Acosta stated, "In our common air we have found our common ground."[15]

In a rare case of grassroots cooperation in Williamsburg that put the common interests of all the neighborhood's longtime residents before their differences, Hasidim and Latinos in Williamsburg succeeded in defeating the incinerator project.[16] Yet this collaboration did not mean that the two communities ceased their competition—and, at times, conflict—over a range of other issues, most importantly, housing. By the time the city decided not to build the incinerator, gentrification had transformed the Williamsburg waterfront into some of the most desirable real estate in the city, and plans for rezoning the area for residential use were moving forward in earnest. Thus, Williamsburg quickly went from a place where New York City literally dumped its garbage to one of its most sought-after sites for luxury development.

In the 1970s, Williamsburg's reputation never quite reached that of the South Bronx, but it was still rough enough that many potential gentrifiers priced out of Lower Manhattan gave it a wide berth. Nevertheless, over the course of the 1980s, the trickle of artists drawn to Williamsburg gradually swelled, creating a scene with its own characteristics, ringleaders, publications, performance and exhibition spaces, along with a gritty outlook that differed from—and defined itself against—the increasingly glitzy art world of Manhattan.[17] It was the members of this initial wave of gentrifiers, most of whom were working artists, who later inspired the Yiddish moniker *artistn*, or "artists," used by Hasidim to refer to all young hipsters who came to live in Williamsburg in the following years and who constituted the Hasidic community's primary competitors for housing in the ensuing decades.

"Paintbrush Pioneers"

The nascent art scene in Williamsburg coalesced around the neighborhood's newly occupied artists' lofts and the freewheeling parties and performances hosted in them. All-night parties were held in abandoned factories such as the Old Dutch Mustard Company building and the Dr. Brown's celery soda factory. Sharon Zukin argued that the growing attraction to these ruin-like spaces reflected an "influential turn in consumer culture that aestheticize[d] the city's gritty authenticity."[18] In waterfront Brooklyn in particular, the " 'masculine' culture of piers and factories" comported with a prevailing ethos of do-it-yourself performances and building remodeling.[19] Cheap apartment rents and empty storefronts nearby meant that it was relatively easy to open new cultural spaces, lending an experimental quality to the atmosphere.

In 1983, a *New York Times* article identified Williamsburg as one of a handful of up-and-coming neighborhoods in Brooklyn where artists were establishing "colonies," a term that suggested that these neighbor-hoods constituted a kind of frontier waiting to be settled.[20] One real es-tate agent quoted in the article said, "Artists are the pioneers in a neighborhood. ... The businessmen follow." For their part, the artists cited in the piece took a devil-may-care attitude to their new neighbor-hood. "It's a graceful way of living if you don't mind being mugged on a regular basis," as one put it. By 1987, the changes afoot in Williamsburg had merited an article whose title, "A Metamorphosis for Old Williams-burg," reflected the dramatic transformation in store for the neighbor-hood.[21] Anticipating the future by two decades, the article reported that real estate developers were eyeing the East River waterfront as an ideal site for thousands of luxury units and were therefore lobbying the city to change the area's zoning from industrial to residential use. Yet at that point, New York City officials were generally reluctant to abandon Wil-liamsburg's still viable manufacturing sector, a view expressed by Wilbur Woods, the director of the Brooklyn Office of City Planning, who called Williamsburg "an active industrial area [that] has been quite stable for the past 25 years," with potential for the manufacturing sector to grow.[22]

Until the eve of its gentrification, Williamsburg's industrial sector was still benefiting economically from the exodus of manufacturing from Manhattan, a process that had been unfolding since at least the 1950s. While global market forces contributed to this phenomenon, Robert Fitch and others have demonstrated how New York City's planners played a key role in the shift from industry to finance, insurance, and real estate (known by the acronym FIRE) in Manhattan. As Fitch put it, "Those who took charge of planning the city—who decided where the subways and highways would run; who zoned its neighborhoods; who granted tax abatements and incentives to its real estate—they weren't indifferent as to whether office buildings displaced factories. They owned the land."[23] In the 1980s, city officials were still not convinced that the "purposeful dein-dustrialization" of Manhattan, as Miriam Greenberg called it, would or should jump the East River and transform Williamsburg.[24]

Gerald Esposito, the district manager of Community Board 1 in North Brooklyn and a lifelong resident of Williamsburg, called his neighborhood "a sleepy town, a forgotten area."[25] One transplant from the East Village, described by the *Times* as a "soft-spoken poet and freelance writer," con-curred: "I chose Williamsburg because I thought it still had the potential of feeling like a small town." Indeed, the article noted that "although Wil-liamsburg has been drawing people from Manhattan with careers in the arts

for at least five years, not a single café or restaurant geared toward that clientele has opened." Some residents remained skeptical that much would
change. One East Village transplant said, "A lot of landlords here try to tell
you this is the next SoHo ... It'll take a long time, if it happens at all." By
contrast, a performance artist expressed concern that the neighborhood
would eventually go the way of its predecessors on the Manhattan side of
the Williamsburg Bridge: "Whenever we see an article about Williamsburg,
we cringe. . . . We see what happened to SoHo and the East Village, and we
don't want it to happen here." Adam Venski, who headed the waterfront
committee of Community Board 1 in Williamsburg and Greenpoint, succinctly expressed both positions to the *Times:* "You've got the wackos who
see the condos coming and think they're going to make millions, and then
you've got the tenants who are scared." Although it took a few years, both
the "wackos" and the concerned tenants turned out to be correct in their
assessments of what the future of Williamsburg would hold.

Not long after this profile appeared in the *Times*, the first cafés and
bars to serve the artistic community were established in North Williamsburg, including the Right Bank, in 1989, and the L Café, in 1992, anchored by the Bedford Avenue L subway stop. Recent arrivals to the
neighborhood also adopted existing working-class bars and eateries as
meeting places, including Teddy's, the Turkey's Nest Tavern, and, until its
closure in 1993, a former longshoremen's watering hole called the Ship's
Mast, at North 5th and Berry, where artists compiled the *Waterfront Week*,
a newsletter serving their growing community.[26] A significant milestone
indicating that gentrification had come to stay in Williamsburg was the
publication of a cover story by Brad Gooch in *New York* magazine in 1992
titled "The New Bohemia: Portrait of an Artists' Colony in Brooklyn."
The article, written very much in *New York*'s house style of neighborhood
ethnography, provided an approving snapshot of Williamsburg, including
interviews with artists and writers and notes taken at loft parties and bars.
It predicted the neighborhood's imminent apotheosis in New York's never-
ending search for the new and cool.[27] As one artist told the magazine, "In
the seventies, it was SoHo. In the eighties, the East Village. In the nineties
it will be Williamsburg."[28] But perhaps what stood out most in the piece
was news of Williamsburg's shockingly low rents. Miriam Greenberg argued that by merging "advertising and editorial content seamlessly," *New
York*, from its founding in the late 1960s, spoke not just to the "culturati"
but also to advertisers and investors interested in current and upcoming
trends. In the magazine's profile of Williamsburg, the neighborhood's low

rents and artists were being not only reported on, but also publicized and marketed. Looked at this way, "The New Bohemia" functioned as a hip advertisement for the rent gap—and the attendant opportunities for real estate development—waiting just across the East River from Manhattan.

In Gooch's deft telling, Williamsburg was "a hotbed of free thought" inhabited by contrarian artist "refugees, forced by speculative rents in the East Village to move outside Manhattan." He identified a "Williamsburg style" of "Fluxus-style works" inspired by both community spirit and the area's dilapidation. Although fledgling art galleries were open for business, Williamsburg's new residents "prefer[red] the obscurity" of Brooklyn to Manhattan's art-world rat race. These artists' impact on the future of the neighborhood's housing stock was already a hot issue. One member of Community Board 1 told Gooch, "They want to gentrify the area with condos, which would lead to a domino effect, changing the neighborhood." By contrast, the chairwoman of the waterfront committee, which later became instrumental in Mayor Michael Bloomberg's 2005 rezoning, said, "I'm fourth-generation in this neighborhood. I don't need someone who moved in five years ago to tell me about gentrification."

Not everyone was sold on Gooch's portrait of the neighborhood as the next big thing. One Brooklyn resident complained in a letter to the editor of *New York:* "Williamsburg is a squalid urban wasteland. Any attempt to portray this crumbling section of Brooklyn as anything more is insensitive to those trapped in its ugliness. . . . An authentic description of Williamsburg could not be complete without mentioning the almost constant sounds of random gunfire in the evening, the singsong sales pitch from crack-dealers, and the pounding bass from car stereos. Nor should the junkies, the crack vials, and the all too common pools of blood on the sidewalk that result from drive-by shootings be overlooked."[29] Despite—or for some, undoubtedly, *because* Williamsburg still had a reputation for danger—the article confirmed what a certain set of young, artistically inclined New Yorkers had begun to realize: Williamsburg, not Lower Manhattan, was the place to be. In his memoir about living in the neighborhood during the 1990s, the writer Robert Anasi recalled, "Williamsburg was a dog whistle that people like me were starting to hear, summoning us from every corner of the city. The *New York* article was only the declaration of a self-evident truth: we couldn't afford the [East] Village anymore."[30]

The early 1990s saw a steadily increasing flow of new residents over the old "Jew's Highway," the Williamsburg Bridge, from Manhattan. What these self-styled bohemians found when they arrived on the

Brooklyn side of the river was a neighborhood that no longer struck fear in the hearts of aspiring urban "pioneers." As Anasi, who moved to Williamsburg in 1994, put it, "By 1995 you could walk home from the L at night and not get jumped by a crackhead."[31] The improved safety of the neighborhood did not mean that the rough reputation of the old Williamsburg was completely forgotten, however, especially since it lent a sense of street credibility to newcomers seeking authentic urban living without too much actual physical danger.

Predictably then, the originally small "colony" of working artists who settled in Williamsburg during the 1980s was joined—and eventually, to a large extent, displaced—by a second wave of hipsters beginning in the 1990s. A majority of these newcomers were not working artists but recent college graduates and young professionals, especially in creative, media, tech, and other cognate fields, who had moved to Williamsburg from other parts of New York City and, increasingly, from elsewhere in the United States and beyond. This second wave of gentrifiers initially concentrated on the North Side of Williamsburg in an area bound by Grand Street to the south and McCarren Park (the traditional border with Greenpoint) to the north, generally avoiding the South Side (Los Sures) between Grand and Broadway, where Puerto Ricans and Dominicans were in the majority, and making almost no inroads into the Hasidic Triangle, the area of South Williamsburg between Broadway, Flushing, and Kent, which lay beyond.

On the streets of the North Side, these new residents opened and patronized numerous shops, restaurants, bars, cafés, yoga studios, musical venues, and galleries, which took over empty spaces or replaced holdovers from the not-so-long-ago days of old Williamsburg. Although most hipsters were not professional artists, they nevertheless embraced a distinctive aesthetic that defined itself over and against the cultural mainstream and, significantly, found primary expression in modes of consumption that encouraged types of entrepreneurial activity that, in turn, spurred further gentrification.

One way of understanding the successive waves of gentrification that transformed Williamsburg from the 1980s to the 2000s is that during the first phase, when artists dominated the scene, most of the new residents would still travel to the East Village or elsewhere in Manhattan to go to clubs and restaurants, returning to Brooklyn to produce their art and to sleep. In the 1990s, when the profile of many of the gentrifiers shifted from artists to hipsters, the scene in Williamsburg had grown to the point

that many of the new residents could happily remain in the neighborhood for their entertainment and leisure activities and eschew going into
Manhattan. In the 2000s, many of the hipsters who had arrived in the
1990s were priced out of the neighborhood by newer residents who
worked in the city's booming financial and real estate industries, and by
well-publicized—and frequently mocked—"trust funders" or "trustafari-
ans," whose parents paid their rent or bought them apartments.[32] By way
of illustration, the *New York Times* reported that during the "boom years"
preceding the financial crash of 2008, one mortgage broker who had financed hundreds of deals in the neighborhood stated that "40 percent of
the mortgage applications he reviewed for buyers in Williamsburg included down-payment money, from $50,000 to $300,000, from parents."[33]

During this third phase, many of the businesses established by hipsters
in the 1990s were replaced by second- or third-generation establishments
that were larger, better financed, and, in some cases, corporate owned.
Williamsburg was no longer just a place where local hipsters stayed rather
than going to a club, bar, or restaurant in Manhattan. It had become a hot
destination in its own right for people throughout New York City and for
visitors and tourists from around the globe, rivaling and even eclipsing the
East Village.[34] Kathe Newman and her colleagues noted that between
2003 and 2007, the number of bars, restaurants, and clubs that catered to
an "upscale clientele" increased from nine to fifty-three, and the total market value of properties in a Bedford Avenue commercial corridor from
North 10th Street to North 5th Street in Williamsburg increased by 224
percent.[35]

Housing Crisis in Williamsburg

The arrival of gentrification in Williamsburg during the 1980s coincided
with a drastic reduction in federal spending on public housing under the
Reagan administration. Peter Dreier summarized the change: "In his first
year in office Reagan halved the budget for public housing and Section 8
to about $17.5 billion. And for the next few years he sought to eliminate
federal housing assistance to the poor altogether."[36] Reflecting this
broader retrenchment, no new public housing projects were built in Williamsburg over the course of the 1980s, a dramatic departure from the
1960s and 1970s, when thousands of affordable units were added to the
neighborhood through this type of construction. Moreover, as a result of
a successful lawsuit brought by Latino and African American residents al-

leging that racial discrimination in the tenanting of public housing in Williamsburg had gone unchecked for decades, Hasidim were at a great disadvantage in applying for any openings in the neighborhood's existing projects. These factors, combined with the rapidly expanding size of the Hasidic population, created an intense housing crisis in the community, one exacerbated as housing costs in Williamsburg began to climb more than in any other gentrifying neighborhood in the city. Between 1990 and 2010–2014, the average rent in Williamsburg went up 78.7 percent compared with 53.2 percent in Central Harlem, 50.3 percent in the Lower East Side/Chinatown, and 44 percent in Bushwick—the next three highest neighborhood increases—and 22.1 percent in New York City in general.[37]

In 1989, Ari Goldman reported in the *New York Times* on an incident in which a group of fifty Hasidic men chased a twenty-four-year-old African American man whom they suspected of robbing and slashing an elderly Hasidic man in the elevator of one of Williamsburg's public housing projects; upon catching him, they beat him into unconsciousness. Aware of the long history of accusations of Hasidic vigilantism in the neighborhood, Goldman wrote, "There is a tradition in the Williamsburg section of Brooklyn, a tradition almost as old as the sidecurls, beards and broad-brimmed hats that the Hasidic men who live there wear. The tradition is that when someone cries 'Chaptzum'—the Yiddish equivalent of 'Grab him!'—everyone obeys."[38] Had the article been written even a decade earlier, the mugging and its violent aftermath would have been the chief takeaway. Yet Goldman ended his article with a comment from an anonymous Hasidic resident that pointed in a very different direction and spoke to the changes transforming the neighborhood: "The number one problem here is not crime. The number one problem here is housing."

In September 1990, *Der Yid* addressed the intensifying housing crisis facing the Hasidic community in a stinging editorial titled "A Burning Problem," which, among other things, accused city officials of unfairly restricting Hasidic access to public housing and ignoring the impact of such policies on young families:

> If indeed there used to be free city apartments [in NYCHA buildings] now they use various ruses and tricks so that no Jewish families can get an apartment. The situation is unbearable. ... The city leaders don't want to acknowledge the difficult fact

that in Williamsburg two families often live in one apartment because parents can't rent apartments for their newly married couples. Other Jewish families live ten, eleven, twelve and even more people in one narrow apartment. It doesn't bother [city leaders] at all.[39]

The editorial offered a historical perspective on the contemporary housing crisis in Williamsburg, presenting it as the culmination of a decades-long process that began with the construction of the Brooklyn–Queens Expressway through the heart of the Jewish community in the mid-1950s. Since then, the area occupied by the neighborhood's Jews had steadily shrunk as non-Jewish, primarily Latino, residents came to occupy more and more territory. At the same time, in the so-called Hasidic Triangle in South Williamsburg, the population had increased dramatically because of high birth rates. As a result of these factors, the Hasidic community found itself hemmed in geographically while continuing to grow demographically. To make matters worse, the editorial claimed, the city was aware that Hasidim could not simply pick up and leave Williamsburg, and therefore made little effort to improve conditions in the neighborhood:

> The lack of apartments is a general problem [in New York City]. But you see it most intensely in Williamsburg. The borders of Jewish Williamsburg have, over the years, shrunken dramatically. ... Years ago, Jewish families lived in a long and wide swath of the Williamsburg neighborhood. They lived from the streets of the South Side to those of the North Side and also lived on the more distant streets all the way to Bushwick. Today Jewish Williamsburg has been fenced into a small triangle. The city has torn up streets that had been inhabited exclusively by Jews, and built highways and other projects. The end result is that many Jewish homes were destroyed, and non-Jewish residents took their place.

The editorial concluded, "There may be a lack of apartments in all other neighborhoods, but it is not equal to Williamsburg. It is a well-known fact—and the municipal authorities have to be aware of it, and know it!—that the Jewish residents of Williamsburg have nowhere to go."

In explaining why so many Hasidim refused to abandon Williamsburg despite the lack of affordable housing, the editorial offered a set of spiritual, rather than material, reasons: "The religious and Hasidic Jewish families in Williamsburg are connected heart and soul to the neighborhood. Here is their source, here are their roots, and they cannot leave it. Here their children, boys and girls, study, and here are their rebbes and spiritual leaders. Williamsburg is the 'city and mother in Israel' which is famous throughout the whole world, and for that reason no Hasidic or religious family wants to leave it." From the perspective of *Der Yid*, the Hasidic community had transformed a rundown neighborhood in Brooklyn into a veritable *ir ve-em be-yisrael*, or "city and mother in Israel," a lofty designation traditionally applied to iconic Jewish communities in cities such as Vilna, Bialystok, and Salonika.

As revealing as what the editorial in *Der Yid* mentioned is what it did not, namely, gentrification. Although gentrifiers had been settling in the neighborhood for at least a decade by 1990, they were still concentrated in the blocks of North Williamsburg, which seemed a world away from the Hasidic Triangle south of Broadway, and they had yet to inspire a backlash from the community or its press. This changed in the following years as the pace of gentrification quickened and its effects—including rising rents and housing prices—began to be felt by Hasidic residents. Whereas in previous decades Hasidim could focus all of their criticism on external actors—the city government, the local Latino community, criminals—the situation was now more complicated. For among the most important figures participating in the gentrification of Williamsburg were Hasidim.

As with the gentrification of any neighborhood, real estate was at the core of the dramatic changes that Williamsburg experienced during the last decades of the twentieth century. And from the beginning of this process, members of the large and growing Hasidic community, located only a few blocks south of the hipster North Side, played a key role. The story of how Hasidim in real estate became major players in the transformation of Williamsburg and other neighborhoods in Brooklyn begins with the simple but powerful fact that Hasidim benefited from being there. Hasidim had remained in Williamsburg during the preceding decades of extensive white flight, economic decline, high crime, and governmental divestment from urban areas. In the years when the neighborhood was considered blighted and many buildings were abandoned, to be taken over by the city, members of the Hasidic community purchased cheap properties, including warehouses and factories, which they kept in operation as long as it was profitable to do so, as well as residential buildings, which they rented to low-income tenants. Thus, in the early stages of gentrification, when the rent gap in Williamsburg was first being recognized, these long-standing Hasidic property owners, as well as other Hasidim who realized the neighborhood's potential and bought up buildings, were well positioned to capitalize on the economic opportunities presented by gentrification, and they brought their experience and capital from Williamsburg to other neighborhoods in Brooklyn.

Hasidic real estate owners and developers were aided by their tight social networks, which allowed them to share information, pool resources, and raise capital from small investors. (Banks were frequently reluctant to lend to them.) The geographic proximity of Hasidim to the North Side gave them an enormous logistical advantage in scouting new properties and keeping abreast of unfolding developments in the neighborhood. In addition, Hasidim in Williamsburg had enormous financial incentives to become heavily involved in real estate development at the time. The population of Hasidim in the neighborhood, and particularly of young families, had reached the point where the creation of new sources of income, employment, and housing were critically important: several of the most important forms of employment and revenue for the Hasidic community in Williamsburg, the diamond and garment industries, had been experiencing significant decline.

Another factor that contributed to the growing sense of economic anxiety among Williamsburg's Hasidim as gentrification took hold was the bipartisan passage of the Personal Responsibility and Work Opportunity Reconciliation Act of 1996, or "welfare reform," as it was popularly called. At the time, roughly a third of the Hasidic community in Williamsburg received some form of public assistance, including Aid to Families with Dependent Children, food stamps, Supplemental Security Income, housing subsidies, Medicaid, and Home Relief (a state program created in the 1930s). Many Hasidim who received aid were employed but supplemented their low incomes—for example, as teachers—with governmental benefits. Critics had long accused the Hasidic community of gaming the system by setting salaries artificially low so that employees could qualify for assistance. Hasidim responded that many of these critics simply refused to believe that members of their community could be poor, a view that reflected skepticism about the existence of Jewish poverty in general. As Chaim Stauber, a prominent member of the Satmar community, told the *New York Times* in a 1997 article on how the new welfare law might affect Hasidic Williamsburg: "The myth is that there are no poor Jews. . . . But Jews, like others, have plenty of people who meet all the criteria for welfare."[40]

The Gentrification of Mayer Schwartz

Against this backdrop, real estate development represented an extraordinarily timely opportunity, one that quickly drew the attention of a growing number of local Hasidim, including many who had no previous experience in the industry. An iconic example of the pioneering role played by Hasidic developers in the gentrification of Williamsburg's North Side was the conversion, in 1999, of the Mini Mall located at 218 Bedford Avenue between North 4th and 5th Streets. Because of its high visibility, the Mini Mall came to serve as a model for the kind of mixed commercial-residential development (businesses on the street level, apartments above) that came to dominate much of the neighborhood over the course of the next decade.

Although located only half a mile from Broadway, the traditional border of the Hasidic Triangle, "the mini-mall that redefined Bedford Avenue," as *New York* magazine put it in 2010, felt like a world away when it was first developed.[41] Until it was repurposed as a hipster marketplace that "housed an artisanal-cheese shop, a wine store, a bookseller with Guy Debord window displays, a Tibetan tchotchke store, a vinyl-heavy indie-record emporium, a Mac-friendly computer shop and, of course, a coffeehouse," the building that became the Mini Mall was the prosaically named Real Form Girdle Factory, operated by the in-laws of the site's developer and co-owner, Mayer Schwartz, a Satmar Hasid then in his late twenties.

Decades before it became the commercial beachhead for the gentrification of North Williamsburg, the Real Form Girdle Factory had played a modest role in the Allied struggle against the Nazis, when its owner, Meyer Dorfman, produced both girdles and nets to mask antiaircraft guns.[42] In 1965, the factory briefly gained national notoriety when its new owner, the prominent television evangelist Rex Humbard, was criticized for reaping untaxed profits from the enterprise. (Humbard, who sold the factory in 1973, told the *New York Times*, "I wasn't saving any souls directly with Real Form Girdle.")[43] Like many industrial properties in Williamsburg, the Real Form Girdle Factory was later purchased by a local Hasidic family, at a time when the area was seen as blighted and dangerous. They maintained it as a garment business, one of a dwindling number of its kind, on an otherwise desolate strip of the city. But by 1997, the hulking machines that were the workhorses of the factory had become almost worthless. The apparel business had dried up, and larger sweatshops and factories had moved to China and Central America; small workshops that had failed to modernize went out of business. Yet at that moment, when many Hasidic businesses were folding, Mayer Schwartz, the son-in-law of the owner of Real Form Girdle, had a vision for the property that would transform not only his building but also the entire neighborhood around it.[44]

At the time, Schwartz was in his twenties and had never held a job. Born and raised in Borough Park, he moved to Williamsburg after he married at age eighteen and entered kollel, an institution of intensive Talmud study for newly married men, often for just a year or two. Schwartz, by contrast, spent a decade in kollel, distinguishing himself as an intelligent pupil who could parse the densest Talmudic discussions. The cerebral lifestyle of kollel is typically subsidized by a young man's in-laws, and for Schwartz this money came from the knitting factory run by his father-in-law, who had inherited it from his own father-in-law. (Schwartz also lived in a section 8 apartment at the time.) The factory was co-owned and overseen by Schwartz's two brothers-in-law, one of whom lived in England. The factory was losing money, and they decided to sell.

After a developer came to look at the property, Schwartz told us he thought, "If someone else is going to renovate it, why not me?" He had overheard a snippet of conversation about artists moving into factories. He understood that change was afoot in the neighborhood, even if not yet on the South Williamsburg streets surrounding the kollel. "I only knew Talmud," Schwartz said. "But Talmud teaches you critical thinking. To a very large extent. 'Why did he say that? Then why did he say the other thing?' Always looking at it from all angles." Schwartz prided himself on thinking outside the box. Later, in his early thirties, he published a concordance of sayings of the Baal Shem Tov, the founder of Hasidism.[45] But in the late 1990s, Schwartz's attention was drawn to what he called the "simple logic" of the real estate business. In any case, he understood something that his in-laws did not. He decided he could get more money per square foot than the six dollars that other landlords were asking, and he let his father-in-law know: "That day when I told him that, I said, 'Tomorrow I'm not going to kollel.' "

Instead of diving back into Talmud study the next morning, Schwartz took to the streets to learn more about the artists, walking north on Bedford, away from the Hasidic neighborhood, toward the factory. But while still near home, he ran into his friend Gary Schlesinger, who later became a notable Hasidic community activist and member of Community Board 1, which includes Williamsburg. "Bedford and Ross, Bedford between Ross and Wilson, I remember where I was," Schwartz recalled of the encounter. He pressed Schlesinger for information that could help him: "I said, 'I'm looking to know a little more about these artists.' He said, 'You know Nachman Brach?'"

Everyone knew Nachman Brach. After Rabbi Yoel Teitelbaum passed away, in 1979, Brach had become a major supporter of the rebbe's widow, Alta Faiga, who was embroiled in disputes over his successor. Since the Teitelbaums lacked living children or grandchildren, it was not clear who would inherit the crown of the largest and most economically and politically powerful Hasidic court in the world. In the last ten years of the rebbe's life, after a stroke had left him partially paralyzed, the *rebbetzin* Alta Faiga, as his primary caretaker, gained stature in the community. When the rebbe's nephew, Moshe, was crowned Satmar Rebbe in 1980, Brach and others close to the *rebbetzin* formed a splinter group that derived authority from Alta Faiga.[46]

Brach's position didn't win him many friends in the Satmar community, where devotees of the *rebbetzin* were a minority. This was especially true after she bequeathed to Brach the rebbe's former Williamsburg residence and shul—located on the same block of Bedford between Ross and Wilson where, years later, Schwartz was told to ask Brach about the artists.[47] The sprawling property was across the street from the newly crowned Satmar Rebbe's house, and a protest at Brach's gates in 1990 ended, in old Brooklyn fashion, with an Oldsmobile burning in the street. Yet as the succession disputes wore on and fractalized in the ensuing decades, Brach's original position, and his tenacity at feuding with the new Satmar Rebbe, made him seem less like a pariah and more like a figure whose independence of mind was admirable, even enviable, at least to some within the community.

Born in 1950, just a few years after his parents arrived in the United States as refugees, Brach epitomized a new generation of American Hasidim. Brach and his peers never knew the horrors of war or the trauma of the Holocaust. On the contrary, Brach was educated in newly opened religious institutions, very much the product of the Satmar Rebbe's vision to create a pious and vibrant Hasidic community in the United States. He had also been hardened by the crime endemic to the neighborhood, once grappling with an armed assailant who tried to rob him with a twelve-gauge shotgun.[48] In an early sign of the generosity that would come to characterize his relations with others, Brach gave a stereo set to the African American Good Samaritan who wrested the shotgun away from the would-be robber.

By that point, Brach had become a successful importer and seller of electronics, starting a company called Granada, and along the way, he had acquired some dilapidated warehouses on the fringes of the Hasidic enclave in Williamsburg. One of these buildings was a former pasta factory at 475 Kent Avenue, a block from the waterfront, where Brach kept a shambolic office, stored electronic equipment, and, around Passover season, baked matzah in the basement. "Go see Nachman Brach," Gary Schlesinger told Schwartz the day they met on the street in front of the building where yeshiva *bokhers* (students) once threw bottles at Brach's gates. "He has a building with a matzah oven in the basement and artists living upstairs."

Schwartz walked right over to see Brach in his Kent Avenue office. "I didn't know him from beans," Schwartz remembered. But he knew Brach's son-in-law's brother, and Schwartz's own father-in-law had some status in the Pupa Hasidic community. And so the two soon made the type of personal connection that often greases the wheels of social interaction and, frequently, business. Schwartz convinced Brach to drive with him to see his father-in-law and try to persuade him that the knitting factory could be converted into artists' lofts. Schwartz also asked Brach to bring along a handy young artist who knew how to build out raw industrial space. Later that day, Schwartz, Brach, and a thirtysomething sculptor named George Mansfield rode together to see Schwartz's father-in-law.

While Mansfield didn't remember taking the ride—"I'm sure it happened," he said—by that time he already had ten years of loft construction under his belt, including four with Brach and other Hasidic building owners.[49] Around 1993, then living in the Meatpacking District in Manhattan, Mansfield, who was originally from Long Island, and another artist friend responded to an ad for industrial space in the *Village Voice*. When they went out to Meserole Street, in East Williamsburg, to see the space, Brach met them on the street. Brach was a big man who wore oversized glasses and pinned his gray-and-white beard so it looked shorter. He was "disheveled," Mansfield remembered. Brach was also known to mumble. "You could hardly understand a word he said." But after "sort of a handshake," Brach threw the men the keys and gave them a floor of the factory for around fifty cents a square foot, twice what he was getting before. Mansfield set to work building walls and installing plumbing, none of it with city approval, although it was later grandfathered in when the Loft Law was extended from Manhattan to Brooklyn.

One time, Brach, who often appeared disorganized, failed to cash a rent check for three months. "So I went down to his office," Mansfield remembered. "I said, 'Here. You apparently didn't cash this check. Maybe you lost it, I don't know, but here's another one.' And he looked at me like I was crazy to have fessed up to that. And from there on, he and I really became close and he immediately considered me a mensch, as he put it." Later, when Brach saw what the artists had done to their floor, he was blown away. As sweatshops closed on other floors of Brach's Meserole building, and in other factory buildings he owned in the neighborhood around it, Brach started to rent out floors to Mansfield and his partner, who rehabbed them and sublet them to other artists. "It became sort of a business," Mansfield said. Eventually, "we probably had in the range of 100,000 square feet of rental space–factory space in Williamsburg."

When Schwartz's father-in-law heard this story from Brach and Mansfield, he was impressed. But when he was told that people were willing to pay twelve dollars a square foot, he balked: "Can't be. You're hallucinating." So they took him to a converted loft space on South 4th Street in a building owned by Motke Dov Halberstein, later an established real estate developer in Bushwick. "Look," they said, "this is how you have to build it. There's nothing to it." Still, when told how much artists were paying, Schwartz's father-in-law said, "You're lying." Later recalling his father-in-law's initial obliviousness of the changes happening around them in the neighborhood, Schwartz stated, "Not only was he not aware, no one was aware. People can't get out of their box." Despite their misgivings, Schwartz convinced his relatives to make a verbal deal that would allow him to develop the property with Mansfield. The deal was not sealed with a handshake, which Hasidim typically avoided, according to Mansfield. "The handshakes annoyed the crap out of me," Mansfield remembered. "It's considered an oath of some sort they shouldn't make with another person. If there were a handshake, it was a begrudging handshake." Instead, Schwartz and his family members all signed the new document, written in Hebrew, in front of a lawyer, and Schwartz's father-in-law held up an item of value to demonstrate his commitment to the deal.

Years later, Schwartz and Mansfield disagreed in separate interviews about whose idea it was to develop the family factory into stores that would directly appeal to the neighborhood's new artistic residents.

Schwartz cited his own predilection to think outside the box. He told us he had thought at the time, "No, let's do something fun. Let's do something that is actually going to create value for the building and create the neighborhood." Mansfield, however, recalled, "When I kind of saw the space, I thought, 'Let's do something interesting here.' And so I came up with this idea to do a mini-mall and keep all the stores relatively small so that it could be affordable and so startup businesses could get a leg up and open a place and it could be something unique." Mansfield added that it was only after talking to him that "Mayer began seeing it."

They also disagreed about the level of Schwartz's worldliness. Schwartz said, "I didn't drive a car, I didn't have a driver's license, I didn't know how to use a fax machine, forget about a cell phone." But Mansfield remembered Schwartz already gravitating toward cell phones and the Internet. "I remember that he's the first person that told me about Google," said Mansfield. "He's like, 'Yeah, why don't you just Google it.' I'm like, 'What the hell is this Google?' " The two decided to put in an Internet café and, later, a "Wi-Fi kiosk," in the mini-mall. But both Schwartz and Mansfield agreed that they were inspired by the disjuncture between the intense interest among young people in the neighborhood and the lack of amenities that catered to neighborhood newcomers. There was "nothing" there, Schwartz remembered. "The only establishment for yuppies was the L Café and Planet Thailand."

Because of its high visibility, the Mini Mall on Bedford Avenue between North 4th and 5th Streets served as a model for the kind of mixed-use development that became the norm in the neighborhood. As a sign of the far-reaching changes that Schwartz and Mansfield predicted for Williamsburg, the latter got the owner of Whole Foods on the phone and tried to see whether the chain would move in. (He was told the neighborhood wasn't ready yet; a Whole Foods opened in Williamsburg in 2016.) Instead, they cultivated local artist-run shops such as a bookstore and a yoga studio. Earwax Records had been in the neighborhood since 1990 but Mansfield convinced the owner to move into his building, which, in his words, "legitimized" the development. They also allowed galleries to use space free of charge. Not everyone was happy with the changes that the pair were promoting, however. In 1998, "YUPPIE GO HOME" graffiti appeared up and down Bedford Avenue. (It prompted a counterstrike in the pages of the *Williamsburg Gazette*, which argued, "Yuppies Can't Go Home.")[50]

The partnership between Schwartz and Mansfield transcended intercommunal tensions. "At first," Mansfield recalled, "I thought he was just going to be another Hasidic guy that didn't know what to do with their place, and I would take the lease out on it, you know, take a twenty-year lease on it and move on, just be the landlord." But Schwartz proved to be both professionally savvy and deeply interested in the results of his investment. Mansfield called Schwartz "a uniquely curious guy" who clearly stood apart. He and Mansfield developed what Mansfield called "a real fondness for each other." The pair was featured in a cover story in *Crain's New York Business* magazine about the "diverse developers," including Hasidim, Koreans, and Puerto Ricans, who were converting their properties into lofts.[51] "Manufacturing is down the drain," a worldly wise Schwartz told the *Crain's* reporter, sounding a bit like another, more famous cocksure New York developer with a penchant for speaking candidly to the press. As Mansfield told us, "Nachman [Brach] kept saying, 'Mayer thinks he's a bigwig now, he's doing all this stuff. I taught him everything he knows.' But it was kind of in jest."

The media attention to the new development in Williamsburg was well justified. *Crain's* reported that rent for a 750-square-foot loft had gone up in just a few years from $225 per month to $1,400, an increase of more than 500 percent. Significantly, the trade journal quoted a broker who said that for a year she could not get a sale in Brooklyn to any Manhattan developer because locals were doing their own conversions. By the end of 1999, Mansfield had bought a building in Beacon, New York, up the Hudson River, where he soon moved after reading about just-announced plans to build the Dia Beacon art museum there. Schwartz parlayed his fortune into other local real estate investments. He explained to *New York* magazine the thrill that Hasidim got from initial real estate success. "Once they turned their family factory into condos," he said of entrepreneurial Hasidic developers like himself, "they got this know-how—'Hey, let's buy the building next door.' Before you know it, you're on this crazy real-estate roller coaster."[52]

Schwartz rode the real estate roller coaster to its next stop, in Bushwick, where in 2003 he converted an old theater into a residential building marketed directly to artists. That year, the Opera House Lofts, as Schwartz named the development, were the focus of "Neighborhood on the Verge?," a long *New York Times* article on gentrification in Bushwick. The *Times* noted, "The hundred or so artists, actors and dancers who live in the Opera House Lofts lack some of the swagger of their peers to the west [in Williamsburg]. What they share with their new neighbors in Bushwick is an uneasy feeling that the fate of their community is undetermined."[53]

While developing and managing the Opera House Lofts, Schwartz became closer to artists personally than he had before, and much closer than the typical developer. He hung out with his tenants and threw barbecues for them. On a whim, he hired a tenant named Taylor Clark as a broker, despite his lack of experience. Clark remembered the experience: "I was a babysitter and a skateboarder ... I had been living at the Opera House close to a year when I met Mayer at a building meeting. Shortly after, based on his perception of my personality and ability, in combination with my adoration of the Opera House, Mayer asked me if I wanted to market and show apartments."[54]

The following year, Schwartz opened what he called "my masterpiece," a development that he named Castle Braid, after the factory in the novel *A Tree Grows in Brooklyn*. Castle Braid was an artist-loft-inspired concierge apartment building near the Central Avenue M stop in Bushwick. Like the Mini Mall in Williamsburg, Castle Braid was full of amenities for creative types, including a screening room and a space for band practice. Art made by residents was displayed on the building's walls, doors, and façade. "I love art and I love artists," Schwartz told the *New York Daily News*.[55] Castle Braid's website crowed about the building: "[It] isn't just an apartment building—it's a vision of a seamless interplay between the individual and the vibrant collective they've helped to create. In a world custom-built to enable the artist, you may finally be free to inhabit the role you've always known was yours to play." Meanwhile, on the blog that Schwartz had begun to maintain, he wrote, "I don't think there is yet another building in the WORLD like this."[56]

In Castle Braid, Schwartz sought to foster a community from scratch by providing the accoutrements of the creative lifestyle.[57] After the building was constructed but before anyone moved in, Schwartz held an art exhibition in the empty building to promote community art and, in the words of the curator, Leia Doran, "help find creative tenants for landlord Mayer Schwartz."[58] Someone from a local Bushwick arts nonprofit, quoted in an article titled "The Art of Gentrification, the Art in Gentrification," took issue with Schwartz's project: "It's clear when you walk in the door that this is about marketing apartments, not the art itself, and the local arts community that is being presented as an 'amenity' to potential renters."[59] Schwartz received criticism from the activist group Occupy Bushwick, too, for receiving a 421-a tax abatement but not providing affordable housing, and for allowing Castle Braid's Twitter account to advise residents not to give to panhandlers, for example, "You have nothing to feel guilty for!" and "Some will never learn to be self-reliant if they depend on government to feed and house them from cradle to grave."

While Castle Braid drew the ire of these critics, it made a large impression on other Hasidic developers in the neighborhood, including Yoel Goldman. According to Schwartz, Goldman, who would become one of the biggest Hasidic real estate developers in Brooklyn, told him that he had gone into Castle Braid to look around and had been inspired to put common areas in his own new buildings and to invest millions in amenities in order to attract a hipster clientele. By that point, Schwartz had become more enmeshed in the community of artists he had helped foster in Bushwick; he regularly attended art openings and was even developing his own app. Mayer Schwartz, the erstwhile kollel student who had helped pioneer gentrification in Williamsburg, had become gentrified.

The Kibbutz on Kent Avenue

George Mansfield didn't refurbish the eleven garbage- and pigeon-filled floors of 475 Kent, but he put Nachman Brach in touch with the artists who would do it. Eve Sussman, Lee Boroson, and Simon Lee were the first artists to sign a lease at 475 Kent. Years later, speaking in his apartment-*cum*–art studio on the ninth floor of 475 Kent Avenue, whose large windows provided sweeping views of the Manhattan skyline, Boroson said he had moved to Williamsburg in 1993, when the neighborhood was, as he recalled, not scary but still crime ridden. At the time, a few galleries, such as Pierogi, anchored the arts community. Brach had advertised available loft space in his building, perhaps inspired by his success with Mansfield at the Meserole Street property. Seeing one of the ads, a friend of Boroson asked him, "Why don't you look at that building?" Boroson remembered that the structure "looked like a wreck," but he called the number on the ad and soon went over to meet Brach.[60] At that point, in addition to Brach's business headquarters, the eleven-story former pasta factory housed only a seasonal matzah bakery in the basement and two floors of storage for the car-stereo business run by Morris Hartfeld, a longtime friend of Brach.

"I couldn't understand a word he said," Boroson remembered of Brach. Brach showed him the seventh floor, which he had cleared of debris. There was no heat or plumbing, lights dangled from the ceilings, and every other floor was filled with salvage and scrap. "This is completely insane," Boroson thought. But the windows were in good shape,

Nachman Brach, owner and landlord of the building that housed the
"Kibbutz on Kent Avenue," 2008 (Photograph by Robin Bruce Drysdale)

and the location was great, so he followed Brach down to his basement
office, with its wood paneling, dropped ceiling, and papers everywhere,
and called up his friends Eve and Lee. They signed a ten-year lease with
Brach, who promised to help them with the build-out, especially the
roof, water, and sewage. Significantly, Brach let the artists use his charge
account at Certified Lumber, a Hasidic-owned hardware store for contractors just across the street, where Boroson remembered charging
around $6,000 worth of sheetrock.

Over time, the artists built out not only the raw industrial space in
the old factory but also a community that Eve Sussman would call a
"vertical village," prompting a group of resident photojournalists to dub
the building "The Kibbutz." The trio of original artists rented three
floors and sublet space on them to other artists. Over the years, artists
eventually moved onto other floors as well, creating a hub for the creative world in Brooklyn and hosting innumerable events, open studios,
and rooftop parties. As the building's artistic community matured and
grew to more than two hundred people, Brach went about his usual business on the lower floors and could be regularly seen idling in his minivan

outside on trash night, obsessing over the proper placement of garbage on the street for pickup. He was "cheap" in his apparent reluctance to invest in the building's upkeep, according to a history written by residents, but also "benevolent."[61] Brach even made his way into the art of some of his tenants, such as a script in which "the main character is a bumbling but sweet Hasidic landlord." While Brach may have appeared penurious, the one characteristic he was widely known for, aside from his dishevelment, was his generosity. This soon became apparent to residents. For example, Brach let a hunchbacked former addict named Jose sleep in the basement for years. He also gave an electrician a lot of the building's potentially valuable old wiring. "Nachman took care of a lot of people," Boroson noted. Mansfield also pointed out, "He didn't live large, and he wasn't ostentatious at all. He gave most of his money away. He obviously had a big family and took care of everyone around him." Brach carved out a small pied-à-terre for Mansfield, free of charge, at the Meserole Street loft building as a token of appreciation.

In a sense, the artistic and Jewish lives of the building went on side by side, only occasionally intruding on each other. Thanks to Brach's seasonal matzah bakery in the basement, the whole block smelled like burning wood in the weeks before Passover. Brach made *shmura* matzah and spelt matzah for people with allergies. According to tradition, *shmura* matzah should be made with water drawn from a well, so Brach had one dug in the basement. Boroson, who is Jewish and whose family emigrated from Romania to Williamsburg in the 1880s (although he grew up elsewhere) got a free box from Brach every year.

Residents of 475 Kent have written about the building's one, creaky freight elevator and its "penchant for breaking on the Shabbos."[62] Boroson recalled, "I used to have to go find him at shul [synagogue] if the elevators stopped working or a truck blocked someone in." The shul was on Bedford, and if Brach couldn't be found there, Boroson would go to his house on Ross. As if living over a matzah bakery weren't enough, Brach's property also included, right next to 475 Kent, a Hasidic girls' school that he doted on and contributed large amounts of charity to. The worlds of the girls' school and the "kibbutz" barely intersected, except when artists were occasionally reprimanded for not closing their blinds while walking around naked.

Despite their dramatically different lifestyles, local Hasidim and the artists at 475 Kent sometimes banded together over shared concerns about developments in the neighborhood. In 2000, Simon Lee looked into getting a permit to store a boat in an inlet of the East River across from the building and learned of the city's plans to construct an electrical power plant on a barge in that location. Outraged by the lack of community input, he and other artists helped organize the community to protest and scuttle the city's plans. Deborah Masters, a sculptor living on the seventh floor, met with a Satmar rabbi to help spread the message to the Hasidic community. A local paper reported, "Community groups had to create and distribute thousands of flyers in Yiddish, Spanish, and English in order to tell residents of the hearings, and then had to hire buses to get them there."[63] Brach arranged for a number of buses from the girls' school to bring dozens of artists to a downtown Brooklyn protest.

But by 2001, one issue overshadowed all others in Williamsburg: gentrification. By that point, Eve Sussman had become a leader in city-wide housing activism, working closely with the Brooklyn LiveWork Coalition and the New York City Loft Tenants. The city's plans to rezone the waterfront were of particular concern to residents of 475 Kent, as was gentrification on nearby blocks. In 2001, Sussman told the *Brooklyn Rail*, "We're under siege from all sides. The neighborhood is at war. They are trying to destroy the culture we've created."[64]

Yet it was not gentrification per se that threw the artists' world into turmoil just a few years later. In the summer of 2007, at the Meserole building where Mansfield first met Brach, a lit cigarette ignited a fire that required dozens of firefighters to help put out the blaze. In the smoky confusion, a twenty-three-year-old firefighter from Greenpoint named Daniel Pujdak fell to his death. The city initially issued Brach three fines for having converted the space to residential use without having acquired the proper permits. But six months later, on a cold January night in 2008, five city departments, including fire and police, surprised residents of 475 Kent with a mandatory order to vacate. It was the Friday before the Martin Luther King Jr. Day long weekend, and no reason was given. After searching the entire building, the agencies announced that Brach's basement grain silo was a potential spontaneous-combustion hazard. Rumors circulated that the whole operation was retaliation against Brach for Pujdak's tragic death at his Meserole Street property. But Brach didn't bear the brunt of the city's actions; his artist tenants did. Forced to leave the building for five months in the middle of winter, some of them never returned. When the city allowed the remaining tenants back into the building in May, most of their ten-year leases were expiring, which sowed confusion and led many of them to switch from subletting to renting directly from Brach with shorter leases of three-to-five years.

The shorter leases, lease buyouts, and direct renting pointed to something many residents didn't want to admit, namely, that Brach had other plans for the space. By that point, Brach had suffered a stroke and had stopped visiting 475 Kent. In 2017, he sold the property, minus the school, which he had had legally separated from the factory building. The sale was made to a pair of Israeli investors, Shlomo Melchior and Assi Arev, who were known for their prior partnerships with the Kushner real estate family. A few artists with rent-stabilized leases, such as Lee Boroson and Eve Sussman, remained in the building as the new owners developed high-end units around them, using the artists' presence as a selling point. The abandoned pasta factory that Brach had purchased years earlier for around $800,000 sold for $56 million.

In October 2017, Mayor Bill de Blasio held a press conference in Sussman's 475 Kent loft, using the building as a symbol of citywide gentrification. At a podium set in front of Sussman's suspended speakers, and next to her workspace and an old car tire, de Blasio announced plans for a sweeping expansion of protections for the city's 10,000 loft tenants. After an introduction from Sussman, the mayor began by saying, "This is another example of people standing up to protect what's great about this city," adding later, "This is about protecting neighborhoods."[65] De Blasio asked the audience to consider the "moral implication" of evicting loft tenants, calling it "one of the wrongs that had to be righted." In a press release for his presentation at 475 Kent, de Blasio explained, "We are looking to protect every affordable home in this City, including the nearly 3,000 remaining spaces converted into homes and studios by artists before these neighborhoods became fashionable."[66] The building at 475 Kent still stood, and some artists still lived and worked within it, but the community, the matzah factory, and the creative spirit were gone. The "Kibbutz on Kent Avenue," now in the hands of Israeli capitalists, had gone the way of most kibbutzim.

CHAPTER SIX
The War Against the Artists

A T FIRST GLANCE, twenty-first-century Williamsburg and first-century Judea would appear to have little in common. Yet the Jewish zealots who stubbornly resisted the Roman occupation against all odds two thousand years ago, and the Hasidim who launched a zealous campaign against gentrification in the fall of 2003, were both participating in a millennia-long tradition of Jewish apocalypticism. Both groups saw themselves as the "righteous remnant" of a Jewish people under siege by invaders—Romans and gentrifiers—and threatened from within by Jewish collaborators. In the case of Williamsburg, these collaborators were willing to build luxury units for "artists" in the streets bordering the Hasidic enclave rather than affordable housing for members of their own community. At stake in both cases was the future of the "holy city," either Jerusalem or, as the Hasidic anti-gentrification activists frequently referred to their corner of Williamsburg, the "Jerusalem of America." Hasidic anti-gentrification activists explicitly viewed their efforts to save Williamsburg through the heroic, ultimately tragic lens of ancient Jerusalem and its righteous defenders.

Between 2003 and 2004, Hasidic activists in Williamsburg waged an unprecedented war against gentrification. This struggle, which Hasidim referred to as the *milkhemes artistn*, or "war against the artists," unfolded on the streets of the neighborhood, where anti-gentrification activists held large-scale demonstrations, hung banners on buildings, and posted broadsides. It was also waged in the pages of Yiddish-language newspapers, where Hasidim published fiery editorials and cynical cartoons; and in the community's synagogues and schools, where they strategized, fired up supporters, led penitential prayers, and shunned members seen as collaborating with the gentrifiers. On the one hand, the campaign was inspired and shaped by the specific socioeconomic conditions in Williamsburg and New York City at the turn of the second millennium. Yet, the Hasidic war against the artists also reflected deep-seated tendencies that have characterized the Satmar community since the pre–World War II period in Europe, as well as much older apocalyptic elements that have punctuated Jewish history during moments of crisis and communal rupture for more than two thousand years.

For most of the 1980s and 1990s, gentrification in Williamsburg was concentrated on the north and east sides of the neighborhood, areas with few if any Hasidic residents—places where Hasidic landlords and developers could make money without impinging on their own community. By the end of the 1990s, however, the effects of gentrification were beginning to be felt in earnest in the streets bordering the Hasidic enclave. As gentrification spurred a dramatic increase in housing costs throughout Williamsburg, and as more and more property was developed into luxury condominiums rather than affordable housing, gentrifiers began to encroach physically on the Hasidic Triangle. Many Hasidim started to fear that the virtual walls they had carefully erected to prevent spiritual and moral contamination by outsiders were in danger of being breached and that this incursion, combined with rising real estate costs, might ultimately compel their community to abandon the "holy city of Williamsburg."

In 2002, a little over half a century after Rabbi Yoel Teitelbaum and his followers first settled in Williamsburg, 52,700 Jews called the neighborhood home, out of a total population of 151,600 residents. Of these Jewish residents, 94 percent identified themselves as Orthodox, which, in the context of the area, meant that almost all were Hasidic.[1] From 1991 to 2002, the percentage of Jewish households in Williamsburg as a proportion of the neighborhood's total population increased dramatically, from 8 percent to 38 percent.[2] Because of the large number of children in Hasidic families, an astounding 54 percent of people living in Jewish households in Williamsburg were age seventeen or younger, the highest percentage within any county in or around New York City. In addition to being overwhelmingly young, the Jewish population of Williamsburg had a strikingly high poverty rate: 61 percent of Jewish households earned less than 150 percent of the federal poverty level; 64 percent earned less than $35,000 a year; and only 5 percent earned $100,000 or more annually.[3]

The high level of poverty in Williamsburg's Hasidic community was also reflected in the fact that the neighborhood's Jews had the lowest rate of home ownership (23 percent) versus renters (77 percent) of any Jewish community in the New York area, making it particularly vulnerable to the dramatic rise in rents associated with gentrification. One study of Williamsburg estimated that between 1991 and 2005, the average market rent rate in the neighborhood increased 43 percent. The study noted further that the highest levels of rent burden were in East and South Williamsburg, where Hasidim were concentrated, and that homeowners, too, were heavily affected in these areas, with approximately one-third of them spending "more than 60 percent of their income on housing."[4]

Within this environment of economic vulnerability and housing pre- cariousness, some members of the Hasidic community began to liken gen- trifiers in Williamsburg to the ancient Babylonian and Roman conquerors of Jerusalem *and* to the 9/11 terrorists. And who, in the minds of these Ha- sidic critics, were the gentrifiers? First, it is important to note that Hasidic sources from the early 2000s, including newspaper articles, broadsides (known as *pashkevilin* in Yiddish), billboards, and speeches, did not employ the terms "gentrification" or "gentrifiers" to describe the threat facing the Hasidic community. Instead, they all used the word *artistn*, which the Ha- sidim of Williamsburg employed to refer to hipsters or gentrifiers more generally (the typical word for "artist" in Yiddish is *kinstler*). Thus, *artistn*, the plural of *artist*, did not necessarily refer to working artists, but was likely inspired by contact between Hasidic landlords and actual artists dur- ing the first phase of the North Side's gentrification and was later applied by Hasidim to members of subsequent waves of gentrifiers, whether they were working artists or, as was increasingly likely over time, not.

It is unclear when this use of *artistn* first became part of the Hasidic lexicon in Williamsburg, though it was in circulation in the late 1990s, when, for example, it appeared in a letter to the editor published in the December 11, 1998, edition of *Der Yid*.[5] The author of the letter, identi- fied as "M. Weiss of Williamsburg," referred to a notice published several weeks earlier in the same newspaper that had decried the phenomenon of *heymishe* (that is, Hasidic) Jews renting apartments to *artistn*. Weiss took a more sanguine view of the *artistn*, however, noting that the lack of housing in the neighborhood was affecting them along with the Hasidim and that "in regard to the '*artistn*' themselves, concerning whom I have a little personal knowledge, many are normal." The answer to the real estate crisis, according to Weiss, was not to focus critically on the *artistn* but rather to "build Jewish housing."

Unlike the local Latinos or the Hasidim, the *artistn* were not initially perceived as a politically coherent community, in the traditional sense of that idea in the neighborhood. As Rabbi David Niederman of the United Jewish Organizations put it to us when asked about the collective identity of the *artistn*, "I don't even understand what that means. It's not like they have a distinct community. There are a few thousand—I don't even understand the relationship."[6] In certain key respects, however, *artistn* did represent a discrete and, in comparison with other groups that had settled in the neighborhood over the years, powerful community. Largely white, middle or upper class, post-ethnic, and—at least overtly—nonreligious, these ambassadors of conspicuous consumption represented a phenomenon previously unknown to the gritty streets of Williamsburg. And yet it was precisely these characteristics that made the *artistn* intriguing to some members of the Hasidic community, especially those who had been exposed to the wider world, including via the Internet, despite the best efforts of Hasidic authorities to severely limit or even ban its use. For Hasidim dissatisfied with their community or just curious about the world across Broadway, the *artistn* represented an alternative lifestyle that could be embraced or merely experimented with.

Because of their relative wealth, perceived lack of religious affiliation, and post-ethnic whiteness—unlike, for example, the Polish immigrants of nearby Greenpoint or the Italian Americans of East Williamsburg—the *artistn* embodied a racially and economically privileged identity that was potentially accessible to younger Hasidim, in particular, if they were willing to give up the physical and behavioral markers that distinguished them from whites in general. Indeed, the physical proximity of *artistn* gave Hasidim the opportunity to observe, and even participate in, certain aspects of a white urban bourgeois lifestyle without having to leave Williamsburg. In this respect, the *artistn* represented a much bigger threat to the social fabric of Hasidic Williamsburg than Latinos or African Americans ever did, since those groups were similarly impoverished competitors for limited governmental resources whose explicitly nonwhite identity represented a racial "step down" for the racially ambiguous Hasidim.

Significantly, the arrival of the *artistn* and their lifestyle in Williamsburg coincided with the broader, though highly uneven and contested, embourgeoisement of Hasidic communities in Brooklyn and beyond. This phenomenon manifested itself in a variety of ways, including the opening of high-end food stores that resembled kosher versions of Whole Foods; the embrace of new cuisines (sushi, gourmet pizza) that were far afield of traditional eastern European Jewish fare; and the placement of glossy advertisements for luxury goods in Hasidic publications. Moreover, despite the vehement attempts of Hasidic leaders to limit or even ban the use of the Internet among community members except for business purposes, many Hasidim continued to surf the web, and in the process, they were increasingly exposed to a wide variety of consumer goods and lifestyle choices. By the turn of the twenty-first century, therefore, no Hasidic community, even the most conservative, could isolate itself from the material temptations of contemporary bourgeois culture.

In Williamsburg there had long been tension between, on one hand, the enduring legacy of Rabbi Yoel Teitelbaum's fiery critique of luxury (*luksus*, in Yiddish), his personal asceticism, and his insistence on especially stringent norms of modesty, and, on the other, the reputation of Satmar and other Hungarian communities among their Hasidic peers for enjoying well-made food (much of it Jewish variations of traditional Hungarian favorites) and for appreciating certain material luxuries (fancy chandeliers, elegant women's clothing and accessories), even as they were also more religiously conservative and had higher poverty rates than more moderate Hasidic groups such as Bobov in Borough Park.[7] To a significant degree, this tension had a gendered dimension, as a Hasidic woman from Williamsburg noted to the authors: "It's ironic that though Reb Yoelish did, indeed, condemn *luksus*, his wife [Rebbetsin Alta Faiga Teitelbaum] actually brought 'balabatishkeit'—living well and dressing well—into the Satmar mindset. Well, it was *already* in the Hungarian mindset, but there's no question that she encouraged it. She herself had a beautiful home, and the convalescent home she built for new mothers was a model in luxury. Her parties, too, were very fancy."[8]

Against this complex backdrop, the gentrification of Williamsburg intensified the anxiety felt by some Hasidim—particularly men, who were already prone to taking zealous positions when it came to issues like women's modesty, changes to the traditional educational system, or Internet use—that the holy community founded by Yoel Teitelbaum was being inundated with *gashmiesdike zakhn* (Yiddish, "material things") that threatened to erode the elevated spiritual status that they had consistently worked hard to achieve in the years following World War II.

By the early 2000s, several generations of Hasidim in Williamsburg had been raised in a Manichean environment in which spiritual leaders, beginning with Rabbi Yoel Teitelbaum, cast certain groups as enemies of the community. Over the years, these enemies had included Zionists, who were frequently condemned for literally doing the work of Satan and endangering the physical and spiritual well-being of Jews everywhere, and even for bringing about the Holocaust through their sins. They had also included members of other Hasidic groups, such as Belz and Lubavitch, who were attacked—both discursively and, in some notorious instances, physically—by Satmar Hasidim, either because they were perceived as being insufficiently anti-Zionist or because they were seen as trying to proselytize members of the Satmar community.

By contrast, Latinos and blacks never inspired the same kind of animus, even though members of these communities and Hasidim sometimes came into open conflict in Williamsburg and frequently possessed dismissive or outright racist and anti-Semitic views of one another. From the perspective of many within the Satmar community in Williamsburg, individual Latinos and blacks might be dangerous as potential perpetrators of street crime, but collectively they did not pose an existential threat to the Hasidic community as a whole. Indeed, even during the depths of New York City's crisis in the 1970s, Hasidim in Williamsburg achieved a modus vivendi—albeit one marked by resentment, housing lawsuits, and sometimes intergroup violence—with the neighborhood's Latinos and African Americans, a sort of truce that enabled the Hasidic community not only to remain in what many outsiders considered a blighted area but also to thrive and grow there. Against that history, the demonization of the *artistn* that some Hasidim in Williamsburg engaged in at the height of the anti-gentrification campaign of 2003 and 2004 should be viewed as almost akin to the community's traditional approach to existential enemies like the Zionists rather than to its pragmatic attitudes toward Latinos and African Americans.

Apocalypse in Williamsburg

A number of factors contributed to the palpable sense of anxiety that enveloped Hasidic Williamsburg in the early 2000s. First, the United States witnessed a predictable upsurge of both Christian and secular millennialism surrounding the year 2000, including the so-called Y2K crisis, which was covered in the Yiddish newspapers that served the Satmar community.

Though millennial mania was not a major factor in the apocalyptic mood that later took hold in Williamsburg around the issue of gentrification, it may have helped create a receptive atmosphere. Within the Satmar community in particular, several events undoubtedly raised tensions during this period. In 1999, Rabbi Moshe Teitelbaum, the elderly and ailing Satmar Rebbe, sparked a struggle over succession when he named his third son, Zalman, to be the leader of the local Williamsburg community, while his first-born son and, until then, presumed heir, Aaron, maintained control over the Satmar town of Kiryas Joel.[9] In the midst of Moshe Teitelbaum's decline, in June 2001, Rebbetzin Alta Faiga Teitelbaum, the highly venerated and controversial widow of Rabbi Yoel Teitelbaum—described by Samuel Heilman as "the closest thing there has been to a female Hasidic rabbi"—passed away, having led a zealous minority faction of the community known as the Bnei Yoel since her husband's death in 1979.[10] Thus, as Satmar Hasidim in Williamsburg welcomed in the new millennium, they were facing profound uncertainty and, increasingly, open conflict over the future leadership of their community and its many institutions.

Within this tense climate, another event took place in 2001 that inspired a sense of apocalyptic dread in New York City, and in Hasidic Williamsburg in particular. The terrorist attack on the World Trade Center on September 11, 2001, prompted a wide variety of responses; religious communities in the United States and beyond interpreted the event through the lens of their own distinctive worldviews and histories. Yet none of these communities experienced the attack in the immediate and visceral way that the Hasidic enclave in Williamsburg did. Located just across the East River from Lower Manhattan, with a clear view of the destruction, Hasidic Williamsburg not only witnessed the attack as it unfolded but also experienced a variety of impacts for years thereafter.[11]

One of the first salvos fired in the Hasidic campaign against the *artistn* was an article published on November 7, 2003, in both *Der Yid* and *Der Blatt*, with the title "We Are Still on September 10."[12] It explicitly likened the danger posed by gentrifiers to the terrorist attacks on 9/11. The article opened with a description of the sense of dread in the United States following 9/11 and then segued into a fictional account of a Hasidic father driving his family back to their home in Borough Park from a celebration in Kiryas Joel. Not long ago, the father had lived in Williamsburg, but now, as they passed the neighborhood, he observed the changes wrought by gentrification and "started to describe [them] with grief and longing; tears streaming from his eyes: Who could have

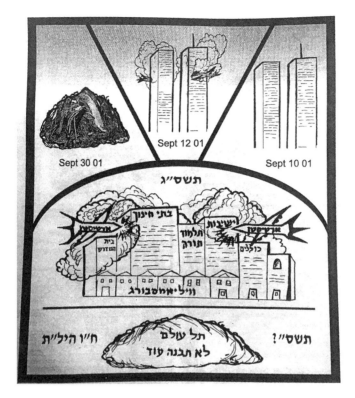

Cartoon depicting planes labeled *artistn* crashing into Hasidic Williamsburg,
in a reference to the 9/11 attacks on the Twin Towers, *Der Yid*, 2003
(Courtesy of *Der Yid*)

believed that Williamsburg would be left a *midbar shemama* [desert wasteland] that no Jew can enter?"

For the anonymous author of the article, the existential threat posed by gentrification loomed on the horizon for Hasidic Williamsburg as ominously as the planes that had crashed into the World Trade Center on 9/11. To make this link more explicit, the article was accompanied in both newspapers by a cartoon with before, during, and after images of the plane attacks on the Twin Towers. Below this appeared a second cartoon depicting two planes crashing into the skyline of Williamsburg and its clearly labeled Jewish institutions. Finally, below that was an image of a pile of rubble where the Jewish community had once stood. In the coming months, Hasidim who participated in demonstrations against gentrification in Williamsburg would return to this theme, circulating a Yiddish-language leaflet with a hand-drawn picture of the World Trade Center collapsing, accompanied by the warning "How long did it take the Twin Towers to fall? Eight seconds. How long will it take for Williamsburg??? God Forbid."[13] And yet the article in *Der Yid* ended on a hopeful note: "Dear Jewish brothers! We are still on September 10. We can still save everything. It will be extremely difficult but it is still possible. . . . Do not say that it cannot happen, because September 11 also seemed like an impossibility."

Other Hasidic newspaper accounts from the fall of 2003 clarified why the *artistn* were so dangerous. On October 24, *Der Blatt*, a Yiddish newspaper established by Elimelech Deutsch in 2000 to serve the followers of Rabbi Aaron Teitelbaum—by this point, *Der Yid* was seen as a media organ for Zalman's disciples in Williamsburg—described an *asife*, or official gathering of leaders and religious authorities, convened to discuss threats then confronting the community.[14] Haredi leaders had held such gatherings in response to perceived crises for more than a century, most famously in 1912, when they met in Katowice, Poland, to found the Haredi umbrella organization Agudas Yisroel. The practice continued when Hasidim and other Haredi Jews immigrated to the United States. In May 1961, for example, Rabbi Yoel Teitelbaum convened a *kinus klali*, or general assembly, of rabbinic leaders at the Hotel St. George in Brooklyn to debate the problems then affecting the Haredi community in the United States, including the growing popularity of Zionism, a perceived decline in women's modesty, and creeping materialism.[15]

Now, in 2003, according to *Der Blatt*, the most serious threat facing the Hasidic community in Williamsburg was gentrification. "As is known, in the last few years, Williamsburg has become utterly plagued by 'artistn,' " the newspaper noted, "whose presence has, lamentably, increased in the neighborhood day by day, via their purchase or rental of apartments in Williamsburg and also through shopping in the neighborhood's stores with their lewd appearance and licentious clothing."[16] A week later, on October 31, *Der Yid* published an article covering the rabbinic assembly, providing its readers with some historical context for the gentrification of the neighborhood: "The gathering was convened on account of the problem that, in the last few years, has impacted the 'city and mother in Israel,' Williamsburg: the so-called *artistn*, who originally used to live in Manhattan, have begun to cross the Williamsburg Bridge and to settle on the Brooklyn side near the bridge, conquering neighborhood after neighborhood, and after conquering the 'North Side' and 'Greenpoint' they are now approaching the borders of the holy Jewish city of Williamsburg."[17]

In a theme that was repeated by Hasidim over and over in the coming months, *Der Yid* depicted gentrification as a hostile invasion by alien forces who threatened to cross the unofficial border of the enclave, breach its figurative walls, and destroy the "holy" community of Hasidic Williamsburg. The image of gentrifiers as invaders in *Der Yid* echoed numerous scholarly sources on the subject; for example, Peter Williams in 1986 described gentrification as the "remorseless march of invaders."[18] Hasidim in Williamsburg appear to have developed their own theory of gentrification—without ever employing that term—based on their experiences of the phenomenon on the ground as well as on their highly dualistic worldview.

A key element in this worldview, one that inflected the Hasidic response to gentrification with a sense of profound urgency, was that at least some Hasidim had come to view their enclave in Williamsburg as a sacred space, a "holy Jewish city," as they put it, whose potential destruction by the *artistn* was only the latest link in a chain of catastrophes that had affected the Jewish people for millennia. For these Hasidim, the threat posed by gentrification was not merely economic or physical but also spiritual and moral. As the article in *Der Yid* put it:

> Of course, the artists' invasion of Williamsburg is a terrible problem, in spiritual [*be-rukhnius*] and physical [*be-gashmius*] terms. Both on account of their way of life—if you can call it that—which is among the worst of all the nations [i.e., peoples] and because they pay a much higher price for an apartment, and this threatens to create the danger that owners of buildings will start to turn over their apartments to them and expel the Hasidic community which has bled so much for the apartments. The worry is even greater still that the entire settlement in Williamsburg, which was built with blood and sweat over a period of so many years, will possibly go aground and be destroyed.[19]

Other articles elaborated on the view that Williamsburg, or at least the *heylike vinkl* (holy corner) where Hasidim had established their enclave, was now sacred territory. For example, on November 21, 2003, *Der Blatt* published an article by an author identified as Sh. B. Margolis entitled "Save Williamsburg from Their Hands," which described the neighborhood as the "Jerusalem of America," a place made spiritually pure by the Satmar equivalent of the "greatest generation," namely, the pious Holocaust survivors from Hungary who settled there in the 1940s and 1950s:

> How could this reality [gentrification] come to pass in the "city
> and mother of Israel"? Williamsburg, the city that is full of sages
> and scribes, the Jerusalem of America, this holy settlement where
> hundreds of rabbis, sages, and holy men came as refugees after
> the terrible Holocaust, where they settled and sanctified and pu-
> rified the environment . . . where the streets were so pure all
> year, pure from every impure thing . . . from television and other
> forbidden things to look at, pure of *treyf* [non-kosher] and con-
> taminating Zionist newspapers, pure of Zionism.[20]

Thus, in addition to an invading army, one of the chief ways that Hasidic
critics portrayed the *artistn* was as a spiritually contaminating force or even
a disease, one that would undo or reverse the sanctification of the neighborhood that Rabbi Yoel Teitelbaum and his followers had painstakingly
achieved in the years following World War II. This idea underlay the frequent references to the *artistn* as a kind of "plague" that had achieved a
foothold in Williamsburg and threatened to contaminate the entire population unless heroic efforts were taken to stop it. For example, in the conclusion to his essay in *Der Blatt*, Margolis invoked the biblical disease of
leprosy to depict gentrification: "With a resolute struggle we can still
merit that our holy city of Williamsburg will be preserved from this malig-
nant leprosy [Leviticus 14:44], this infectious plague called *artistn*."

For a community built on a religious ideology that distinguished in
all spheres between the sacred and profane and that viewed physical and
spiritual states as intimately related, the *artistn* were perceived as a moral
and, therefore, a mortal danger. As the October 31 article in *Der Yid* described them, once again invoking a biblical image to indicate the profound nature of their threat: "[The *artistn*] have no shame, bringing with
them the greatest filth from Manhattan like Sodom and Gomorrah. . . . It
has been demonstrated that on the 'North Side,' where they have already
lived a long time, they have taken over the entire street and have introduced businesses where the most *treyf* and worst newspapers and greatest
filth are sold."[21]

Ironically, one of the most dangerous qualities of the *artistn*, and one
that distinguished them from the other groups that had traditionally resided in Williamsburg alongside the Hasidim, was their perceived friend-
liness: "A large part of the '*artistn*-problem' is that they seek to get along
with their neighbors and they lure others to their lifestyle, which is a
great danger both for adults and even more for children."[22] Whereas La-

tino, black, and white ethnic residents of Williamsburg had long coexisted with the Hasidic community and were generally content to live parallel lives with their Hasidic neighbors, interacting when necessary, the *artistn* were constantly disrupting the delicate intergroup balance in the neighborhood by ignoring—or simply being ignorant of—the invisible walls that existed around the Hasidic enclave. This problem was particularly acute in streets shared by Hasidim and *artistn*, where Hasidic critics expressed grave concern over the possibility that friendly hipsters would negatively influence Hasidic children playing outside on the Sabbath, or that even their most mundane "customs" would contaminate the environment. Thus, for instance, an unsigned article in *Der Blatt* on November 21, 2003, lamented the hipster practice of keeping dogs as pets and walking them in the neighborhood (many Hasidim, like a majority of eastern European Jews before immigrating to the United States, viewed dogs as unclean, physically dangerous, and, generally speaking, goyish, or gentile): "Another worry concerns the lowly custom of the *artistn* to take their dogs for a walk every morning around the entire block where they live, in order for it to urinate on the street."[23]

Undoubtedly, the greatest moral concern expressed by Hasidic critics regarding the *artistn* was how their presence might negatively affect the community's many children. On November 14, 2003, for example, *Der Yid* published a full-page announcement in which it asked its readers, "Can we imagine how difficult it will be to educate our children when thousands [of people] belonging to this lowly element are living among us?"[24] A week later, Sh. B. Margolis put it more passionately in *Der Blatt:* "Concerning them [the children] I cry, that is the reason for the grief and the sadness . . . for the thousands of Jewish children who look upon the situation with brokenness and despair and ask, 'How is this faithful city become a harlot [Isaiah 1:21], this loyal city turned into a prostitute?' How can this be? How can people let this happen?"[25]

In classic rabbinic fashion, Margolis cited a biblical verse in order to liken the current situation facing Hasidic children in Williamsburg, the "Jerusalem of America," to the moral corruption of ancient Jerusalem at the time of the prophet Isaiah. As is often the case with such midrashic interpolations, the surrounding biblical verses, which Margolis did not cite, were as important to conveying his message as the one that he did. Thus, Isaiah 1:19–20 declares the consequences for those residents of Jerusalem who do not repent: "If you are willing and obedient, you shall eat the good of the land; But if you refuse and rebel, you shall be devoured with the sword," and Isaiah 1:23 states the root of the problem: "Your princes are rebellious, and companions of thieves; every one loves bribes and follows after their rewards." While the "sword" wielded by God to punish the disobedient residents of Jerusalem might take the form of Babylonians—or, later, Romans—the real cause of the crisis was the moral decline of the city's Jewish inhabitants and their turning away from the path of righteousness in order to seek crass material benefit. This greed, according to Hasidic critics, was the real source of the current crisis in Williamsburg and the reason that the "sword" of the *artistn* now perilously hung over the community.

Collaborators

Though some Hasidim criticized the *artistn* for causing housing prices to rise in Williamsburg and for exposing Hasidic children and others to their supposed licentiousness, they also agreed that gentrification would never have become such a threat without the active collaboration of members of the Hasidic community. The willingness of these people to abet gentrification was linked by critics with a more general moral decline within the neighborhood and a weakening of communal bonds. In his essay in *Der Blatt*, for instance, Margolis noted that in the past, Williamsburg had stood out for its piety even among other Haredi neighborhoods in New York City. He noted that when the Satmar Rebbe publicly condemned Agudas Yisroel as insufficiently anti-Zionist, the Haredi organization was unable to gain a foothold in Hasidic Williamsburg despite its inroads elsewhere, because of the united opposition of the local community. Similarly, for decades, women's clothing that was permitted in other Haredi neighborhoods remained prohibited in Williamsburg, and no storeowner would think of carrying "Zionist newspapers." But now, Margolis bemoaned, "it has become clear that in the last few years, terrifying breaches in the wall around Williamsburg have occurred which are the direct cause of the current *khurbn*."[26] Here the author employed the Yiddish term *khurbn*, traditionally used to refer to the destruction of the ancient Temples in Jerusalem and, later, to the Holocaust, to describe the catastrophic effects of gentrification in Williamsburg.

According to the prophet Isaiah, the transgressors in ancient Israel had brought Jerusalem to ruin because "every one loves bribes and follows after their rewards"; so, too, Hasidim who aided the *artistn* in Williamsburg were doing so for financial gain, according to Margolis: "And now today some of our own people, Hasidic Jews and residents of Williamsburg, our friends 'from among you and in your midst' . . . are ready to betray thousands of their brothers and thousands of Jewish children and thousands of small *kheyder* pupils for a bit of money and to hand over our holy city to the lowliest elements that our world possesses." Margolis pleaded, "Dear brothers? Where are we? Have we not learned even a little concerning how cheap and lowly money is? Have we then not seen how the greatest philanthropists in the world have become paupers overnight? What kind of honor for money is ruling over us? What kind of esteem for the wealthy do we have here? Why are people silent and keeping quiet? Where are the men of war?!"[27]

Particularly galling to Margolis was the dramatic contrast between the veneration of wealth among some members of the current generation of Hasidim and the antimaterialism and simple piety of the "men of war" who had founded the Hasidic enclave of Williamsburg. To emphasize the contrast and, hopefully, shame his readers into action, Margolis cited a public lecture given by the Satmar Rebbe. "Once upon a time the worst evil one could say about a person is that he had sold himself for money," the rebbe said. "When people said about someone that he had done something wrong just so he could make money, it was considered fearfully demeaning and shameful for the one who had 'sold himself for his lust of money.' " By contrast, "Today, unfortunately, the bowl has been overturned on its mouth, money has entirely become a justification. . . . Whatever is difficult about someone's behavior, inspires the justification 'He makes money this way.' . . . My teachers and masters! The question is, until when? How much longer? What is the amount that we will suffer for money?"[28]

Der Yid expressed the same biting sentiment in a cartoon published on November 7, 2003, featuring an image of a moving truck emptying out Hasidic-occupied buildings in Williamsburg. The caption read, "We must move from our hard-earned apartments because Mr. [So-and-so] has built here for that group [meaning gentrifiers]." Beneath this image was one of an overweight Hasidic developer standing next to newly constructed or renovated buildings with the English signs "Books," "Bar," "Newstand" [*sic*], and "Pool," accompanied by the Yiddish-language thought bubbles "Ha, ha, ha," and "Oy, I will make a killing, another hundred million dollars."[29] A week later, the newspaper published a full-page announcement that identified Williamsburg as only the latest in a series of iconic Jewish neighborhoods in New York City that, it implied, had been literally sold out by greedy Jewish landlords: "The South Bronx—1950.

Cartoon depicting a Hasidic developer with the text, "Oh, am I going to
make a killing, another hundred million dollars." Above, it reads,
"We have to move from our hard-earned apartment because Mr. . . . builds
here for that bunch," *Der Yid*, 2003 (Courtesy of *Der Yid*)

Brownsville—1955. East New York—1960. Crown Heights—1970.
Williamsburg—200?! Will we let Williamsburg follow in the footsteps of
all these neighborhoods that became extinct because some landlords sold
them out for money?"[30]

The stereotype of the greedy Jewish landlord has long been an anti-
Semitic staple, which makes the critique and caricature of greedy Hasidic
(and more broadly, Jewish) landlords in the pages of a Hasidic-owned
Yiddish-language newspaper all the more striking. Some observers indis-
criminately applied the same stereotype to Hasidic landlords and developers who became prominent in the Brooklyn real estate scene, often
after getting their start in Williamsburg. This trope is anti-Semitic not
because there are no greedy Hasidic landlords—of course, as with any

group, there are—but because it assumes that Hasidic landlords are in-
herently predisposed to greed and rapaciousness because they are Jewish.
By contrast, the internal Hasidic critique of individual Hasidic landlords
accused of selling out their own community for the sake of money
turned the anti-Semitic stereotype on its head by casting their behavior
as immoral and fundamentally un-Jewish. This critique accomplished
something else important by illuminating a historical reality that has
long been occluded by the stereotype of the greedy Jewish landlord,
namely, that poor and working-class Jews, including many Hasidim, suffered as the result of processes like redlining, blockbusting, and, most recently in neighborhoods such as Williamsburg and Crown Heights,
gentrification.

The War Against the Artists

Hasidic critics were clear about the existential threat posed to their enclave in Williamsburg by the *artistn* and their Hasidic collaborators.
What remained for these Hasidic opponents of gentrification was to
spell out a detailed course of action for members of their community to
follow. One of the first steps in the campaign against the *artistn* took the
form of a Yiddish- and Hebrew-language *pashkevil* (broadside) posted on
the streets of Williamsburg in October 2003 by an organization identifying itself as HaVaad leHatsolos Vilyamsburg, or the Committee to Save
Williamsburg; it consisted of important householders in the community
committed to fighting gentrification. The broadside, which was dated the
first of the Jewish month of Cheshvan in the year 5764, or October 27,
2003, stated in Yiddish, "It has come to our attention that a resident of
our city has sold two lots at 176/178 Division Ave. to someone who is
not a resident of our city [meaning Williamsburg] and for a high price
that creates the danger that the project will be built for *artistn*, God forbid."[31] In response, the broadside continued in Hebrew:

> We have come to triple and strengthen our warning that no one
> may rent or sell an apartment or loft to those people in our
> neighborhood, nor should they sell them lots. And this even in-
> cludes someone who sells to a Jew and knows that he in turn will
> build for them [gentrifiers] or if he transfers it to a Jew at a price
> that proves that it is intended for them, the law is that it is as if
> he had sold it to them. And he who transgresses this matter will,

along with his sons and daughters, be shunned from the synagogues, Torah institutions, and schools in Williamsburg.

Reverting to Yiddish, the broadside added a further "warning" that a
Hasid was going around to neighbors in Williamsburg, offering "to buy
their houses in order to build on the lots," and that no one should sell to
him. Finally, it provided a telephone number that residents could call to
report infractions.

On October 31, 2003, *Der Yid* published an article which described the
precedent-setting case of a Hasidic transgressor, or *poyrets-geder*—literally,
one who has "breached the fence"—whose "apartment was located in the
midst of a project that was thickly inhabited by Jews, yet he was willing to
sell it to *artistn*. He sent around a letter to all the real estate brokers and
placed his apartment on the market with a price that only *artistn* could afford."[32] The case was brought to the attention of a council of rabbis, who
deliberated for a long time before arriving at a series of decisions.

First, the rabbis pronounced an "emergency prohibition," binding on
individuals and developers alike, against selling or renting property on
the open market, including apartments, houses, and empty lots.[33] As in
the broadside, the prohibition included cases in which persons were not
attempting to sell property directly to *artistn* but had set a price that
members of the Hasidic community could not afford. Second, the rabbis
stated that in the coming days, they would send a delegation to convey
their prohibition to Hasidic developers and landlords on the South Side
of Williamsburg who might be tempted to sell or rent to *artistn*. This
part of the plan was accompanied by a "sharp warning" that if such people chose not to comply, "they and their children and grandchildren
would be excluded from the communal organizations and educational institutions in Williamsburg." Regarding the Hasidic apartment owner
whose case had been brought before the rabbis, "[They] entreated [him]
to lock the door before the destroyer, lest it provide an open door in the
heart of Williamsburg to this vulgar group [the *artistn*]. If not, then he,
his children and grandchildren would be excluded from all the holy community institutions in Williamsburg." The rabbis also endorsed the
Committee to Save Williamsburg; the opening of an office dedicated
specifically to fighting gentrification; and a "wide-ranging and extensive
campaign to educate the masses." Every head of a Hasidic household in
Williamsburg would be asked to donate $36 to the "struggle to rescue
the city of Williamsburg."

On November 7, 2003, Hasidic opponents of gentrification took an even more radical step in their campaign by placing a full-page announcement in *Der Blatt* publicly declaring war against the *artistn*. The newspaper identified the source of the decision as "the Organization of Activists and Religious Functionaries of Williamsburg founded in 2003 to save our neighborhood of Williamsburg in the city of Brooklyn." It declared: "According to the call of the great rabbis of our city, each and every resident is obligated to do everything in his power to stop the invasion of the lowly 'artistn' in our neighborhood. We therefore proclaim the **'War Against the Artistn' Campaign'** " (bolding in the original).

The newspaper announcement continued with the statement "The first steps in the war against the artists will be as follows," and then listed a series of actions closely reflecting those mentioned a week earlier in *Der Yid* (such as creating a delegation to warn developers and landlords, opening an office dedicated to the campaign, requiring a minimum donation from Hasidic householders, etc.) but also added a few new "steps." Those steps offered a window onto the important role that public shaming—or the threat thereof—played in the insular Satmar community in Williamsburg. The promised actions included "publishing the names and addresses of the transgressors, in order that all of Williamsburg will be able to send letters via post and appeal to them not to contaminate the environment with *artistn*, and subsequently, according to the instruction of the rabbis, to hold demonstrations in front of the transgressors' homes" and "publicizing the names of the communal institutions and organizations that accept donations, great and small, from the transgressors."

In the same edition, *Der Blatt* published an article titled "War Against the Artists Campaign Proclaimed by the Organization of Activists and Religious Functionaries of Williamsburg," in which it explicitly exhorted community members to prevent an irreparable breach in the virtual walls surrounding their enclave: "With God's help, we will succeed in causing the evil decree of the *artistn* to pass by our camp, to guard the wall of our city from becoming cracked and broken."[34] Significantly, the article was accompanied by photos of the new Steiner Studios, then being built at the Brooklyn Navy Yard on the East River waterfront directly adjacent to the Hasidic enclave.

Der Blatt had previously (in 1999) condemned the idea of the "thoroughly depraved movie industry" establishing itself "right on the threshold of . . . the 'Jerusalem of America.' "[35] The message to readers was clear: the movie studio was only the beginning of what Hasidic residents of the neighborhood could expect if their war against the *artistn* were to fail. As the *New York Times* breezily put it in a 2003 article about the Navy Yard studio—which neglected to mention any possible effects it might have on the Hasidic enclave and the longtime Latino residents—"Hey, the line forms right on the waterfront, you New York City movie dreamers. Who's ready to sign up for a Steiner Studios safari à la the Universal Studios Tour?"[36] It speaks volumes about the profound gulf between the Hasidic community in Williamsburg and the city's cultural elites that precisely when the former's newspapers were declaring war against gentrification, the latter's newspaper of record was fantasizing about a movie studio "safari" along the Brooklyn waterfront.

The decision by Satmar activists to employ the image of "war" to describe their campaign against gentrification is not surprising. First, it jibes with the long-standing Jewish apocalyptic tradition of portraying conflicts between the forces of good and the forces of evil in bluntly martial terms. Second, the Satmar declaration of holy war against the *artistn* reflects the classic rabbinic distinction between the categories of discretionary war (Hebrew, *milhemet reshut*) and religiously commanded wars (*milhemet hovah* and *milhemet mitzvah*), just as Christian and Muslim jurists have debated the nature of just war and jihad.[37] Finally, and closest to home, Satmar Hasidim and their antecedents have consistently employed militaristic language and imagery in their conflicts with opponents since at least the end of the nineteenth century.[38]

David Myers has outlined three cases in which Satmar Hasidim waged what they explicitly described as religiously "commanded wars" against opposing factions within the Jewish community. The first case occurred during the 1880s when the followers of the Yetev Lev, Rabbi Yekutiel Yehudah (1808–1883), engaged in a heated power struggle with a group of rabbinic opponents in Sighet; the second unfolded during the 1920s, when supporters of Rabbi Yoel Teitelbaum promoted his candidacy for town rabbi in a heavily contested election in Satmar. It was the third and final case, however, that had the closest connections with the war against the artists.

In the late 1980s, a group of Hasidic parents in Kiryas Joel, the Satmar village in Orange County, New York, sought to create a public school district to provide instruction for special-needs children in the community. They and their allies successfully lobbied for the passage of a state law creating the school district in 1989, only to see the U.S. Supreme Court rule in 1994 that the state law violated the Establishment

Clause of the First Amendment.[39] In addition to critics who opposed the district on constitutional grounds, some members of the Hasidic community rejected it on religious grounds. As Myers wrote, "For these groups, the creation of a public school district, intended for Hasidic children, within the carefully circumscribed boundaries of the *shtetl* was sacrilege. It would allow for streams of polluted foreign values to flow into the community. To blunt the thrust of this dangerous plan required a war, an 'obligatory war' (*Milhemet hovah*)."[40]

The intracommunal battle against the Kiryas Joel school district anticipated in several key ways the war against the *artistn* in Williamsburg, which took place only a few years later. Both cases involved a group of Satmar Hasidic zealots who launched a campaign against what they saw as an "invasion" of their holy community by alien forces; both directed most of their animus against a faction of their own community that they condemned for aiding and abetting this invasion; both stressed the moral contamination faced by the community's children; and both published declarations of "obligatory war" in which they blamed the current breach in the community's walls on the traditional Jewish concept of the "decline of the generations" (Hebrew, *yeridat ha-dorot*).[41] Finally, both the war in Kiryas Joel and the war against the *artistn* in Williamsburg were waged by some of the same zealous men, including Rabbi Avrohom Chaninah Leitner, a prominent Satmar educator and polemicist popularly known as the Montevideo Rav, who would play a key role in the war against the artists.[42]

For there to be no confusion within the Hasidic community about what constituted the holy territory of their enclave or, put differently, the borders of the turf that they were obligated to defend, the Committee to Save Williamsburg created a map of the neighborhood that was published in newspapers and posted in broadsides in the streets of the neighborhood. The map outlined two discrete zones: a white zone, located in the historical heart of South Williamsburg, where Hasidim were forbidden from selling or renting entirely to "the element"—that is, *artistn*—and a gray zone, which was not yet part of the Hasidic enclave but could be connected to it via future development. There, Hasidim were allowed to rent to *artistn* with short-term leases, but only after the seller had determined that he could not rent it to "our brothers, the sons of Israel. [Otherwise] it is understood that it is forbidden to sell there."[43]

On November 28, 2003, *Der Blatt* published an article about what it described as the "*artistn*-map which drew the borders of Williamsburg, indicating where it was forbidden according to the great rabbis of the city to rent or sell apartments to *artistn.*"[44] The article noted that a controversy had already erupted over the map because some members of the community felt that its borders had been drawn to protect the real estate projects of certain powerful Hasidic developers: "According to the critique being leveled in the street and before the Organization of Activists and Religious Functionaries of Williamsburg, the map was especially drawn up with political interests in mind so as to exclude certain projects from the mapped-out borders, to enable certain rich entrepreneurs to sell or rent entire projects to *artistn.*" Thus, while the stated goal of the map was to draw the borders of the Hasidic enclave, it ended up revealing fault lines within Hasidic Williamsburg, fault lines reflecting stark differences in socioeconomic status and influence between the haves and the have-nots. The incipient controversy over the map also laid bare what had perhaps been the fundamental tension within the Satmar community in Williamsburg since its founding, namely, the dialectic between an intense and uncompromising religious ideology, on the one hand, and an equally intense pragmatism, on the other.

Ground Zero: The Gretsch Building

In the same period that the "*artistn*-map" was making the rounds in the neighborhood, Hasidic activists launched a series of public gatherings and demonstrations against gentrification. The immediate target of their ire was the cavernous Gretsch Building, a former guitar factory located at 60 Broadway, right on the border of the Hasidic enclave. Like the nearby Schaefer Landing site on Kent Avenue, which was then being developed into luxury condominiums, the Gretsch Building was a relic of Williamsburg's long history as an industrial center. Unlike the former Schaefer brewery, however, which was being developed in partnership with the United Jewish Organizations and would include a percentage of affordable housing units, the Gretsch Building was owned by a pair of Orthodox, but not Hasidic, Jewish brothers from elsewhere in Brooklyn who intended to build luxury apartments priced at $550 a square foot, well out of the range of almost all Hasidic buyers at the time. As the tallest building on Broadway, the Gretsch development loomed large as a symbol of the kind of rapid gentrification that had caused average sales prices in the neighborhood to rise by 19 percent between June 2003 and June 2004.[45]

At the beginning of November 2003, concerned Hasidim gathered in the Kahal Yetev Lev d'Satmar Congregation on South 8th Street, right

Aron Friedman, the managing editor of *Der Yid*, Williamsburg, 1993
(Photograph by Maud B. Weiss; copyright Maud B. Weiss/
Gina Kehayoff Verlag)

around the block from the Gretsch Building, to protest the "scandalous in-justice of selling out our city and forsaking it for a couple of dollars," as an article in *Der Yid* put it. "Residents of Williamsburg should commit them-selves to struggle for the future of the neighborhood and to ensure that Williamsburg will remain, with God's help, a 'city and mother in Israel' until the arrival of the messiah."[46] *Der Yid* reported two weeks later that "hundreds of Jews had protested in front of the Gretsch Building in Wil-liamsburg," where they listened to a Satmar rabbi named Aaron Taub de-liver a speech in Yiddish in which he "called, in the name of the entire public, upon builders to have mercy upon our city and not to destroy the entire city on account of money," while another speaker declared in English that "we request that the city fathers pass a law that all the housing that is currently being rezoned should only be rezoned for 'affordable housing.' "[47]

A week later, *Der Yid* reported on an even larger demonstration, by more than a thousand Hasidim, in front of the Gretsch Building. Rabbi Aaron Taub opened the rally by paraphrasing a verse from the book of Es-ther in which Mordechai takes to the street to mourn after learning of Ha-man's plan to kill all the Jews in the Persian Empire.[48] Taub's message to the gathered Hasidim was clear: like the Jews of the Purim story, the Hasidic community of Williamsburg faced immanent destruction and needed to be saved, or as Taub declared to the crowd, "Let us all cry rescue!" Another speaker at the rally, Rabbi Avrohom Chaninah Leitner, condemned the Jewish developer of the Gretsch Building in no uncertain terms: "People say that the buyer is a Jew from Flatbush. He is not concerned with the protests of the Jews from Williamsburg, but with the Holy Torah he must reckon. The Holy Torah states, 'Cursed be he who makes the blind go astray in the way. And all the people shall say: Amen.' All who do this are cursed and excommunicated." (The verse is Deuteronomy 27:18.)

Rabbi Avrohom Chaninah Leitner (1929–2007) was one of the Hasidic activists who, in 1995, formally declared a "commanded war" against the supporters of the public school district in Kiryas Joel. Long before that, Leitner had earned a well-deserved reputation for zealotry, especially when it came to Zionism, which he condemned as the greatest threat of all to "Torah true Judaism."[49] Born in Grossvardein (Oradea, Romania), Leitner was imprisoned in the community's ghetto by the Nazis but managed to escape and make his way to Palestine via Turkey. Vehemently opposed to the creation of the State of Israel, Leitner immigrated to the United States, where he became one of Rabbi Yoel Teitelbaum's closest disciples in Williamsburg, even helping him edit his landmark anti-Zionist book, *VaYoel Moshe*, in the late 1950s. At the behest of the Satmar Rebbe, Leitner spent 1960 to 1964 in Montevideo, Uruguay, where he served as the leader of the city's small Satmar community. Even after he returned to Williamsburg and became the head of the Binyan Dovid Yeshiva, Leitner was popularly known as the Montevideo Rav because of his sojourn in South America. Over the years, Leitner participated in numerous protests against Zionism, including speaking in 1980 at a rally in Washington, D.C., in opposition to Israeli prime minister Menachem Begin's meeting with newly elected president Ronald Reagan.

In the fall of 2003, Leitner turned his considerable polemical energies against those Jews whom he considered collaborators with the *artistn* in Williamsburg. Before the massive protest in front of the Gretsch Building, Leitner gave a fiery speech in Congregation Yetev Lev D'Satmar, on South 8th Street, in which he invoked the Halakhic (legal) principle known as *din rodef*, or "law of the pursuer," to stress the grave consequences for any Jew who helped the *artistn* gentrify the Hasidic enclave in Williamsburg: "The people who are renting to *artistn* are causing many to sin, and he who causes someone else to sin is greater [i.e., worse] than he who kills someone. They have the legal status of a *rodef* [pursuer], concerning whom it is a commandment to kill. In truth, people would need to tear him to pieces [literally, "rip him apart like a fish"], only people cannot do this. In any case, each and every one who can do it is obligated to pursue and hinder them. This is certain: tomorrow people are going to protest, and each and every person is obligated to go protest. May God help that this will come to pass and all the evil will at present be annulled and we will merit the coming of the complete redemption."[50]

The law of the pursuer appears in the Babylonian Talmud Sanhedrin 73a, which states that a bystander is obligated to stop (literally, "save") a "pursuer" from murdering another individual by killing him first.[51] In his jeremiad against gentrification, Leitner argued that the law of the pursuer applied to Hasidim in Williamsburg who abetted the *artistn*, because they were guilty of causing others to sin by exposing them to moral contamination, which, according to another legal principle invoked by Leitner, made them even worse than murderers. While Leitner believed that such a "pursuer" deserved to be stopped by any means necessary, including death, he acknowledged that given the circumstances of living under American law, this was impossible. Instead, other Jews had to "pursue and hinder" them in nonlethal ways.

In the coming months, Hasidic activists attempted to maintain pressure on what they considered the beachhead for gentrification in their "holy corner" of Williamsburg. On the façade of a building across the street from the Gretsch Building, Hasidim hung a large banner declaring, "The neighborhood is NOT welcoming the Gretsch building. We need AFFORDABLE housing!" On January 4, 2004, Hasidim held a protest on South 8th Street against luxury development in Williamsburg and demanded more affordable housing in the neighborhood. The date chosen for the rally was fraught with symbolism and revealed the degree to which some Hasidic activists viewed gentrification through the lens of the long history of the Jewish people. In 2004, January 4 coincided with Asarah be-Tevet (the tenth day of the Hebrew month of Tevet), a traditional Jewish fast day commemorating the siege of Jerusalem in 589 BCE by the Babylonian ruler Nebuchadnezzar II, which eventually culminated in the destruction of the First Temple in 587 BCE. By holding the rally against gentrification on this day, Hasidim were explicitly drawing a parallel between the threatened destruction of their own *kehila kedosha* (holy community) in Williamsburg and the foundational catastrophe experienced by the Jewish people, namely, the *khurbn beys ha-mikdesh*, or "destruction of the Temple" in Jerusalem. The rally reflected an ancient Jewish tradition of assimilating contemporary events—in particular, catastrophes and experiences of redemption—to paradigmatic episodes from the Jewish past.

At the rally, Hasidic activists distributed a traditional *segulah* (protective invocation), in Hebrew, intended to ward off the invading army of gentrifiers that threatened to destroy the sacred precincts of Williamsburg, like a biblical plague sent by God to test his people:

> For the Protection of
>   Our City of Williamsburg
>   From the Plague of the Artists
>   Master of the Universe, have mercy upon us and upon the borders of our village and do not allow the persecution to come inside our home; please remove from upon us the plague of the artists, so that we shall not drown in evil waters, and so that they shall not come to our residence to ruin it. Please place in the hearts of the homeowners that they should not build, God forbid, for these people, and strengthen their hearts so that they can withstand this difficult test and so that they will not sell for the lure of money.[52]

The Hebrew text employed a series of phrases to draw a spatial and moral contrast between the Hasidic enclave—"our city of Williamsburg," "the borders of our village," and "inside our home"—and the dangerous realm that lay beyond—"the impurity and immorality that is growing in the world" and "the lowly American soil." Rather than focusing on the negative economic impact of real estate development in Williamsburg, the prayer emphasized existential and apocalyptic concerns, warning that new luxury buildings were part of a veritable invasion, a breaking down of the carefully constructed barriers between the Hasidic "camp of Israel" and the outside world.[53] In its Manichean depiction of the struggle over gentrification, the flyer strongly echoed Rabbi Yoel Teitelbaum's dualistic view of the world and appeared to confirm his fears concerning the possibility that the Hasidic community of Williamsburg might one day be contaminated by the culture of the surrounding city.[54]

In January 2004, *Der Yid* published lengthy excerpts of a speech given by Rabbi Yekusiel Yuda (aka Zalman Leib) Fulop at the rally opposing the Gretsch development. Fulop was a member of the Satmar *bes din*, or rabbinical court, in Williamsburg and therefore wielded significant influence within the community. He frequently weighed in—and typically took a hard line—on controversial issues.[55] In his speech at the rally, Fulop drew a parallel between the destruction of Jerusalem by the ancient Babylonians and the current "siege" of Williamsburg, the "Jerusalem of America," by the Babylonians of today, the "worst gentiles, the impure and lowly ones," namely, the *artistn:*

> Today [the 10th of Tevet] is a day of judgment on which people fast even if it falls on the Sabbath. Today people say the *slichot* [penitential prayers] "On this day the King of Babylon laid siege to Jerusalem" [Ezekiel 24:2]. This is speaking about the holy corner, "the Jerusalem of America," Williamsburg. The holy city where the holy rebbe, may his memory be for a blessing, purified the atmosphere in Williamsburg from the impurity of America so that people could establish here upstanding Jewish generations. Everyone knows that in the home country [eastern Europe], people were terrified of America, and people knew that when someone traveled to America, he was in [spiritual] danger. With God's help, people purified a corner, but now, due to our many sins, a bitter decree hangs over this holy corner. The biblical verse "On this day the King of Babylon laid siege to Jerusalem" is being fulfilled. The worst gentiles, the impure and lowly ones, have laid siege to our holy city, the Jerusalem of America . . . and they want to destroy our city.[56]

In the remainder of his remarks, Fulop addressed the grave consequences for those Hasidim who helped the *artistn*, including ending up in *gehenom* (basically, the Jewish equivalent of hell) after they died. Nor could such Hasidic collaborators hope to spiritually launder their impure money by donating some of it to charity, for such money was fundamentally *treyf,* and therefore it was as impossible to use it for holy purposes (educating children, building Jewish institutions), as forbidden as it would be to serve pork at a Sabbath meal:

> Everyone who has a part in this must understand clearly that they are sinners and are causing many to sin. . . . Those who cause thousands and thousands of Jewish children to sin will never leave *gehenom!* . . . They are bringing the worst impurity to this holy corner! What do they get from their millions? The money is *treyf* money, it

is ugly money. . . . With such money they cannot build any institutions, with such money they cannot educate their children.

Whereas other Hasidic critics in this period exhorted opponents of gentrification to publish the names and addresses of offenders, establish an office, raise funds, and so on, Rabbi Fulop stressed the need for a concerted spiritual response, focusing on penitential prayer and repentance:

> People must entreat the Master of the Universe to "let fear and terror fall upon them" [Exodus 15:16] that they [the gentrifiers] should not come here, and that God should send *hirhur teshuva* [stirrings of repentance], both for the sellers and for their enablers who seek to make excuses for them. . . . Each and every one must take it upon themselves—without an oath—to recite at least one chapter of Psalms each day concerning the bitter decree. May God help the Jewish children so that they shall be saved from this desperate situation.[57]

In February 2004, several months after Hasidic activists first declared the war against the *artistn* in Williamsburg, the *New York Times* published an article titled " 'Plague of Artists' a Battle Cry for Brooklyn Hasidim," about the atmosphere of crisis enveloping the neighborhood: "[Hasidic] community members say, real estate agents and would-be buyers have knocked on their doors offering to buy their homes for at least double the $200 per square foot they are used to paying. Many fear that if even a few agree to that, market rates and property taxes will soar, leading to an unraveling of the community's tightly woven fabric."[58] The *Times* reported that Hasidim were particularly upset that the developers of the Gretsch Building were Orthodox Jews who had purchased the property from a local Satmar Hasid. As Maier Katz, a Hasidic protester put it, "If it's not a Jew, it's not our business, we can't do anything. . . . If it's a Jew, we can do something." Sam Brown, a Satmar real estate investor, added, "We made it very clear for the seller and buyer, in all kinds of language, to explain that they should not do this because it's hurting the interests of the community . . . they were ignoring our pleas." The *Times* also noted that the developers of the building were going out of their way to accommodate Hasidic sensibilities: "A plan to add balconies was scrapped to reduce the chance that scantily clad residents would be visible on them; tinting was added to windows on two sides for the same reason. When the Hasidim balked at an idea for an enclosed swimming pool because people in bathing suits might step out onto the sidewalk, that plan was discarded, he [one of the developers] said, adding that a rabbi from the community gave the project his blessing."[59]

Despite these efforts to placate Hasidic critics, fierce local opposition to the conversion of the Gretsch Building continued into the summer of 2004. On June 16, an estimated crowd of more than three thousand Hasidim, including hundreds of yeshiva students bused in from elsewhere in Brooklyn, held a massive rally at the intersection of Wythe Avenue and South 8th Street. The *New York Post* described the scene: "A sea of black . . . seeing red in Williamsburg . . . Local Hasidim protested the skyrocketing prices of housing in Brooklyn's hippest neighborhood."[60] David Heimlich, a Hasidic protester and real estate broker, explained his opposition by referring to the community's investment in infrastructure: "We've been living here for 40 or 50 years, we've invested tens of millions of dollars for institutions, schools, synagogues." Rabbi David Niederman, director of the UJO, "stressed the fight was not Jew against non-Jew," adding, "There is nobody in the entire area who can pay $500 to $700 [per square foot] for their apartments, I don't care if they are Hasidic, Hispanic or artists." He "blamed developers both outside and inside the orthodox community who he said were trying to make a fast buck."

It is notable that among the protesters at these rallies were Hasidim involved in the real estate industry. The opposition of such people to the Gretsch Building and similar luxury developments in the neighborhood indicated the emergence of a split within the Hasidic community in Williamsburg over the direction of real estate development and its relationship to gentrification. For many Hasidim, real estate speculation was acceptable, even desirable, as long as it took place on the North Side of Williamsburg and did not—directly, at least—impact the Hasidic enclave in South Williamsburg. As gentrification proceeded in Williamsburg, however, some Hasidic real estate developers were willing to build even when doing so would clearly raise prices in the Hasidic enclave, decrease the availability of affordable housing for their fellow community members, and introduce morally problematic influences into the neighborhood. The stakes for the Hasidim in Williamsburg could not have been higher, for as a Hasidic mortgage broker named "Motl" who lived around the block from the Gretsch Building put it to us, "Goyim can live wherever they want. But we *yidn* [Jews] must live together in the same place. We cannot just move."[61]

Hasidic Housing Discrimination or Grassroots Activism?

Among the most vexing and provocative questions raised by the Hasidic war against the artists was whether it constituted illegal housing discrimination by members of the Hasidic community in Williamsburg or whether it was one of the most radical grassroots struggles against gentrification waged by any local community in the history of New York City. Put differently, was the Hasidic campaign against gentrification an effort to encourage illegal residential segregation, or was it an attempt to protect a deeply rooted community with many low-income members from being displaced by wealthier newcomers? Or was it perhaps both?

To answer these questions, or at least appreciate the complexities underlying them, it is first necessary to situate the Hasidic campaign against gentrification within the broader history of housing discrimination in the United States. One striking element in the campaign was the map of Williamsburg created and distributed by Hasidic activists identifying zones in which Hasidic residents were either prohibited from renting or selling property to *artistn* (the so-called white zone) or were permitted to offer *artistn* short-term leases, but only after first ensuring that there were no Hasidim interested in buying the property (the gray zone). The creation of a map with color-demarcated zones to encourage residential segregation will undoubtedly remind some readers of the maps employed in the infamous practice known as redlining.

Beginning with the passage of the National Housing Act of 1934, the federal government—and some private entities—drew maps of municipalities in which neighborhoods were given different letter ratings (with "A" being the best and "D" the worst) based on their racial and ethnic composition, supposed desirability, and other factors. In the maps, the borders of these neighborhoods were outlined in different colors depending on their letter rating, with the "best" areas outlined in green and the "worst" ones outlined in red—hence, the origin of the term "redlining." Residents of redlined neighborhoods had great difficulty getting mortgages and other services, since the Federal Housing Administration (FHA) both refused to provide insurance to lenders and discouraged them from doing business in such areas. Not surprisingly, many of the redlined neighborhoods, especially in the older cities of the Northeast and Midwest, were inhabited largely by African Americans. Less well known is that in a number of places, including Brooklyn, heavily Jewish neighborhoods such as Williamsburg were also redlined. Predictably, the result of redlining was to concentrate poorer residents and racial and ethnic minorities in "undesirable" neighborhoods, and wealthier white residents in "desirable" ones, and, concomitantly, to cause the housing stock and infrastructure of redlined areas to decline from a lack of financial investment.

Although both strategies employed color-coded maps to promote forms of residential segregation, redlining and the Hasidic campaign against gentrification had little else in common when it came to the racial and class dynamics involved. A closer parallel, perhaps, was the use of restrictive or exclusionary covenants to preserve and promote racial, ethnic, or religious segregation. These kinds of private covenants or deed agreements became especially popular following the U.S. Supreme Court decision in *Buchanan v. Warley* (1917), which declared racially restrictive zoning ordinances unconstitutional. (The decision relied on the sanctity of property rights and not the possible unconstitutionality of racial discrimination, which the Court did not address.) Unable to rely on municipal zoning to enforce segregation, many private home-owner associations and real estate developers around the country drew up deed agreements or covenants that prohibited a buyer of property from selling or leasing to members of particular ethnic, racial, or religious groups, including African Americans, Jews, Italians, Mexicans, and Asians. Not only did the federal government tolerate this practice, but the FHA explicitly promoted it, for example in its *Underwriting Manual* in 1938, which stated, "If a neighborhood is to retain stability, it is necessary that properties shall continue to be occupied by the same social and racial groups," and even included a model restrictive covenant that recommended "prohibition of the occupancy of properties except by the race for which they are intended."[62]

Like the restrictive covenants adopted by homeowner associations, the Hasidic campaign against gentrification sought to preserve the existing character of the enclave by preventing residents from selling or leasing to a particular group of outsiders. Yet unlike the authors of such covenants, the Hasidic activists who waged the war against the artists never called for the emendation of deed agreements or other documents to accomplish their goal. In 1948, the U.S. Supreme Court had ruled in *Shelley v. Kraemer* that exclusionary covenants were unenforceable under the Equal Protection Clause of the Fourteenth Amendment. While Hasidic activists may not have known the relevant case history, they were undoubtedly savvy enough about real estate law—indeed, the Yiddish newspapers in Williamsburg published virtual primers on zoning regulations, mortgage types, and so on—to avoid anything resembling a restrictive covenant. Instead, the architects of the campaign made moral, spiritual, and economic arguments to persuade Hasidim in Williamsburg not to sell or lease to *artistn* and threatened potential transgressors with public shaming, shunning, and the prospect of suffering for their sins in *gehenom* if they did.

In 1968, the passage of the Federal Housing Act made it illegal to refuse to sell or rent on the basis of membership in certain protected classes. Initially, these classes were limited to race, color, religion, sex, and national origin; in 1988, disability and familial status (such as the presence of children under eighteen years old or a pregnant woman in the household) were added to the list of protected categories. In addition to these federal provisions, the City of New York passed its Human Rights Law, which prohibited housing discrimination based on an expanded list of protected classes, including age, alienage or citizenship status, color, disability, gender identity, marital status and partnership status, national origin, pregnancy, race, religion or creed, sexual orientation, as well as additional protections based on lawful occupation, lawful source of income, the presence of children, and status as a victim of domestic violence, stalking, or sexual offenses.

Were *artistn* members of a legally protected class according to either of these statutes? At first glance, the answer appears to be no, since being a hipster or a gentrifier more generally—both possible definitions of the Yiddish term—was not a matter of belonging to a particular race, religion, sex, and so on. Even if one wanted to argue that most—though not all—*artistn* were white, it was not their race or color per se that led to the Hasidic campaign against them, but rather their supposed immorality and their economic impact on the neighborhood. It is also important to note that Hasidic activists were not calling for housing discrimination against *artistn* because they were non-Jews; indeed, they were no happier about the prospect of Jewish *artistn* moving into Williamsburg than they were about their gentile counterparts. In other words, the war against the artists was clearly, even proudly calling for housing discrimination within the borders of the Hasidic enclave, but not against a class of people explicitly protected from such discrimination under existing federal or local laws. Nor does it appear that any *artistn* ever attempted to file a lawsuit against Hasidic landlords or developers in Williamsburg for engaging in housing discrimination against them, although Brooklyn Legal Services did attempt, unsuccessfully, to demonstrate such discrimination on behalf of black and Latino plaintiffs.

Rather than the prism of illegal housing discrimination, we might view certain aspects of the war against the artists through another, very different lens, namely, as a grassroots effort by members of an "indigenous" local community to prevent their threatened displacement by gentrifiers. Thus, for example, instead of redlining, we might fruitfully compare the white and gray zones in the anti-gentrification map created by Hasidic activists in Williamsburg to the "neighborhood anti-gentrification zones," proposed by New York state senator Adriano Espaillat in his 2016 campaign for the Thirteenth Congressional District, comprising Harlem, the rest of Upper Manhattan, and a small section of the Bronx.[63] Espaillat's campaign website stated: "In order to address the vital issue of preserving neighborhoods in the face of such overwhelming forces, Congress should establish federal gentrification mitigation zones supported by the federal Department of Housing and Urban Development (HUD). These neighborhoods would be identified based on their history as a working-class area, with a connection to immigrant or minority communities, where property values have increased at a certain percentage above the average for the rest of the city, and in which the pre-existing population shows signs of being displaced." Similar to the gray zone of the Hasidic-designed map, where landlords were required to offer the option of leasing to Hasidic residents of the neighborhood before opening it up to *artistn*, these proposed federal gentrification mitigation zones would include a "right of first refusal for sale of residential buildings," meaning that "tenants of a particular residential building within the zone should have an automatic right of refusal any time the building owner seeks to sell that building."[64]

Indeed, viewed through the wider lens of anti-gentrification activism in New York City, the Committee to Save Williamsburg may be seen as a pioneering organization in what would eventually become a borough-wide phenomenon in Brooklyn. The movement took in numerous neighborhood-based anti-gentrification groups, such as the Greenpoint-Williamsburg Tenant Anti-Displacement Collaborative, the Crown Heights Tenant Union, the Flatbush Tenants' Coalition, the Movement to Protect the People (which focused on Lefferts Gardens and Crown Heights), and, in 2015, more than a decade after the Hasidic campaign was launched, the Brooklyn Anti-Gentrification Network, which was established as "a people of color-led, mass-based coalition of tenants, homeowners, block associations, anti-police brutality groups, legal and grassroots organizations working together to end the rampant gentrification and displacement of low to middle income residents of Brooklyn, New York."[65] Ironically, it was the Movement to Protect the People, a Brooklyn anti-gentrification organization that some accused of engaging in anti-Semitic rhetoric, that most closely resembled the Hasidic war against the artists in its confrontational methods, harsh criticism of gentrifiers and suspected community collaborators (whom it called "Uncle Toms"), emphasis on cultural loss and negative economic impacts, and concern for the effects of gentrification on local children.[66]

Although many Hasidim in Williamsburg, Crown Heights, and elsewhere in Brooklyn were involved in opposing gentrification in their neighborhoods, the Brooklyn Anti-Gentrification Network, which served as an umbrella organization for numerous local groups, did not include any Hasidic organizations. Their glaring absence reflected a number of interrelated factors. First, most Hasidic anti-gentrification activists were concerned with protecting only their own enclaves rather than forming alliances to oppose gentrification per se. In a few notable cases, such as the anti-incinerator movement in Williamsburg and the aftermath of the Crown Heights riots, Hasidim in Brooklyn collaborated with their black, Latino, and even artist neighbors for the greater good of the entire neighborhood, but that kind of cooperation did not happen with the struggle against gentrification, at least not in the early 2000s. Instead, the long and bitter history of competition between Hasidim and other ethnic groups over affordable housing in Brooklyn, along with the contemporary pressure to find such housing in a climate of governmental retrenchment and private-sector real estate speculation, appears to have encouraged a zero-sum attitude among many Hasidic anti-gentrification activists. Rather than working together with other community organizations, the most passionate and vocal Hasidic activists preferred to go it alone, an approach that reflected the fact that many of the most radical Hasidic anti-gentrification activists came from the most intensely isolationist circles within the Satmar community and therefore were ideologically opposed to collaborating with others unless absolutely necessary.

Yet it was not only the separatist or zero-sum attitudes of the Hasidic activists that may have kept them from participating in the broader struggle against gentrification in Brooklyn. Anti-gentrification organizations in Brooklyn typically omitted Hasidic areas from their lists of threatened local communities. For example, a flyer announcing the creation of the Crown Heights Tenants Union in 2014 called for "an end to the rigged system that pushes out long-term Black, West Indian, and Latino tenants," yet did not mention the large Lubavitcher community in the neighborhood, even though many longtime Hasidic residents of Crown Heights were being driven out because of rising real estate prices.[67] Another grassroots group, the United Neighbors Organization, whose mission was to fight "for affordable housing in Williamsburg and Greenpoint, Brooklyn," noted in 2012: "Williamsburg and Greenpoint are now known as two of the hottest neighborhoods in New York. . . . But in reality, this community is the home of hundreds of Latino, African-American, Polish and Italian working families that are at risk every day of losing their homes from the increasing waive [*sic*] of gentrification and real state [*sic*] speculation." Strikingly absent from this list of affected residents were local Hasidim, even though large numbers of them were also being forced to abandon Williamsburg for the same reasons.[68]

The significant presence of Hasidic landlords and developers throughout northern and central Brooklyn—including some on the Crown Heights Tenants Union's "Worst Landlord Watchlist"—contributed to a sense among some housing activists in the borough that Hasidim, in general, were on the wrong side of the gentrification divide, regardless of the fact that many Hasidic community members were being priced out of the same neighborhoods. This created a kind of cognitive dissonance when it came to Hasidim and gentrification in Brooklyn. In addition, the bad behavior of some Hasidim involved in the Brooklyn real estate industry tapped into deeply rooted and widespread anti-Semitic stereotypes regarding Jewish economic exploitation in general, and the figure of the "Jewish landlord" in particular. Rather than seeing exploitative Hasidic landlords as corrupt individuals—the way they might see exploitative landlords of other backgrounds—some critics viewed them through the lens of these stereotypes and indicted the entire Hasidic community.

Aftermath

The "war against the artists," which began in 2003, ended with neither victory nor defeat. Indeed, it never really ended at all, even though the intense media campaign and the large public demonstrations that had characterized the initial phase, between 2003 and 2004, were not sustained. In the ensuing years, passionate opposition to gentrification continued unabated in certain circles of Hasidic Williamsburg and, arguably, become even more desperate as real estate prices climbed higher and higher and demographic pressures increased with every passing year, factors that combined to exacerbate a long-standing housing crisis in the neighborhood. Employing a combination of moral persuasion and threats, the war against the artists succeeded in convincing or at least intimidating some members of the community into following anti-gentrification directives when it came to renting or selling to gentrifiers. Moreover, the campaign created a climate in which Hasidic developers were forced to consider the needs of the *heymish* (literally, "homey") community, as Hasidim often referred to themselves, when buying or building on sites in Williamsburg or its immediate environs. The Committee to Save Williamsburg continued to be active throughout the decade, and as late as 2015, Hasidim in the neighborhood were still decrying—and debating—the ongoing threat of gentrification in gatherings, public demonstrations, the Hasidic press, and new, Yiddish-language forums on the Internet.

Despite its successes, however, the war against the artists did not halt the march of gentrification in the neighborhood, particular along its northern border of Broadway and on the stretch of Kent Avenue near the Williamsburg Bridge. In this area of prime real estate, developers with increasingly deep pockets—many of them from New York City's most powerful real estate firms or from elsewhere in the United States or abroad—competed with one another to build ever grander and more expensive projects, even as the demand for affordable housing in Williamsburg increased yearly. At the same time, tensions intensified over the area beyond Flushing Avenue, the traditional southern border of the Hasidic enclave, which was now dubbed "New Williamsburg" by Hasidim, who found themselves in a veritable race with gentrifiers to buy property there and develop new housing.

A number of factors undermined the effectiveness of the war against the artists in both the short and long term. Despite all efforts to stop the Gretsch Building from being transformed into luxury condominiums, the project went ahead as planned. Instead of serving as a symbol of the Hasidic community's ability to maintain the integrity of its borders, therefore, the Gretsch Building became a looming monument to the power of money even in the face of staunch community opposition.

Rather than being inspired or persuaded by the campaign against the gentrifiers, some members of the Hasidic community in Williamsburg were turned off by its emphasis on morality. Hasidic critics of the war against the artists also disagreed with the unremittingly pejorative way that the *artistn* were being portrayed, took a more moderate stance than the Hasidic activists when it came to other issues (for example, women's modesty), did not agree with the campaign's strong-arm tactics, and viewed the activists as hypocrites who looked the other way at real estate deals that benefited members of their inner circle. One Hasidic resident of Williamsburg succinctly expressed to us the cynicism that some community members felt toward those who had led the war against the artists: "[They] care about 'their holy city being destroyed,' but if they have a chance to make money, they suddenly realize that there's enough holiness to go around, even if a little gets destroyed. And the fact is that the ones who owned properties, or could afford to invest in properties that the hipsters wanted, were the people who tend to be close to the rabbis, part of the *hanhalah* [administrative or leadership class], big *tsedakah* [charity] givers, etc. These are the people who ultimately make the rules."[69]

The death of the Satmar Rebbe, Moshe Teitelbaum, in 2006, which greatly intensified the heated conflict between supporters of his sons, Aaron and Zalman, also helped shape the Hasidic community's response to gentrification in the following years. Rather than forming a united front against the gentrifiers, members of both factions fought over the more than $1 billion in communal property in Williamsburg. Real estate deals within the neighborhood became increasingly politicized by the festering intracommunal conflict, and Hasidic developers belonging to one camp were accused of aiding the *artistn* by their opponents, who, in turn, were accused of unfairly opposing these projects because of their own sectarian interests. And so on. Finally, the landmark passage of the Greenpoint-Williamsburg Waterfront Rezoning in 2005 transformed the landscape of the neighborhood and introduced a new era of real estate development, which some termed "hyper-gentrification." The rezoning attracted many new players, including major foreign investors and developers, to the blocks directly bordering the Hasidic enclave. This had the dual effect of decreasing the leverage of the Hasidic community while increasing the financial incentives for Hasidic developers to build market-rate projects that would appeal to *artistn* rather than to other Hasidim.

CHAPTER SEVEN

A Fruit Tree Grows in Brooklyn

I N A TREE GROWS *in Brooklyn*, Betty Smith's classic 1943 novel of poverty and childhood resilience set in Williamsburg, a central motif is a mythical plant called the "Tree of Heaven." Growing only from concrete, the tree magically predicts the spread of tenements in the neighborhood. When one of these trees appears on a building's property, people know that the building will soon become dilapidated. Once the tree takes root, "poor foreigners seeped in and the quiet old brownstone houses were hacked up into flats, feather beds were pushed out on the window sills to air and the Tree of Heaven flourished. That was the kind of tree it was. It liked poor people." Although the tree is cut down, it miraculously grows again. In a Hasidic twist on Smith's story, another kind of tree came to haunt Williamsburg in the first few decades of the twenty-first century. Rather than marking the decline of the neighborhood, however, fruit trees became a symbol of how, even as Hasidic developers in Williamsburg emerged as major players in the booming Brooklyn real estate market, they remained deeply rooted in the particular beliefs and practices of their community. On another level, fruit trees served as a particularly apt metaphor for the Satmar community in Williamsburg, whose symbol was the date palm, a fruit-bearing tree that could not be cut down or uprooted.

Like Smith's Tree of Heaven, fruit trees inspired wonder and fear among many Hasidic residents of Williamsburg, who considered cutting one down to be strictly forbidden by long-standing custom, even if not by Jewish law.[1] For those Hasidim in the burgeoning real estate business, fruit trees could hold up deals, delay construction, and cost millions of dollars in overruns or lost labor.[2] Hasidic property owners built staircases and even entire buildings around fruit trees to avoid damaging them.[3] In one case in Williamsburg, a desperate Hasidic developer pleaded with the local rabbinic court to help him figure out what do with a lot he had purchased for several million dollars, only to discover later that it contained a fruit tree. He lamented that other Hasidim did not want to purchase the property because they would then face the same problem, yet he could not sell the land to a non-Hasidic developer, because community members would condemn him for abetting gentrification. In a *New York* magazine profile, a Hasidic landlord described his experience with fruit trees:

Some people really don't give a shit about fruit trees. But most of the Hasidic Jewish people will not cut down a fruit tree. There's one house in Borough Park where they cut down a fruit tree and there was nine fires over there in the last two years. Sometimes weird stuff happens. So we had a building, and the only way it's working for us is if the fruit tree comes down. We spent $50,000 doing the plans and then found out there's a fruit tree. We didn't know about it. So we had to sell the building. It's the only way I'm going to sell a building.[4]

The prohibition against cutting down fruits trees is a particularly striking example of how Jewish legal rulings, mystical beliefs, and folk practices profoundly shaped the way that Hasidim in Williamsburg engaged in real estate development. But it is only one of many. Even as they mastered the finer points of financing, zoning regulations, and the Fair Housing Act, Hasidic real estate developers also needed to ensure that their business practices accorded with their community's norms and traditions, sometimes requiring them to lose significant amounts of money in the process.[5] Many Hasidim, for instance, held that hired non-Jewish builders could not work on the Sabbath and holidays, or that certain days of the week and month were inauspicious times to begin construction. In other cases, Hasidim drew on the rich trove of Jewish folk and magical beliefs to facilitate success or avoid disaster from the

Hasidic house built around a fruit tree to avoid cutting it down, 2020
(Photograph by Eli Wohl)

evil eye and other destructive forces. In this regard, many Hasidic developers from Williamsburg swore by the power of amulets inspired by the
Kerestirer Rov, Rabbi Yeshaya Steiner (1851–1925), to stop rodent infestations. Steiner was said to have miraculously cured a mouse problem in
a tiny town in northeastern Hungary, and by the early 2000s his distinctive portrait could be seen throughout Brooklyn, tacked to the tall green
wooden fences around construction sites. In all of these ways and more,
the new class of Hasidic developers sought to bridge two worlds by har-
monizing their religious beliefs with their real estate practices.

"Fortis of Solitude"

The story of Louis Kestenbaum, whose Fortis Group conducted numerous high-end real estate deals in New York City during the 2000s, exem-
plifies the ways in which an emerging class of Hasidic real estate
developers in Brooklyn sought to negotiate the demands of their community with those of the real estate industry. Born in a displaced-persons
camp in Milan after World War II, Louis was the son of Zvi Kesten-

baum, the Holocaust survivor who founded the Opportunity Development Association, the Williamsburg community organization whose lobbying efforts, as outlined in chapter 3, secured Hasidim status as a legally recognized "disadvantaged minority group."[6] We met with Kestenbaum in the boardroom of his office in the Walentas family's Two Trees Management building in Dumbo (Down Under the Manhattan Bridge Overpass), another heavily gentrified neighborhood, two miles west of Williamsburg at the foot of the Manhattan Bridge. Hard copies of the *Real Deal*, a New York City real estate trade publication, were on display in the waiting room, and his assistant offered kosher catering and tea. We were joined by Louis's son Joel, the president of Fortis, and their non-Hasidic Jewish assistant David, who began working for the family under Zvi at the ODA.

Louis and Joel Kestenbaum represented different generations of Williamsburg Hasidim. The father leaned forward in his chair while speaking animatedly, occasionally punctuating his points by banging his fist on the table, while the son, sporting a deep tan, chimed in from behind an iPad. In a wide-ranging conversation, we discussed how being a Hasidic Jew affected his work in the real estate business. When asked about fruit trees, Louis's eyes widened and he sat up straight. He said that he would never cut down a fruit tree or arrange for a non-Jew to do so, and that he had backed out of very good deals because a fruit tree had been found on the property. "I spent hundreds of thousands of dollars on my home in Miami Beach to avoid touching a fruit tree," Louis said. His son Joel joked, "Want to buy some properties with fruit trees?"

In the interview, we discussed the arc of his career as well as the transformation of Hasidic Williamsburg that had occurred in the same period. At one time, Louis said, "Williamsburg was like a ghetto. Everybody lived in one place and dressed one way, like a shtetl." Then, "fortunately and unfortunately the [real estate] market changed." Louis was one of the people to experience the drastic changes in the neighborhood in a fortunate way. He initially went into the apparel business, and the factory buildings that this line of work necessitated were later critical to his transition into real estate. In 1984, Louis Kestenbaum purchased 184 Kent Avenue, a former grocery warehouse, for his garment business on the North Williamsburg waterfront, for $56,000. The building was designed by Cass Gilbert, the noted architect of the iconic Woolworth Building in Manhattan and the U.S. Supreme Court Building, but had fallen into disrepair. Kestenbaum told us that the neighborhood was then

Hasidic construction site featuring a portrait of Yeshayah Steiner,
the Kerestirer Rov, known for miraculously curing mice infestations,
New Williamsburg, 2018 (Photograph by Michael Casper)

so dangerous that people were afraid to leave work at the end of the day. But by the early 1990s, he was letting artists and young professionals build out living spaces in unfinished floors of the 1915 building, which is now on the National Register of Historic Places, in part because of its pioneering use of reinforced concrete. Sensing broader changes afoot in the neighborhood, in 2004 Kestenbaum presciently, and successfully, lobbied the city's Board of Standards and Appeals for a zoning variance that would allow him to convert the building to residential use; in return, he offered to construct a public promenade by the building and donate over $300,000 to a fund for local affordable housing.

Tenants were not pleased with the proposal. As one thirty-one-year-old resident told the *New York Daily News* at the time, "The larger issue is that the whole waterfront will be redeveloped, and this will set a bad precedent."[7] Indeed, just a year later, the city council approved a large-scale rezoning of Williamsburg and Greenpoint, whose upzoned waterfront section, from North 3rd to North 7th Streets, used the already-residential 184 Kent as an anchor. Also in 2004, Kestenbaum expanded his real estate business by forming the Fortis Group with Joel Landau, a Cleveland-based lawyer who was Jewish but not Hasidic. According to a *Real Deal* profile titled "Fortis of Solitude"—a riff on the title of a Jonathan Lethem novel set in Brooklyn—"At the time, Kestenbaum was a sort of one-off developer who also ran a sportswear business. The two decided to team up to build a more official venture. . . . In its first two years, Fortis acquired some $3 billion in cash-flowing properties" outside New York City.[8] Fortis entered the Brooklyn market with the 2011 purchase of a building near McCarren Park. After a successful rehab, they started to develop on the Williamsburg waterfront and then moved into Manhattan. By 2015, when Fortis successfully bid $240 million for the Long Island College Hospital, operated by the State University of New York in Brooklyn (SUNY Downstate Health Sciences University), Louis Kestenbaum had traveled worlds from the Williamsburg of the 1970s, when his father, Zvi, had founded the ODA to provide, in his own words, "services to Hasidic entrepreneurs and other ethnic groups to compete effectively within the American economic mainstream . . . [and] save and revitalize a declining neighborhood in Brooklyn, NY."[9]

In our conversation, Louis Kestenbaum took pains to stress that he was continuing the community service and philanthropy of his father even as he also worked as a developer of high-end real estate. Like his father, Kestenbaum became the chairman of the ODA, which, at the time of our interview, operated six community health care clinics in Williamsburg and two summer clinics in the Catskills. In addition to continuing to operate the ODA, Kestenbaum emphasized that he donated a significant amount of money to the Hasidic community, even opening his doors once a week to receive the needy and give charity to them directly. He mentioned building wedding halls in Williamsburg—named after his parents—that offered complete package weddings, including music, *badkhn* (master of ceremonies), and food for hundreds of guests, for what was considered the bargain price of $10,500. Louis explained that this was both a way to allow less fortunate Hasidim to have "very nice weddings" and also to discourage *luksus* (luxury) among wealthier Hasidim who might be inclined to spend lavishly. Undoubtedly, Kestenbaum was motivated to give back to his community by the central Jewish commandment of *tsedakah* (charity), the desire to honor his father's philanthropic legacy, and the Hasidic expectation that wealthy community members donate to needier ones. And doing so was especially important at a time of increasing criticism, suspicion, and resentment of Hasidic developers and property owners by the Hasidic community. Against this backdrop, Kestenbaum's prodigious charitable giving could be seen as a way to demonstrate that his vast wealth could "trickle down" to the much larger number of financially struggling Hasidim, for whom the luxury-building boom in Williamsburg had only deepened the long-standing housing crisis in the neighborhood.

On the Waterfront

In the same period that Louis Kestenbaum, the chair of the ODA, was developing his waterfront property at 184 Kent, Rabbi David Niederman, the executive director and president of United Jewish Organizations (UJO), another large social-services provider for the Hasidic community in South Williamsburg, was negotiating with city officials and private developers to include affordable housing units in a planned luxury waterfront development to be located a few blocks away on the site of the Schaefer Brewery. These parallel stories reveal the different ways that Hasidic power brokers and activists from Williamsburg became deeply involved in the wave of real estate development spurred by gentrification. In a study of Williamsburg and Greenpoint in this period, Filip Stabrowski argued that local "community-based organizations (or CBOs)," like the UJO, "have gone from grassroots organizations devoted to community organizing and self-help in the face of widespread disinvestment and government neglect to multipurpose agencies involved in the (often conflicting) demands of affordable housing development, social service provision and community organizing." Stabrowski cited Nicole Marwell, who noted that in North Brooklyn, "CBOs have become increasingly important 'meso-level' actors in the 'entrepreneurial city.' "[10] Against the backdrop of this broader phenomenon, which intensified with the rezoning of the Williamsburg-Greenpoint waterfront in 2005, United Jewish Organizations emerged as a pioneer in what some would come to call the "nonprofit industrial complex."

Schaefer Landing, as the development at 440 Kent Avenue was named, was initially hailed as a model for the kind of private-nonprofit collaborations that the rezoning of the waterfront was supposed to encourage. But that praise came from only certain sectors of the local community, and given the ultimately dismal course of affordable-housing construction in the rezoned area, it was premature in its optimism. Like many of Williamsburg's most iconic waterfront sites—for example, the Domino Sugar Refinery at 314 Kent Avenue, which would be developed by Two Trees Management, and the Kedem Wine factory at 420 Kent Avenue, which would be developed by (Eliot) Spitzer Enterprises— Schaefer Landing had deep roots in the area's industrial past. In 1915, the F. & M. Schaefer Brewing Company relocated from Manhattan to the Williamsburg waterfront, where it built a state-of-the-art brewery, part of a wave of construction that transformed North Brooklyn into one of the most important brewing centers in the United States. Surviving the lean years of Prohibition by manufacturing "near beer," Schaefer was both the longest-operating brewery and the last one in New York City by the time it was shut down, in 1976, when operations shifted to a new plant in the Lehigh Valley, taking along 850 jobs in the process.[11] For the next few decades, members of the Hasidic community and, in particular, the UJO had eyed the land—by then owned by the city—as a potential site for developing affordable housing.

In a December 2003 article published in *Der Yid*, Rabbi David Niederman explained: "[The] former Schaefer Brewery Building, which has already been vacant and uninhabited for ten years, is the only piece of land within Williamsburg itself that still belongs to the city. Years ago we began to request that the city should build inexpensive apartments in the area for residents of Williamsburg."[12] But, the article continued, "during the last two years the city has claimed that it does not have the money to dedicate the 'entire' project to low-income residents, and it was even about to sell the land for the full price [in a public auction], where all the developers would be able to compete for the project without any obligation [to develop affordable housing], either to the city or to the neighborhood where the project was located." At that point, the UJO lobbied Ken Fisher, then the city councilman for the neighborhood, and Mayor Rudolph Giuliani, whom *Der Yid* described as "unusually helpful to the Orthodox Jewish public in general and in Williamsburg in particular," to put a halt to the public auction. Instead, the UJO proposed that the city require any future developer to set aside 40 percent of the units built on the site for low-income tenants—the maximum amount possible—and that the UJO be named the official community sponsor of the project. Following negotiations, according to *Der Yid*, the city appointed the UJO as the community sponsor for the development and "in order to create an incentive for the construction of inexpensive apartments, the city gave away the land for these apartments for free, and the developer only had to pay for the part of the land designated for the expensive apartments."

Kent Waterfront Associates, the firm chosen to develop the site, proposed to build "215 owner-occupied luxury units and 140 rental units affordable to families earning up to 60 percent of [area median income], which is $37,680 for a family of four."[13] In addition to "a 40 percent reduction in land cost given by the City in exchange for affordable housing," the developer received a twenty-five-year tax abatement and $8 million in environmental remediation of the area.[14] As the community sponsor, the UJO ran the lottery for the affordable-housing units in the development, opened an office to help people fill out applications, and successfully argued that half of the affordable units should go to residents of the neighborhood.[15] In the days leading up to the lottery, the office of Vito Lopez, the assemblyman for Williamsburg, estimated that between 15,000 and 20,000 people would apply for the 140 affordable units.[16]

Although the UJO could not guarantee that members of the Hasidic community would be successful in the lottery for affordable units in Schaefer Landing, their role as community sponsor meant that local Hasidim would be made aware of the lottery early in the process, that notices would be published in Yiddish (along with Spanish and English), and that they would receive aid in filling out the necessary paperwork. Moreover, the design of the low-income rental units in Schaefer Landing reflected "special accouterments required by the Chasidic community: master bedrooms with enough space for separate beds, pairs of sinks for compliance with Kashrut laws, and an outdoor space for a sukkah [a shelter for use during the holiday of Sukkoth]."[17] As with many luxury buildings in New York seeking tax breaks and other financial incentives, the affordable apartments built in Schaefer Landing would lack the waterfront views of the luxury units and would have a separate, decidedly unglamorous entrance, with its own address.

The choice of the UJO as a sponsor and the accommodation of Hasidic needs in the design of the low-income units raised concerns among the neighborhood's Latino residents that the process was rigged in favor of the Hasidic community. As David Pagan, the executive director of Los Sures, told the *New York Sun*, "We just want to make sure we're not excluded." Others were more pointed in their criticism, such as Jercy Bautista, a longtime resident of the neighborhood, who complained to the newspaper, "The Jews want to control the whole area. . . . It used to be divided between the Jews and Latinos. Now you have the Jews, the Latinos, and people from Manhattan. We cannot all be in the same space."[18] Ultimately, the racial breakdown of low-income tenants in Schaefer Landing would be "43% Hispanic, 42% white, 9% black, and 6% Asian," with an unspecified number of Hasidic tenants.[19] Black and Latino residents would occupy thirty-five of the affordable units with three or four bedrooms, while whites—most likely Hasidim, given their typically large families— would occupy forty-five apartments in that category.[20]

In contrast to the anxiety expressed by Latino housing advocates and residents, city officials and the UJO praised Schaefer Landing as an example of how private-public developments could revitalize the Brooklyn waterfront and provide affordable housing to the neighborhood's low-income residents. In an October 2005 press release from the mayor's office, Assemblyman Vito Lopez declared, "The Schaefer Landing development is an outstanding example of State, City and private-sector collaboration to create affordable housing," and Daniel Doctoroff, the deputy mayor for economic development and rebuilding, stated, "Today, we are one step closer toward reclaiming and renewing Brooklyn's East River waterfront. . . . With Schaefer Landing, we celebrate a project that inspired the historic Greenpoint-Williamsburg rezoning." Rabbi Niederman was equally upbeat about the development: "After so many years, we have finally been able to successfully transform vacant City-owned land into a beautiful housing development that creates low income and market rate housing for all people in our community. . . . The Schaefer development is a wonderful model of what can be achieved when the private, government and not-for-profit sector work together to produce these much needed affordable units."[21]

Several months earlier, in May 2005, the city had approved the Greenpoint-Williamsburg Rezoning Plan, which would play a large role in transforming the North Brooklyn waterfront in the years to come. The plan opened vast areas of the neighborhood formerly dedicated to industrial use to residential development and included an "Inclusionary Housing Program." In return for building new affordable-housing units, private developers would receive a twenty- to twenty-five-year exemption on property taxes under the city's 421-a program, which was now extended to the neighborhood. Officials promised to build more than a thousand affordable housing units on city-owned land in North Brooklyn

Rabbi David Niederman, leader of the UJO, touring
Schaefer Landing, 2006 (Getty Images)

and pledged that private developers would include more than two thousand affordable-housing units in new waterfront buildings and renovated
buildings farther inland.[22]

While the Schaefer Landing development did not inspire the rezoning, it had long been part of the community-based discussions that pre-
ceded the passage of the plan. Planning in Williamsburg had begun in
1989, and Community Board 1 held a series of workshops involving
members of community organizations and local residents throughout the
1990s. In an interview with the authors, the urban sociologist Miriam
Greenberg, then a teacher at El Puente Academy for Peace and Justice
(the "New Visions" high school established by El Puente in 1993), recalled these workshops as, seemingly, an opportunity for community
members to "have a voice in shaping the future of the neighborhood
along lines we had long envisioned." As she recalled:

> We would gather around tables with giant maps and talk about
> community priorities for redevelopment on the waterfront. With
> the help of the Pratt Center for Community Development, we
> educated ourselves on land use and zoning, and created a process
> for people to contribute ideas—including from the Latino, Pol-
> ish, and Hasidic communities. There were many organizers with

lots of knowledge and experience with land use already—who had blocked the siting of an incinerator on the waterfront, converted abandoned lots into gardens, fought to open up parks and pools and to rezone buildings for schools and affordable housing. So we saw the 197-a amendment, itself the result of activist pressure, as a great thing that would enable us to finally put forth a comprehensive vision rooted in local priorities, values, and struggles. There was consensus. It was citizen-planning.[23]

The 197-a amendment to the city charter empowered local community boards to "sponsor plans for the development, growth, and improvement of the city, its boroughs and communities."[24] Community Board 1, in Williamsburg, established a 197-a committee that included Rabbi David Niederman of the UJO, John Fleming from El Puente, and other local leaders and activists who collaborated to develop a plan for the neighborhood that would address the particular needs of its diverse communities and articulate a common vision for its future. In 1998, the committee completed the "Williamsburg Waterfront 197-a Plan; A Matter of Balance: Housing, Industry, Open Space" and submitted it to the City Planning Commission for adoption.[25] Among its major recommendations, the plan called for the city to preserve and create new jobs in "high performance light manufacturing," expand parks and other green spaces, develop affordable housing on the waterfront, and encourage private developers to set aside affordable units in market-rate projects or contribute to an affordable housing fund.[26] In this regard, the plan called for the development of the Schaefer Brewery site as residential or mixed use and stressed that affordable housing units should be included.

Along with these general recommendations, the plan addressed the particular needs of specific groups within the neighborhood, including the construction of housing to "accommodate the need of large and extended families particularly on the South Side and South Williamsburg," which was of special interest to both the Hasidic and Hispanic communities; the study of loft conversions and the development of "mixed-use [sites] that would allow for joint live/work space for artists and small home-based businesses," which appealed to artists; and new homes for El Puente Academy for Peace Justice and the Williamsburg Learning Institute, an adult computer-literacy program then housed in the offices of the UJO.[27]

After it was approved and modified by the City Planning Commission and adopted by the city council, the 197-a plan, according to the

Department of City Planning, was supposed to serve as a "guide" for "future actions of city agencies."[28] While some aspects of the plan did eventually come to fruition, including the new site for El Puente Academy for Peace Justice, most of its major recommendations were never implemented after the city's 2005 rezoning of the Williamsburg waterfront. Particularly frustrating to many community members, especially those who had participated in the decade-long planning process, was that rezoning did not result in a significant increase in the number of affordable-housing units either on the Williamsburg waterfront or in the interior of the neighborhood. Expressing a widely held opinion, Greenberg recalled,

> It was a bitter pill when the community plan we developed—the essential elements of it—was not ultimately used. And instead, they [city officials and developers] did what they did—building luxury high-rises and amenities all along the waterfront. We devoted all of this energy believing it would bear fruit. It's hard to know what else we might have done, given our understanding at the time. With 20/20 hindsight—and looking forward—maybe the same resources could have been used to learn about what was actually being planned and then intervene in order to challenge the process.[29]

Some felt that the city had co-opted the Williamsburg community's activist energies during the 197-a planning process, but that rather than guiding development, the plan had ultimately served as window dressing for the city's neoliberal rezoning of the waterfront.[30]

In 2015, ten years after the Greenpoint-Williamsburg Rezoning Plan was passed, only a tiny fraction of the promised affordable-housing units had been constructed. Stabrowski noted, "Of the 7,218 total units created in the IHP [Inclusionary Housing Program] designated area, only 949 units (13%) were affordable housing [including those in Schaefer Landing]." Over 30 percent of that total were not even newly created units but "existing below market-rent units 'preserved' through refinancing or substantial rehabilitation." On city-owned land, the picture was even more dismal: "Where 1,345 units of new affordable housing were anticipated—only 14 below-market condominium units and two affordable rental units have been completed to date [as of 2015]." During the same period, the Hispanic population of North Brooklyn decreased by

22 percent and "median rent burdens for low income tenants" increased by 6 percent.[31] The bleak statistics led Stabrowski to conclude, "Although the Greenpoint-Williamsburg IHP was deemed a success relative to other IHP 'designated areas' across the city, in the rapidly gentrifying neighborhoods of Greenpoint and Williamsburg it has utterly failed to stem the tide of rising rent levels."[32] Instead of a victory for the grass-roots citizen planning that produced the Williamsburg community's 197-a plan, the ultimate outcome of the waterfront rezoning was the accelerated displacement of that community—further evidence for what Sam Stein has called "the real estate state."[33]

"Be Your Own Broker"

Large-scale developers, including those who had close links to Hasidic social service organizations or were community activists or *askunim*, were not the only Hasidim to become involved in the Brooklyn real estate industry in the 2000s. Far more numerous were the individual Hasidic men and women who became smaller players in different aspects of an industry that had by then come to dominate the Hasidic economy in Williamsburg.[34] To get a better sense of this feature of the Brooklyn real estate ecosystem, whose interconnected web of actors included members of many ethnic and religious communities, we visited an unassuming store-front on a down-market commercial strip in Williamsburg in the summer of 2017. The back room of this business was a place where Hasidim, non-Hasidic Jews, and non-Jews met to discuss a variety of economic activities, including real estate deals. On the day we visited, numerous people moved in and out of the office, including a divorced Hasidic woman involved in real estate and a clean-shaven ex-Hasid wearing a construction worker's neon-colored safety shirt. Everyone was brought together by a non-Jewish woman whom we will call Kathleen. Not a native New Yorker, Kathleen had found employment in the city's municipal agencies until entering the Brooklyn home health care industry, which put her in contact with Hasidic businessmen (many of whom were involved in this sector).

After working with Hasidim in Williamsburg for a few years, Kathleen began to study Yiddish in order to better understand her business partners, who jokingly called her the *goyte* (non-Jewish woman). Similarly, these aspiring Hasidic real estate entrepreneurs took financial self-help courses offered in Yiddish and attended seminars, such as the JCON Real

Estate Summit, to improve their professional networks and knowledge.[35] The sociologist Adam Goldstein showed that the early twenty-first century was a period "characterized not only by a run-up in property prices, but also newly prevalent forms of economic action in which hundreds of thousands of Americans became real estate entrepreneurs, buying millions of homes for short-term profit."[36] Daniel Fridman argued that such entrepreneurs developed a new type of "capitalist economic subject" by seeking financial advice in books, columns, meetups, webinars, and events held in hotel conference rooms.[37] Hasidim actively participated in this global entrepreneurialization of the real estate industry, which contributed to the embourgeoisement of the Williamsburg community.[38]

In 2008, a firm called The Market Specialist used the tagline "Be Your Own Broker" to advertise available properties to Hasidim in the Yiddish press: "A list will be sent to you via an email or fax that will thoroughly describe all the details of every property: the address, how big the apartment is, how many bedrooms, rooms, and many more details. . . . Be the first to know when a new apartment or house comes on the market."[39] Aspiring Hasidic entrepreneurs could also participate in a seven-week crash course in Yiddish and English for real estate professionals in Williamsburg, Borough Park, and Monroe offered by Aron Gottlieb, the principal of a real estate investment firm called Diversified Capital, based in Lakewood, New Jersey. Gottlieb covered everything: financing, negotiation, closing, property management, and leveraging. According to his website, "The course is designed to give the *heimishe tzibbur* [Orthodox Jewish public] a very informative education about investing in real estate . . . specifically geared to the *heimish* mindset."[40] In one video, Gottlieb cautioned, in Yiddish, "Overnight [success] is *geshmak vi kigel* [tasty as kugel] but an investment demands patience to be able to achieve full success." As part of his course, Gottlieb offered students a 450-page Yiddish-English dictionary of real estate terminology.

On the day we visited the storefront in Williamsburg, Kathleen opened up to us about her experience of working with Hasidim in the neighborhood. Her first encounter with the community was as a home health aide, tending to women with numerous children (who were sometimes told by their mothers not to look at Kathleen when she entered the apartment, because of her supposedly immodest appearance). Kathleen noted the poverty she saw in many of these Hasidic homes, including in the neighborhood's public housing projects, adding that the projects in Williamsburg were the cleanest and safest she had seen in her work throughout "the Bronx, Harlem, and Brooklyn," because "everybody knows they have to get along." As the owner of several small businesses in Williamsburg, Kathleen had learned that real estate was "a good way to unload cash."

Another person present in the back room was a young man we will call Aaron, who grew up in Brooklyn's large Syrian Jewish community. Aaron sat behind a desk, wearing a blue suit with a handkerchief poking out of the breast pocket, and gave his perspective on working with Hasidim as a real estate jack-of-all-trades. "Developing and selling are completely different things," he said. "A developer will go to a broker and ask, 'What's hot right now? Three-bedroom? Two-bedroom?' And they build accordingly." In Aaron's telling, Hasidim developed properties in one of two ways. In the first scenario, they secured all the financing before beginning construction, from banks or private investors, who sometimes had what he called "old money" inherited from the diamond trade. In the other scenario, Hasidic developers consulted with brokers to pre-sell as many units as they could up front, typically at least 40 percent of the projected total. Once the building was finished, often by Hasidic-owned construction firms, developers then turned the building over to brokers, often Israelis or other non-Hasidic Jews, to sell or rent the remaining units. In an article titled "The Coolest Place in Brooklyn: The Full Story," published by the Israeli newspaper *Haaretz* in 2014, Guy Hochman, the Israeli owner of a Bushwick-based real estate firm, explained the relationship between Hasidic developers and Israeli brokers in the neighborhood: "The Satmar Hasidim are the real players in this market. They are more creative than anyone else. In my opinion, they are the ones who invented this neighborhood. We Israelis arrived after them. And the division is more or less like this: The Satmars are the big developers and we Israelis are the sellers or the renters of their apartments."[41] Much had changed since the days when Rabbi Yoel Teitelbaum turned his fierce opposition to the State of Israel into a rallying cry for his followers to build the Hasidic enclave in Williamsburg.

After Kathleen left the room, Aaron, who had *smicha* (rabbinic ordination) from a well-respected Brooklyn yeshiva, confided to us that while doing business with Hasidim, "ninety-nine percent of the time it helps to be Jewish." But he added that Hasidim will do business with anyone. Aaron explained that while being Jewish increased the chance of mutual trust, at the same time, "If you screw someone over, you're out of the community and out of business." Aaron also highlighted the role of African Americans in the world of Brooklyn real estate. Hasidim sometimes partnered with African Americans, who could get special deals or incentives from the city because of their minority status, he said, giving the example of a female African American real estate developer and de Blasio campaign contributor who did extensive business in Williamsburg with Hasidic investors.

The storefront represented the multiethnic Brooklyn "real estate ecosystem"—to borrow a phrase from David Madden and Peter Marcuse—in which Williamsburg Hasidim operated.⁴² Most commonly, Hasidim worked with Syrian Jews, non-Hasidic Orthodox Jews, secular American Jews, Israelis, and a range of non-Jews, including African Americans and Latinos. In his sociological study of real estate networks in Brooklyn, Clement Thery described these networks of "small and independent housing actors" who bought, sold, managed, and mortgaged properties outside the traditional large-scale real estate firms.⁴³ These actors typically worked in low-income black and Latino areas of the borough and often conducted their business without a brick-and-mortar office.⁴⁴ Larry, the small-time Jewish investor who served as Thery's primary informant, partnered with other Jews, including Syrians, Hasidim, and Israelis, as well as Italians, Russians, Albanians, Poles, Dominicans, African Americans, and Jamaicans, who had a distinct advantage when approaching the mostly older Caribbean homeowners in northern and central Brooklyn, sometimes on behalf of Hasidic buyers, whom these sellers frequently viewed with suspicion.⁴⁵

The Rise of the Hasidic Real Estate Mogul

While some Hasidim in the real estate industry were small-time hustlers and entrepreneurs operating in obscurity, other Hasidim became major developers whose highly visible projects, such as waterfront hotels, drew the rapt attention of the New York media. Some of the most successful Hasidic developers emerged from the cutthroat world of Brooklyn wheelers and dealers, while others, such as Mayer Schwartz, inherited buildings that they were able to convert into lucrative developments or, like Louis Kestenbaum, were able to parlay ties to the Hasidic establishment in Williamsburg to help them launch careers in real estate. The 2005 Brooklyn waterfront rezoning freed up many Hasidic-owned industrial spaces for conversion into residential use. The housing market crash a few years later, which one New York state representative called "a subprime tsunami," exacerbated what was already a high rate of foreclosures in Brooklyn, especially near Hasidic Williamsburg.[46] According to data published by the Federal Reserve Bank of New York in 2008, a zip code including Bedford-Stuyvesant had the highest percentage of defaulting subprime loans—more than 25 percent—in the borough of Brooklyn, followed closely by zip codes that included Williamsburg and Bushwick.[47] While many real estate players of all backgrounds pulled out of their Brooklyn investments in the wake of the economic crisis, Hasidic landlords and developers from Williamsburg actually increased their portfolios during this period by purchasing large numbers of foreclosed or distressed properties with cash financing from local Hasidic investors at a time when banks had dramatically reduced their lending.

By taking advantage of their geographic proximity to gentrifying areas and the distinctive lending practices of their community, a number of Hasidic real estate developers in Williamsburg emerged from the recession stronger than ever. A broker who focused on the Brooklyn market later recalled one such developer: "He was one of our top two buyers in the early years of the recovery. . . . Most of what he was buying was 20 units and less in these emerging neighborhoods. [He was] buying when no one else was buying. They [Hasidic developers] were the ones cutting checks when you couldn't get financing—when these neighborhoods looked nothing like they do today."[48] Mark Maurer, a real estate journalist, noted of Hasidic developers: "[They were] buying and flipping and employing, you know, 1031 at a deferred tax exchange to kind of move profits from one deal to the next. This is something that we're seeing with this community especially."[49] Section 1031 of the federal tax code allows for a deferral of taxes on income derived from real estate when those profits are subsequently reinvested in the purchase of other properties. This created an incentive for Hasidic developers and investors in Williamsburg to keep their assets in real estate and to continue engaging in a high volume of deals, leading Maurer to conclude, "These developers are just accelerating the pace of gentrification."

As Williamsburg Hasidim began to establish a greater presence in the New York real estate world, they increasingly drew the attention of the media. At the forefront of this trend was the *Real Deal*, a real estate news website and magazine that touted itself as the "bible" of the real estate industry.[50] Founded in 2003 by the Iranian-born publisher Amir Korangy, the *Real Deal* made a regular beat out of the business deals and, to the limited extent possible, personal lives of Hasidic developers, whom they treated with a mix of respect and wry amusement. The lionizing of New York real estate moguls was hardly a new phenomenon. Indeed, it had been a favorite topic of local media outlets since at least the 1970s, perhaps best illustrated by *New York* magazine's annual section "The Power Game."[51] This reportage transformed prominent developers such as the Rudins and Tisches into public figures, and they used their wealth and power to transform the city's image and cultural institutions. Following in these footsteps, the *Real Deal* confirmed what many observers in Brooklyn had already known or suspected by the 2010s: local Hasidim had become "some of the industry's most active and powerful players."[52] The *Real Deal* also emphasized the major differences between Hasidic developers and established multigenerational New York City Jewish real estate families such as the Tisches, Rudins, Walentases, Ratners, LeFraks, Spitzers, and Kushners: "Unlike their Grill Room–dining, art-collecting Manhattan counterparts, [Hasidic developers] prefer to stay in the shadows, their connections to properties masked through a network of frontmen and a labyrinth of limited liability corporations (LLCs). Most have no websites, and some have never been photographed."[53]

One of the distinctive features of the Hasidic real estate industry in Williamsburg was the extensive use of LLCs by property owners who sought to maintain anonymity. A single unassuming store called Lee Avenue Shipping and Communication, located at 199 Lee Avenue in the heart of Hasidic Williamsburg, was home to hundreds of private post office boxes, each apparently associated with a different LLC. According to the *Brooklyn Paper*, "For years, the address has sent shivers through the spines of tenants throughout North Brooklyn: 199 Lee Avenue."[54] As a result of this reputation, the storefront also became a symbol of landlord corruption and a lack of transparency for tenant activists, who traveled to Hasidic Williamsburg to stage protests and hold press conferences.

Rather than seek publicity, like many Manhattan-based real estate families, Williamsburg's Hasidic real estate moguls preferred to be part of a "clandestine empire," according to the *Real Deal*, whose practically anonymous members formed "a who's who of Brooklyn real estate: Simon Dushinsky and Isaac Rabinowitz's Rabsky Group; Joseph Brunner and Abe Mandel's Bruman Realty; Yoel Goldman's All Year Management; Joel Gluck's Spencer Equity; Joel Schwartz; the Hager family; and Joel Schreiber's Waterbridge Capital."[55] By 2016, Hasidic developers had invested over $2.5 billion dollars in five Brooklyn neighborhoods, and ten LLC addresses associated with Hasidic development companies each had at least $100 million in purchases from 2006 to 2016. The article was accompanied by a graph titled "Hasidic Brooklyn's Big Spenders," which showed, against a backdrop of the Brooklyn skyline, developers' net worths, organized by LLC address and measured in stacked fedoras—not, in fact, the preferred headgear of Williamsburg's Hasidic men.

One figure who exemplified this "clandestine empire" was Simon Dushinsky, a Hasidic immigrant from Israel who enjoyed a rapid rise in the Brooklyn real estate scene in the 2010s as the head of the Rabsky Group. Although Dushinsky developed prominent properties such as the former Rheingold Brewery site in Bushwick and major new construction projects in downtown Brooklyn, Gowanus, and in his adopted home of Williamsburg, real estate observers struggled to find information about him. Most sources agreed that he had entered the real estate business in Brooklyn by tapping local private financing as well as large creditors such as Bank Leumi, of Israel, and the Spanish bank BBVA.[56] In addition to detailing his aggressive financing and successful partnerships, the real estate press identified characteristics that set Dushinsky apart from other developers, portraying him as a "progressive thinker" with an encyclopedic knowledge of zoning code and building regulations.[57] Meanwhile, an investigation by ProPublica, the nonprofit news organization, concluded that "there is little doubt that the Rabsky Group broke the law" by charging tenants in one of its Williamsburg buildings, The Driggs, excessive rent, or as Leticia James, then the New York City public advocate put it, "It is clear that this unscrupulous landlord is violating rent-stabilization laws."[58] When asked to comment on these accusations, "the Rabsky Group—which owns many other buildings in its home borough of Brooklyn—did not respond to calls, emails and a hand-delivered letter."[59]

The same real estate websites that covered the apotheosis of Simon Dushinsky hailed the rise of another "mysterious developer who's transforming Brooklyn," Yoel Goldman, a Satmar Hasid from Williamsburg.[60] As with Dushinsky, reporters stressed how difficult it was to locate photographs of Goldman. But his company, All Year Management, was too prolific to ignore. Among its projects was the white modernist William Vale hotel on North 12th Street, which towers over North Williamsburg. One of the reasons that the press was drawn to Goldman's story was that he had not inherited money but rather got his start by buying multifamily buildings in Central Brooklyn neighborhoods before they became gentrified. Funding his purchases with the help of private investors from within the local Hasidic community, Goldman built up a large portfolio of mid-range properties during the 2008 recession. When financing became available again, he was well positioned to secure loans from large banks, and in a sign of his meteoric rise, he eventually went on to issue "roughly 1.7 billion shekels, or $485 million, in low-interest, publicly traded bonds on Israel's Tel Aviv Stock Exchange," catapulting him into a different class of developer.[61] Like Dushinsky, Goldman became embroiled in legal troubles, the *Real Deal* reported, in his case facing accusations from Israeli bondholders that he "misappropriated company funds, which they say caused their bonds to lose value."[62]

Another developer who worked—at least for a time—with both Simon Dushinsky and Yoel Goldman was Toby Moskovits, an Orthodox Jewish woman from Flatbush, Brooklyn. Calling herself "an accidental entrepreneur, an accidental developer," Moskovits noted, "I started in real estate towards the end of 2008, after the market had crashed."[63] While a self-described outsider in the real estate world, she found a niche as an insider in the Williamsburg market, relying in large part on her credentials as an Orthodox Jew with local ties. Moskovits stated, "I'm a neighborhood developer. My family has very deep roots here in Williamsburg."[64] Although she grew up in Flatbush, her father had an apparel business on Kent Avenue and North 10th Street in "a factory they probably should have bought but just rented." When she began working in Williamsburg, she realized that her local knowledge was an asset she could leverage. "My family happened to have a business in Williamsburg in the '80s," she said, "and I was somewhat familiar with the areas where these real estate developments were."[65]

Moskovits became CEO of Heritage Equity Partners, which, the company website stated, was "founded during the downturn in 2008 with a focus on emerging neighborhoods" and "played a significant role in driving the development and evolution of Williamsburg, Clinton Hill, and Bushwick."[66] As a developer, Moskovits oversaw the construction of the so-called American Apparel Building, the Quarry Building, and the Williamsburg Hotel, and the restoration of the historic St. Vincent de Paul Catholic Church, all on the North Side of Williamsburg. Another of her major developments, at 25 Kent Avenue between North 12th and North 13th Streets, was originally financed by Simon Dushinsky and Yoel Goldman before the partners had a falling out and Moskovits brought in other investors, according to *Crain's New York*.[67]

Toby Moskovits was Orthodox and had a BA from Touro College in New York and an MBA from Bar-Ilan University, outside Tel Aviv—both

Orthodox Jewish institutions. By contrast, a Hasidic woman named Chany Rosen became a notable real estate professional despite the greater limitations placed on women in her community. In Rosen's case, she took advantage of the new opportunities created by the booming Brooklyn real estate market, as well as her own family connections, to go from working as a teacher to becoming a successful player in the industry. In a glowing profile, the *Real Deal* described Rosen as "the upstart expeditor on defying expectations, all-nighters and Chanel," in reference to the forty pairs of $750 Chanel ballet flats she owned.[68] Expeditors serve as liaisons between developers and the Department of Buildings (DOB), helping clarify blueprints and zoning; they also lobby city officials to solve real estate related problems and help close deals. The magazine emphasized Rosen's self-made image: "Whether it's going to housing court, bidding on foreclosed homes or overseeing renovation work for her former employer, Elliot Frankel, Rosen worked hard to teach herself the real estate business."

Rosen partnered with her brother, Yoel Bochner, also in real estate, to form Cavalry Associates. "I deal with a lot of stop-work orders and vacate orders," she said. "Not in our developments—we own properties in Brooklyn and thank God those go smoothly—but a big chunk of my clients are people coming to me with messes that need cleaning up."[69] Being a Hasidic woman presented challenges to entering the business world that went beyond having five children at home. The profile reported that some Hasidic landlords refused to work with her until they realized that she could help them. "I guess their project is more important to them than the fact that I'm female," she mused. And despite running a multimillion-dollar company, she said, "I don't drive—women in our community don't drive, so Uber, Lyft and Juno are my go-tos."

Unlike the male Hasidic developers profiled by the *Real Deal*, who studiously avoided publicity and whose images could not be found on the Internet, Rosen was featured in a publicity video produced by the magazine called "A Day in the Life of Chany Rosen," which recalled the kind of brash self-promotion of an earlier generation of New York City real estate moguls (for example, *The Lew Rudin Way*, a documentary narrated by Sidney Poitier about the developer once popularly known as "Mr. New York").[70] Ironically, contemporary Hasidic media prohibited the publication of any images of women, with one newspaper even going so far as to edit out the face of then–secretary of state Hillary Clinton from a photo of President Barack Obama and his advisers in May 2001.[71] In a video that could not be watched—at least openly—by any of her male Hasidic co-workers, Rosen dispensed with the stereotype of the Hasidic stay-at-home mom and related that her work day began at four in the morning and ended late at night, with a sacrosanct break in the evening to focus on her family. "It's so important that when I'm running all this [the business]," Rosen explained, "the home front should be just as well taken care of. A mom is just a mom."[72]

Death of a Landlord

Of all the roles that Hasidim came to occupy in the real estate industry in Brooklyn, the most controversial was that of landlord. Long before gentrification arrived in the neighborhood, Hasidim from Williamsburg owned residential and commercial properties. Indeed, as we have seen, this fact helped them become significant players in local real estate early on. By the 2000s, the number of buildings owned by Hasidim had expanded dramatically, as had their geographic distribution in Brooklyn, including in poorer neighborhoods far removed from Williamsburg. Increasingly, black and Latino renters in these areas contended that many Hasidic landlords were not only engaging in exploitive or illegal behaviors but were also actively displacing longtime low-income residents in favor of gentrifiers with deeper pockets. This perception was particularly widespread in Bushwick, directly abutting Williamsburg. As "Mariel," an older Latina resident of the neighborhood, stated to Rosemary Ferreira, who conducted a study of the phenomenon in 2014 (like many of the residents interviewed by Ferreira, Mariel employed the phrase "los judíos," or "the Jews," to refer to Hasidic landlords collectively): "I have seen that it has changed tremendously. My neighborhood used to have people from different Latino nationalities. . . . But now all of these people have been displaced and have moved out. Now the white people are moving in and the Jews have bought all of the properties and all that's left is my building. All of these new people that have come, the Jews are bringing in from different states." On the basis of her interviews, Ferreira concluded, "For some of the older women, the migration of white gentrifiers into Bushwick is not the source of their worries when it comes to gentrification. Instead, older women believe that the real root of the problem rests in the displacement and denial of housing Latinos face due to the discrimination inflicted upon them by Jewish landlords."[73]

Some Hasidic landlords in Brooklyn—like those belonging to other ethnic or religious communities in the city—were guilty of corrupt or criminal business practices and, in the pursuit of higher rents, many contributed to the gentrification of historically poor and working-class neighborhoods and the extensive displacement of longtime residents. Some also took advantage of members of their own community and, in doing so, worsened the housing crisis in Hasidic Williamsburg. Regardless of whether they engaged in such behaviors, however, Hasidic landlords frequently came under fire in ways that recycled long-standing anti-Semitic stereotypes regarding Jewish economic exploitation and greed. In light of this phenomenon, the challenge was—and is—to describe Hasidic landlords, including, or perhaps especially, those whose behavior justly deserved criticism or condemnation, without sugarcoating or dehumanizing them, reducing them to caricatures, or implying that their behavior was somehow essentially Jewish.

The death of Menachem "Max" Stark, a thirtysomething Hasidic landlord from Williamsburg whose tragic murder provoked a storm of publicity, illuminates the human complexity behind the one-dimensional stereotypes. One winter night in 2014, Stark, who owned the Greenpoint Motel and dozens of other residential buildings in North Brooklyn, left his Williamsburg office and was abducted by two men in a van.[74] His partially burned body was later discovered in a dumpster in Long Island, and the autopsy reported he had died of asphyxiation from pressure on his chest. It was later revealed in court that the kidnappers had worked for Stark as contractors. They claimed that they accidentally killed Stark while menacing him so that he would pay them long-owed money for work done on one of his buildings. (The men were convicted of second-degree murder, among other charges, in 2019.) While not defending the assailants outright, the broader New York media framed the connection between Stark's line of work and his ultimate end in sensationalistic terms.[75] A number of news outlets, including the *Village Voice*, referred to Stark as a "slumlord" in their coverage of the case. Most notoriously, the *New York Post* ran a front-page article, three days after Stark's abduction, with the headline "Who Didn't Want Him Dead? Slumlord Found Dead in Dumpster."[76] Rabbi David Niederman of the UJO in Williamsburg expressed outrage at the media coverage. "There are many buildings, governmental and non-governmental, that have violations against them," he said. "He owed money? Show me one person in real estate or in business that doesn't owe money. And great people go bankrupt. Show me one airline that hasn't been bankrupt, and emerged."[77]

A more complicated portrait of Menachem Stark began to appear in the media, too. An article in the *New York Times* headlined "A Developer Is Mourned and Vilified in Brooklyn" called Stark "a lightning rod for fuming tenants and neighborhood activists across north Brooklyn"—though the only tenant quoted in the article said he was " 'furious' to see Mr. Stark maligned in the media," adding: "Besides being very nice, the building was well maintained. I knew Max well and I was horrified. . . . My fellow neighbors were, too."[78] In fact, some of Stark's tenants remembered him fondly as a person, even as they noted his negligence as a landlord, especially when it came to upkeep and repairs. One commercial renter told a reporter that Stark was friendly and gave her a good deal, adding, "In Brooklyn, people know the value of their properties, but he was really flexible and not at all money-hungry."[79] In a piece on the website *Gothamist* entitled, "Why I (Sometimes) Miss Williamsburg's Infamous Murdered Slumlord," Jesse Jarnow reminisced about Stark's disarming Yiddish accent and jovial outlook. "It'd be wrong to call Max 'beloved,' " Jarnow wrote, "but he could border on endearing. He was just the landlord, and a pretty tolerable one at that. Max was a daily presence in our lives during those years, as the Morgan Avenue stop transformed around us from the East Williamsburg Industrial Park into an extreme model of Brooklyn gentrification."[80]

To learn more about Stark, we conducted interviews with some of his former tenants, including one who observed that despite his faults as a landlord, Stark could also be accommodating when it came to the rent. "The one thing that I will give him credit for is if he came to the door, and you didn't have the rent, he would let it fly," he noted.[81] Another tenant, whom we will call Molly, lived in one of Stark's buildings for more than half a decade. Molly observed of this period, "Over six years there were a number of serious issues. But in general—it was a pretty great apartment in a neighborhood that I loved." By way of explanation, she added, "Real estate in all of New York is a nightmare. Getting an apartment is hard and stressful, and this city is filled with rats and bugs and people who break into buildings. I was twenty-four and working on films twelve-plus hours a day for not much money. Everyone was so short on time and money, so we just dealt with it."[82]

Molly's introduction to the hard-boiled reality of Brooklyn real estate came in 2009 when she was working two jobs while still in college. She had landed a $500-a-month room in a four-bedroom apartment on the third floor of a prewar building on Franklin Avenue in Bedford-Stuyvesant, the neighborhood where most of her friends lived. Soon after Molly moved in, the problems began to appear. The stove leaked gas and eventually broke, never to be replaced. The gas meter was illegally locked in the closet. Mail carriers could not enter the building, forcing tenants to retrieve mail from the post office before it would be returned to sender, leading to a number of lost paychecks. Although mail carriers could not get in, workers often entered unannounced to make seemingly unnecessary "improvements." Once, they removed the radiators and left huge holes in the walls, along with piles of dirt and sheetrock dust, for three chilly fall months. Rats came in through the holes, adding to the menagerie of mice and bedbugs, which the landlord's office staff was reluctant to treat. There was no heat until late November every year, much later than the October 1 date by which heat legally must be available in New York City. A leak from the apartment above caused the ceiling to cave in. After three years, Stark raised the rent significantly, even though Molly and others believed that the apartment was rent stabilized. Stark then threatened eviction if she and her roommates did not sign a new lease immediately. Perhaps worst of all, one of Molly's roommates was robbed at gunpoint after someone followed her through the front door of the building, which had a faulty lock. Molly told us that the building's super and his bosses "expressed no concern for her, and the door wasn't fixed for another year after that."

One of the most vexing issues for Molly and other building residents was that they could not get in touch with their landlord. In fact, for a long time after moving in, they were not even sure who their landlord was. Most communication went through two Hasidic women named Esty and Frady. Rent had to be dropped off in person at the Greenpoint Motel, a notorious single-room-occupancy hotel known as a meeting place for recent ex-cons and rumored to be the source of Greenpoint's bedbug infestation of the early 2000s. Molly had some phone numbers to call in case of an emergency, but said, "We didn't know who we were talking to." One day, Molly's roommate paid a visit to Esty and was surprised to learn that she was just out of high school. "It also turns out that Esty is not our landlord, but just someone that works for our landlord," the roommate informed Molly. "Our landlord is the guy that changed the locks last week." That man was Menachem Stark.

The War Against the Artists II

Like their non-Hasidic counterparts, many financially strapped Hasidic renters in Williamsburg during this period found themselves at the mercy of their landlords, forced to put up with increasing rents, shoddy maintenance, or dangerous conditions in their apartments. The lack of affordable housing in the neighborhood pushed Hasidim and non-Hasidim into a competition for available units. Esther Ungar, a mother of three who lived near the Williamsburg Bridge in the Hasidic Triangle, explained these challenges to the Orthodox *Ami* magazine in 2014: "One of the main reasons that rentals are not affordable [in Williamsburg] is because there is fierce competition between members of our community and the artist community. . . . The artists are willing to pay double the amount of money that we can for a rental and are willing to live in tiny apartments."[83]

The 2008 financial crash created new economic opportunities for Hasidic real estate investors with access to capital, but it added severe strain to most Hasidic households in Williamsburg. This inverse relationship between the success of Hasidic real estate developers and owners and the struggles of everyday Hasidim was exacerbated by the relationship of landlord and renter, which sometimes included predatory rental practices within the Hasidic community. Typically, Hasidim rented and sold apartments to one another differently from how they did so when renting to individuals outside the community. After the crash of the housing market, a January 2010 analysis of the previous year's economic woes appeared in *Di Tsaytung*, a Yiddish weekly published in Borough Park. Signed with the pen name, "Investor" (*investirer*), the writer compared square-footage prices in different parts of Williamsburg, noting, "One of the 'hot' areas in New York, when real estate was going so well, was Williamsburg. We're of course not talking about the Haredi area in Williamsburg, where everything goes according to a different calculation. . . . The story is different for the other [hipster] part of Williamsburg, in the north half of the neighborhood."[84]

While generally intended to produce lower prices for Hasidim than the prevailing rates elsewhere in Williamsburg, the "different calculation" practiced in the Hasidic enclave did not always work in favor of Hasidic renters, or at least not everyone in the community agreed that it did. One of the practices that became a bone of contention in Williamsburg was *shlisl gelt*, or "key money," a sum that renters were expected to pay to landlords when they moved into an apartment to help with its ongoing maintenance. In return, tenants who paid *shlisl gelt* were supposed to receive a form of eviction protection, perhaps for their lifetime. With roots in eastern Europe, *shlisl gelt* was practiced in Hasidic communities around the world.[85] Yet not everyone was happy with the arrangement, as one Williamsburg Hasid explained to us: "Landlords used to ask for a bulk sum just for the right of leasing a decent apartment. They would claim it's for money they put in, such as a new kitchen, a fresh coat of paint, etc. But really, it was just a way of bilking the tenant."⁸⁶

The practice received significant pushback within the Hasidic community around the time that gentrification intensified in Williamsburg and some Hasidic landlords began to rent to artists, thereby worsening an already tight housing market. Amid rising competition for rentals in South Williamsburg, one Hasidic resident wrote to *Der Yid* to complain about what he called the "Williamsburg *minhag*" (custom) of *shlisl gelt*. Signing his name S.F., the letter writer said that he had married three and a half years ago but had yet to find an unfurnished, and therefore less expensive, apartment: "The apartment owner believes, just like all the others, that as long as the demand is great—and it is, there is a lack of apartments here—they can take however much [the market] allows." In addition, landlords expected prospective tenants to have a section 8 voucher, which S.F. tried but failed to obtain: "Every apartment that we learn about is 'section 8 preferred.' The apartment owners simply say, 'If you don't have section 8, it's not interesting to even talk about it.'" He concluded with an admonishment of Hasidic landlords in Williamsburg: "What will you landlords say when you are told in the World to Come, *shlisl gelt* is demanded from you for your entry into Heaven? If you don't have it, you'll have to go back to your furnished apartment until you've finally saved up!"⁸⁷

A few weeks later, *Der Yid* ran a response from a Brooklyn reader who wanted to clarify some of the issues at stake. This letter, signed A.N., began, "The first thing that I want to make clear is likely not known by a lot of people. That is various laws. The first and most important is that there is a strong law against *shlisl gelt*."⁸⁸ A.N. continued, "When you rent an apartment to a non-Jew, you don't have any choice. And everything must be done according to the law, right? Is it not a great shame that when you rent an apartment to a *heymishe yid* [Hasidic Jew], your approach has nothing at all to do with these laws? Because your neighbor, friend, relative, etc. won't be a snitch, you take advantage of him?" A.N. emphasized that rental practices in Williamsburg differed from those in other Hasidic communities: "In Borough Park, Monsey, Kiryas Joel and also other settlements no such thing exists, that a 'tenant' has to renovate an apartment or give *shlisl gelt* to the landlord because he renovated the apartment. Why does it have to be different in Williamsburg?" He asked, "Where are the rabbis? Where are the *askunim* [activists]?" The problem, A.N. argued, was landlords' greediness in the tight rental market. Some landlords, he wrote, had the chutzpah to ask tenants for more *shlisl gelt* after two to three years of renting:

> Now, to all the developers who are building new apartments: are the costs of construction higher in Williamsburg than in other neighborhoods? No! But the people know that you "must" raise money because there is a large demand here. Then you can make a hundred thousand dollars of profit on every apartment. Why not! But what would happen if you made a little less profit, and people who need apartments would be happy and a little healthier. All of these things cause heart attacks, nervous breakdowns, and other things.

A.N. noted that some landlords asked for more than the legally allowable rent in rent-controlled apartments: "Even after the mortgage was paid, he wanted more pocket money from it! Why do people have to do this? Is it Jewish? Do people no longer have any feeling for a fellow Jew? I get red talking about it. . . . How can a Jew sleep well in a luxury apartment when it is financed by a pure tenant who tortures himself to make a living? . . . to live in *luksus* [luxury] while profiting off of another man's sweat and blood!" A.N.'s solution to the situation in Williamsburg would have been welcomed by rent-burdened New Yorkers well beyond the Yiddish readership of *Der Yid:* "We need to work to build apartments for 'middle- and low-income' earners. It's high time people should be protesting against the ethical breach of ripping someone off." A.N. concluded by exhorting "those who have the right connections" within the Hasidic community to work to solve the problem, for, he stressed, "it is truly a mitzvah of *pikuach nefesh,*" or a Halakhic matter of life or death.

In response to the great need for housing in their community, as well as the growing sense of resentment toward them, some Hasidic developers built apartment buildings specifically for Hasidim while developing other buildings for high-earning neighborhood newcomers. The most prominent example in Williamsburg was the so-called Dushinsky Houses on Kent Avenue. In 2015, at the same time that the Rabsky Group filed plans to build a number of luxury condominium developments on the Brooklyn waterfront, the firm made plans to turn a site on Kent Avenue into housing with four-bedroom units, a sign that Hasidim were the target market.[89] In one of the buildings, units were listed for under $400 a square foot, or about half the going market rate at the time in the rest of

Williamsburg.⁹⁰ "Most of us are not after the over-priced studio apartments that are springing up like mushrooms after the rain," one Williamsburg resident wrote. "We want to purchase a home at an affordable price even if it's a 3 bedroom apartment on the eighth floor of the Dushinsky housing complex on Kent Avenue."⁹¹

By 2015, the apartment crisis in Hasidic Williamsburg had reached the breaking point, and community leaders felt compelled to directly address it, as they had a decade earlier when they launched the war against the artists. They called together a "historic *asife*," or large public gathering, of rabbis and community activists. "History repeats itself in Williamsburg," an article in *Der Yid* declared.⁹² But this time the main issue was not small-time Hasidic landlords renting to artists in South Williamsburg, but rather large-scale Hasidic developers building luxury high-rises for well-heeled newcomers. Organized in May 2015, the *asife* carried the "double goal" of compelling Hasidic developers to build housing within the old Hasidic enclave and to "expand the borders of Williamsburg." Some of the reasons offered for the new "war" were similar to those of a decade earlier: "Williamsburg is becoming bit by bit an 'immodest city,' " the article stated, "and more non-Jewish elements are attracted to the neighborhood and may eventually overwhelm the noble and holy neighborhood until it is unrecognizable, God forbid."

The rabbis and activists proposed a new plan, "Williamsburg for Williamsburg," in order "to accommodate the numerous couples who get married every year." They emphasized the need to "expand Williamsburg" by buying up property across Flushing Avenue in Clinton Hill and Bedford-Stuyvesant all the way to the border of Crown Heights and incorporating this new territory into their enclave, "with its true Jewish grace and splendor." In a follow-up article, *Der Yid* assured its readers, "*Askunim* [activists] are working on all fronts to try to alleviate the difficult apartment crisis in the city by expanding the borders of the *heymishe* [Hasidic] neighborhood," adding, "If we have the courage, and are ready to spread out a bit, then there are so many houses and streets that can be filled up. And some years from now, people won't believe it [when you say], 'Remember when no Jew lived on such-and-such a street?' The same thing happened in current Williamsburg."⁹³ The article recommended that Hasidic residents move one street over, and then a year later a few people should move one street beyond that, and "in general begin to buy right and left wherever there are available homes for sale." Sounding a hopeful note for the future, it predicted that home prices would "automatically" drop. Help was available in the community: "And if you don't believe it, the *askunim* can spread out maps, analyze the streets, and point with their fingers: 'Right here, look! Here there are apartments you can readily acquire!' " The article concluded, "A loud call goes out to Williamsburg residents: 'Spread out! Drag yourselves out a bit beyond our borders! More apartments exist, you just have to want to go!" ending on a riff on God's exhortation to Abraham in Genesis 12:1, "*Go forth from the street of your fathers to the street that I will show you!*"[94]

But whereas the rabbis sanguinely encouraged their followers to simply buy buildings in new areas, rank-and-file Hasidim found this to be cold comfort in light of their pressing economic problems. Commentators on online Hasidic message boards called on community leaders to contribute more than just words to the apartment crisis. One poster on the Yiddish-language message forum Kave Shtiebel (coffee house) demanded that community leaders reallocate funds to housing in Williamsburg.[95] In a remarkable rejection of the traditional Hasidic power structure, this commentator articulated what amounted to a new set of negative commandments, indicting rabbinic leaders for investing time, money, and energy in the wrong places, including building mikvehs in Ukraine, refurbishing Jewish cemeteries in Hungary, posting "notices in the newspapers against short and colorful dresses," and organizing anti-Internet rallies, among other grievances.

Yet none of the individuals who posted criticism—however sharp—regarding the complicity of Hasidic leaders in helping create or exacerbate the housing crisis in Williamsburg suggested that Hasidim should ally themselves with similarly affected members of other local communities in order to fight luxury development and advocate for more affordable housing. The deeply rooted imperative to keep grievances within the Hasidic community apparently outweighed any benefits that might have been gained through such intercommunal alliances.

CHAPTER EIGHT
The Holy Corner

WHEN WALT WHITMAN COMPOSED "Crossing Brooklyn Ferry," in 1856, he could watch the boats plying the East River from his office window at the *Williamsburgh Daily Times* on Broadway in what is now the Hasidic neighborhood, only a few miles from Fort Greene, where a public housing project today bears his name. Admiring the ferries that connected Manhattan and Brooklyn before the construction of the Williamsburg Bridge, Whitman predicted, "A hundred years hence, . . . others will see them, / Will enjoy the sunset, the pouring-in of the flood-tide, the falling-back to the sea of the ebb-tide." A century later, Whitman's love for this corner of Brooklyn was shared by another local poet: Yom Tov Ehrlich, who became the unofficial bard of Hasidic Williamsburg in the years following World War II. Ehrlich, who worked as a diamond polisher by day and a *badkhn* (wedding master of ceremonies) by night, composed beloved Yiddish-language tributes to the neighborhood, including "Williamsburg," in which he declared, "Oh! Williamsburg! She has no equal. She is water of life, Jerusalem for the exiled Jew."[1]

Like the gritty waterfront of Whitman's time, Hasidim found beauty and transcendence in the hardscrabble blocks of what they called, with both reverence and affection, their *heylike vinkl*, or "holy corner." Despite its physical proximity to Lower Manhattan, South Williamsburg had long been viewed as a dangerous slum, even a no-man's-land, by the monied interests of the city, who, according to Satmar ideology, posed a much greater existential threat to the Hasidic community than poor Latino and African American residents. With the arrival of gentrification, however, the barriers between the Hasidic enclave and the outside world, erected by poverty, crime, and systemic neglect over the decades, began to come down. What remained in place was what the British anthropologist Mary Douglas called the "wall of virtue" that enclave cultures like Hasidic Williamsburg assiduously seek to maintain between insiders and outsiders.[2]

Gentrification did not affect Hasidic Williamsburg in a vacuum. Instead, it intersected with, and in some cases intensified, other phenomena transforming the community—and other Haredi enclaves—in the same period. These changes included growing embourgeoisement and, with it, greater consumerism; the widespread use of the Internet, despite the ongoing campaign against it by religious leaders; new attitudes toward the body, reflected in new health, fitness, and beauty practices; intracommunal critiques of the Hasidic educational system; and controversies over sexual abuse and whether it should be reported to outside authorities. The anthropologist Ayala Fader also identified what she calls a "crisis of *emune* (locally translated as 'faith') . . . the sense that more and more were either leaving their communities altogether, going 'OTD' (off the *derech* [path]), or living what community members called 'double lives': practicing religiously in public for the sake of families, while secretly exploring secular socialities and subjectivities online and off."[3]

Hasidim in Williamsburg responded to these changes in a variety of ways, reflecting the diversity within the community, ranging from fear and anger to ambivalence and, even, delight—though this last had to be expressed circumspectly lest it lead to condemnation or worse. The case of Hasidic Williamsburg reveals that even in enclaves that seem to be the most extreme in Douglas's terms, not everyone sees "everything in black and white," as she put it, and certainly not all the time. Rather, even as the most zealous members of the local Hasidic community tried to double down on their traditional isolation and fortify the "wall of virtue" between them and the gentrifiers, others in Williamsburg adopted a live-and-let-live attitude to the newcomers and sought compromise on some issues, while still others viewed gentrifiers' growing presence in the neighborhood and the many changes they brought with them as an opportunity to engage in new, and in some cases forbidden, activities and experiences.

In interviews conducted by the authors in 2008, Hasidim in Williamsburg expressed a diversity of attitudes toward the *artistn* whom they encountered in their daily lives on both sides of Broadway and in a variety of settings.⁴ Younger Hasidim, in particular, stated that they were not personally bothered by the *artistn*, or as one young Hasid put it, "Half the Jews will tell you they like the artists." Two young Hasidic men interviewed on Broadway and in McCarren Park declared that "*artistn* are very friendly people," and a middle-aged Hasidic woman in a butcher shop in South Williamsburg stated, "They're nice people." An employee at the upscale Hatzlacha ["Success"] food market on Flushing Avenue—itself a nod to the impact of gentrification in the Hasidic enclave—told us, "This is a supermarket for everyone ... There is no problem with *artistn* shopping at the store."

But other Hasidic residents of Williamsburg, especially those belonging to the older generation, expressed far more critical views. One middle-aged Hasidic woman near the J subway train stop on Hewes Street opined that "some [*artistn*] are real lowlifes" who "eat in public, cackle loudly, kiss in the street, and worse." An old man interviewed in a corner store in South Williamsburg condemned *artistn* en masse as "not honest people" and responded, "I would become sick," when asked what he would do if he heard that his son were mixing with them. The same man expressed a view repeated by numerous Hasidim of all ages when he emphasized that the biggest problem posed by the *artistn* was "the women, the girls," specifically, as another Hasidic man on Broadway put it, that female *artistn* dress "immodestly." The threat posed by the *artistn* did not lie solely in their immodest dress or behavior, but also in the possibility that younger Hasidim might be tempted to emulate them; as one Hasid put it, "People are afraid the *artistn* will teach the young people things about the world."

Just as his forebears had done before him, Rabbi Zalman Teitelbaum, who became leader of the largest Satmar faction in Williamsburg following the death of his father, Moshe, in April 2006, responded to the moral threat of gentrification by exhorting his followers—known colloquially as "Zalis"—to reinforce the community's "wall of virtue." According to a *New York* magazine profile of Hasidic Williamsburg published in May 2006: "They put questions to their rabbi: What should we do with our teenage girls who peer covertly at these artists? Why do these artists never put curtains on their windows? Can we force them out? Zalmen, they reported, meditated a moment. 'You must close your curtains and pray and remember what it is to be Satmar,' he said. 'This is our shtetl, and our walls must go high.' "⁵

God's Police

In Hasidic parlance, breaches in the community's walls of virtue were known as *pritsus*, a word whose Hebrew root means "to break through" and whose opposite was *tsnius*, or "modesty." While *pritsus* most commonly referred to infractions of a sexual nature and was therefore translated as "licentiousness" in English, the term was applied to other kinds of excess as well, including certain kinds of eating and other uses of the body. Mary Douglas argued for a parallel between the human body and the social body: anxieties regarding one often find expression in anxieties over the other, and regulation of one frequently mirrors or symbolically informs regulation of the other, especially when it comes to openings and entrances of different kinds.[6] We should not be surprised, therefore, that Hasidic authorities had long attempted to police the behavior and fashion choices of members of their communities in order to enforce their conception of modesty.[7] Women were a particular focus of this regulation, not only because they might lead Hasidic men astray as a result of their supposedly immodest behavior or dress, but also because they were viewed as more susceptible than men to the temptations of fashion.[8] Even among Hasidic rebbes, Rabbi Yoel Teitelbaum of Satmar earned a reputation for extreme strictness—a legal approach known as *khumre*—when it came to anything connected to modesty. In Williamsburg, Teitelbaum insisted on separate entrances for men and women at various communal buildings, declared that Satmar women should cover their hair with scarves—that is, go *gebindn*—rather than a wig (a common alternative among many Orthodox women), and even established his own line of opaque panty hose called "Palm" (the meaning of "Teitelbaum"), which he required female members of his community to wear.

In the years following Teitelbaum's death, in 1979, zealots within Hasidic Williamsburg, as in other Haredi enclaves around the world, adopted ever-stricter attitudes toward women's modesty. As in many traditionalist societies, the struggle over women's bodies became a proxy for broader anxieties concerning the perceived threats of modernity. Increasingly, the most extreme elements in Haredi communities employed the threat of violence and other forms of intimidation to silence the voices of more moderate community members who opposed their views.[9] Referring to this phenomenon, one member of a Haredi community observed, "It's a small group that gained power from the fact that most people want to go about their daily lives. . . . They're emboldened by the inactive silent majority."[10]

In Williamsburg, Hasidic zealots under the auspices of a *vaad ha-tsnius* (committee on modesty) or in more informal groups attempted to police Hasidic bodies as well as the boundaries of the enclave. While some in the community avidly supported these activities, others took a more critical, or at least neutral, stance. Yosef Rapaport, a Hasidic journalist, observed to Joseph Berger of the *New York Times*, "There are quite a few men, especially in Williamsburg, who consider themselves Gut's polizei [God's police]. . . . It's somebody who is a busybody, and they're quite a few of them—zealots who take it upon themselves and they just enforce. They're considered crazy, but people don't want to confront them."[11] Deborah Feldman, who was raised in Williamsburg and published a memoir titled *Unorthodox: The Scandalous Rejection of My Hasidic Roots*, declared, "Many within the community call it the Taliban as a joke. They answer to no one. They can get away with whatever they want."[12] Yet in speaking with Berger, Rabbi David Niederman, the head of the United Jewish Organizations in Williamsburg, downplayed the significance of the neighborhood's zealots while also avoiding an endorsement of their activities: "These are individual people who decide to take on this crusade. You see posters telling people do this and do that. It does not represent an authorized body."[13] Niederman had in mind the numerous posters or broadsides, known as *pashkevilin* in Yiddish, that warned Hasidic women in particular to behave modestly in public, a catchall admonition that referred to proper dress but also targeted comportment, such as how Hasidic women should act when encountering a man on the sidewalk, whether they should use a cell phone in public, drive a car, and so on.[14]

It was no accident that zealots in Williamsburg focused their attention on the external signs of *pritsus*, or licentiousness. Since the community's founding in the 1940s, the religious leaders of Hasidic Williamsburg had always put great stock precisely in the external aspects of their community's collective identity. Together, these external elements were often referred to as Hasidic *levush*, a term that literally means "dress," but that also conveyed the broader idea of appearance. According to several Hasidim we interviewed, the most important thing for remaining a member of the community in good standing was not whether one believed in God or even whether one followed the Torah's laws in private, but whether in public one wore the Hasidic *levush* in the broadest sense of the term. As one put it, "Many remain with the Hasidic *levush* but at home are not *shomer shabbes* [do not follow Sabbath laws] or don't believe in God."[15] Adherence to these external markers might not demonstrate an inner belief—and in some cases, they most certainly did not—but they did symbolize a commitment to the collective identity and survival of the community, the continuity of Jewish tradition, and the authority of Hasidic leaders. Perhaps more than faith in God, these three factors had always been paramount in sustaining the Hasidic enclave in Williamsburg, and they help to explain why zealots devoted their energies to policing aspects of *khitsoynius* (exteriority) rather than more interior phenomena such as correct belief.[16]

As gentrification and creeping consumerism transformed the physical landscape of Hasidic Williamsburg, the neighborhood's zealots increasingly employed broadsides, as well as public protests and threats of boycott, to target businesses they viewed as transgressing community norms. In 2007, for example, a glatt kosher ("glatt" indicates that a slaughtered animal's lungs were smooth, without adhesions) food truck named Sub on Wheels, or as it was soon dubbed by Hasidic critics, the "fress-truck" (*fress* is a Yiddish term for eating boorishly), was established by a Hasid named Nathan Lichtenstein, who was born and raised in Williamsburg but later moved to Monsey, in Rockland County. Lichtenstein parked his truck at the intersection of Lee Avenue and the Brooklyn–Queens Expressway in August of that year and began selling eastern European Jewish favorites such as knishes, cholent, chicken soup, and kugel as well as standard American fast-food dishes, including hamburgers, hotdogs, French fries, and "Philly Steaks" (absent the traditional cheese, because of the Halakhic prohibition against mixing milk and meat). By then, food trucks were already an iconic symbol of gentrification in hipster neighborhoods across the country, including North Williamsburg, where a veritable fleet parked daily on Bedford Avenue and sold gourmet ice cream, tacos, falafel, and other dishes.

Yet Sub on Wheels was the first—and perhaps the last—food truck to set up shop on the Hasidic side of Broadway. Initially, Lichtenstein's truck, which served food from six to midnight, five nights a week, did brisk business among the neighborhood's Hasidim and others, despite the presence of some Hasidic protesters.[17] In the following months, Sub on Wheels became a cause célèbre among Hasidic fans before its opponents eventually forced Lichtenstein to close.[18] Some of the same zealots soon went on to deface advertisements for a local Hasidic butcher shop and a neighborhood restaurant named Grill on Lee, which contained images of food that they deemed morally decadent. As the Hasidic website *Vos Iz Neias* explained, "The motivation behind the incidents is spiritual. Ads featuring highly detailed images of tantalizing food—and businesses hawking an unnecessarily wide variety of food, such as the now-shuttered Sub on Wheels, once parked along a Williamsburg street—are seen as excessive and indulgent by austerity-minded activists, who are alarmed by what they see as an intrusion of secular, pleasure-oriented values into their community."[19]

In May 2011, nearly one hundred protesters targeted Iris Beauty Salon & Spa, which had recently opened a branch on Lee Avenue in Williamsburg after first drawing Hasidic women from the neighborhood to its popular site in Crown Heights. The opening of a beauty shop owned by a Lubavitcher Hasidic woman from Crown Heights in the heart of Williamsburg reflected the greater contact between members of both communities now that the tensions between Satmar and Lubavitch that had erupted in violence during the 1970s and 1980s had dramatically declined. Hasidic women from Williamsburg regularly visited Crown Heights— sometimes walking through Bedford-Stuyvesant, which was viewed as much safer than before—where they ate at one of the new restaurants that dotted the neighborhood, went shopping, or availed themselves of wellness-related services at places like Iris. But the more permissive standards in Crown Heights, especially when it came to women's modesty, were seen as a threat by some men within Williamsburg, who drew the line at having a beauty salon in their own enclave, particularly on a central street like Lee Avenue.

Not satisfied with just protesting in Williamsburg, however, local zealots also traveled to Crown Heights, where, given the more relaxed relations between the two communities, they felt safe enough to gather in front of the Iris salon on Kingston Avenue, the main commercial strip of the neighborhood. In a nod to the different language politics of Crown Heights, the protesters held English-language signs with a few key words in Hebrew—rather than the Yiddish broadsides they posted in Williamsburg. These signs sought to shame bystanders by emphasizing the image of Williamsburg throughout New York City as a kind of holy fortress, even by broader Hasidic standards: "Please!! Why should you be the FIRST to start such a business in public, thereby breaking the *tsniyus* [modesty] fortress in our community" and "Please respect our desire to live by higher standards of *kedusha* [holiness]!"[20] In response, many Hasidic residents of both Williamsburg and Crown Heights rejected the message of the protesters, with some dismissing them as "Williamsburg Taliban."[21]

In February 2013, zealots in Williamsburg targeted another local business with a female clientele for alleged modesty infractions. The *New York Daily News* reported that the neighborhood's *vaad ha-tsnius* had posted broadsides encouraging Hasidic residents to boycott a new women's clothing store called Pastel on Lee Avenue because its large plate-glass windows allowed male passersby to observe female customers from the street. The article quoted Moshe Spira, the manager of Grill on Lee, who defended the storeowners: "It is not right. . . . [They are] trying to make a living for them and their family." Spira added that the same group had targeted his restaurant: "When we opened the store, they put up flyers. . . . They made a protest saying, 'Don't eat here.' We were the first fast food restaurant in the neighborhood. They were saying men and women can sit together and are on line together [which they opposed]. We just ignored them and they moved on."[22]

Against this backdrop of surveillance and intimidation, the numerous bars, clubs, and cafés that gentrification had brought to the hipster side of Williamsburg were particularly tempting to Hasidim who desired an alternative to the highly policed spaces of their enclave.[23] In interviews conducted by the authors at the height of this gentrification-inspired interaction, Hasidim in Williamsburg expressed a range of opinions concerning whether it was ever acceptable to patronize a bar. One middle-aged respondent dismissed fellow Hasidim who went to bars as "bums, one in five thousand," and a young Hasid stated, "If I went to a bar it was only 4 or 5 times, just to have a good time," adding, "It doesn't interfere with my Judaism." Another young Hasid, a shopkeeper, said that he sometimes went to a pool hall "just outside [Hasidic] Williamsburg," but added that the older generation was opposed to such activity. Several Hasidim mentioned going to the Turkey's Nest, an old-school neighborhood bar on Bedford Avenue in North Williamsburg, or to a bar on McGuinness Boulevard in Greenpoint to watch the New York Mets on television; another Hasid admitted that he frequented a Williamsburg bar so regularly that he had been nicknamed the "Mayor" by other patrons.

Bars were not the only places where Hasidim from South Williamsburg went to engage in activities that pushed the boundaries of what was seen as acceptable or that were condemned by some in their community. In 2010, for example, the *Jewish Week* published an article titled "Pumping Iron for the Payes Set: In Williamsburg, Chasids and Hipsters Are Increasingly Working Out Alongside One Another," which profiled the workout regimen of a Hasidic restaurant owner from Williamsburg named David Lowey, "in his full Satmar regalia": "Tzitzit dangling from his black pants and payes swinging over his ears, the 290-pound 26-year-old breathed heavily, as he scrolled through the day's Daf Yomi Talmud

page online, from a touch-screen computer panel in front of him."[24] All
of the Hasidim interviewed for the article stressed the health benefits of
exercise and the endemic problem of obesity in Hasidic Williamsburg,
rather than other aspects of the experience that conflicted with the norms
of their community—for example, the desire to be more physically attractive, to look at other people's bodies while exercising, and to be seen
themselves. By framing their membership in the gym in purely utilitarian
terms, they hoped to ameliorate the potential threat posed by these behaviors to their sense of themselves as good Hasidim, and to soften the
negative impact on their reputations within the Hasidic community if
they were discovered. As a Hasid who would only identify himself as
"Yoel" put it, "I for sure hide it from them [my community] because I
should spend my evenings learning Torah in shul and not in gym. I would
never be able to make good shidduchim [marriage matches] with my kids
if this would be public."

When asked about the newfound pursuit of physical fitness by some
men in the community, "Malkah," a Hasidic woman from Williamsburg,
linked the phenomenon with changing conceptions of Hasidic masculinity.[25] In the past, Malkah told us, men in Satmar and other Hungarian
Hasidic sects were expected to eschew an interest in fine food, fashion,
fitness, and other *gashmiesdike* (material or worldly) concerns that were
typically dismissed as the purview of women. As an example, Malkah
mentioned that at weddings—whose lavishness had long been regulated
by communal decree to prevent a kind of *luksus* (luxury) "arms race"—
men's tables had traditionally lacked the centerpieces found on women's
tables, and men were served only a fish appetizer, while women were
served more elaborate dishes. Now, however, a growing number of men
desired better food at weddings, and their tables were increasingly decorated with centerpieces as well. Malkah linked the gruff demeanor and
"lack of manners among the older generation of men"—something that
frequently drew the ire of outsiders—with the rough conditions that
many had endured in Europe or in postwar Williamsburg: "They [mem-
bers of the older generation] were tough. But now [younger Hasidic
men] want to have nice things and look good. I hate to say it because it's
not PC [politically correct], but the new generation of men in their
twenties, they're kind of emasculated. They're not macho like the older
generation." To Malkah, the newly fit Hasidim were actually less masculine, at least by the traditional standards of the community, than their
predecessors. While the latter may have avoided physical exercise, they

were not afraid of hard work, including physical labor, nor were they averse to employing their fists to defend their turf when they deemed it necessary.

Walls of Virtue

In an interview conducted in April 2008, Rabbi David Niederman, the president of the United Jewish Organizations (UJO), spoke passionately about the struggle to keep his enclave free from negative moral influences in the face of gentrification. "People got together and tried to rebuild our religious community from the ashes [of the Holocaust]," he stressed. "We try to keep as much [of] an insular community [as possible] under the circumstances." Niederman emphasized that Hasidim wanted neighbors and visitors to "try to respect the religious character" of the neighborhood, but added, "You cannot tell someone what to do. It's not like we're putting up posters."[26] And yet a few years later, that was precisely what some Hasidic business owners on Lee Avenue in South Williamsburg did in an effort to require all customers to observe the community's standards of modesty. Seven Hasidic-owned businesses posted signs in their stores, headed by the English phrase "Dress Code for Store" and followed by a statement in Hebrew—probably intended for Israeli tourists who sometimes visited the neighborhood—"Here One Enters Only in Modest Clothing" and then, in both English and Spanish, "No Shorts / No Barefoot / No Sleeveless / No Low Cut Neckline / ALLOWED IN THIS STORE."[27]

The signs represented a milestone in the history of Hasidic Williamsburg, one that reflected the growing perception among some residents that their holy enclave was under siege. No longer content to police just their own community members, these Hasidim and their supporters now sought to regulate the dress of non-Hasidic customers in their business establishments, too. For years, it had been common in Haredi neighborhoods in Israel to post signs warning female visitors to dress modestly.[28] While condemned by other Israelis, this policing of women's dress was tolerated by the state as one of many accommodations made to Haredim. Unlike Mea Shearim or Beit Shemesh, however, Williamsburg is in the United States, where the First Amendment protects both religious expression and freedom of speech. Courts have frequently understood the latter to include dress, though certain dress codes have been deemed legally permissible as long as they do not discriminate on the basis of race, sex, or religion. Within this wider context, the gentrification of Williamsburg had transformed the neighborhood into a virtual laboratory for thorny questions of religious freedom and its limits.

In August 2012, the New York City Commission on Human Rights filed a complaint against the storeowners, charging that the signs violated the New York City Administrative Code, since they "expressly intended to deny patrons the advantages, facilities and/or privileges of a public accommodation based upon their gender and creed."[29] In an interview with *Vos Iz Neias*, a Haredi-run news website, Clifford Mulqueen, the deputy commissioner and general counsel of the city's Commission on Human Rights, explained, "There is nothing wrong with a dress code, per se. . . . But there is something wrong with a public accommodation trying to impose its religious beliefs on other people."[30] Hasidic storeowners quickly secured legal representation from Kirkland & Ellis, one of the country's largest law firms. Devora Allon, an attorney for the firm, told the Israeli newspaper *Haaretz* that she was representing the Hasidim pro bono because of the case's "implications for religious rights, and for religious freedoms." Regarding the merit of the complaints, Allon stated, "The complaints do not allege discriminatory intent, and that is what the human rights law outlaws. . . . The signs do not actually discriminate between men and women, and apply equally to men and women."[31]

Informally advising Allon was Marc Stern, associate general counsel of the American Jewish Committee (AJC), a Jewish advocacy organization established in 1906. Stern pointed out that numerous private clubs elsewhere in the city had dress codes that prohibited "shorts and a halter top," arguing, "The only bias I see in these lawsuits is a stereotype by the City Commission of Human Rights that 'all Hasidim must be guilty of discrimination because they're all misogynists' . . . How is it, within three miles of the city commission's office, there are God knows how many restaurants with different gender-based dress codes, and the city commission doesn't pursue them?"[32] In the *Jewish Week*, Deputy Commissioner Mulqueen responded to these claims of a double standard by emphasizing that Hasidic storeowners had "posted a sign that basically indicated that customers had to obey the Jewish laws of modesty. . . . Dress codes are OK. . . . Telling someone to wear a jacket is saying we want a certain kind of clientele here; we want to project a certain image. It has nothing to do with a protected class. Whereas telling someone they have to abide by certain rules of the Jewish faith crosses the line into [establishing] a protected class."[33]

The claim that the city's Commission on Human Rights was discriminating against the Hasidic storeowners, and not that the storeowners were discriminating against potential customers, was also supported by Eric Rassbach, the deputy general counsel of the Becket Fund for Religious Liberty, which described itself as "a non-profit, public-interest legal and educational institute with a mission to protect the free expression of all faiths."[34] In an article in the *New York Times*, Rassbach derided the Williamsburg case as an example of "the power of government to suppress Orthodox religious practices," and in the *Jewish Week*, he asked, "How is it discrimination and a human rights violation when the request is made by a poor chasidic Jew but perfectly fine if posted in an upscale establishment? You may disagree with what an owner of a restaurant or business wants you to do, but disagreement is not discrimination."[35]

The battle lines in the Williamsburg case reflected a broader struggle taking place in legislative bodies and courthouses across the United States over the government's ability to regulate religious expression or compel action in the face of individual religious objections. In a landmark decision in 2014, the U.S. Supreme Court decided in *Burwell v. Hobby Lobby Stores* that closely held for-profit companies that objected on religious grounds were not required to provide their female employees with contraceptive coverage as mandated by the Affordable Care Act, "if there is a less restrictive means of furthering the law's interest."[36] While politically and religiously conservative groups such as the Family Research Council and the U.S. Conference of Catholic Bishops lauded the decision as a victory for religious freedom, many civil liberties organizations and women's rights groups decried what they saw as the Court endorsing religiously justified discrimination, or as the ACLU put it, "With increasing frequency, we are seeing individuals and institutions claiming a right to discriminate—by refusing to provide services to women and LGBT people—based on religious objections. The discrimination takes many forms."[37]

As in *Hobby Lobby*, the intersection of women's bodies and religious beliefs was at the center of the New York City Human Rights Commission's complaint against the Hasidic storeowners in Williamsburg. Although the Hasidim formally denied that they were targeting women in their signs, that was how the Human Rights Commission interpreted their actions, undoubtedly because of the well-documented attempts by Hasidim in Williamsburg and elsewhere to police women's modesty. Could these Hasidim be compelled to accept patrons in their stores whose clothing violated their religious norms? Or, in this case at least, was the patrons' right to dress as they wished trumped by the right of the Hasidic business owners to follow the dictates of their religion? If the city could establish that women, in particular, were the intended targets of the signs, did that determination change the equation?

Ultimately, these questions were never debated in court. In January 2014, seventeen months after the complaint was first filed, the administrative law judge in the case took both parties aside and encouraged them to come to a pretrial agreement. The city withdrew its lawsuit and waived the fines, and the Hasidic store owners agreed to "state clearly that they did not discriminate on the basis of gender or race."[38] Patricia L. Gatling, the New York City Human Rights commissioner, released a statement in which she explained the terms: "Pursuant to the proposed agreement, representatives from the stores agreed that if they were to post new signs in their windows, they would say that while modest dress is appreciated, all individuals are welcome to enter the stores free from discrimination. The Commission is satisfied that the store owners understand their obligations under the NYC Human Rights Law."[39] Just as the city spun the agreement as a victory, Hasidic activists did the same, with Rabbi David Niederman of the UJO declaring in a public statement:

> I am gratified that this case is finally over and that the seven small businesses of Lee Avenue have been vindicated. It was an outrage for this case to be brought in the first place and even more shocking that as recently as this morning, the New York City Human Rights Commission had the chutzpah to try and impose a $75,000 fine against local businesses that did nothing wrong.
>
> If you go to a [sic] upscale restaurant, there is a dress code. Yet when small businesses in Williamsburg do the same, they are attacked and threatened with fines that would put them out of business?[40]

Bokhers of Summer

Like the neighborhood's bars, fitness clubs, and stores, McCarren Park, located on the border between North Williamsburg and Greenpoint, became a site where Hasidim interacted with other residents after the area's gentrification. In 2008, a group of Hasidic yeshiva *bukherim* (unmarried young men) in their late teens and early twenties even formed a softball team, the Stormers, to compete in the Greenpoint Softball League, whose members came from a wide variety of backgrounds, including hipsters and Latinos. Members of the team stated that negative attitudes toward sports, widely held in their part of Williamsburg, made the Roberto Clemente Ballfield on Division Avenue between Wythe and Kent Avenues, located right in the Hasidic enclave, an undesirable spot to play softball. Reflecting this attitude, an administrator at the Pupa yeshiva, interviewed in front of the institution's offices on Bedford Avenue in the Hasidic section of Williamsburg, emphasized that members of the team were an extreme minority. "How many of them are there, 12? What does it matter?" he said.[41]

On the one hand, the yeshiva administrator was justified in downplaying the significance of the team. After all, the number of players was minuscule compared with the thousands of students in the Hasidic school system in Williamsburg, Kiryas Joel, and elsewhere. But seen within the longer history of the Hasidic community's attitude toward ball playing and the broader context of gentrification in Williamsburg, the team's creation was yet another sign of how much the enclave was being affected by new cultural influences. When Rabbi Yoel Teitelbaum arrived in New York Harbor in the fall of 1946, Hank Greenberg, the great Detroit Tiger slugger, was chasing his fourth and final American League home-run crown. In 1934, Greenberg had become a hero to millions of Jews around the country when he refused to play on Yom Kippur. Greenberg and, after him, the Dodger pitcher Sandy Koufax came to symbolize the possibility of being Jewish *and* American, a dramatic departure from the historical situation in Europe. As Philip Roth noted in a *New York Times* essay in 1973: "For someone whose roots in America were strong but only inches deep ... baseball was a kind of secular church that reached into every class and region of the nation and bound us together in common concerns, loyalties, rituals, enthusiasm, and antagonisms."[42]

So complete was the romance between American Jews and baseball in the 1940s that even Orthodox and Hasidic schoolboys played the game in Williamsburg, a phenomenon that Chaim Potok transformed into a key plot element in *The Chosen*, his novel about Jewish life in the neighborhood during this period. Recalling these years, Yonah Landau, a disciple of Yoel Teitelbaum, noted, "It was then customary for even the Hasidic Talmud Torahs [elementary schools] to 'play ball' in the American fashion."[43] Not surprisingly, it did not take long for Teitelbaum to turn his attention to the practice. As Landau observed,

The Rebbe, may the memory of the righteous be a blessing, was a great opponent of these kinds of games which were practiced by the nations of the world. At a gathering of teachers, the Rebbe . . . explained that children should play games that they will outgrow over the years. This is not the case with a game such as playing ball that grows along with the children. Because it is popular in the wider gentile street, they will also retain an interest in it when they become adults. Jewish children should not play such games. With time, the previously mentioned schools followed the example of Satmar in the matter of ball playing, as with dress and other Hasidic customs. Today a ball is prohibited in all Hasidic Talmud Torahs without exception.

Hasidic leaders in Williamsburg were opposed to uses of the male body that made Jews seem more like the biblical figure of Esau—gentiles were supposedly defined by their physicality—than like his brother Jacob, considered to be the ideal of Jewish spirituality and learning. Similarly, they cautioned that too much emphasis on the male body might lead Hasidim to imitate the sinful Zionists, who had broken with the traditional masculine ideal of rabbinic Judaism and replaced it with the so-called Muscle Jew of Max Nordau. For these reasons, Rabbi Yoel Teitelbaum and his followers sought to tightly regulate or prohibit certain athletic activities among Hasidic schoolboys, a stance that made Satmar more similar to Haredi communities in Israel, which confronted Zionist ideals of masculinity daily, than to the American Haredi mainstream, which tended to have a more relaxed attitude toward sports.[44]

For Rabbi Yoel Teitelbaum, baseball was particularly problematic because it served as a pathway to acculturation. Childhood engagement with the game could lead to a lifetime of interest, which in turn could inspire Hasidim to see themselves as belonging to a wider community of fans (for example, the so-called Yankees Universe), have idols who were not Jewish religious leaders, and engage in activities (such as watching games and following pennant races) considered *bitul Torah*, or a waste of time, instead of studying. Nevertheless, some Hasidim did become diehard baseball fans over the years, and members of some sects even played the game recreationally, especially in the summer bungalow colonies in the Catskills, where communal restrictions on athletic activities were often looser than in Brooklyn and where, beginning in 1977, Hasidim and Orthodox Jewish men played together in the Orthodox Bungalow Baseball League.[45]

In Hasidic Williamsburg, by contrast, organized ball playing was frowned on, and for most of the community's history, the temptation to do so was limited by the woeful lack of parks in the neighborhood. In the early 1990s, when Latino residents lobbied the city to turn a lot in the Williamsburg Urban Renewal Area into a baseball field, Hasidim proposed that low-income housing be built on the site instead. As a Hasidic activist named Isaac Abraham stated, "I think the whole world would agree that housing would serve a better purpose. . . . If a kid doesn't have a roof over his head, you can't just throw him into a park to play baseball."[46] At the time, relations between Hasidim and Latinos in South Williamsburg had reached a nadir after decades of fighting over public housing and other issues, leading the *New York Times* to compare members of the communities to "urban Hatfields and McCoys."[47] Seeking compromise, the city built the Roberto Clemente Ballfield in 1998, in honor of the famous Puerto Rican slugger, and a year later it completed construction of the adjoining Jacob's Ladder Playground, which became popular with Hasidic children and their caretakers.[48]

The gentrification of North Williamsburg played a decisive role in the creation of the Hasidic softball team. Before the neighborhood's transformation, McCarren Park was widely perceived as dangerous by many residents of the Hasidic community. "No one played baseball before the artists moved in," one member of the Stormers declared. "I have nothing against Hispanics, but it was dangerous when it was a Hispanic neighborhood. Artists make it safer." Jim Sherman, longtime director of the Greenpoint Softball League, viewed the Stormers as an important addition to the community league, which he said represented all ethnicities and "never has any racial stuff" or anti-Semitism on the field—a statement confirmed by Hasidic players.[49]

During the summer months, the team, originally named the Blue Socks but later called the Stormers, practiced in the park daily. After one scrimmage observed by the authors, a half-dozen Hasidim in good spirits razzed the other dugout in Spanish. Their opponents called back in jest, "*Judíos*, play ball! *Judíos*, play ball!" Among them was Hector, who recalled with a smile his first encounter with the Stormers: "I wasn't expecting them to be that good. But they all can hit. They all can field." The Hasidic members of the team—which also included three Dominicans and an African American, who all worked with one of the Hasidim—played in long-sleeved white dress shirts and black pants, trading dress shoes for sneakers and black hats for baseball caps during games. Most

A member of the Stormers, a Hasidic softball team that participated
in the Greenpoint Softball League in McCarren Park, 2008
(Photograph by Michael Casper)

hid their athletic hobby from their parents, who assumed they were going
out to learn Torah. "No one would like to know their kids are playing
with goyim in the park," Moishe, the twenty-year-old third baseman, admitted in an interview. "But they don't know that they're not the bad
kind." Citing Yoel Teitelbaum's aversion to sports, another Hasidic ball
player declared, "Rabbis don't like it, but they got a job to do." He added
that his parents know about his unorthodox hobby, but found it "better
than doing other bad things." A nineteen-year-old player named Itsik explained: "I like to play, because it's like hypnosis. I can forget about the
world." He mentioned that his family was especially strict. And if his father were to find out he played softball? "I would be *geshlugn* [beaten]."[50]

Marienbad on Metropolitan Avenue

Gentrification helped make possible another form of physical recreation
that was not prohibited by the Hasidic community, but had to be strictly
regulated. In contrast to baseball, which Hasidic critics in Williamsburg

had long viewed as quintessentially American and a slippery slope to assimilation, teaching one's children to swim was required by the Talmud, and in fin-de-siècle Europe, visiting spas such as Marienbad and Carlsbad (both now in the Czech Republic) became a widespread and ritualized element of Hasidic leisure culture, including among the Satmar Rebbe and his circle of followers.[51] A century later, in Williamsburg, a very different kind of spa became popular among members of the local Hasidic community for aquatic exercise, relaxation, and socializing. This time, however, it was not Hasidic rebbes and their entourages who were at the center of the activity, but Hasidic women of different ages, most of them mothers or grandmothers, who, for a few hours a week, turned the Metropolitan Pool on Bedford and Metropolitan Avenues in North Williamsburg into their own version of Marienbad.

The Metropolitan Pool began to attract Hasidic women after the city renovated its swimming pool and exercise facilities in 1997, some of the capital improvements spurred by gentrification.[52] In deference to requests from Hasidic women, the pool designated women-only swimming hours for several days a week, during which a special curtain was drawn to block visual access to the pool by people entering from the street, and a female lifeguard was posted.[53] An evocative first-person account published in 2003 by Annie Bruno, a non-Hasidic woman who moved to the neighborhood in 1992, captured the atmosphere in the Metropolitan Pool during one of the women-only swim sessions:

> I was a little startled when the Hasidic women started coming in, their shaved heads in puffy old-fashioned shower caps, their bodies draped in flowered housedresses with long sleeves, the kind that snap or button down the front, with two patch pockets at the thigh. Their only traditional pool accessory that I could see were flip-flops, which they lined up carefully along the tiled wall. . . . More and more women kept coming, and I realized that there was going to be very little swimming going on. I imagined that this was their hour away from duties and children and prayers, when they could all sit in a huge bath together and talk freely. Even their bodies were as free as they could be: No wigs, no stockings.

Bruno added, "I don't know if it was their hairlessness or their playfulness together, but they exuded innocence, which was probably the desired effect of the shaving and the covering up. They didn't look anything like the contained, competent Hasidic women I would see on the subway, pushing their well-behaved toddlers in strollers and wearing shiny, chestnut-colored wigs, mid-calf skirts, and well-made shoes."[54]

In an interview with us, Malkah, a middle-aged Hasidic resident of Williamsburg, noted that at least some of the Hasidic women who began to make use of the Metropolitan Pool in the late 1990s had previously swum at the 14th Street Y on First Avenue during its own women-only hours.[55] Unlike the Metropolitan Pool, however, the YMHA was much less conveniently located in Manhattan, rather than just down Bedford Avenue, and, moreover, it typically had male lifeguards.[56] While this deterred some Hasidic women from swimming there, it clearly had not dissuaded all of them, including Malkah, who also recalled rumors that one Hasidic woman from Williamsburg even swam during the regular, mixed-gender hours.

Malkah added that in the 1950s, some Hasidic women of her mother's generation would swim at public beaches in Miami and elsewhere, even though men were present. This reflected the more flexible attitude toward women's modesty that then existed among many of the recent Hasidic immigrants from Europe and that Rabbi Yoel Teitelbaum and his most zealous admirers strove to counter. These followers included Rabbi Hananya Yom Tov Lipa Deutsch (1905–1991), a disciple and relative of Teitelbaum who published a collection of responsa from Haredi rabbis around the world that prohibited mixed bathing or swimming.[57] Citing a common set of Talmudic sources, these authorities agreed that the activity was prohibited by the Torah—the highest level of prohibition—and that if a Jewish woman persisted in engaging in it despite being warned, her husband was allowed, even obligated, to divorce her.[58] Teitelbaum issued numerous warnings against the practice, beginning in 1936, when he told followers in Satmar that those who engaged in mixed swimming "should not be mentioned in a holy *shul* [synagogue]."[59] In 1958, Teitelbaum became embroiled in a major controversy when a hotel owner in Jerusalem announced plans to build the first mixed-swimming pool in the holy city, prompting heated demonstrations by local Haredim. Amid a lobbying campaign that included pleas to the United Nations and President Eisenhower, as well as ads in the *New York Times* and other newspapers, Teitelbaum called for large protests against the pool to take place in Manhattan and Washington, D.C., where roughly five hundred Satmar Hasidim from Williamsburg gathered in front of the White House.[60]

Long before the Metropolitan Pool established women-only hours, therefore, mixed-gender swimming was a powerful symbol of *pritsus*, or licentiousness, for leaders of the Hasidic community in Williamsburg and a flashpoint for activism. Although Hasidic women and men were prohibited from swimming together, this did not prevent women and girls in the community from learning how to swim in the upstate summer camps, bungalows, and hotels that quickly became popular among Hasidic residents of Williamsburg in the postwar period. There, not only did Hasidic women and girls learn to swim, but some also became trained water safety instructors and lifeguards. Later, a number of these women became regulars at the Metropolitan Pool, and because of their deep dedication to both the physical and the social dimensions of the swimming sessions, they mobilized to save the women-only hours when they were threatened, gathering signatures on petitions, speaking at meetings of local Community Board 1, and confronting Mayor Bill de Blasio at a public forum in Borough Park.[61]

When the regular female lifeguard went on vacation in the summer of 2013 and was replaced by a man, Hasidic women stopped visiting the pool and protested to local officials. As Rose Herschkowitz, a fifty-seven-year-old Hasidic woman who swam at the pool with her eighty-six-year-old mother, stated at a Williamsburg and Greenpoint Community Board 1 meeting: "There are hundreds of [Hasidic] women who come to the sessions. . . . When there's a male we don't come. It's for modesty. . . . A lot of women cut their membership to the pool because of the lost months of swimming."[62] Liam Kavanagh, the city's first deputy commissioner for parks and recreation, responded, "We don't have a formal policy, but we can't commit to providing a female lifeguard because it would run against the establishment clause [of the First Amendment of the U.S. Constitution] of providing a service on the basis of a religious belief."[63] Of course, concern could have just as easily been expressed regarding the legality of the women-only hours. And that was exactly what happened after an anonymous complaint was filed with the New York City Commission of Human Rights on December 1, 2015, prompting the city to give signals that it was going to suspend the women-only hours at the pool.[64]

In the following days, supporters and opponents of the women-only hours squared off against one another. Prominent advocates included local Hasidic women such as Rivka Friedman, Scheindal Kraus, Esther Weiss, Esther Erp, and Henny Herzog, who regularly used the pool; the veteran Williamsburg activist Rabbi David Niederman, the president of the UJO; Democratic New York state assemblyman Dov Hikind of Borough Park; and Jan Peterson, an iconoclastic feminist and longtime resident of the neighborhood who had founded the National Congress of Neighborhood Women in Williamsburg.[65] Peterson, who served as chair of the Women's Issues Committee of Community Board 1, argued that it was necessary to "look at this as a women's issue" and as a local issue: "The swimming hours were a real gift to this community."[66] In a series of public pronouncements, Hikind sought to hoist progressives on their own petard: "What happened to being culturally sensitive? I thought we were in the midst of a 'Progressive Era,' where we do everything we can to be more accepting of cultural differences. In no way is this program for separate gender swimming meant to be discriminatory. Anyone, regardless of their race or religion, is more than welcome to take advantage of the facility's services. We call upon the City and the Parks Department to reverse this decision and ensure the continuation of this program."[67] Elsewhere, Hikind emphasized that the women-only hours embodied the principle of cultural sensitivity, which was important to progressives: "The whole idea of being culturally sensitive to other people's differences. That's what we're all about. That's what being progressive is. Why deprive this group of women, hundreds of women who come during the course of the week?"[68]

The arguments made in favor of the women-only hours at the Metropolitan Pool reveal remarkable parallels with those made by Agudas Yisroel, a Haredi political party in Israel, in its campaign to convince the Israeli government to create a gender-segregated beach in Tel Aviv in 1966. As Shayna Weiss showed, the Chief Rabbinate of Israel, a state institution, had unsuccessfully lobbied the Tel Aviv municipality to end mixed swimming, on Jewish religious grounds. It was only when Agudat Yisrael shifted arguments away from religion and, instead, emphasized the language of rights and the accommodation of minorities that the campaign was successful. In the words of Weiss, "According to the Agudah, the city of Tel Aviv was obligated to enable Haredim to access the beach just as their secular brethren, because members of the ultra-Orthodox community were tax-paying citizens. ... Religion became marginal, as a civic discourse was adopted to argue the value of a separate beach."[69] Whether supporters of the women-only hours in Williamsburg were aware of this precedent in Tel Aviv or whether they simply arrived at the same strategy via a similar political calculus, the resulting arguments were nearly identical. Taken together, both cases illuminate how concerns that are fundamentally religious can be transmuted into claims regarding rights and cultural diversity, thereby dramatically shifting the discursive and political terrain and potentially producing very different outcomes.[70]

Critics of the policy at the Metropolitan Pool included local swimmers frustrated with the limited number of all-access hours or with trying to swim laps while Hasidic women socialized in the lanes.[71] Some swimmers were bothered on principle. As Doug Safranek put it, "I'm happy that these women have a place to swim, but strictly speaking it isn't fair. It's an extreme religious group that has a standard of modesty and decorum the rest of the culture doesn't share."[72] Another swimmer, Barbara Campisi, expressed sympathy for the Hasidic women—albeit while perpetuating an inaccurate stereotype regarding their freedom of movement—but still felt that the current arrangement did not adequately address the needs of others who used the pool: "I feel for them. They can hardly leave their homes. I want them to be able to swim. But it's just gone too far."[73] But not all swimmers objected. Robert Taylor spoke in favor of the women: "It doesn't bother me that I have to get out of the pool to respect other people's religious expression. Being tolerant of other people's religious and personal expression is an important part of being in New York."[74] Arlene Rosado, a non-Hasidic woman who swam at the pool precisely because of the women-only hours, went further: "[When] you're in that pool you realize this isn't a Hasidic thing. Someone who's never been there, they see more Hasidic than any other religion or race, they might take it as that[,] interpret as that. There are black women, Arab women, Chinese, other Hispanic. There are a lot more Hasidic women than any other group. That's only because they're right here . . . it's convenient."[75]

Despite these arguments, some critics drew a bright constitutional line between the government's tolerance of religious expression and what they considered an illegal endorsement of it. Donna Lieberman, the executive director of the New York Civil Liberties Union, told the *New York Times*, "People have every right to their beliefs and to limit their swimming in accordance with those religious beliefs. But they have no right to impose a regime of gender discrimination on a public pool."[76] Similarly, after the city appeared to reverse itself as a result of pressure from supporters, the *Times* published an editorial on June 1, 2016, that lambasted the decision as "unmoored from the laws of New York City and the Constitution, and commonly held principles of fairness and equal access" and calling it "a capitulation to a theocratic view of government services."[77]

Hasidic women lining up for women-only hours at the Metropolitan Pool in
Williamsburg, 2019 (Photograph by Caroline Ourso)

The editorial led supporters of the women-only hours to cry foul, since,
as the journalist Seth Lipsky first noted, the *Times* had published an article three months earlier that celebrated separate swimming hours for
Muslim women at a public housing project in Toronto.[78] The article described the culturally sensitive housing project, with "the aquatic center
as its centerpiece," as "a scathing indictment of the meager efforts by
New York, London and other cities that have failed to protect middle-
and working-class residents from the displacement wrought by gentrification," and praised its efforts "to create a session that allows only women
and girls to relax in the hot tub, swim laps or careen down the water slide,
a rare bit of 'me' time treasured by many of the neighborhood's Muslim
residents."[79] In *Tablet* magazine, Yair Rosenberg noted that similar accommodations had been made for Muslim women in several cities in the
United States, including Seattle, San Diego, and St. Paul, adding, "It is
exceedingly odd that the national paper of record only excoriated the
practice of sex-segregated swimming when it became aware of religious
Jews engaging in it, and even then, omitted the identical practices of religious Muslims."[80] That sentiment was shared by the Orthodox Jewish

Public Affairs Council, a Hasidic-run advocacy organization in Rockland County, which asked, "If it is great when the wishes of women in the Muslim community are accommodated, why is it a problem when the same is granted to women in the Orthodox Jewish community?"[81]

It was a question that the *Times* chose not to address in its pages, perhaps because it would have required a frank—and uncomfortable— exploration of whether Hasidim were, in fact, covered differently by the media from members of other religious communities, even when they engaged in identical practices. Like concurrent debates over infant cir- cumcision, kosher and halal slaughter, and religiously required head cov- erings, the controversy over separate swimming hours—a potential precedent for other prescribed forms of gender segregation—not only placed Hasidim and devout Muslims on the same side of the issue but also served as a harbinger for other complicated challenges to constitu- tional norms regarding religion and state that would likely become more frequent as previously small or disenfranchised religious communities grew in size and confidence in the United States.

In July 2016, city officials announced a compromise on the women- only hours at the Metropolitan Pool, reducing them by half, from eight to four hours per week. The decision placated at least some critics, including a longtime Metropolitan Pool swimmer named Catherine Fukushima, who praised the Human Rights Commission for having "come to a very fair and balanced decision that takes into account the needs of all the dif- ferent aspects of our diverse community."[82] It also allowed the Hasidic es- tablishment in Williamsburg to declare victory and laud Mayor Bill de Blasio, especially in comparison with his predecessor, Michael Bloomberg, who had run afoul of the community on a number of fronts. "Heaven and Earth between Bloomberg and de Blasio," trumpeted a headline in *Der Yid* after the decision was announced. "Haredi Jews also have Human Rights!"[83] In a measure of how complicated politics could be in New York City, the article defended the proudly progressive mayor, who had long cultivated Haredi votes and donors, for standing up to his own liberal al- lies, who, it complained, typically ignored the rights of Haredim: "Unfor- tunately, you hear today from many liberals who defend all rights, except for the rights of Haredi Jews. Mayor de Blasio stands out for his sympathy for the Haredi public, even when the powerful liberal interests tear him apart for it."

At a press conference held at the Metropolitan Pool, Dov Hikind demonstrated the degree to which liberal ideals such as human rights, women's rights, and cultural diversity could be deployed to defend a practice that was fundamentally rooted in a patriarchal and separatist religious culture. "This is a human rights victory for women," he said. "It's about respecting the cultural differences between people, that's the beauty of New York."[84] His words were a far cry from the legal responsa on mixed swimming published by Rabbi Deutsch in his compendium *Sefer Taharat Yom Tov*, among them one by Rabbi Yitshak Tsvi Sofer, the *av bet din*, or head of the rabbinic court, of Temeshvar in Jerusalem. According to Sofer, mixed swimming was a symbol of a much broader—and from his perspective, disturbing—trend, namely, the political empowerment of women: "If we examine the past we see that the terrible *pritsus* of mixed swimming that prevails now throughout the world was once considered disgusting and abhorrent in the eyes of the nations. ... Yet, after the First World War, the corrupt view emerged that women should have equal obligations and rights as men regarding all political and practical matters of life. The result of this heresy that spread throughout all these territories was to change the order of the world that God had ordained."[85]

Dov Hikind was not alone in depicting the battle over the Metropolitan Pool's women-only hours as a human rights struggle or in claiming that Hasidic—or Muslim—women had a constitutionally protected right to expect the city to accommodate their religious beliefs as long as doing so did not overly burden other residents.[86] Among those who offered support in case the conflict resulted in a legal battle was the First Liberty Institute, which described itself as "the largest legal organization in the nation dedicated exclusively to protecting religious liberty for all Americans," and had taken on numerous cases around the country, "defending the fundamental right of every individual—of any faith—to follow their conscience and to live according their religious beliefs."[87] Of course, there were also critics of the compromise, such as Donna Lieberman of the NYCLU, who did not accept this reasoning and argued that the city was essentially endorsing religion in violation of the Establishment Clause of the First Amendment, or as she put it bluntly after the decision was announced, "It has all the earmarks of a religious exemption. People have every right to go swimming in a gender-segregated environment pursuant to their religious beliefs, but not on the taxpayer dime."[88] Caught between these two positions, a short while later New York City cut the women-only hours at the Metropolitan Pool again, this time to only two a week, prompting Hasidic women and their supporters to restart their protests.[89]

At a Community Board 1 meeting in February 2017, female Hasidic activists emphasized the health benefits of swimming and complained that the pool was now being underused during the former women-only swim times. Esther Weiss, who had swum at the pool for decades, noted that she had gathered petitions in support of the women-only hours and that "women have the right to swim without men." Rivka Friedman, who identified herself as the daughter of a Holocaust survivor, argued that "Hassidic women are like any other minorities and they are entitled to their rights, too," and Henny Herzog, a lifeguard and water safety instructor, stressed the inclusiveness, of a sort, of the segregated swim times: "The women who use the swim time are a part of the diverse community that use the pool. Every woman is welcome."[90] As in the case of the Muslim women in France who first became politically active during the head scarf controversy in that country, Hasidic women in Williamsburg became activists for the first time in the history of their community in order to defend a religiously obligated practice that critics considered sexist and oppressive.[91] And like many of their Muslim counterparts, these Hasidic women did not invoke religious duty to make their claims but, rather, the liberal language of rights.

CHAPTER NINE

Two-Way Street

I N CITIES AROUND THE world, one of the most common—and controversial—spatial transformations that accompanied gentrification during the first decades of the twenty-first century was the construction of bike lanes.[1] Like gentrifying neighborhoods in Portland, Los Angeles, Washington, D.C., and other cities during this period, Williamsburg was no exception. What was different, however, was the presence of the large Hasidic community in South Williamsburg, an area that linked gentrifying areas to the south (Clinton Hill, Fort Greene, Bedford-Stuyvesant, Dumbo) with those to the north (North Williamsburg, Greenpoint) and that included a crucial segment of the rapidly developing Brooklyn waterfront.

Beginning in 2004, the city held a series of public workshops to discuss the development of a greenway along the Brooklyn waterfront.[2] The following year, the rezoning of the Williamsburg-Greenpoint section of the waterfront set the stage for the construction of bike lanes on several of the main arteries that traversed the Hasidic enclave. Once installed, the bike lanes were a stark reminder that the traditional borders of Hasidic Williamsburg had been breached, and in practical terms, they served as a conduit for the daily passage of numerous riders through the neighborhood. The ensuing controversy and the sensationalist media coverage it inspired revealed unique features of what took place in Hasidic Williamsburg while also illuminating important parallels with other gentrifying neighborhoods in the city, as well as

around the country, where the creation of bike lanes provoked conflict between longtime residents and newcomers.

For decades, the Satmar community had sought to regulate and, in
certain contexts, prohibit bike riding by its members. According to one
Hasidic source, when asked about the subject in the 1970s by one of his
followers, Rabbi Yoel Teitelbaum had expressly prohibited Satmar children from riding bicycles to and from school.[3] Yet unlike ball playing,
which he also sought to limit, bicycling was not only a leisure activity but
also an important mode of transportation, one that could easily have been
adopted by Hasidim in Williamsburg for practical reasons. The vast majority of Hasidic residents of the neighborhood—unlike those in the Hasidic enclave in Antwerp, Belgium—rejected bicycling for transportation.
Instead, over the years, the Hasidic community in Williamsburg developed a pervasive and entrenched culture of driving automobiles. The reasons for this included the typically large number of children in Hasidic
families, which encouraged the use of minivans, SUVs, and, in an earlier
generation, station wagons. All of these children attended private religious schools, which relied on fleets of yellow buses to shuttle them back
and forth. The extensive family and business ties between Hasidim in
Williamsburg and those in other neighborhoods in Brooklyn, as well as
in communities such as Kiryas Joel, New Square (New York), or Lakewood Township (New Jersey), meant that Hasidic residents of the neighborhood relied on their own vehicles or on private buses to attend
weddings and other functions, to travel to bungalows during the summer,
to commute to work, and so on. In addition, many Hasidim avoided using
subways, either out of fear of crime, especially during the period of New
York City's decline, or because they wanted to avoid crowded, mixed-gender settings and immodestly dressed riders.

Long before city officials decided to install bike lanes in the neighborhood, therefore, many residents of Hasidic Williamsburg had developed a strong attachment to driving, one that reflected the community's
distinctive character but was also shared by members of other working-
and middle-class urban neighborhoods across the United States, where
opposition to bike lanes crystallized during the same period. As the anthropologist Adonia Lugo observed in regard to a bitter conflict over
bike lanes in a traditionally African American neighborhood in Washington, D.C.: "Access to driving is seen as a very important status symbol [in
such communities]. . . . Sometimes people feel threatened when they feel
a [bike lane] project will reduce their access to driving."[4] It is important

to keep this broader context in mind as we examine how the "Williamsburg Bike Lane Battle" unfolded and was represented in the media.[5]

By the time Mayor Michael Bloomberg appointed Janette Sadik-Khan to be New York City's new Department of Transportation (DOT) commissioner, in 2007, bike lanes had been installed earlier in the year on Wythe and Bedford Avenues, right in the heart of Hasidic Williamsburg. Six years and hundreds of miles of bike lanes later, Bloomberg described Sadik-Khan as being "like the child that Robert Moses and Jane Jacobs never had: an urban visionary determined to reshape the streets of New York, but with an abiding concern for the health of neighborhoods and the safety of their residents."[6] By contrast, critics of her ambitious bike lane program accused her of overreach; John Cassidy, a writer for the *New Yorker*, even compared her to Louis Antoine de Saint-Just, and Bloomberg to Maximilien Robespierre, the French revolutionaries who led the Terror.[7]

Almost immediately after being appointed commissioner, Sadik-Khan turned her attention to the Williamsburg waterfront, whose landmark rezoning in 2005 had made possible the construction of high-rise luxury developments in an area previously notable for its factories and warehouses, Hasidic educational institutions, the cavernous used-clothing emporium Domsey's, the Italian restaurant Giando, and, once the sun went down, sex workers who plied their trade in the shadow of the Williamsburg Bridge. Running through this changing landscape was Kent Avenue, long used as a truck route; it was there that Sadik-Khan sought to install what she described in her memoir as "a bike super highway connecting with Dumbo, Fort Greene, and Greenpoint . . . a local link in a biking greenway that one day will link neighborhoods along Brooklyn's fourteen-mile waterfront."[8] In April 2008, representatives of the Department of Transportation presented this vision to Community Board 1 in Williamsburg-Greenpoint, whose members voted 39–2 to approve construction of the greenway along the local waterfront, including a protected bike lane on Kent.

Later that fall, as details of the proposed bike lane became public with the release of a "concept plan" for the greenway, put together by planners at the Brooklyn Greenway Initiative and the Regional Plan Association, opponents in the Hasidic community expressed their concerns at a meeting of Community Board 1 in September 2008.[9] Media outlets focused on the community's objections to scantily clad riders biking through their neighborhood. A few days after the meeting, for example,

the *New York Post* published an article on the brewing conflict, its provocative headline, "Hasid Lust Cause," reflecting a long-standing tendency
in the media to highlight the sexual dimension of news stories involving
the Hasidic community in Williamsburg.[10] Of course, to some degree
this framing simply reflected the importance of sexual modesty among
Hasidim and the attempted regulation of immodest dress and behavior
by zealous members of the community. It is also a truism that sex sells,
especially in the tabloid media, and most especially when it came to a
highly insular religious community whose very modesty helped provoke
sometimes lurid speculation by others.

And yet even the article in the *Post* indicated that sex was only one aspect of what was going on in Williamsburg. Hasidim expressed concern
that bike lanes would cause parking problems, traffic congestion, and potentially dangerous conditions for the neighborhood's many children. The
Post reported: "Hasids said during a Sept. 8 community-board meeting that
the lanes on Bedford and Wythe avenues should be eliminated if the neighborhood has to accept being part of the greenway [along Kent Avenue]."[11]
In other words, Hasidim were suggesting a trade-off to the city: our community will accept a bike lane on Kent Avenue, enabling you to achieve
your vision of a greenway, if you get rid of the bike lanes on Bedford and
Wythe, which go straight through the middle of our neighborhood.

Later the same day, other media outlets published pieces riffing on
the *Post* article, with salacious headlines such as "It's 'Hasids vs. Hotties' in
South Williamsburg" and "Hipster Hottie Bicyclists vs. Hasids in South
Williamsburg?"[12] The latter piece, which appeared on the popular real estate blog *Curbed New York*, prompted over one hundred comments, most
of which were highly critical of Williamsburg's Hasidic community, to say
the least, and many of them expressing virulently anti-Semitic views.
Among other things, posters to the site referred to Hasidim as the
"Brooklyn Taliban" and suggested that they be sent to Iran or "back to Israel"; described them as "smelly weirdos" or "freaks"; mocked their clothing and their supposed propensity to solicit prostitutes ("tranny
hookers"); and asked whether "New York City should set up a gated community on the same order as the Warsaw ghetto and see how the sids [*sic*]
like living there." In addition to a number of comments that critically
compared Hasidim to burqa-wearing Muslims, one poster confessed that
Hasidim were even "scarier" than the African American and Latino residents of East New York: "South Williamsburg scares me more than East
New York. And I'm white." Only a few posters to the site questioned the

profound anti-Semitism in the comments section, with one arguing that since Hasidim were longtime residents of Williamsburg, they should have a greater say regarding its infrastructure than newcomers: "Wow. So much racism and intolerance exhibited here. The Hasidic community has been in W-Burg long before it was 'hip' to be there. Please respect their right to have the neighborhood they want. After all the Hasids are not moving into your neighborhood, we are moving into theirs." Comments on the article were closed after someone asked, "Is it possible that we could clone Hitler from some remaining DNA?"

Mainstream media coverage fanned these flames by focusing almost exclusively on the modesty issue and ignoring the ways in which Hasidic opposition to bike lanes was not merely a product of the community's particular religious outlook but also a reflection of much broader social forces affecting neighborhoods around the city and the country at the time. Rather than portraying Hasidic Williamsburg as one of a group of urban communities that were resisting bike lanes for a variety of reasons, including their close association with gentrification, concerns over parking and safety, and the longtime reliance of community members on cars, the media tended to treat the neighborhood as a unique phenomenon and an outlier.

And yet only two years before the bike lane controversy began in South Williamsburg, members of Community Board 2, in neighboring Clinton Hill and Fort Greene had voted to reject the construction of a bike lane; Anthony Ibelli, a board member, dismissed cyclists as "thugs on two wheels."[13] Similarly, in the fall of 2008, just as the struggle was heating up in Williamsburg, the installation of a new bike lane on Grand Street in Manhattan prompted business owners in Little Italy and Chinatown to mobilize against it, prompting one publication to ask, "Will New Grand Street Bike Lane Kill Little Italy?"[14] Within a few years, bike lane controversies had erupted elsewhere in the city: in Woodside, Queens; in Staten Island, where the city removed a lane after installing it; and in Park Slope, Brooklyn, which became the site of what Sadik-Khan later described as "the biggest bike controversy of all—one that engaged some of New York City's most powerful figures in a highly public, bitter, and vitriolic battle."[15]

Therefore, while the Hasidic community's concern over immodesty was distinctive, in other respects the opposition of some of its members to bike lanes resembled that of other communities in New York City, especially in the outer boroughs, as well as in other cities profoundly affected by gentrification in this period. In Washington, D.C., for example, some African American residents fought a series of planned bike lanes on the grounds that they would severely limit parking for churchgoers and thus, as the United House of Prayer complained to the District Department of Transportation, "infringe upon 'its constitutionally protected rights of religious freedom and equal protection of the laws.' "[16]

Significantly, Haredi media sources were as quick as their mainstream counterparts to cover the brewing bike lane controversy in Williamsburg.[17] *Vos Iz Neias* published an article on the topic that inspired nearly a hundred and fifty comments.[18] Some posters to the site were highly critical of Hasidic activists for bringing up the issue of modesty at all, with one writing, "It was so stupid to bring up the Modesty issue. . . . This will backfire strongly. . . . The safety issue was simple and politically correct. . . . Do our spokespeople have heads??" By contrast, other comments focused on the *pritsus*, or licentiousness, that bike lanes would bring into the neighborhood. One commenter wrote, "Pedestrians can close their eyes or look away not to see this *'pritzus,'* but unfortunately we the drivers have an obligation to see the road . . . so we are forced to see the *pritzus* of the hipsters, which is the lowest of the low." The supposed moral decline of Hasidic Williamsburg brought about by gentrification, either relative to its glorious past or to other Haredi communities, inspired a number of comments. Others stressed that Williamsburg was not Kiryas Joel, New Square, or Mea Shearim (a Hasidic neighborhood in Jerusalem), spatially segregated and culturally homogenous Haredi enclaves where it was possible to regulate people's behavior. Several pointed out that bike lanes were simply a part of living in exile: "This is ridiculous— we're in *golus* [exile]—deal with it."

Many posters on *Vos Iz Neias* framed the conflict in terms of rights. Some asked how Hasidim would feel if other residents of the city tried to make them conform to their own standards of dress, or as one put it, "How would *frum* [Orthodox] people feel if others tried to regulate their dress in their neighborhoods? 'Sorry in order to walk in this area you must were [*sic*] short shorts and no head covers, your *kippas* [head coverings] and long coats offend our values!' The streets of New York belong to all its people and it's not our place to tell goyim how to dress in public. End of story. If the bike lanes are unsafe we can fight them on those ground nothing else will work." Yet others argued that just as the "hipsters" had the right to lobby for bike lanes, so too did Williamsburg's longtime Hasidic residents have the right to oppose them: "I live in Williamsburg, and I'm flabbergasted on many of the above comments. . . . Yes, hipsters have the same rights as us—but, the lanes don't have to pass in the CENTER of our neighborhood; let it pass on the outskirts."

A few posters praised Hasidic activists such as Isaac Abraham and Shimon Weisser, a member of Community Board 1, for organizing public opposition to the bike lanes, but others attributed the presence of bike lanes to the failure of Hasidic leaders who had squandered precious time and energy on infighting when they should have been confronting "this plague on us, called hipsters." Some posters bitterly criticized their fellow Hasidim for selling out to the gentrifiers and only afterward complaining about their immoral behavior: "First all the people rented all their vacant apartments to the yuppies and they didn't care to rent it to their poor brothers now there is the out cry *oi vei tznius* [oy vey, modesty]." Other posters predicted: "Eventually the entire Williamsburg will be sold to the hipsters, because at some point we will have no choice but to move out." The existential threat posed by gentrification to the Hasidic community in Williamsburg was stressed by a poster who wrote, "The hipsters are the ones dictating what in our community should be. I actually did some research as to who these hipsters are, and was surprised to find that many who live in Williamsburg are quite powerful people; some are editors of magazines, famous artists, and children of the privileged of America. Williamsburg's leaders have no clue who they are up against. I, a *poshiter Yid* [simple Jew], cannot confront its leaders; that's why I'm crying out here."

The range of these responses reflects the range of Hasidic positions on the bike lanes in Williamsburg. Some community members viewed the bike lanes as an additional sign of the moral decline of the neighborhood, spurred on by gentrification; others were more concerned with the economic impact of gentrification than with its moral dimensions; and still others viewed the bike lanes as just another consequence of living in exile or of living in the United States, where the same laws that protected the rights of bike lane advocates also enabled Jews to practice their religion with a kind of freedom they had never enjoyed elsewhere.

Like the bike lanes themselves, the emergence of *Vos Iz Neias* and other Haredi-run websites—despite the ongoing attempts of community leaders to ban or severely limit Internet use in general, and these websites in particular—was a sign of how the virtual walls between Hasidim in Williamsburg and the outside world became both more porous and more difficult to police in the first decade of the 2000s. Nevertheless, this new reality did not stop the Hasidic establishment of the neighbor-hood from seeking to articulate an ideologically coherent and practically effective strategy for dealing with the bike lanes, as it had done regarding many other issues affecting the community for decades. Thus, a week after the story of the bike lane controversy broke in *Vos Iz Neias* and the mainstream media, *Der Yid*, the Yiddish newspaper of record for Hasidic followers of Rabbi Zalman Teitelbaum, leader of the largest Satmar fac-tion in Williamsburg, addressed the topic head-on.

The article, "Bike Lanes and Train Lines," framed the issue of bike lanes within the broader context of the Hasidic community's relationship to forms of transportation in Williamsburg and in other neighborhoods around the globe.[19] Moshe Yida Deutsch, the article's author, began by declaring that the "problem" posed by bike lanes was both "spiritual" and "physical." Spiritual, because the bike lanes were being used by people who wore revealing clothing; physical, because the lanes created traffic delays and eliminated a great deal of parking, among other problems. On the latter basis alone, Deutsch argued, "it would be legitimate to oppose such 'lanes' even if it had nothing to do with the religious feelings of the residents."

In opposing the bike lanes, however, Hasidim had to accept certain realities, according to Deutsch, and to proceed in a way that would mini-mize clashes with others. First, Deutsch noted, Hasidic critics of the bike lanes could no longer accurately claim that the lanes only "served people from the outside, that is to say, not residents of Williamsburg," for one simple reason: "The regrettable thing is that the definition of 'Williams-burg resident' has, in recent years, taken on an entirely different form and, yes, in the quarter known as Williamsburg live, unfortunately, such people who use 'bike lanes' in their daily lives." Second, Deutsch cited the Talmudic dictum that it is "difficult to live in big cities" (Babylonian Talmud Ketubot 110b), to indicate that in a metropolis like New York, Hasidim had to expect that they would be exposed to things that did not jibe with their moral code. Finally, Deutsch enjoined his readers to remember that they were still living in exile, albeit a kind that would have been unrecognizable to their ancestors: "We Jews must remember, after all, that we are in *golus* [exile]. In former times, people would shut the Jewish population in ghettos. And prima facie, no one would make a 'bike lane' in a walled in and enclosed ghetto for the use of outsiders. Today people do not live in a ghetto and the yoke of *golus* is in general lighter than in those dark times."

As for what the community could do, Deutsch reminded Hasidim that since they were living in exile, they were "not free to exercise control over public places." At the same time, they should not simply take a quietistic approach to the problem. Rather, members of the community should demand that their concerns and desires be treated with the same seriousness as those of the citizens who were lobbying for the bike lanes, or as he put it, "If the principle of opening 'bike lanes' is to enable citizens to benefit from public streets, then the same principle must also acknowledge the loss that the other part of the citizenry suffers on account of this and find a way to balance the opposing positions." This political negotiation, moreover, should be conducted by experienced *shtadlanim* (intercessors), representatives of the Hasidic establishment: "What is left for us to do is *shtadlanus* [intercession] with the hope that, with heaven's help, the community spokesmen will succeed in annulling the aforementioned decree."

Thus, the course of action implicitly endorsed by Williamsburg's Hasidic establishment was to avoid force, lobby behind the scenes, and accept that any outcome was likely to involve some degree of compromise. In the coming months, as tensions built around the bike lanes, Hasidim in Williamsburg overwhelmingly followed this approach. Though a few physical confrontations between bikers and Hasidic drivers were reported in the press, it was unclear whether these were connected with the controversy over the bike lanes or were simply the kind of traffic encounters that occurred daily on streets throughout the city; none of them involved the violent targeting of women deemed "immodest." Nor were there any reported cases of Hasidim attempting to physically sabotage bicyclists in Williamsburg, unlike some bike lane opponents in other parts of New York City who spread tacks or pulled wires in front of riders.[20]

The measured approach endorsed by *Der Yid* and embraced by Hasidim in Williamsburg contrasted dramatically with the growing number of violent assaults perpetrated by Haredi vigilantes in Israel during this period against women and girls perceived to be immodest.[21] For those aware of Satmar's long history of confronting threats in Williamsburg "by any means necessary," as Malcolm X put it, the community's restraint regarding the bike lanes was striking and, for some, disappointing. In general, the embourgeoisement of the Hasidic community in Williamsburg had made its members less prone to public expressions of violence. As one reader of *Vos Iz Neias*, which continued to cover the bike lane controversy as it unfolded, unhappily observed regarding this transformation, "I live in Flatbush and I oppose these sick bike lanes especially in *frum* [Orthodox] areas where the women drive *untniosdik* [immodestly]. Im [*sic*] surprised the Satmars of today are so passive. If they tried bike lanes with women dressed not modestly in [M]eah [S]hearim there would be crushed bikes. I respect the real Jews in [M]ea [S]hearim because they are the real deal not the materialistic *heimisha* [religious Jews], yes assimilated types [in Williamsburg]."

Yet as other posters to *Vos Iz Neias* had noted when the story of the bike lanes was first reported, Hasidic Williamsburg was not Mea Shearim, nor was it the same community that had earned a reputation in the 1970s and 1980s for meeting threats with fists as well as with *shtadla-nus*. First, the embourgeoisement of the Hasidic community in Williamsburg—driven in part by new real estate wealth generated as a result of gentrification—may have diminished the appetite for direct physical confrontation that characterized the enclave when it was more hardscrabble. Second, the marked increase in media scrutiny of the neighborhood spurred by gentrification, as well as the near ubiquitous ability to create videos with smartphones, meant that actions taken by Hasidim that previously would have gone unrecorded were now subject to viral dissemination and could be used in criminal prosecutions and other legal proceedings. This point was especially salient when Hasidim confronted well-organized media-savvy outsiders such as pro-bike-lane activists. Third, even the most zealous Hasidim may have treated the largely young white middle-class people who biked through the neighborhood with kid gloves, because they understood that the newcomers possessed a kind of cultural capital that Latinos, African Americans, and even other Hasidim did not. This capital could readily translate into increased attention and action by the media, police, and politicians. Finally, unlike the residents of Haredi towns and neighborhoods in Israel, Hasidim in Williamsburg lived in a cosmopolitan city where people of all walks of life mingled daily, and like most New Yorkers, they had learned to basically ignore others whose appearances were radically different or even, by their communal standards, offensive.

Despite the opposition of Hasidic activists in Williamsburg, the city proceeded with its plan to create a two-way bike lane on Kent Avenue at the end of October 2008 and installed signs prohibiting parking or stopping at any time on the street. Within weeks, it became apparent that many non-Hasidic business owners were upset with the bike lanes for their own reasons, including a lack of access to loading docks, difficulty in receiving deliveries, and the elimination of around five hundred

PRICE $7.99   THE   APRIL 11, 2016

NEW YORKER

New Yorker cover titled "Take the 'L' Train," referring to the subway
line to Williamsburg used by Hasidim and hipsters alike, 2016
(Tomer Hanuka, *The New Yorker* © Condé Nast)

parking spots, which contributed to a drastic decline in revenue for some businesses.[22] Compared to what the *Wall Street Journal* later described as the "turf war—or *shtetl* feud" involving "Hasids vs. Hipsters," or what *New York* called "the Clash of the Bearded Ones," the growing opposition of merchants and other business owners—including some who could have easily been described as hipsters—to the Kent Avenue bike lane, received little media attention, and what it did receive was presented factually and nonsensationally.[23]

In the coming months, the protracted struggle over the Williamsburg bike lanes became a synecdoche for the narrative of the "clash of cultures," as the *Brooklyn Paper* put it, which came to dominate media coverage of the neighborhood. The *New York Times*, the *Wall Street Journal*, the *New York Daily News*, the *Atlantic*, the *Forward*, the *New York Post*, *New York*, the literary magazine *n+1*, and many Brooklyn-based publications and real estate blogs published pieces on the issue. Eventually, the controversy inspired a documentary film, *Hasidics and Hipsters: A Battle on Bikes*, and a play, *Division Avenue*.[24] Within these works, bicyclists served as a stand-in for hipsters, who, in turn, signified gentrifiers generally.[25]

While the clash-of-cultures narrative accurately reflected some of what was taking place on the ground in Williamsburg, and was articulated by at least some of the neighborhood's Hasidic residents, it flattened the differences within demographic groups in Williamsburg while ignoring what at least some members of the different groups had in common. Perhaps most important, one thing that Hasidic opponents and non-Hasidic supporters of the bike lanes in Williamsburg shared was that both groups included well-organized and media-savvy activists skilled at employing direct action to generate publicity and apply political pressure in support of their causes. As one poster on *Vos Iz Neias* bluntly put it, "Bikers are as organized as chasidim, if not more so."[26]

The first move in what became a yearlong struggle between activists from both sides of the issue was taken on November 24, 2008, following a fractious transportation town hall organized by two local politicians, Diana Reyna and David Yassky. Isaac Abraham, who was running as a candidate to replace Yassky on the city council, publicly announced a direct action by Hasidic school bus drivers to protest the new "no stopping" prohibition on Kent Avenue: "We will ask all the drivers: 'When you pick-up or drop-off our children, put your bus in an angle, block the entire street, wait 'til the parent gets to the door of the bus, [and] slowly—very slowly—take your child off or put it on the bus, [and] don't rush to get back on the sidewalk.' One day the traffic will be backed up all the way to Long Island City to [the] Department of Transportation Headquarters, traffic will come to a halt."[27]

By December 5, mounting pressure from neighborhood residents and business owners had prompted a number of local politicians, including Reyna, Yassky, and Brooklyn borough president Marty Markowitz, to sign a letter requesting that the city modify the design of the Kent Avenue bike lane to restore some of the eliminated parking and allow stopping in certain zones.[28] In response to these developments, Time's Up! which described itself as "a grassroots environmental group that uses educational outreach and direct action to promote a more sustainable, less toxic city," issued a press release announcing that on December 17, the organization's "Bicycle Clowns" would be riding through the neighborhood to "defend the new bike lane and future greenway connector in Williamsburg . . . [and] use theater to comically draw attention to the serious danger faced by cyclists without safe, protected bike lanes."[29] And the clowns did ride.[30]

A few weeks later, on December 28, Hasidic activists placed a four-by-eight-foot Detour sign in a warehouse parking lot near the intersection of Kent Avenue and Broadway, the unofficial border of Hasidic Williamsburg. The semiofficial-looking sign declared in alternating black and white print against an orange background, "IMPORTANT NOTICE TO ALL DRIVERS FROM THE RESIDENTS OF KENT AVE.—DETOUR ROUTE—DUE TO THE BIKE LANE AND PARKING PROBLEM CREATED BY NYC DEPARTMENT OF TRANSPORTATION. WE URGE ALL DRIVERS TO USE WYTHE AVE. AS YOUR ALTERNATIVE ROUTE SO YOU HAVE NO DELAYS WHEN THE BUSES ARE PICKING UP AND DROPPING OFF KIDS. THE BUSES WILL BE IN AN ANGLE BLOCKING THE ROAD AND THE BIKE LANE FOR SAFETY."[31] Two days later, on December 30, the sign was removed, but not before it had inspired another attention-grabbing article in the New York Post titled "Hasid Street Fight."[32] Despite its pugnacious-sounding headline, the article noted, "Hasid community activist Isaac Abraham said the decision to hang the sign has nothing to do with the battle between the Hasids and hotties, however. He says it's about protecting kids from bikers who ignore traffic laws."

By this point, Hasidim who commented to the press about the bike lanes invariably stressed that their opposition was due to safety concerns and traffic issues rather than immodesty. As Leo Moskowitz, a Hasidic resident of Schaefer Landing, put it, "There are people who are trying to play that the nudity is the issue, but it's not. The main concern is the

safety of our kids. There are lot of institutions and families on that Bedford Avenue stretch, and we are always really concerned about the kids
being picked up and dropped off. There are sometimes small accidents
where the cyclists are violating the law because they don't stop for flash-
ing school buses."[33] In fact, all these concerns, including ones regarding
immodesty, existed in the Hasidic community—as well as plenty of indif-
ference to the bike lanes and even some quiet support—but Hasidic activists had learned that publicly complaining about immodesty not only
did not help their cause, but also catalyzed the opposition. Isaac Abraham, who had initially expressed concern regarding the bike lanes' potential for bringing immodestly dressed riders to the neighborhood,
went on to distance himself completely from the issue in the documentary *Hasidics and Hipsters: A Battle on Bikes*, in which he said, "There was
one stupid moron—who is absolutely an imbecile—that made a statement in public that the problem is with the dress code of the women. If
you look at the guy who said this, he should really be in the zoo. I have
no better words for this guy."[34]

Instead of complaining about immodest bikers, Hasidic activists had
learned that traffic and safety concerns resonated with non-Hasidic critics
of bike lanes around the city and also provided a politically palatable
justification—some would say cover—for the Department of Transportation
to make changes to the biking infrastructure in Williamsburg. Over the next
several months, Community Board 1 meetings continued to erupt in heated
debate. Then, in the spring of 2009, the Department of Transportation un-
veiled a new design for the Kent Avenue bike lane that restored loading
zones and hundreds of parking spaces. In her retrospective account of this
period, Janette Sadik-Khan argued that although the changes may have been
inspired by critics, the outcome was actually a victory for bike lane advocates.
"We expected pushback to the proposal, which also changed Kent from a
single traffic lane in both directions to a one-lane, one-way car traffic street,"
Sadik-Khan wrote. "But that didn't seem to faze neighborhood opponents
when they saw how much parking would be restored. Through community
consultation, a street design was negotiated that was more radical than the
one it replaced. Had we started by proposing what we ultimately built on
Kent, we would have been tossed from the Williamsburg Bridge."[35]

Pushback came half a year later, however, in December 2009, after
city workers eliminated the fourteen-block section of the Bedford Avenue bike lane that ran through Hasidic Williamsburg, sparking cynical
speculation that Michael Bloomberg had made a backroom deal with

Hasidic power brokers in order to shore up support in the community in advance of the upcoming mayoral election.[36] At the time, New York City officials refused to acknowledge on the record that they had cut a deal with the Hasidic community over the bike lanes in Williamsburg. Seth Solomonow, a spokesman for the Department of Transportation, described it laconically as "part of ongoing bike network adjustments in the area."[37] Writing in 2016, however, Sadik-Khan and Solomonow suggested that there had, in fact, been an understanding, maybe even a downright quid pro quo, that Hasidim would withdraw their opposition to the Kent Avenue bike lane if the city removed the one on Bedford:

> The downside to the [Kent Avenue] redesign was the controversial erasure of the bike lane on Bedford. It was hard to explain how this seeming retreat actually advanced the biking agenda. But with the new Kent Avenue lane, we have the best bike lane in Brooklyn just a couple of blocks parallel to the one we removed from Bedford. . . . A single action instantly stanched a potentially deep political wound and made possible hundreds of miles of future bike lanes in New York City. And to this day, hundreds of people still bike down Bedford Avenue daily in the blank space where the bike lane used to be—just as it is legal to bike on any other city street. Stretch pants, short-shorts, miniskirts, and all.[38]

The elimination of the bike lane on this particular stretch of Bedford Avenue was a goal—arguably *the* goal—of Hasidic activists from the beginning of the controversy over Kent Avenue, and with good reason. Whereas Kent Avenue ran along the mixed residential and industrial edge of the neighborhood and was bordered on one side by the Brooklyn Navy Yard, Bedford Avenue was one of Hasidic Williamsburg's two iconic thoroughfares (along with Lee Avenue), lined with brownstones, including the former home of Rabbi Yoel Teitelbaum, long-established businesses such as Spitzer's Kosher Bakery, and important Jewish institutions, including the Pupa yeshiva, whose numerous school buses made frequent stops to drop off and pick up students. Thus, the Bedford Avenue bike lane had considerable symbolic and practical significance, raising concerns among some Hasidic residents about not only immodestly dressed bikers but also potential accidents involving pedestrians, especially schoolchildren, as well as problems with parking and traffic flow.

Bike lane in Hasidic Williamsburg with Jewish school bus in the background, 2009 (Photograph by Brian Branch-Price/TheFotoDesk)

At the same time, many cyclists valued the Bedford Avenue bike lane precisely because it ran through one of the most scenic streets in the neighborhood rather than a semi-industrial truck route like Kent Avenue, and because it provided a direct link to both the Williamsburg Bridge and the main commercial strip of North Williamsburg. Whereas Hasidic activists viewed the elimination of the Bedford Avenue bike lane as part of a broader compromise involving their acceptance of the redesigned bike lane on Kent Avenue, biking activists took it as a major step backward for both traffic safety and the environment, and a provocation that had to be confronted head-on, which they did in a series of direct-action protests.

A few days after the Bedford Avenue bike lane was sandblasted, activists who later identified themselves to the press as "self-hating Jewish hipsters" used the cover of night to repaint the lane and then posted a video of their action online. On December 13, members of the Time's Up! Clown Brigade organized a "New Orleans-style funeral procession" to commemorate the demise of the bike lane.[39] And a week later, *Candy Rain,* "a porn magazine for women, made by women," sponsored a topless "freedom ride" through South Williamsburg to protest what Heather Loop, its chief organizer, decried as the Hasidic community's intolerance: "If you can't handle scantily clad women ... live in a place where you can have your own sanctuary, like upstate."[40] Although winter weather forced the "freedom riders" to abandon their plans of cycling naked, they remained defiant. Loop declared, "I feel like they're forcing their beliefs on us. It's in the Bill of Rights to not force your religion on anybody." Calisha Jenkins, another participant, argued, "They're essentially moving it [the bike lane] because they don't want to look at girls dressed like sluts. And I want to dress like a slut."[41] Paul Steely White, the executive director of the nonprofit Transportation Alternatives, opposed the bike lane removal but also criticized the "freedom ride" for being unduly confrontational. "A bike lane on Bedford Avenue is an issue of transportation and road safety," he said. "Rhetoric or acts that pit neighbors against one another are not just irrelevant to this discussion, they are flat-out offensive. A bike ride of people in provocative undress doesn't make Bedford any safer, and undermines efforts to bring north Brooklynites together to solve this problem."[42]

One of the most provocative figures to become involved in the bike lane controversy in Williamsburg was Baruch Herzfeld, variously portrayed in the media—with varying degrees of accuracy—as a "lapsed Satmar," a "neighborhood gadfly/clown/activist/businessman," a "classic *macher* and motormouth with a foot in both the Hasid and hipster worlds," an "impish ... ex-Orthodox bike activist," and a "self-appointed liaison between the pro-lane hipsters and anti-lane Satmar Hasidim."[43] A graduate of Yeshiva University, a Modern Orthodox institution located in Upper Manhattan, and the brother of two Orthodox rabbis, Herzfeld opened and ran the Traif Bike Gesheft—"unkosher bike business"—on South 6th Street near Broadway for several years.

Herzfeld donated space in the Traif Bike Gesheft to Time's Up! and presented himself as the "spokesman" for the activists who repainted the Bedford bike lane, though he stated that he had not participated in the action himself. When, in December 2009, Mayor Michael Bloomberg attended a climate change conference in Copenhagen, a city so linked to bike-centered urban planning that it inspired the term "Copenhagenization" to describe the phenomenon, Herzfeld credulously declared, "How can Mayor Bloomberg go to Copenhagen and pose as a green mayor after this? He's a hypocrite, and I believe his office directed the DOT to remove this bike lane as a political favor for the rabbis, who want to keep South Williamsburg a ghetto enclave."[44] In numerous interviews with the press, Herzfeld argued that there was a gulf between Williamsburg's Hasidic leaders, whom he derided as puritanical "Talibanowitz," and the community's rank-and-file members, whom he claimed were not only more tolerant of the hipsters' presence in the neighborhood but also open to bike riding if given the opportunity.[45]

To this end, Herzfeld created a free bike-lending program, or *gemach*, specifically for local Hasidic residents and sought to turn the Traif Bike Gesheft into a meeting place for Hasidim and hipsters, one "decorated with a Magen David shaped out of adjoining rubber chickens, artistic graffiti and a Yiddish message reminding Satmar residents to come borrow bicycles."[46] Transportation Alternatives, which had criticized the topless bike protest for being unnecessarily divisive, publicly supported the Traif Bike Gesheft. As Wiley Norvell, a spokesman for the group, told the *Forward*, "It's definitely the kind of bridge building that north Brooklyn could really use right now. It's been a tough year—there's no doubt about that. This is the sort of thing that could help us get back to a much more civil place."[47]

Despite their differences, activists representing a variety of camps came together on January 25, 2010, to debate the Bedford Avenue bike lane at Pete's Candy Store, an iconic hipster bar and performance space in North Williamsburg.[48] Moderated by Baruch Herzfeld, the debate included Caroline Samponaro from Transportation Alternatives, Heather Loop and Lyla Durden of the topless bike protest, and Isaac Abraham, the Hasid whose energetic activism and—ultimately failed—candidacy for the city council had inspired the *Brooklyn Paper* to describe him as the unofficial "Mayor of South Williamsburg."[49] Abraham and his fellow debaters disagreed on practically everything that night, but the fact that they had all gathered in one spot to discuss the bike lane revealed the degree to which they all belonged to the same activist universe in Williamsburg.[50]

CHAPTER TEN

New Williamsburg

A S GENTRIFICATION AFFECTED EVERY corner of Williamsburg, the dramatic growth of the local Hasidic population, along with the deepening housing crisis in the community, created a desperate need to find new housing, particularly for young families, who increasingly found themselves competing with non-Hasidic newcomers. With Hasidic expansion essentially blocked on the enclave's northern border because of high prices and competition, these demographic pressures led Hasidim to look beyond Flushing Avenue, Williamsburg's traditional southern border, to the largely African American neighborhoods of Bedford-Stuyvesant and Clinton Hill. There, in the span of a few short years, Hasidim engaged in one of the fastest and most complete transformations of any area of New York City since the remarkable population shifts and neighborhood changes of the 1960s.

"New Williamsburg," or Nay Vilyamsburg, as the area came to be known among Hasidim, was initially envisioned as a contiguous extension of "Old Williamsburg," to be realized through a combination of intense lobbying, individual zoning variances, and, ultimately, the large-scale rezoning and redevelopment of formerly industrial tracts for residential usage. As a Hasidic bookseller on Lee Avenue told us, the Hasidic community of Williamsburg was "shrinking in one direction [on its northern border] and growing in another [on its southern border]."[1] By 2013, the *Forward* was reporting on the dramatic change in an article titled, "Ultra-Orthodox Jews Spread into Once-Black Brooklyn Neighborhoods." Moishe, a Hasidic construction site manager, observed, "Ten years ago there were no Jews living here. . . . Then they changed the zoning. Now it is going heavy."[2]

In 2015, *Der Yid* weighed in, providing its Hasidic readers with a brief history of the nearly half century of housing development and community expansion that had culminated in the creation of New Williamsburg. The description reveals how conscious the Hasidic establishment was of its enclave's borders and its precise spatial relationship to other neighborhoods in Brooklyn:

> In the early 1970s the apartment situation in Williamsburg had already become a bit tight. Then the [Taylor Wythe and Roberto Clemente] projects in Williamsburg started to be built, and then came Bedford Gardens. In the 1980s and beginning of the 1990s, a lot of developments were built on the South Side of Williamsburg—what we now call "Old Williamsburg." Until then the border of Williamsburg to the southeast side was Heyward Street. In the early 2000s, an apartment crisis once again forced . . . a great move from Williamsburg's Flushing Avenue to the first streets in Bedford-Stuyvesant: Park Avenue, Myrtle Avenue, Willoughby Avenue, Dekalb Avenue, and even Lafayette Avenue. The borders extended bit by bit in various other places, like Clinton Hill. In other words, *heymisher* [Hasidic] Williamsburg expands accordingly more and more. . . . If you look forty years ago, you'll see how it was, with a little crumb compared to today's Williamsburg. Every ten years Jewish Williamsburg spreads out a little more.[3]

The Flushing Avenue Corridor

The roots of New Williamsburg can be traced to the 1990s and early 2000s, when Hasidim began to cross Flushing Avenue and settle in parts of Bedford-Stuyvesant and Clinton Hill—traditionally, the two neighborhoods met at Classon Avenue—which until then were home to a mix of light-industrial, commercial, and residential buildings. Very few Hasidim moved into the area's famous brownstones and architecturally significant row houses, which defined a neighborhood described as having "perhaps the largest collection of intact and largely untouched Victorian architecture in the country, with roughly 8,800 buildings built before 1900."[4] The reason for this was simple: by the time Hasidim began their expansion into the area, non-Hasidic gentrifiers were purchasing its many brownstones for higher prices than most Hasidic buyers could afford, a phenomenon portrayed memorably in Spike Lee's iconic film *Do the Right Thing* in 1989.

Yet Hasidim who made the short trip across Flushing Avenue from South Williamsburg had a profoundly different historical relationship to Bedford-Stuyvesant than the gentrifiers who arrived from elsewhere in New York City, other parts of the United States, and, increasingly, abroad. For decades, the northern section of Bedford-Stuyvesant bordering Williamsburg had been home to Hasidic businesses and educational institutions as well as to a small number of Hasidic residents.[5] In fact, Hasidim had been rooted in the area of Bedford-Stuyvesant adjoining Williamsburg—where they initially joined a long-standing non-Hasidic Jewish community—since their arrival from Europe in the 1940s. Hasidim retained a presence in Bedford-Stuyvesant for years thereafter, even as the community's population center remained concentrated in South Williamsburg and as Bedford-Stuyvesant became emblematic, for many observers, of the urban crisis then affecting cities across the nation.[6]

Despite their institutional presence in the neighborhood, however, until the late 1990s most Hasidim considered Bedford-Stuyvesant an inhospitable area in which to live. Even a homeless Hasidic couple profiled by the *New York Times* in 1990 refused to live in the Marcy Houses, a massive housing project in Bedford-Stuyvesant with twenty-seven six-story buildings and 1,705 apartments located on twenty-eight and a half acres of land bordered by Flushing, Marcy, Nostrand, and Myrtle Avenues. As the article explained, "They applied for public housing, and were assigned to a project in the Bedford-Stuyvesant section of Brooklyn. For Hasidic Jews living in Williamsburg, also in Brooklyn, that might as well have been on Mars. Synagogue, yeshivas, kosher food—everything that defines their strictly ordered life—would have been hopelessly distant. 'We refused it because we are Jews,' said the woman. 'Nothing is there for us.' " Instead, the couple "landed on an upper floor of a Williamsburg synagogue in a room barely large enough for two torn mattresses," along with a "dozen other homeless people."[7]

The Marcy Houses had an especially fearsome reputation among residents and neighbors during the 1980s. One prominent native son of the projects, the Grammy Award–winning rapper Jay-Z (born Sean

Carter in 1969), who lived in the Marcy Houses in this period, described the rough-and-tumble nature of the area in songs such as "Where I'm From," "Marcy to Hollywood," and "Chill," in which he defiantly proclaimed, "I'm from murder murder Marcyville." Lyrics such as these indicated the entrenchment of turf warfare in the area. As Jay-Z rapped in "Hard Knock Life," the song that earned him his first Grammy nomination, in 1999, "I'm from the school of the hard knocks / We must not let outsiders violate our blocks."

According to Jay-Z, the blocks around the Marcy Houses had always included "pockets of Hasidim," who were part of the complex social fabric of the neighborhood. The authors' conversations with locals along the Flushing Avenue corridor confirmed Jay-Z's recollections. One longtime African American resident of the Marcy Houses told us, "Hasidics have always been here—for years, if not decades."[8] Similarly, Jay-Z, whose nickname derived from the local J/Z subway line, recalled in his 2010 memoir, *Decoded*: "There are no white people in Marcy Projects. Bedford-Stuyvesant today has been somewhat gentrified, but the projects are like gentrification firewalls. When I was growing up there, it was strictly blacks and Puerto Ricans, maybe some Dominicans, rough Arabs who ran the twenty-four-hour bodegas, pockets of Hasidim who kept to themselves, and the Chinese dudes who stayed behind bullet-proof glass at the corner take-out joint."[9] In the music video that accompanied "99 Problems," a hit single from *The Black Album*, released in 2004, Jay-Z rapped over different scenes filmed in and around the Marcy Houses (the location is clearly demarcated in a variety of ways), including shots of a school bus with Hebrew writing, indicating its ownership by the Hasidic Pupa yeshiva, and one of a bearded Hasidic man walking toward the camera. Like the shots of Jay-Z in the Marcy Houses, a police lineup, church worship, break dancers on the street, dogfighting, and so on, the Hasidic visual references were deployed in the video to create a sense of "ghetto authenticity."

By the 1990s, Hasidim in Williamsburg had become victims of their own demographic success: large families and rapid generational turnover had produced intense competition for the limited supply of available housing within the borders of the Hasidic Triangle.[10] In response to this ever-growing housing crisis, Hasidim overcame their previous reluctance and initiated a massive wave of construction near the Marcy Houses. Hasidic real estate developers and housing advocates sought individual variances from the city to rezone a large number of commercial parcels for residential usage. Until then, much of the Flushing Avenue corridor, which stretched from the Brooklyn–Queens Expressway to the Marcy Houses, was lined with chop shops, warehouses of all sizes, parking lots, and small factories. Some of these lots were sizable and, just as importantly, served as a geographic link between the densely populated Hasidic enclave in South Williamsburg and the plentiful, undervalued properties in Bedford-Stuyvesant and Clinton Hill. "Building by building," the *Daily News* reported about this period, "the Board of Standards and Appeals, a little known quasi-judicial agency, granted the zoning variances in Williamsburg and Bedford-Stuyvesant."[11] By 1999, about 385 units had been built on the largely industrial stretch along Flushing Avenue, and 433 more were up for review by the Board of Standards and Appeals.

The redevelopment of the Flushing Avenue corridor was directly linked with ongoing political negotiations over affordable housing in Williamsburg. Following the 1996 resolution of a lawsuit known as *Williamsburg v. Giuliani*, in which community organizers sued the city for negligence over the sandblasting of lead paint off the Williamsburg Bridge (described in court records as "by all accounts . . . a public relations and public health fiasco"), Mayor Rudolph Giuliani's administration sought to improve relations with the neighborhood's communities by proposing to build more than eighty two-family houses for low-income residents in the predominately Latino section of Williamsburg, to be overseen by Los Sures.[12] In addition, the city committed $3 million to create a new day care center to be administered by Nuestros Niños, another community organization, for the many children on the South Side whose mothers were now obligated to participate in "workfare" programs under President Bill Clinton's new welfare reform law. In an apparent quid pro quo, the city granted United Jewish Organizations the right to facilitate construction of up to 1,600 market-rate condominiums on former sites of light manufacturing along Flushing Avenue. These apartments would be legally available for anyone to purchase, but certain design features—for example, multiple bedrooms for large families and kosher-friendly kitchens—made them especially appealing to Hasidic buyers, and their prices put them out of reach for most Latino and African American residents of the neighborhood.

Thus, the transformation of the Flushing Avenue corridor initially grew out of a political bargain brokered by the Giuliani administration that sought to secure support from two critical constituencies in Williamsburg and help solve an acute housing shortage in one fell swoop. The *New York Times* described the multiple benefits and beneficiaries of the plan: it ended "a stalemate on the future of housing in the overcrowded, often emotionally volatile neighborhood [of Williamsburg]"; it provided "politi-cal benefits for the Mayor in an election year"; and it amounted "to a major achievement for the Hasidim, who are desperate for housing and whose forays into traditionally Latino sections of the neighborhood have provoked concern and protests."¹³

Although the city's plan focused on ten blocks of land located along Flushing Avenue that were mostly owned by Hasidim, the *Daily News* re-ported in October 1997 that the broader goal of the Hasidic community was to develop a contiguous area that would stretch into the heart of Bedford-Stuyvesant. "Part of the rezoning is designed to create a residen-tial corridor connecting it to Williamsburg," the newspaper stated. "One official involved in negotiations said there is an informal understanding that the Hasidic community will redirect its growth south of Flushing Ave. [into Bedford-Stuyvesant] and away from Williamsburg's Hispanic South Side with Broadway as a dividing line."¹⁴ A full-page ad in Yiddish placed by the UJO in *Der Yid* that same month invited readers to a rally with Mayor Giuliani, whom it called "Williamsburg's best friend in City Hall" because of his enthusiastic support "for the construction of apart-ments, to expand the possibilities to build thousands of new apartments and enlarge our neighborhood."¹⁵

While the city-brokered deal was initially seen as a victory for Williamsburg-based Hasidic and Latino affordable-housing leaders such as Rabbi David Niederman of the UJO and David Pagan of Los Sures, it triggered concerns among longtime African American residents of Bedford-Stuyvesant. The *Daily News* reported, "In the cacophony of housing politics, trying to settle problems for Hasidim and Hispanics in Williamsburg has angered black leaders in Bedford-Stuyvesant. The lat-est deal among Hispanic and Hasidic leaders, who have battled apartment by apartment for decades, includes a major rezoning of manufacturing land for residential use with areas targeted for each group."¹⁶

Increasingly, homeowners in the area complained that they were being harassed by prospective Hasidic buyers, and renters expressed con-cern that they would eventually be priced out of their apartments by rap-idly rising rents.¹⁷ Residents employed in the area's numerous industrial and commercial enterprises worried that they would be forced to find work elsewhere as landlords received variances from the city to redevelop their properties into more profitable apartment buildings. Such concerns were well founded, given the heavily industrial character of the area. Ac-cording to the Pratt Institute Center for Community and Environmental

Development, until the residential construction boom that began in the late 1990s, nearly 60 percent of the land in the area around Flushing Avenue was devoted to manufacturing, supporting a local rate of industrial employment that was "three times that of New York City as a whole," whereas only 10 percent of the property in the area was residential.[18]

Hasidic leaders justified the community's expansion into the northern part of Bedford-Stuyvesant on the grounds that its members were bringing long-needed development to a historically underpopulated, crime-ridden, and "blighted" area. Rabbi David Niederman told *City Limits*, "There is prostitution, drug-dealing. We're bringing back life to the neighborhood."[19] Yet this bleak portrait was vehemently rejected by many locals, as the article made clear. "This is not some bombed-out area. It is very safe—that's why people are moving here," declared Melvin Foster, president of the Neighborhood Stabilization Task Force, a community group concerned with Hasidic expansion.

Despite growing local opposition, between 1995 and 2000 the city's Board of Standards and Appeals approved more new construction in the Flushing-Bedford area than anywhere else in the city.[20] In 2001, the city council approved resolutions that changed the zoning of a fifteen-block stretch along Flushing Avenue from industrial to residential use, including a special mixed-use area, unleashing yet more development.[21] This particular set of rezoning resolutions, according to Nicole Marwell, "opened the door for Hasidim to expand across their traditional southern boundary, Flushing Avenue."[22]

While the city had hoped that facilitating Hasidic construction in Bedford-Stuyvesant would ameliorate tensions between Hasidim and Latinos in South Williamsburg, it created a new set of problems. Hasidic development raised the ire of local housing activists, who sued—unsuccessfully—to stop the changes in zoning, claiming, inter alia, that Hasidic developers had engaged in illegal discrimination by advertising new units only in Yiddish-language newspapers, thereby excluding other potential buyers.[23] In 2000, Raun Rasmussen, an attorney with South Brooklyn Legal Services who led the lawsuit, asserted, "It's illegal to develop housing for one group. . . . Nobody can say that [they are building for Hasidim only], even though everybody knows it is."[24] For his part, Rabbi David Niederman of the UJO responded, "It really hurts. . . . Instead of working together and developing a better place for both communities, they are fighting. It means depriving families and children who live in unbelievable and undesirable conditions an opportunity to have decent housing."[25] A decade and a half later, in

Massive Hasidic development across Flushing Avenue from the Marcy Houses,
2013 (Photograph by Michael Casper)

2016, Rasmussen, then the head of Legal Services NYC, recalled of the
failed lawsuit, "We thought it was a violation of the Fair Housing Act to be
marketing and ultimately renting to exclusively Hasidic families." Nevertheless, he admitted that housing advocates could not prove that non-
Hasidim had sought to purchase units in the buildings and been rejected
on the basis of their membership in a legally protected group, the basis for
demonstrating discrimination, according to the law.[26]

Clinton Hill

In the same period that Hasidim from Williamsburg were beginning to
develop the Flushing Avenue corridor, they established their first satellite
on the border of Bedford-Stuyvesant and Clinton Hill. Like Bedford-
Stuyvesant, Clinton Hill had long had a reputation for urban decay. Indeed, the area had struggled with poverty and blight for most of the
twentieth century, as Frank McCourt, who was born into an Irish family

there in 1930, wrote about in *Angela's Ashes*, his best-selling memoir.[27] Deterioration continued over the following decades, culminating with the decommissioning and closure of the adjacent Brooklyn Navy Yard in 1966.[28] By then, Clinton Hill had become a predominantly black neighborhood.[29]

Despite, or perhaps because of, the neighborhood's economic decline, Clinton Hill experienced gentrification as early as the 1970s. But as Lance Freeman noted, it took a different form, at least initially, from the kind seen in other parts of the city: "Whereas the term *gentrification* conjures up images of an influx of whites rapidly displacing poorer minority residents . . . this is not an accurate depiction of what occurred in Clinton Hill or nearby Fort Greene." In those neighborhoods, the earliest gentrifiers were African American professionals and artists.[30] Over time, their ranks were supplemented by others, including art and design professors and students from the nearby Pratt Institute.[31]

Hasidic families did not move into the neighborhood to meet the challenge of fixing up a brownstone with charming architectural details, nor were they drawn to the proximity of the Brooklyn Academy of Music and other cultural institutions. Instead, Hasidim were looking for affordable housing that was close to the Hasidic enclave of South Williamsburg. In this sense, they were somewhat like the first generation of artists in North Williamsburg, who arrived in the neighborhood from the East Village seeking inexpensive housing and more space. And just as the establishment of Williamsburg's hipster community began with the conversion of old factories into housing, Hasidim began their move into Clinton Hill by converting a former factory into apartments.

Hasidim established their first outpost in Clinton Hill in 1996 when a cluster of families from Williamsburg began moving into the former Bommer Hinge factory at the intersection of Classon and Willoughby Avenues, a block from the Pratt Institute, which was one of the neighborhood's most important institutional anchors. At 128,636 square feet, the building was large enough to house 85 families, or over 600 people, and represented the first development of its kind outside the boundaries of Williamsburg proper, signaling the creation of a new "frontier" for the Hasidic community. By the time the building was renovated, with Hasidic residents in mind, the area around Classon Avenue had become a target for gentrification by others, buoyed by Pratt's redevelopment of the neighborhood. Yet Hasidim hoped that they would be able to purchase much of the property in the area and that the blocks between the "satellite" building on Classon Avenue and Williamsburg proper would eventually be filled in with other residential developments. At the time, Rabbi David Niederman of the UJO said, "We will be closing the gap between Williamsburg and Clinton Hill."[32]

As plans for the renovation of the factory proceeded, one Hasid told a member of the Pratt Community Council that the location of the building was a good omen, since it sat diagonally across from a church named Saint Mary's, which some Hasidim understood as the meaning of Satu Mare (the Romanian name for Satmar), although Satu Mare actually means "big village."[33] Despite its linguistic dubiousness, the Hasidic effort to find meaning in the name of their new settlement reflected an old Jewish tradition—known as name midrashim—whereby hidden meanings are discovered in the names of otherwise mundane geographic sites. Over the centuries, name midrashim have helped transform historically non-Jewish places into Jewish territory, at least in the local Jewish imaginary, even if not on official maps. In this way, New Williamsburg began to take shape in the consciousness of Hasidim who sought to make it an extension of the enclave they were leaving behind. Eventually, Classon Avenue even produced its own "Classoner Rebbe."

Separated from Hasidic Williamsburg by nearly half a mile, the building on Classon Avenue posed new challenges and opportunities for the first Hasidic families who moved into it. In a *New York Times* article titled "Hasidic Pioneers Set Forth from Williamsburg to Seek Space Across a New Frontier," one Hasidic couple described life in the building: " 'We are cut off to a certain extent,' Mr. Kohn said, and Mrs. Kohn does not allow her children to walk the five blocks to Williamsburg alone or to play outside at night. At the same time, she said, her children had learned to greet strangers of all kinds. 'In Williamsburg, if the children see a black worker, they run away,' she said. 'Here, the kids are not afraid.' "[34] Significantly, the article's headline borrowed the same settler-colonial terms— "pioneers" and "new frontier"—that the *Times* had used to describe the gentrification of other Brooklyn neighborhoods, including Williamsburg, since at least the 1980s.

Despite this parallel, there were striking differences between the way in which artists had initially taken up residence in loft spaces in Williamsburg and the way in which Hasidim transformed the former Bommer Hinge factory into living space. In the former case, individuals, often by word of mouth, learned about promising spaces where they could live and work, and negotiated directly with landlords, who often rented to them illegally at first and then frequently sought higher-paying tenants when the factory or warehouse was legally zoned for residential usage. By contrast, the residential development of the Bommer Hinge factory was brokered by Rabbi David Niederman of the UJO, who encouraged Hank Camuso, the site's developer, to create units that would be particularly attractive to Hasidim and, concomitantly, much less appealing to other potential buyers. According to the *New York Times*, "The factory's developer, Hank Camuso, said that after meeting Rabbi Niederman, he agreed to rehabilitate the property specifically for the Hasidim. That meant modifying architectural plans to include religious amenities, like two kitchen sinks for kosher food, as well as a synagogue with a separate area for the women," and space for families with many children. In return, Camuso could rely on the UJO to advertise the units to members of the Hasidic community in Williamsburg and arrange "generous financing terms with banks," including down payments of only 10 percent.[35]

Almost immediately, the Classon Avenue factory development inspired complaints from longtime residents concerned that it would set a problematic precedent for the neighborhood. Thus, for example, Sharonnie Terry, the head of the housing commission for Community Board 3, which oversaw the area where the factory was located, told the *New York Daily News* in 1997 that "board members were not told of plans to turn the Classon Avenue factory into apartments for Hasidic families when okaying a zoning variance for residential use," and that "Bed-Stuy residents fear being shut out of developments targeted for Hasidim."[36] By the summer of 1999, when the *New York Times* ran a follow-up article on the Classon Avenue factory conversion, community groups and tenants' associations in northern Bedford-Stuyvesant were actively trying to block further Hasidic development in the area, on multiple fronts. "Fearing they will be slowly isolated . . . residents of Bedford-Stuyvesant talk of how their corner bodegas will be replaced by kosher groceries," the *Times* reported, "and how their longtime friends will be pushed out by a religious community. Realistically or not, they fear becoming second-class citizens who are ordered around on their own streets."[37]

Multiple local residents complained of being harassed by Hasidim who wanted to purchase their property, and a member of Community Board 3 told the *Times*, in a veiled threat, "If the Hasidics move in, bias incidents could flare up, because nobody here is going to stand by and be manhandled." Peter Crisci, the bishop of the Cathedral of St. Lucy, stated, "People are afraid because of all the zoning changes from commercial to residential, and because the Hasidic community is buying all the available residential properties. .... They are afraid that these people are coming into the community not to build it up, but to create a community within a community, and that doesn't work." In response, Rabbi David Niederman defended Hasidim as good neighbors and suggested that critics were essentially being discriminatory in their own right. "It is basically saying, 'Stay out of here,'" Niederman said. "I would hate to characterize why, but what has been said at various meetings is scary. ... I would venture to say to any of them, 'Come to Williamsburg, come into the housing projects, and tell us we are not good neighbors. We have African-Americans, Latinos, everybody, and everybody feels safe and secure. ... We want to make this area a better place to live for everyone."[38]

Local African American residents expressed frustration in other ways about what they considered to be the unfair Hasidic appropriation of available land and resources. For example, *Our Times Press*, an African American paper that serves central Brooklyn, reported: "A city-owned vacant lot earmarked for the long-sought-after sanitation garage for Bedford-Stuyvesant has turned into a parking lot for the Satmar Hasidic Jewish sect that utilizes it to park their school buses, work vans and other transportation buses."[39] The paper noted that "since 1985, Bedford-Stuyvesant residents have been advocating" for the construction of a sanitation facility on the city-owned site as a solution to garbage collection problems that had long plagued the neighborhood. Many African American residents were initially hopeful, the paper added, when the Department of Transportation took over the nearly 50,000-square-foot lot on Nostrand Avenue between Park and Flushing Avenues, but were subsequently disappointed when the site was leased to the Satmar community.

Another article in *Our Time Press* highlighted tensions between members of the two communities. "A cultural and economic turf war between African-Americans and Hasidim [*sic*] Jews continues to brew in Bedford-Stuyvesant with the park attached to the Marcy Public Houses along the Myrtle Avenue corridor being the latest battleground," the newspaper announced. "The difficulty began about a year ago, according to Marcy Houses Tenants Association President Naomi Colon, when about 40 Hasidim [*sic*] Jewish kids from the Satmar sect, who has been buying up, developing and moving into a large swath of northern Bedford-Stuyvesant, took over a basketball court. 'They seemed to think when their kids go on the playground our kids had to leave,' recalled Colon."[40] In turn, Hasidim complained that they had become the target of hate crimes and multiple cases of harassment in the neighborhood, including the defacement of homes with swastikas.[41] Hasidim also faced the widespread perception, expressed in a variety of ways, that they did not belong in Bedford-Stuyvesant and Clinton Hill and should remain on the north side of Flushing Avenue, in Williamsburg.[42]

Despite these rising tensions, many Hasidim from Williamsburg continued to seek opportunities to purchase and develop real estate in both Bedford-Stuyvesant and Clinton Hill throughout the 2000s. For them, expanding across Flushing Avenue was the only practical alternative to leaving the area entirely. Although the housing crisis of the late 2000s slowed new real estate development in many parts of the city, including Williamsburg, it created opportunities for both Hasidic and non-Hasidic buyers in Bedford-Stuyvesant, which was among the ten city neighborhoods with the highest rate of foreclosure filings between December 2009 and December 2010.[43] In 2008 alone, Bedford-Stuyvesant had fifty-seven foreclosures, the second-highest number among Brooklyn neighborhoods.[44] These foreclosures opened up undervalued and previously unavailable housing stock, which fueled gentrification in Bedford-Stuyvesant and, in a more limited geographic area, Hasidic expansion south of Flushing Avenue.

Hasidic residential developments in the area were initially understood to be geographic and cultural extensions of South Williamsburg. Over time, however, as the Hasidic neighborhood that took shape in the northern parts of Clinton Hill and Bedford-Stuyvesant came to be known as New Williamsburg, the area took on a distinctive character. One of the starkest differences between Old and New Williamsburg was the housing stock. Unlike the many cramped, aging apartments and public housing projects of Old Williamsburg, New Williamsburg had a high concentration of new, spacious, well-appointed apartments designed to serve every need of a young Hasidic family. These multi-bedroom apartments contrasted also with the studio and single-bedroom apartments then being constructed in large numbers along the waterfront and on the border between the Hasidic Triangle and the rapidly gentrifying South Side of Williamsburg. As a local resident named Esther Ungar told *Ami* magazine in 2014, "This year, a huge building full of studio apartments went up right across the street from us [in South Williamsburg]. Each studio is being rented out for $2,500 per month. Artists are willing to pay that amount for a bedroom and kitchenette, but such an apartment is obviously not practical or affordable for a *frum* family."[45]

Over the years, Hasidim had effectively created a parallel rental market within Williamsburg. They did so by renting apartments via word of mouth or advertisements in Yiddish-language publications and, especially when new construction was involved, as in New Williamsburg, by adding features such as kosher-friendly kitchens, a balcony for a sukkah, and multiple bedrooms. These features not only were designed specifically for Hasidic needs, but also discouraged non-Hasidic renters. In addition to these distinctive design elements, the Hasidic rental market had lower prices than the neighborhood's non-Hasidic market. For example, in October 2014, *Ami* magazine reported that two-bedroom apartments in the traditional Hasidic Triangle (or what it called "Original Williamsburg") went for "about $1,500" a month, and three- and four-bedroom apartments went for "well over $2,000," and in New Williamsburg, monthly rentals for the same kinds of units were "about $1,900" and "about $2,300."[46] In the same month, the *MNS Brooklyn Rental Market Report* listed average monthly rents in Williamsburg's non-Hasidic market as $3,103 for a one-bedroom and $3,746 for a two-bedroom (it did not cite prices for three- and four-bedroom apartments because of their rarity), and in Brooklyn as a whole, they were $2,580 and $3,345.[47] In other words, Hasidic renters in both Old and New Williamsburg paid significantly less than others in Williamsburg—and in Brooklyn, in general—even as the community's large families and high poverty rate still meant that many of its members were rent burdened. Moreover, rental costs were higher in New Williamsburg than in the traditional Hasidic Triangle, even though this was offset to some degree by the extensive use of section 8 vouchers by Hasidic renters in the area.

Hasidim were involved in the local real estate market not only as buyers, developers, landlords, and renters. The side streets between Bedford and Nostrand Avenues in New Williamsburg were dotted with numerous Hasidic-owned businesses in the construction and home design industries (such as Kitchen Expo, Lion HVAC Supplies) that appealed to both Hasidic and non-Hasidic customers in the neighborhood. In addition, Hasidim were employed as contractors, truck drivers, electricians, carpenters, and plumbers, forming a large Hasidic working class that served as a counterpoint to the community's wealthy developers and that harked back to an earlier era when New York City's outer boroughs were home to hundreds of thousands of working-class Jews before they migrated to the suburbs and entered the middle and upper classes.

Much of the housing that was built for Hasidic buyers and renters in New Williamsburg had a distinctive exterior architectural style that set it apart from the rest of northern Bedford-Stuyvesant and Clinton Hill. Although the neighborhood's existing housing stock consisted mainly of

Hasidic-run tire shop on an industrial stretch of Park Avenue,
New Williamsburg, 2019. Signs warn in English against using
foul language, and in Yiddish against non-employees entering
the place of work. (Photograph by Michael Casper)

prewar apartment buildings, triple-deckers, and brownstones—the last
were particularly prized by wealthy gentrifiers—the large Hasidic
developments that rapidly filled former industrial lots in the area were
described by one observer as "a solid wall" of buildings that "won't win
any design awards, with their looming, protruding window cages and diagonally cascading balconies" on which Hasidic families could build
small sukkahs that would, per Jewish law, have nothing above them.[48]
The scale of these largely unadorned buildings, some of which contained
businesses or synagogues at street level, turned many of the streets in
New Williamsburg into veritable pedestrian canyons. Moreover, once a
certain number of Hasidic families moved into a particular block, it was
common for a tipping point to occur, resulting in the kind of dramatic

turnover last seen in the neighborhood at the height of white flight during the 1950s and 1960s with the arrival of large numbers of African Americans and Latinos.

Many of the buildings in New Williamsburg were designed by a small number of architects who worked extensively with the Hasidic community and helped give the neighborhood its distinctive aesthetic. Foremost among them was Karl Fischer (1949–2019), a prolific architect whose style was lambasted by critics as "grim" and "characterless," earning him the title, in the *New York Post*, "New York's most loathed architect."⁴⁹ Fischer, who redesigned the Gretsch Building and Schaefer Landing, credited his success to long-standing relationships with the Hasidic communities in Brooklyn and Montreal. "I started off working with the Hasidic community on Kent Avenue, doing their housing," Fischer said. He had a personal connection with Williamsburg Hasidim that made him a favorite among community members: he was born in the Hungarian village of Gemsze, about forty miles from the town of Satmar. Despite the traditional limitations on secular education, in at least one case the Hasidic community produced its own architect, Chaim Fishman, a Vizhnitz Hasid whose office was in Borough Park. In an interview, Fishman compared the study of Talmud with mastering the intricacies of zoning regulations.⁵⁰

Other differences between Old and New Williamsburg were not architectural but cultural, and to some degree they reflected the younger demographic profile of many Hasidic residents south of Flushing Avenue. For example, in April 2012, on the Yiddish-language Hasidic web forum Yidishe Velt (Jewish World), a user with the handle "Moyshe Kornfeld" suggested that New Williamsburg residents were more likely to use the Internet—despite prohibitions against it by Hasidic religious leaders—than residents of Williamsburg proper. In a discussion beginning with a post entitled, "Old Williamsburg a Little Sheep Surrounded by 70 Wolves," Moyshe Kornfeld presented maps that showed broadband Internet usage in both areas. While up to 20 percent of households in Old Williamsburg were shown to use broadband, usage was much higher in New Williamsburg. "I have long known that Old Williamsburg is the Jerusalem of America," Moyshe Kornfeld wryly noted, "but that New Williamsburg is the Tel Aviv of America was a surprise to me."⁵¹

Many of the businesses that opened in New Williamsburg catered to young families with small children and at least some disposable income, members of the emerging Hasidic bourgeoisie, whose tastes were a far cry from the spartan ideal that Rabbi Yoel Teitelbaum had championed in his decades-long campaign against *luksus* (luxury). Instead, the Hasidic-owned establishments that came to dot Bedford Avenue and the side streets of both northern Bedford-Stuyvesant and Clinton Hill owed more to contemporary trends in consumption than to traditional Satmar conceptions of piety. Indeed, many promoted a lifestyle that would have been unrecognizable, even anathematic to the founders of the Hasidic community of Williamsburg, who espoused Rabbi Moshe Sofer's dictum "the new is forbidden by the Torah."

By the 2010s, Hasidic residents of New Williamsburg could join a kosher wine tasting at the Wine Cave or eat at Sushi K Bar, "one of the first pioneers of the Kosher sushi market," as it proudly advertised itself on its website: "Way, way before the many kosher sushi joints you see around today, Sushi K Bar was providing the community with their sushi fix. We wanted to make sure that our sushi was not only the freshest, but also had the highest level of Kashrus possible."[52] They could visit Café Latte Kosher for an espresso or satisfy their sweet tooth at the Ice Cream House or Viennese Classic Confections, which specialized in high-end chocolates.

Chestnut, which bragged, "We Have It All," offered customers a stylish, kosher version of Whole Foods. The growing number of Hasidim interested in health food and alternative medicine could peruse the shelves at the Sage Health Food Market, where during the summer of 2019 they could find "Kosher Gold" cannabinoids, which had not only a seal guaranteeing lab-tested "Purity & Potency" but also a hechsher, or kosher certification. Those in need of a "lymphatic massage" or a "coffee enema" could walk a few blocks to Your Health Success Center or cross Bedford Avenue and visit the Gan HaTeva [Garden of Nature] Wellness Center, where they could "discover the perfection G-d provides through nature and enjoy the most perfect version of you."[53] All these businesses gave the lie to the oft-repeated claim that Hasidic Williamsburg was an unchanging island or premodern shtetl in Brooklyn, cut off from external influences.

At the same time, the youthful demographic created a burgeoning market for businesses providing more traditional goods and services for weddings, newly married couples, and families with young children, including Homemaker's Haven Kallah [Bridal] Store, The Chasunah [Wedding] Depot, Dimensions Better Maternity Wear, Little Luxury Home of Baby Accessories & Necessities, Royal Family Shoes, Baby Palace, and even, for a brief period, a branch of the upscale international chain United Colors of Benetton, which specialized in children's and babies' clothing. Significantly, the names of these stores explicitly promoted *luksus* in a way that once would have been impossible in the Hasidic community of Williamsburg.

Predictably, not everyone in the broader Hasidic community was happy with the bourgeois character of New Williamsburg. This included a small contingent of Hasidic protesters who showed up at the 2013 opening of Moishe's Place, a restaurant on Bedford Avenue whose sign hinted at the "golden arches" of McDonald's but whose eclectic menu included Chinese, Middle Eastern, American fast food, and classic deli options in addition to a few of the traditional eastern European Jewish dishes (such as brisket and chicken soup) that most outsiders probably associated with Hasidic cuisine. Chanting "*gevalt*" (emergency), the protesters condemned Moishe's in Yiddish for encouraging Jews to eat like gentiles (*goyishe fress*) and for being a "hangout" (they used the English term) where men and women could socialize together.[54] Greatly outnumbered by Hasidic supporters of the restaurant, however, the protesters were eventually dispersed by the police, and Moishe's opened for business, quickly becoming a mainstay in the neighborhood.

In comparison with the bustle of New Williamsburg, Old Williamsburg seemed slower paced, especially during the summer months, when many residents went upstate. Many of the businesses on Lee Avenue, the neighborhood's main commercial strip, had been around for decades and retained their long-standing character. But even there, the effects of embourgeoisement and the influence of gentrification could be seen in the design and marketing of businesses like Pastel or Panini ("To make ordering easier & faster we've created our own mobile app") or in the new, modish sign "Baked Goods to Excite! Since 1959" that Sander's Bakery, a neighborhood institution, put in its front window to appeal to the growing number of tourists—many on organized tours—who made it a regular stop.[55]

Despite its embrace of sushi, cannabinoids, lattes, and wellness, the commercial culture of New Williamsburg still differed from that of hipster Williamsburg. One of the most striking contrasts was in the almost fetishistic way that many businesses in New Williamsburg employed terms like "luxury" and "royal," while on the north side of Broadway, businesses such as Simple Goods, Martha's Country Bakery, Blue Collar, and Miss Favela embraced an aesthetic of working-class authenticity that was itself a sign of elite status. In comparison with the extreme luxury in hipster Williamsburg, whether understated or, in the case of the high-rise developments on the waterfront, in your face, the invocations of luxury in New Williamsburg seemed almost quaint.

Despite the differences between Old and New Williamsburg, the Hasidic establishment made efforts to ensure institutional continuity between the two areas. In January 2009, the UJO began converting a storefront on Myrtle Avenue into a branch office, which opened in January 2010. According to the UJO's website, the organization served "the communities of Williamsburg, Clinton Hill and Bedford-Stuyvesant" and "the greater Williamsburg area."[56] At the same time, UJCare, another organization serving the Hasidic community, opened its only office one long block away, on Park Avenue, near Clinton Hill. UJCare shared a building with the ParCare Community Health Network, another health care provider. "The community expanded. There happens to be more space in this part of town," said Gary Schlesinger, ParCare's chief executive officer, by way of explaining the building's New Williamsburg location. "A younger population has moved out to this part of town. In the past few years they built up this part, built a couple thousand apartments."[57]

Community organizations and health care facilities were not the only Hasidic institutions to mushroom in New Williamsburg. Myrtle Avenue, once widely known among local residents as "Murder Avenue" because of its high crime rate, became dotted with Hasidic synagogues and study houses. The Pupa Hasidic sect established a large school at the corner of Bedford and Lafayette Avenues, and Rabbi Asher Anshel Scher, the Classoner Rav, named in honor of the avenue that serves as the border between Clinton Hill and Bedford-Stuyvesant, and the site of his first study hall, settled in a building on Franklin, between Myrtle and Willoughby, identified by a Hebrew sign reading, "Kahal Beys Mordkhe D'Classon."

Borderlands

Beginning in 2008, in a series of interviews, we asked Hasidim and non-Hasidim in the area to describe the borders of New Williamsburg. One Hasid told us, "We have a border. But not an official border." In 2013, the Ustrikover Rebbe, whose *shtibl* (small synagogue) was located on Skillman Street in Bedford-Stuyvesant, between Lafayette and Dekalb, told us that the limit of New Williamsburg was Lafayette between Bedford and Franklin Avenues.[58] A Sikh construction worker employed by Hasidim at a site on Franklin between Myrtle and Willoughby said that the new Jewish area was bounded by Flushing, Lafayette, Classon, and Nostrand. An African American resident said that Hasidic settlement ran "from Spencer to the projects"—the nearby Lafayette Gardens Housing

Project on Classon Avenue—but predicted that it would not extend past Spencer Street: "It's harder to gentrify over there."[59]

While informal definitions prevailed, official and semiofficial borders for New Williamsburg were also being delineated. In May 2009, a notice in the Hasidic newspaper *Di Tsaytung* showed a map of Brooklyn Community Board 2, bordered by Flushing, Classon, Fulton, and Flatbush Avenues, with the message, in Yiddish: "The area in 'New Williamsburg' where alternate side parking is suspended for almost two months."[60] Also in 2009, a Yiddish newspaper article titled "Good News for Those Who Use the G Train: Of Special Interest to New Williamsburg Residents" was accompanied by a detail of the subway map showing G train stops beginning with Broadway and moving south. As one comment on a thread on the Yiddish-language message board Kave Shtiebel put it: "We call it *Nay Vili* [New Willi] but on the map it is Clinton Hill."[61] Meanwhile, a demographic study prepared by David Pollock in 2013 for the Jewish Community Relations Council of New York asserted matter-of-factly that Hasidic Williamsburg was no longer limited to the borders of the neighborhood. "Expanding southward and eastward," the study stated, "Hasidic Williamsburg now includes significant portions of the neighborhoods of Williamsburg, North Side–South Side, Bedford [Stuyvesant and] Clinton Hill."[62]

Some of the most striking evidence for the dramatic expansion of the Hasidic enclave beyond its traditional borders comes from federal census data between 2000 and 2010.[63] Beyond documenting the explosive increase in the Hasidic population in the Flushing Avenue corridor and New Williamsburg, this data reveals that the Hasidic population in Old Williamsburg increased at a much slower rate during the same period and even appears to have declined in one census tract. Overall, this pattern suggests that there was little room for expansion in the core census tracts where Hasidim had been living since the 1940s, and therefore that the community sought new areas in which to settle. This was especially the case for young families with children, for whom it was almost impossible to find adequate housing in the core census tracts of Old Williamsburg.

Fayge, a middle-aged Hasidic mother, explained to the authors that during the early 2000s, the numerous children of married Hasidic couples who belonged to the postwar baby boom of the 1950s and 1960s started to come of age and marry. This large cohort produced an intense need for new housing. Once these grown children moved out, either to New Williamsburg or elsewhere, the population of certain parts of Old Williamsburg experienced a decline because households that once had

Hasidic boys across the street from the Marcy Houses public housing project in the Flushing Avenue corridor, 2019 (Photograph by Jackson Krule)

eight, ten, or even more members now had far fewer, and in some cases were reduced to a single, older couple. Besides a lack of housing stock, other factors contributed to the slower pace of growth or, in some areas, decline. Most importantly, the increasingly high cost of living in New York City encouraged many Hasidim to move to Kiryas Joel, Monsey, and other heavily Hasidic areas in upstate New York, as well as to Lakewood Township and Jersey City. Meanwhile, Hasidim were largely unable to move into Williamsburg's public housing projects, and some Hasidim who occupied units in the projects decided to move out, for a variety of reasons, according to Hasidic residents we spoke with, further affecting the overall Hasidic population of Old Williamsburg.

Despite the major expansion of the Hasidic community across Flushing Avenue between 2000 and 2010, not everyone was convinced that the creation of New Williamsburg would be enough to solve the community's housing woes. Some Hasidim called on their fellow community members to abandon the neighborhood for greener—and less expensive—pastures. In the fall of 2007, for example, *Der Blatt*, the Yiddish paper associated with Satmar's upstate faction, announced in a front-page article timed to coincide with the weekly biblical *parsha* (portion) in which God instructs Abram to leave his native land (Genesis 12:1–17:27): "Young people ... need to realize that it's time to come out from under their mothers' apron. We need to learn how to practice *parshas 'Lekh lekha'* in today's times," referring to the Hebrew name of the portion, which roughly translates as "Leave!" The article went on: "All supposed worries that people have about dragging themselves to new locales are false."[64]

Aron Friedman, managing editor of *Der Yid*, the competing newspaper associated with followers of Rabbi Zalman Teitelbaum, leader of the largest Williamsburg faction of the Satmar community, told us at the time that the housing situation was "a very big crisis" but that "nobody should say, 'We should all move out.' "[65] However, Sam Weider, the editor of *Der Blatt*, defended the dramatic editorial. "We need apartments," he said. "The ones that are built are very expensive. We have to move out because we don't have apartments in the neighborhood."[66] Weider said the community was continuing to grow rapidly and suggested that some families, but perhaps not all, should move upstate because new affordable housing in the city would not meet the ever-growing demand. In Brooklyn, he said, "[You have a] small tiny apartment. You can't move and there's no peace of mind." Weider dismissed the possibility that by encouraging financially strapped Hasidic residents to leave Williamsburg, the newspaper was engaging in internecine politics between rival Satmar factions.

Based on a combination of geographic and demographic criteria, we identified seven census tracts as constituting the core area of the traditional Hasidic enclave in Williamsburg.[67] In these tracts, the overall white population, which closely approximated the number of Hasidim, went from 23,641 in 2000 to 29,061 in 2010, and the total population went from 33,670 to 34,596. Throughout the area, the percentage of Latino residents declined significantly, except in the census tracts where housing projects were located; there, their numbers, along with those of black residents, increased modestly. By contrast, the Hasidic population increased throughout the core area except in the two census tracts that might be described as the "heart" of the enclave, where it grew by 2.2 percent in one tract and declined by 4.4 percent in the other, probably indicating an aging Hasidic population and a lack of available housing for young families.

Meanwhile, in the three South Williamsburg census tracts that bordered Flushing Avenue—the Flushing Avenue corridor—the Hasidic population grew dramatically, thanks to a veritable wave of new housing construction.[68] Since much of the area had previously been zoned for industrial and commercial usage, its total population was only 5,273 in 2000, which had more than doubled to 12,890 by 2010. Over the same period, the number of white residents—here also a good proxy for Hasidim—went from 3,626 in 2000 to 11,808 in 2010, while the population of Latinos, the only other significant demographic group in the tract, declined. When we turn to New Williamsburg proper, the demographic transformation is even starker. The borders of New Williamsburg coincided almost exactly with an area comprising two census tracts in 2000, which in turn were combined to form a single census tract in 2010, one bounded by Flushing Avenue to the north, Myrtle Avenue to the west, Taaffe Place to the west (one block east of Classon Avenue), and Nostrand Avenue to the east (the western boundary of the Marcy Houses).[69]

In 2000, the area that would become New Williamsburg over the next decade had a total population of 1,838, which ballooned to 6,008 in 2010. The number of non-Hispanic whites went from 144 to 4,703 in this period (an astounding increase of 3,166.0 percent), while the number of blacks decreased from 202 to 182 (a decline of 9.9 percent) and the number of Latinos went from 1,440 to 988 (a decline of 31.4 percent). While the census did not provide figures on the Hasidic population per se, other data serve as useful proxies for gauging their presence in the tract. Thus, for example, out of a total of 1,282 households in the area, 1,028 were family households, and of these, 893 were living with their own children under eighteen years of age. The number of families consisting of married couples with their own children under eighteen made up 61.1 percent of the population, compared with 17.5 percent in Brooklyn and 16 percent in New York City as a whole. There were 1,189 children under the age of five, accounting for 18.7 percent of the total population of the census tract, compared with 7.4 percent in Brooklyn and only 6.5 percent in New York City. Similarly, there were 1,246 children between the ages of five and nine, or 19.6 percent of the total population, compared with 6.4 percent in Brooklyn and 5.7 percent in New York City. The median age of the white, non-Hispanic population was an extraordinarily low fourteen years old, compared with thirty-four in the rest of Brooklyn and thirty-eight in New York City as a whole (and 37.7 among Latino residents of the tract). Undoubtedly reflecting the presence of many young Hasidic families in the area, there were 143 six-person households and 340 households with seven or more persons. Finally, the average household size was 4.78 persons, with the figures for owner- and renter-occupied units nearly identical, at 4.79 and 4.77 persons. This compared with a Brooklyn average of 2.69 persons and a citywide average of 2.57 persons.

Among white households in the New Williamsburg census tract in 2010, 61.1 percent were living below the poverty level, which increased to 77.3 percent among households with seven or more people. Significantly, most housing units, 1,002, were renter-occupied, compared with 256 that were owner-occupied. White householders occupied 764 of the rental units and 210 of the owner-occupied units. In summary, federal census statistics revealed that the population of New Williamsburg was dominated by young Hasidic families with numerous children; they tended to rent rather than own their apartments, and most were living below the federal poverty line.

In the same way that the growth of the Hasidic community in South Williamsburg was catalyzed in the 1960s by the construction of new public housing projects that became home to numerous Hasidic residents, the creation of New Williamsburg in the 2000s was made possible by the Hasidic community's striking use of the section 8 program (aka housing choice vouchers) to subsidize the cost of apartment rentals. Beginning in 1974, when Congress passed legislation to create a private-market-based alternative to public housing projects, section 8 vouchers became an increasingly important mode of providing affordable housing to the needy. By 2015, more than twice as many people were using section 8 vouchers than were living in public housing projects across the nation.[70]

For Williamsburg's Hasidic community, section 8 became an especially important way for young renters to afford housing in the 2000s. Because vouchers were in such high demand, local waiting lists were often closed. When, as sometimes happened, the lists were briefly opened to new applicants, the UJO would quickly get the word out and help Hasidic residents of Williamsburg apply in the thousands. Similarly, Hasidim from the neighborhood traveled to other locales when their waiting lists opened, and applied there (section 8 vouchers are portable as long as certain conditions are met), a phenomenon facilitated by the creation of a dedicated Twitter feed called @sec8heymish, which notified Hasidim of such openings, and by the coordination of buses to provide transportation to the sites.

The result of these well-coordinated efforts was revealed by a study conducted jointly by WNYC and the *New York Daily News*: "In 2014 about 3,300 households in this community [of Hasidic Williamsburg] paid rent with help from a Section 8 voucher. That's more than twice as many as there were in 2000."⁷¹ Moreover, according to a survey done in 2014 of federal census tracts in the area with high concentrations of Yiddish speakers, those in New Williamsburg had the greatest use of section 8 vouchers by residents, demonstrating the degree to which the program had helped create the burgeoning rental market in the neighborhood. In sharp contrast to other parts of New York City where vouchers were common, such as the outer reaches of the Bronx, WNYC reported that Hasidic Williamsburg had become "one of the heaviest concentrations of Section 8 housing in the city, right in the middle of one of the hottest real estate markets in the city." It was a tightly coordinated effort: "They've done it through a combination of political influence, aggressive organization, and community members who provide both supply and demand."

Despite the success of the local Hasidic community in navigating the section 8 program, it was still not enough to satisfy the huge need for affordable housing. Esther Ungar, a young Hasidic mother of three in Williamsburg, described to *Ami* magazine how difficult it was to get a voucher in 2014, and the lengths to which Hasidim would go to acquire one: "[Section 8] is almost impossible to get at this time. One of my friends, who wanted to ensure she'd be able to pay her rent in the future, has applied for and received Section 8 assistance in Arizona! She is moving there with her husband and two children with the hopes of returning one day when she can legally transfer her Section 8 slot to Brooklyn."⁷²

The widespread use of section 8 by Hasidim was facilitated by another factor, one that had played a critical role in their decision to move into public housing projects in Williamsburg during the 1960s: the striking lack of stigma surrounding the program in the community. Even as section 8, like public housing before it, became a mark of racialized scorn—a historical process that the *Washington Post* described in an article headlined "How Section 8 Became a Racial Slur"—many Hasidim in Williamsburg enthusiastically embraced the program as "a building block for their community," according to Rabbi David Niederman of the UJO, who added in an interview with WNYC, "That's what I'm saying. There's no stigma."⁷³

While the demand for section 8 vouchers was driven by the increase in young Hasidic families, the supply was met by Hasidic real estate developers who viewed the rental of units to Hasidim in the housing program as a communal duty, even a religious obligation, and one that might help offset their construction of luxury units for the open market. As Rabbi David Niederman of the UJO stated to WNYC, "There's a language that we can talk and say [to Hasidic developers], look, housing is so scarce [in Williamsburg]. Don't come in over here and basically destroy your neighborhood. Okay? Develop something that is available to the local [i.e., Hasidic] market."[74] The report added that this was "a story that stands in stark contrast to the way Section 8 works in the rest of the city where people with vouchers typically get pushed to the margins because most landlords don't want to rent to them."

Not everyone was sanguine about the extensive use of section 8 by members of the Hasidic community in Williamsburg. Critics charged that some Hasidic renters gamed the system by paying Hasidic landlords money under the table in addition to the subsidy provided by the voucher and the rent allowed under the law, a maximum of 40 percent of total household income.[75] Yet the WNYC report placed such instances of Hasidic malfeasance within the broader context of the affordable-housing crisis then affecting the entire city, which contributed to cases of section 8 fraud in other communities as well. "There's nothing illegal about being hyperorganized," the report narrated. "But there have been cases of fraud. One [Hasidic] man used a section 8 voucher while owning a stake in four different properties. Another man rented from his brother. So they both benefitted from the same voucher, earning them both a short stint in jail. Of course, fraud like this happens all over the city, especially in an overheated real estate market. And the Hasidic community feels that too."[76] Therefore, New Williamsburg, like the Hasidic Triangle nearly half a century before, owed its dramatic growth, in part, to the Hasidic community's unique ability to tap into government-subsidized housing programs.

By 2014, Hasidic expansion beyond Flushing Avenue had become so successful that some members of the community lamented that New Williamsburg had become just as densely settled and expensive as Old Williamsburg. This situation was exacerbated by the intense competition with non-Hasidic buyers as well as by the greater financial incentive for real estate developers, including Hasidic ones, to build for the open market rather than for subsidized renters—and in the case of Hasidic developers, rather than for members of their community. Speaking to *Ami* magazine in 2014, Moishe Zelik, a mortgage broker at ABC Mortgage in Williamsburg, described a situation in which Hasidic demand was far outstripping supply despite the incredible rate of construction in New Williamsburg over the past decade: "At this point even in Bed-Stuy it is becoming more difficult to find something affordable. The hipster community has settled into that area as well, and they are keen on buying the

million-dollar-plus renovated brownstones and brick town houses. . . .
With prime real estate on their hands, some [Hasidic] developers are
opting to build luxury condominiums instead of affordable housing for
the community. The greatest similarity between New and Old Williamsburg is the fact that there is no affordable property to purchase, and absolutely no place to grow."[77]

Broadway Triangle

The largest undeveloped area bordering Hasidic Williamsburg was a legendary plot of land known as the Broadway Triangle. Comprising roughly
thirty acres at the intersection of Williamsburg, Bedford-Stuyvesant, and
Bushwick, it was described by one writer in 2012 as "almost post-apoca-
lyptic, an empty stillness that belies the heated controversy that has surrounded the site for years."[78] For years, the Broadway Triangle included
the largest tract of undeveloped city-owned land in North Brooklyn, and
its contentious history reveals how the development of affordable housing
in Williamsburg was affected by gentrification, rezoning, and the complex
interplay among politicians, activists, developers, and Brooklyn's unique
neighborhood dynamics.

In 1989, New York City created the Broadway Triangle Urban Renewal Plan to develop a tract of land where Pfizer, the largest pharmaceu-
tical firm in the world, had operated since the nineteenth century.[79] After
years of legal wrangling, in 2006 the city selected the UJO and the Ridgewood Bushwick Senior Citizens Council, a nonprofit connected with Vito
Lopez, then a New York state assemblyman and chairman of the Democratic Party of Kings County (Brooklyn), to develop affordable housing on
several parcels on the site. The organizations came up with a proposal that
gave preference to residents of Community District 1, in whose borders
the Broadway Triangle was located, over those in Community District 3,
which it adjoined. Whereas the former was majority white and included
the Hasidic enclave, the latter was majority African American. In 2009,
after the New York City Council approved the plan, the Broadway Triangle Community Coalition, which consisted of more than forty community
organizations, sued the mayor's office and the Department of Housing
Preservation and Development for violating the Fair Housing Act.

The suit alleged that whites had received preferential treatment in the
affordable-housing proposal at the expense of blacks and Hispanics. The
plaintiffs' argument hinged on four assertions: first, that Hasidim were

white; second, that they were not a minority; third, that they were being favored in ways that discriminated against blacks and Hispanics, who *were* minorities; and fourth, that the current plan for Broadway Triangle would perpetuate "existing racial and national origin segregation."[80] As the court documents made clear, however, the identification of Hasidim as white was not entirely straightforward. Indeed, at times it was important for the plaintiffs to be able to differentiate between whites in general and Hasidim in particular, and to highlight certain Hasidic attitudes and practices (regarding elevators on the Sabbath, for instance, or large family size) that distinguished them from whites, blacks, and Hispanics.

The plaintiffs objected that the construction of numerous large multi-bedroom apartments and low-rise buildings was being proposed with Hasidim in mind, and that the preference given to residents of Community District 1 over those in Community District 3 would result in a much larger pool of white applicants for the affordable-housing units.[81] Persuaded by their arguments, Judge Emily Goodman of the New York State Supreme Court issued a temporary injunction in 2009 prohibiting the rezoning of the site or the transfer of city-owned land.[82] Two years later, in 2011, Goodman temporarily blocked the project while expressing support for the plaintiffs' claims regarding discrimination and segregation.[83] In some ways, this case was a replay of the struggle over public housing in the 1970s, when blacks and Latinos successfully accused the city and Hasidim of gaming the system to provide the latter with more affordable-housing units in the projects. And yet the situation in Williamsburg had changed dramatically in other respects, most notably when it came to private real estate development. The neighborhood was now a site for massive new residential construction, much of it consisting of luxury units, and some of the biggest developers were Hasidim.

While the court case dragged on regarding the city-owned lots in the area, private developers were allowed to go forward with construction on their parcels. In 2016, the Hasidic-owned Rabsky Group announced plans for a development on the site of the former Pfizer plant that would have 1,147 apartments, including 344 affordable units, or 30 percent of the total, in order to satisfy the city's recently passed mandatory inclusionary housing requirement.[84] The project immediately sparked a series of protests by black and Hispanic community activists, who charged that the Rabsky Group would show preference for Hasidic residents in the design and allocation of the affordable units. In a July 2017 article in the *Forward* titled "Housing War Pits Ultra-Orthodox Against Latinos in 'Last Cor-

ner' of Booming Brooklyn," Rabbi David Niederman suggested that anti-
Semitism lay at the root of the opposition to the development: "Let me
say what the problem with this project is. The problem is that it's a Jewish
developer. And somebody's afraid maybe, maybe, Jews will also have a part
in that development. That's the bottom line."[85]

Despite the staunch opposition of activists, the New York City Council approved the Rabsky development in October 2017. A few months
later, the city finally settled the lawsuit that had been brought against it
by the Broadway Triangle Community Coalition in 2009. Under the
terms of the agreement, the city removed the UJO and Ridgewood Bushwick Senior Citizens Council as sponsors, promised to redo the bidding
process, increased the number of one- or two-bedroom apartments in
any future project, and split the residential preference equally between
Community District 1 and Community District 3. While Shekar Krish-
nan, an attorney at Brooklyn Legal Services Corporation A, which helped
bring the lawsuit, celebrated the agreement as "a major victory for racial
justice," Rabbi David Niederman condemned it: "The proposed deal is
not a settlement. It is a sell-out to politically-connected biased groups
with a history of using lawsuits to further its anti-Semitic goal of preventing Jewish families in Williamsburg from finding housing."[86]

Meanwhile, two housing activist groups, Churches United for Fair
Housing and Brooklyn Residents Against Segregated Housing, filed a
new lawsuit, in March 2018, to block the Rabsky Group's development,
charging that the city had violated the Fair Housing Act by not performing a racial impact study when it rezoned the Pfizer site.[87] A few months
later, when the Supreme Court of New York tossed out the lawsuit, Judge
Arthur Engoron wrote in his decision, "The Pfizer Project will probably
extend a predominantly white area (Williamsburg) closer to black (Bedford-Stuyvesant) and Hispanic (Bushwick) areas. This appears not to be
the result of some nefarious midnight plot but, rather, the inexorable, on-
the-ground realities of population growth (Hasidic) and income disparity
(White compared to People of Color)" (parentheses in the original).[88]

In March 2019, thirty years after the city first created the Broadway
Triangle Urban Renewal Plan, the saga over who would be allowed to
build affordable housing on the city-owned land in the area finally came to
an end. The New York City Department of Housing Preservation and Development and the Housing Development Corporation announced that
Unified Neighborhood Partners would "construct five new entirely affordable buildings that will have a combined total of 387 new apartments

that will serve extremely low-, very low-, low-income, and formerly home-less households."[89] Unified Neighborhood Partners comprised the St. Nicks Alliance, the RiseBoro Community Partnership, and the Southside United Housing Development Fund Corporation—Los Sures. There was also one other partner—United Jewish Organizations of Williamsburg (UJO). Despite everything—the lawsuits, the protests, and the charges of anti-Semitism—the Hasidic group had still found a way of being included in the development of the Broadway Triangle, and even took credit for it. The UJO tweeted, "We are very happy that @NYCHousing accepted our Housing plan—jointly with our neighborhood partners."[90]

Conclusion
The Camp in the Desert

NO LONGER ISOLATED—OR, from another perspective, protected—by poverty, crime, municipal neglect, and the once-widespread feeling that New York City was in apocalyptic decline, Hasidic Williamsburg has also weathered several decades of some of the most intense gentrification of any neighborhood in the world. Much has changed—and remained the same—since we first began to do the research for this book. The gentrification "frontier" in Brooklyn has moved from Williamsburg and Bushwick to Bedford-Stuyvesant and Crown Heights and beyond. The Hasidic community in Crown Heights, in particular, has experienced many of the same stresses as its counterpart in Williamsburg; as an article on a Chabad-Lubavitch website put it in 2013, "Watching the gentrification of Crown Heights is like watching Williamsburg at warp speed."[1]

Even with skyrocketing real estate prices and their ongoing demographic growth, many Hasidim have remained in Brooklyn by doubling down on the same qualities that enabled their predecessors to establish enclaves in the first place, despite all the odds: fierce resilience, savvy pragmatism, and a powerful sense of communal pride. Like their Puerto Rican and Dominican neighbors in Williamsburg or their Afro-Caribbean neighbors in Crown Heights, these Hasidic residents are a living link to an erstwhile Brooklyn that was nothing like the global brand and hot tourist destination that it is today. For decades, Rabbi Yoel Teitelbaum and his successors assiduously sought to prevent their followers from being contaminated by the influences of the city around them and, in the words of Numbers 23:9, to remain "a people apart." And yet despite the efforts of their leaders, Hasidim in Williamsburg are not merely in the city but also of it—consummate urban dwellers whose street smarts, swagger, and sensibilities not only make them closer to their longtime neighbors than to their co-religionists in the suburbs but also connect them with the broader experience of Jews in the modern period as the "People of the City" par excellence.[2]

At the same time, Hasidim are no longer asking *whether* gentrification will force some community members to abandon Brooklyn. Instead, the past few years have witnessed the departure of many young Hasidic families to places outside New York City. In 2014, *Ami* magazine published a three-part series titled "The Housing Crisis," in which it raised the question, in the title of one article, "Is Moving Out the Answer?"[3] By 2017, *Ami* was drawing on data from the New York State Education Department to track the dramatic growth of enrollment in Jewish schools—a common proxy for Haredi community expansion—in upstate New York and New Jersey and the parallel stagnation of Jewish school enrollment in Brooklyn, "a shift that will likely only increase in the future," according to the magazine.[4] A year later, in an article with the headline "The Exodus: Those Left Behind," *Ami* treated the large-scale departure of Hasidim from the borough as a fait accompli, asking, "As the exodus from Brooklyn continues, what is happening to the communities and people who remain?"[5]

This exodus from Brooklyn, to the extent that it has occurred among some Hasidim, has been driven by soaring prices in the borough, fierce competition over limited housing stock, and the efforts of Hasidic and, more broadly, Haredi real estate developers, brokers, and others to encourage new home construction and purchases outside of the city. Not coincidentally, this includes some of the advertisers in *Ami*.[6] The migration of Hasidim from New York City to its exurbs and surrounding towns has also coincided with broader population declines in America's biggest cities as the urban growth of the 1990s and 2000s that drove gentrification in neighborhoods like Williamsburg began to reverse itself in the twenty-first century's second decade.[7] The result has been dramatic growth in longstanding Hasidic communities in Kiryas Joel, Monsey, and Lakewood as well as in the creation of entirely new enclaves in Bloomingburg, a village in Sullivan County, New York, and Greenville, a traditionally working-class neighborhood with a large African American population in Jersey City, New Jersey.[8] The arrival of Hasidim in these locales, in turn, has generated rising tensions over zoning, public schools, and other issues.[9]

At the end of 2019 and the beginning of 2020, a wave of physical attacks, some of them deadly and almost all of them by African American assailants, swept through Hasidic communities in Jersey City, Monsey, and Brooklyn neighborhoods such as Williamsburg and Crown Heights.[10] The extent to which these incidents reflected underlying anti-Semitism in certain sectors of the black community, local tensions over gentrification, or the broader increase in anti-Semitic rhetoric and violence since 2016—much of it linked to white supremacists, as seen in the deadly synagogue attacks in Pittsburgh and Poway—was hotly debated.[11] For their part, many Hasidim began to fear for their physical safety in ways that harked back to the 1970s or even earlier, as Rabbi David Niederman told the *New York Times*, "We thought the things that happen in Europe would never happen in the United States and definitely not in New York City. But unfortunately, we were in dreamland."[12]

The completion of this book coincided with another, very different event, one that revealed how far Hasidic Williamsburg had come from its early days. While the community has attracted national media attention—much of it exoticizing—since *Life* published a photo-essay on the enclave in 1955, the debut of the Netflix miniseries *Unorthodox* in March 2020 became a global media phenomenon.[13] Based on Deborah Feldman's best-selling 2012 memoir of her Satmar upbringing in Williamsburg, the miniseries represented the apogee of nearly a decade of books written by authors, most of them women, who had grown up and subsequently left Hasidic and other Haredi communities.[14] *Unorthodox* also followed on the heels of *Shtisel*, an Israeli television drama series that achieved great international success, joining a crop of new feature films and documentaries devoted to exploring the lives of Haredim.[15]

Yet it was not just the number and popularity of these media portrayals that suggested a major shift in the relationship between communities like Hasidic Williamsburg and the wider world. While still maintaining their profound insularity in many ways, these communities are now linked with global media and communication networks. Nor is it a one-way street, with others gazing in from the outside. Even as Haredi leaders continue to try to prohibit or limit access to the Internet, smartphones, and other related devices, many community members have become extremely sophisticated users of these technologies.[16] In online forums, blogs, Twitter feeds, news sites, and publications such as *Der Veker* (Yiddish, "The Alarm Clock"), Hasidim are now able to discuss and debate any and all topics, including media portraits of their communities, with the protection afforded by virtual anonymity.[17] At the same time, ex-Hasidim who have left these

306   *Conclusion*

communities comment on and critique these portraits openly, either on their own social media accounts or in mainstream media platforms, as happened immediately following the debut of *Unorthodox*.[18] In some ways, this cultural efflorescence represents a kind of Brooklyn Haskalah (Jewish Enlightenment), with the crucial caveat that many of its participants have remained within the fold. These developments provide further evidence that Hasidic Williamsburg has never been unchanging or "lost to time"—as an article once put it—despite the community leadership's fervent embrace of an ideology that holds that the "new is forbidden by the Torah."

And finally, just as *Unorthodox* was introducing viewers around the world to its highly contested version of Hasidic Williamsburg, Covid-19 began to ravage the community, along with other heavily Hasidic neighborhoods in Brooklyn such as Borough Park and Crown Heights. After many decades of battling figurative "plagues" such as *luksus*, crime, and gentrification, Hasidic Williamsburg was now threatened by an actual pandemic. In the first months of the outbreak, Brooklyn's Hasidic enclaves reported some of the highest rates of infection of any neighborhood in New York City, resulting in the deaths of hundreds of residents and prompting a Hasid named Shulim Leifer to tell the *New York Times* in April 2020, "There is not a single Hasidic family that has been untouched. It is a plague on a biblical scale."[19] Hasidic Williamsburg once again had more in common with poor, heavily black and Latino communities in the city, which were also disproportionately devastated by Covid-19, than with wealthier Jewish areas such as the Upper West Side of Manhattan, which had much lower rates of infection.[20]

Why Hasidic enclaves had such high rates of infection was debated throughout the spring of 2020. The phenomenon was attributed to several causes: limited Hasidic access to the mainstream media in general and to public health announcements in particular; a suspicion of governmental authority among some community members, especially when it came to health-related matters; the public celebration of the carnivalesque Jewish holiday Purim at the start of the pandemic, right before guidelines were widely put in place; the community's large, multigenerational households; and the profoundly social nature of Hasidic communal and religious life, which sometimes led to significant breaches of social distancing, drawing sharp criticism from city officials, among others, and pushback from some within the Hasidic community.[21]

As the pandemic dragged on, Hasidim grappled with ways to limit Covid-19's spread in their communities, and those who had recovered from the illness began to donate blood plasma in large numbers in an effort to help victims nationwide.[22] By the summer of 2020, the public conversation had shifted dramatically. Rather than discussing soaring rates of infection, the media was asking whether hard-hit Hasidic communities in Williamsburg, Borough Park, and Crown Heights, along with largely black and Latino neighborhoods such as Bushwick in Brooklyn, Corona in Queens, and parts of the Bronx, had achieved herd immunity. And yet, only a few months later, in the fall, rates were once again rising in the city's Hasidic communities, prompting new scrutiny.[23]

As we made our final revisions to this book, the situation on the ground was rapidly evolving. After city and state officials implemented new restrictions on the opening of businesses, schools, and houses of worship in several heavily Hasidic neighborhoods, demonstrators took to the streets of Borough Park, protesting against what they considered unfair treatment and, in several instances, engaging in violent attacks against community members whom they accused of being *mosrim*, or "snitches," as well as a Hasidic journalist covering the events. Like their zealous predecessors in decades past, these Hasidic protesters represented a highly vocal—and sometimes violent—segment of the broader community that frequently sought to intimidate other members, in this case the Hasidim who embraced the scientifically supported advice to wear masks and practice social distancing in order to diminish the spread of the pandemic.[24]

Over the decades, Hasidic Williamsburg's supposed inability to adapt has led successive generations of observers to predict the community's imminent demise. Among them was Jerome Mintz, who conducted dissertation fieldwork in the neighborhood between 1959 and 1961 and later published two illuminating books on the subject. In a 1960 letter to Margaret Mead, then the most famous anthropologist in the United States, perhaps the world, a young Mintz sought her "guidance and advice" on how to proceed with what he considered to be a project of salvage ethnography, since, "like the Jewish community in Eastern Europe, it is quite possible that the Hasidic community in the United States will not survive more than a few years in its present form."[25] Sixty years later, this proverbial camp in the desert remains in the same corner of Brooklyn, still waiting until the divinely ordained time to enter the Promised Land.

Acknowledgments

IT IS IMPOSSIBLE TO thank everyone who helped shape this book, which we worked on for over a decade, but a few people deserve special mention.

We greatly benefited from the accessibility and collections of several libraries and archives in New York City. Thanks to Amanda Seigel and the helpful staff at the Dorot Jewish Division of the New York Public Library, which became our home base on visits from California; Douglas DiCarlo of the La Guardia and Wagner Archives at La Guardia Community College; Dwight Johnson of the NYC Municipal Archives; the staff of the National Anthropological Archives at the Smithsonian Institution in Suitland, Maryland; Eddie Portnoy and the archivists at the YIVO Institute for Jewish Research; and Melanie Meyers and the librarians at the Center for Jewish History.

For help and, in some cases, hospitality while conducting research, we thank Rachel Arons, Brenden Beck, Adam Brodsky, Jeremy Butman, Molly Doria, Lucy Kaminsky, Luis Lainer, Naomi Seidman, Dan Shapiro, Moyshe Silk, Lena Sradnick, Matt Weir, Duncan Yoon, and members of the New York Working Group on Jewish Orthodoxies, in particular, Ayala Fader. Gina Kehayoff, Jackson Krule, Kore Yoors, and the editors of *Der Yid* graciously opened their photographic archives to us. We benefited greatly from Eliyahu Stern's thoughtful comments on our manuscript. Special thanks to Rose Waldman.

We received research funding from Swarthmore College and the University of California, Santa Cruz.

This book would not have come together without our agent, Don Fehr; our incredible editor at Yale University Press, Jennifer Banks; and Abigail Storch, Heather Gold, Phillip King, Kip Keller, and the extraordinary editorial team at the press.

It has been a long journey, and we could not have completed it without the loving support of our families. Thank you.

Finally, we are especially grateful to the numerous Hasidim who shared their time and knowledge with us in the homes, *shtiblekh*, and streets of Williamsburg.

Notes

All translations from Yiddish, Hebrew, and other languages are the authors' unless otherwise indicated.

Introduction

1. John Winthrop, "A Modell of Christian Charity" (1630), in *American Sermons*, ed. Michael Warner (New York: Library Classics of the United States, 1999), 28–43, quotation on 42.
2. Alexander Sender Deutsch, *Sefer Butsina Qadisha* (Brooklyn: Tiferes, 1998), 1:79.
3. Interview by the authors, July 15, 2019.
4. Joseph Berger, "Aided by Orthodox, City's Jewish Population Is Growing Again," *New York Times*, June 11, 2012: "After decades of decline, the Jewish population of New York City is growing again, increasing to nearly 1.1 million, fueled by the 'explosive' growth of the Hasidic and other Orthodox communities, a new study has found. . . . Now, 40 percent of Jews in the city identify themselves as Orthodox, an increase from 33 percent in 2002; 74 percent of all Jewish children in the city are Orthodox." Sharon Otterman, "Jewish Population Is Up in the New York Region," *New York Times*, January 17, 2013: "The Jewish population in the New York area grew by 9 percent over the last decade, reversing a longstanding trend of decline. . . . Two-thirds of the rise was propelled by two deeply Orthodox Jewish neighborhoods in Brooklyn with high birthrates—Williamsburg and Borough Park." Similarly dramatic changes occurred in other major Jewish population centers around the world; see, for example, David Connett, "Haredi: Half of Britain's Jews Will Soon Be Strictly Orthodox, Says New Study," *Independent*, October 15, 2015. In Israel, meanwhile, approximately 30 percent of all Jewish babies were born to Haredi families in the early 2000s, and studies indicated that Haredim would constitute 15 percent of the *entire* population by 2025.

5. Irving Howe, *World of Our Fathers* (New York: Harcourt Brace Jovanovich, 1976).

6. Solomon Poll, *The Hasidic Community of Williamsburg* (Brooklyn: Free Press of Glencoe, 1962), 37.

7. Israel Rubin, *Satmar: An Island in the City* (Chicago: Quadrangle, 1972).

8. "King of All Rabbis," *Time* magazine, August 3, 1959, 65: "Unlike other modern Hasidic sects—which are devoted to a kind of cheerful mysticism and have no objections to Israel—Teitelbaum's followers are fanatically opposed to most aspects of modern life."

9. There is a vast scholarly literature on Hasidism. For the most thorough history of the movement up to the present, see David Biale et al., *Hasidism: A New History* (Princeton, N.J.: Princeton University Press, 2017).

10. Jacob Leschinsky, "The Revolution in Williamsburg," *HaTsofe*, April 1, 1956 (Hebrew). Leschinsky incredulously described the "revolution" as "the complete opposite of what our generation experienced in Eastern Europe at the end of the 19th and beginning of the 20th centuries: There lived our pious forefathers and foremothers and we were forced to fight in order to shorten our *peyos* [sidelocks] and our clothes, in order to go with our heads uncovered, and not be satisfied with only learning Gemara [Talmud] and the Pentateuch. And here [in Williamsburg] is the exact opposite: The children fight to keep Kosher, to light candles on Shabbat, to wear *peyos*."

11. For statistics on contemporary Hasidic communities, see Marcin Wodziński, *Historical Atlas of Hasidism* (Princeton, N.J.: Princeton University Press, 2018), 188–199. With 26,078 families, Satmar is by far the biggest Hasidic group in the world. By comparison, the second biggest, Chabad-Lubavitch, has 16,376 families, and the third, Ger, which is the biggest group in Israel, has 11,859 families. Although they are also the largest Hasidic group in Borough Park, London, Montreal, Monsey, Kiryas Joel, and a few other locations, Williamsburg remains the population center for Satmar Hasidim in the world, and no other Hasidic group even approaches their size or influence within the neighborhood.

12. On Satmar's use of the name "kingdom" to refer to the community, see, for example, Elhanan Hertsman, *Malkhus Satmar: Satmarer kenigraykh in Amerike* (Brooklyn: E. J. Hertzman, 1981).

13. Rafael Kadosh, "Extremist Religious Philosophy: The Radical Doctrines of the Satmar Rebbe" (PhD diss., University of Cape Town, 2011), 19 (Hebrew).

14. Deutsch, *Sefer Butsina Qadisha*, 2:192. Yoel Teitelbaum wrote the letter on behalf of the Central Rabbinical Congress of the United States and Canada in support of Jews living in Middle Eastern and North African countries. As president of the Congress, Teitelbaum was invoking the Jewish legal principle known as *dina de malkhuta dina*, or "the law of the land is the law," as well as the traditional Jewish political strategy that the historian Yosef Hayim Yerushalmi labeled "vertical alliance," or the pragmatic cultivation of those in power.

15. See Menachem Keren-Kratz, "Rabbi Yoel Teitelbaum—the Satmar Rebbe—and the Rise of Anti-Zionism in American Orthodoxy," *Contemporary Jewry* 37 (2017): 464.

16. Furious at Satmar's demonization of Israel, Chaim Lieberman, a prominent journalist for the Yiddish newspaper the *Daily Forward*, published *Der rebe un der sotn, satmar un di neture karta in zeyer milkhome af medines Yisroel* (New York, 1959). He sardonically observed, "The Jewish people is the Satmar community, the Jewish land is Williamsburg, and nothing more. . . . The rest can burn. And they, themselves, will gladly ignite it. . . . They gird their loins for war. For real war. . . . With religiosity they do this, only with religiosity, with Torah. . . . A war against the Jewish state! Rabbis sharpen their swords against Jews!" (20–22).

17. Kadosh, "Extremist Religious Philosophy," 35.

18. *Life*, June 13, 1955. Solomon Poll described the community's response to the media coverage: "Many [Hasidim] expressed their dissatisfaction [with the *Life* profile]. They felt that this article should have made fun of nonobservant Jews who left the traditions of their forefathers, but instead it made fun of them, the 'truly religious.' They objected to being called 'archaic,' 'strange figures' who 'belong to another age,' just because they remained true to their traditions" (*Hasidic Community of Williamsburg*, 270). A few years later, in 1959, Harry Gersh wrote in *Commentary* that visiting Williamsburg felt "as if one were in fact traveling to some foreign place." Responding to the persistent tendency to exoticize the Hasidim, a spokesman for the community told George "Gershon" Kranzler, who lived in Williamsburg in the 1940s and 1950s and published three books on the community over the course of forty years, "We are not an exotic tribe of Israel. We are sober, hardworking people who want to live a decent, proper life." Kranzler, *Hasidic Williamsburg: A Contemporary American Hasidic Community* (Northvale, N.J.: Aronson, 1995), 263.

19. Ray Schultz, "The Call of the Ghetto: The Lubavitchers Believe It Takes Only a Little Stoking to Ignite the Spark of Religion in Every Jew," *New York Times*, November 10, 1974. Rabbi Nathan Perilman, the longtime leader of Temple Emanu-El, a Reform congregation in New York City, dismissed Hasidim as "caricatures" and a "grotesque distortion of Judaism." In a 1963 review of Poll's and Kranzler's books on Williamsburg, Zalman Posner admitted that the "average American Jew" viewed the community as "bizarre." Jay Maeder, "Real World Hasidim," *New York Daily News*, October 8, 2001.

20. Simcha Elberg, "Vilyamsburg," *Dos yidishe vort*, May 1954.

21. Hella Winston, *Unchosen: The Hidden Lives of Hasidic Rebels* (New York: Beacon, 2005), xiii: "I had begun to wonder whether the Hasidim themselves had any idea that they were a screen onto which so much Jewish ambivalence was projected."

22. Eli Lederhendler, *New York Jews and the Decline of Urban Ethnicity, 1950–1970* (Syracuse, N.Y.: Syracuse University Press, 2001), 149. Lederhendler argues that although the "participation of Jews from the city in 'white flight,' by all accounts, was significant and the Jewish presence in the suburbs burgeoned" (154), the outflow of Jews lagged that of other white ethnic groups by approximately a decade, and in the end, Jews remained a larger percentage of the overall white population of the city than the Irish, Italians, and other communities. Furthermore, Lederhendler writes, "The *delay in Jewish suburbanization* may have tended to expose them, more than other non-Hispanic whites, to the atmosphere of crisis that developed in the city during the sixties" (emphasis in the original).

23. See, for example, Richard Severo, "Reagan Grants Hasidim 'Disadvantaged' Status," *New York Times*, June 29, 1984.

24. "The Undeserving Poor?," *Forward*, June 21, 2012: "Does the safety net help those who truly are in need, or does it shackle them to the kind of government assistance that stifles motivation and derails self-sufficiency? We're used to hearing that argument play out with regard to racial and ethnic minorities—the so-called Welfare Queens, the undeserving poor. Now it's time for the Jewish community to engage in this delicate, complicated debate. . . . It's the ballooning birthrate in Orthodox families, particularly Hasidic ones, that fuels this trend. . . . This is a poverty of choice, or perhaps more generously, a poverty of default. It is voluntary impoverishment." See also Evan Goldstein, "Israel's Ultra-Orthodox Welfare Kings," *Wall Street Journal*, November 12, 2010; Joe Sexton, "Religion and Welfare Shape Economics for the Hasidim," *New York Times*, April 21, 1997; Ginia Bellafante, "In Brooklyn, Stifling Higher Learning Among Hasidic Women," *New York Times*, September 2, 2016; Ira Stoll, "New York Times Column Smears Satmars as Ignorant Welfare Sponges," www.algemeiner.com/2016/09/05/new-york-times-column-smears-satmars-as-ignorant-welfare-sponges.

25. Stephen Price, "The Effect of Federal Anti-Poverty Programs and Policies of the Hasidic and Puerto Communities of Williamsburg" (PhD diss., Brandeis University, 1979), 81. Price, who lived in Williamsburg in the 1960s and 1970s, noted, "The younger Hasidim spoke a rapid-fire New Yorkese, similar to the younger Puerto Ricans."

26. Karen Brodkin, *How Jews Became White Folks and What That Says About Race in America* (New Brunswick, N.J.: Rutgers University Press, 1998); see also Eric Goldstein, *The Price of Whiteness: Jews, Race, and American Identity* (Princeton, N.J.: Princeton University Press, 2008).

27. Jay-Z, *Decoded* (New York: Spiegel & Grau, 2010), 176.

28. Samuel Heilman, "Orthodox Jews, the City and the Suburb," in *People of the City: Jews and the Urban Challenge*, ed. Ezra Mendelsohn, Studies in Contemporary Jewry 15 (New York: Oxford University Press, 1999), 27: "The dangers of their neighborhoods might be physical, but as they saw it, the assimilative dangers of the suburban milieus were religious and cultural. The

former risks seemed to them small in comparison to the latter. Those inside the haredi enclave in largely African American and Hispanic areas could often feel as if they were protected by a wall of Jewish virtues, as if they were clearly a people set apart and chosen for higher moral rewards. More and more, therefore, the city neighborhoods where the surrounding population was most unwelcoming seemed the preferred locale for haredi life."

29. Bernard Weinberger, "The Interracial Crisis: How Should Jews Respond?," *Journal of Jewish Communal Service* 46, no. 1 (1969): 40.

30. Lance Freeman, *There Goes the 'Hood: Views of Gentrification from the Ground Up* (Philadelphia: Temple University Press, 2006), has stressed the importance of focusing on the experiences of "indigenous residents" in addition to those of gentrifiers, or on impersonal economic forces.

31. Ruth Glass coined the term "gentrification" to describe the transformation of working-class neighborhoods in London by wealthier newcomers: "One by one, many of the working class neighbourhoods of London have been invaded by the middle-classes. . . . Once this process of 'gentrification' starts in a district it goes on rapidly, until all or most of the original working-class occupiers are displaced and the whole social character of the district is changed." Ruth Glass, *Introduction to London: Aspects of Change* (London: MacGibbon and Kee, 1964), xviii. On the key scholarly debates that have emerged since, see Japonica Brown-Saracino, ed., *The Gentrification Debates* (New York: Routledge, 2010).

32. On gentrification as the "revenge" of the monied classes, see Neil Smith, *The New Urban Frontier: Gentrification and the Revanchist City* (New York: Routledge, 1996).

33. Richard Florida, "Bohemia and Economic Geography," *Journal of Economic Geography* 2 (2002): 55–71.

34. Neil Smith, "Gentrification, the Frontier, and the Restructuring of Urban Space," in *Gentrification of the City*, ed. Neil Smith and Peter Williams (New York: Routledge, 2007), 15–24.

35. See, for example, Elizabeth Lesly, "It's Rough in the Diamond District," Bloomberg, May 2, 1993, www.bloomberg.com/news/articles/1993-05-02/its-rough-in-the-diamond-district; Dan Bilefsky, "Indians Unseat Antwerp's Jews as the Biggest Diamond Traders," *Wall Street Journal*, May 27, 2003.

36. Garment-manufacturing job statistics are from a 2012 report by the Design Trust for Public Space, as cited in Carlo Scissura, "Public and Private Sector Investment Is Transforming Brooklyn into New York's Capital of Couture," *New York Daily News*, February 3, 2015.

37. Center for an Urban Future, "The Empire Has No Clothes: Rising Real Estate Prices and Declining City Support Threatens the Future of New York's Apparel Industry," February 2000, 1. See also A. Zimmer, "Real Estate Fears Spread Through Industrial Sector," *Metro New York*, September 20, 2006, and Winifred Curran, " 'From the Frying Pan to the Oven': Gentrification and the Experience of Industrial Displacement in Williamsburg, Brooklyn," *Urban Studies* 44, no. 8 (July 2007): 1429.

38. "Brooklyn, NY—Mishpacha Magazine Profiles Rabbi Niederman of UJO, Calling Him One of the Most Effective Diplomats in the Orthodox Community," *Vos Iz Neias*, January 18, 2010, vosizneias.com/47258/2010/01/18/brooklyn-ny-mishpacha-magazine-profiles-rabbi-niederman-of-ujo-calling-him-one-of-the-most-effective-diplomats-in-the-orthodox-community. "Reb Moishe Duvid [Niederman] expounds 'Our *tzibbur* [public] has always worked hard. Every decade brought its industry, and we were always leaders. First it was in the needle trade, then retail, electronics, and more recently, real estate and mortgages.' "

39. Danielle Wiener-Bronner, "Hasidic Williamsburg Poverty Data Are Bleak, but Some See Reason to Hope," Reuters, June 7, 2013, http://blogs.reuters.com/events/2013/06/07/jewish-poverty.

40. Michelle Cohen, "With $2.5 Billion in Brooklyn Real Estate, Hasidic Investors Are a Formidable Gentrification Driver," 6sqft.com, August 26, 2016, www.6sqft.com/with-2-5-billion-in-brooklyn-real-estate-the-hasidic-community-is-a-formidable-gentrification-driver.

41. Paul Harris, "Brooklyn's Williamsburg Becomes New Front Line of the Gentrification Battle," *Guardian*, December 11, 2010.

42. Pamela Engel, "The Gentrification of Williamsburg, Brooklyn in 3 Maps," *Business Insider*, December 17, 2013; see also Sam Beck, "Knowledge Production and Emancipatory Movements from the Heart of Globalised Hipsterdom, Williamsburg, Brooklyn," *Anthropology in Action* 23, no. 1 (Spring 2016): 22–30.

43. On the urban "authenticity" of Williamsburg and its appeal to gentrifiers, see Sharon Zukin, *Naked City: The Death and Life of Authentic Urban Places* (Oxford: Oxford University Press, 2010), 16.

44. For some examples, see "A Shtetl in South Williamsburg," *Canadian Jewish News*, December 1, 2011, www.cjnews.com/perspectives/opinions/shtetl-south-williamsburg; Meg Miller, "This Brooklyn Neighborhood Has Gone Virtually Unchanged Since World War II," *Fast Company*, February 26, 2016, www.fastcompany.com/3057097/this-brooklyn-neighborhood-has-gone-virtually-unchanged-since-world-war-ii; Jordan Teicher, "The Unchanging Streets of Hasidic South Williamsburg," *Slate*, February 19, 2006, https://slate.com/culture/2016/02/william-castellana-photographs-his-hasidic-neighbors-in-south-williamsburg.html; Alan Feuer, "A Piece of Brooklyn Perhaps Lost to Time," *New York Times*, July 5, 2009.

45. The Hebrew word "Haredi" comes from a root meaning "to tremble," as in "those who tremble at [God's] word" (Isaiah 66:5) and is an umbrella term for a constellation of Jewish groups—Hasidim, Litvaks or Yeshivish, Hungarians, Sephardi Shas supporters—with distinctive origins and characteristics that nonetheless share similar attitudes toward tradition, modernity, and contemporary efforts to "reform" Judaism. The term is often used interchangeably with the English "Ultraorthodox," a label that many Haredim see as pejorative.

46. Deutsch, *Sefer Butsina Qadisha*, 2:300. This biblical text, Proverbs 1:8, is the one most commonly cited to support the importance of following customs.

Chapter 1. A Land Not Sown

1. Henry Miller lived until 1899 at 662 Driggs Avenue in Williamsburg before moving to Bushwick with his family. Yet he visited his old neighborhood for years thereafter. Miller, "Two Williamsburg Remembrances," *New York Times*, October 17, 1971.
2. Jenna Weissman Joselit, *New York's Jewish Jews: The Orthodox Community in the Interwar Years* (Bloomington: Indiana University Press, 1990), 18; Ilana Abramovitch, introduction to *Jews of Brooklyn*, ed. Ilana Abramovitch and Seán Galvin (Waltham, Mass.: Brandeis University Press, 2002), 6.
3. Helen Epstein, *Joe Papp: An American Life* (New York: Da Capo, 1996), 20.
4. According to Jeffrey Gurock, "A 1940 neighborhood survey . . . revealed that 'only about nine percent of adult males in Brownsville attended synagogue with any regularity' " ("Jewish Commitment and Continuity in Interwar Brooklyn," in Abramovitch and Galvin, *Jews of Brooklyn*, 232).
5. Ibid.; see also William Helmreich, *The World of the Yeshivah: An Intimate Portrait of Orthodox Jewry* (Brooklyn: KTAV, 1982), 26–51, and Yonoson Rosenblum, *Reb Shraga Feivel: The Life and Times of Rabbi Shraga Feivel Mendlowitz, the Architect of Torah in America* (Brooklyn: Mesorah, 2001).
6. Frida, telephone interview by the authors, July 23, 2016.
7. Philip Fishman, *A Sukkah Is Burning: Remembering Williamsburg's Hasidic Transformation* (self-published, 2012), 37.
8. Michael Casper, "*Luksus* and the Hasidic Critique of Postwar American Capitalism," in *All Religion Is Inter-Religion: Essays in Honor of Steven M. Wasserstrom*, ed. Kambiz GhaneaBassiri and Paul M. Robertson (London: Bloomsbury, 2019), 171–180.
9. Joselit, *New York's Jewish Jews*, 18. For an evocative firsthand description of what it was like to attend one of the Satmar schools in Williamsburg in the 1950s, see Eli Hecht, *Crossing the Williamsburg Bridge: Memories of an American Youngster Growing Up with Chassidic Survivors of the Holocaust* (self-published, 2004), 9–47; see also Saul Carson, "Satmar Hassidim Build Their Own Town in the United States," *Wisconsin Jewish Chronicle*, September 28, 1962.
10. On this issue, see Kadosh, "Extreme Religious Philosophy," 66: "Examining the writings of the Satmar Rebbe reveals that the *Geulah* [Redemption]—more than any other subject—serves as the cornerstone of his teaching." For another recent comparison of Chabad and Satmar messianism, see Shaul Magid, "American Jewish Fundamentalism: Habad, Satmar, ArtScroll," in *Piety and Rebellion: Essays in Hasidism* (Brighton, Mass.: Academic Studies Press, 2019).
11. Jerome Mintz, *Hasidic People: A Place in the New World* (Cambridge, Mass.: Harvard University Press, 1992), 39. On Teitelbaum's skepticism regarding

Hasidic tales, see Avraham D. Gluck, ed., *Zekher Tsadik Livrakha* (Kiryas Joel, N.Y.: Mazel, 2002), 1:600.

12. On Yoel Teitelbaum's devotion to Moses Sofer, see Deutsch, *Sefer Butsina Qadisha*, 2:116–118. Shlomo Gelbman's multivolume work devoted to Teitelbaum's life, *Sefer Moshian shel Yisrael: Toldot rabenu ha-kadosh mi-Satmar* (Kiryas Joel, N.Y.: self-published, 1988–), explored his rebbe's relationship to Sofer's teachings as well as to those of other important rabbis (e.g., Nahman of Bratslav). On Gelbman and his significance, see David N. Myers, "Remembering the Satmar Movement's Chronicler," *Tablet*, April 3, 2015, www.tabletmag.com/sections/news/articles/remembering-the-satmar-movements-chronicler. See also the extensive references to Sofer's Halakhic rulings in Teitelbaum's responsa collection, *Sefer She'elot u-Teshuvot Divrei Yoel* (Brooklyn: Jerusalem Book Store, 2005).

13. Alan Nadler, "Piety and Politics: The Case of the Satmar Rebbe," *Judaism* 31 (Spring 1982).

14. For a collection of Yoel Teitelbaum's teachings regarding the challenges and opportunities of living in the Exile, see *Sefer mi-torato shel rabenu: Kovets gadol mi-yoter mi-shesh me'ot 'erkhe 'inyanim be-sifre rabenu mi-Satmar*, vol. 1, *Erekh galut*, ed. Shlomo Margaliyot (Brooklyn: Jerusalem Publishing House, 1984).

15. Deutsch, *Sefer Butsina Qadisha*, 2:121.

16. Before World War II, Teitelbaum's approach to Zionism was shared most notably by Rabbi Chaim Elazar Spira, the Munkacser Rebbe, a fellow Hasidic leader and sometime rival from the Unterland region.

17. For examples of Yoel Teitelbaum's instructions to his followers not to accept financial aid from the State of Israel, see the letters in Yoel Teitelbaum, *Sefer Divre Yoel: Mikhtavim: Kovets mikhteve kodesh be-'inyanim shonim* (Brooklyn: Bet mishar ve-hotsa'at sefarim Yerushalayim, 1980), 1:139–141.

18. Fishman, *Sukkah Is Burning*, 37.

19. Yoel Teitelbaum, *VaYoel Moshe* (Brooklyn, 1961), 318n112. The title is from Exodus 2:21–22, "And Moses was content to stay with the man . . . an alien in a foreign land," but is also a combination of his name and his grandfather's name—Yoel and Moshe, respectively; see Teitelbaum, *VaYoel Moshe*, 315n110. Discussions of the Exile and its significance are scattered throughout Teitelbaum's other writings, for example, *Sefer Divrei Yoel al-ha-Torah* (Brooklyn: Jerusalem Book Store, 2014), 1:307.

20. Teitelbaum, *VaYoel Moshe*, 316n110.

21. Yoel Teitelbaum's approach recalls Gershom Scholem's observation that "the [Hasidic] movement as a whole had made its peace with the *Galuth*"; see Gershom Scholem, *Major Trends in Jewish Mysticism* (New York: Schocken, 1961), 336. On the minority rabbinic view that the Exile represented a spiritual opportunity rather than merely a disaster, see Marc Saperstein and Nancy Berg, " 'Arab Chains' and 'The Good Things of Sepharad': Aspects of Jewish Exile," *AJS Review* 26, no. 2 (2002): 302n2; see also Shalom Rosenberg, "Exile and Redemption in Jewish Thought in the Sixteenth Century:

Contending Conceptions," in *Jewish Thought in the Sixteenth Century*, ed. Bernard Dov Cooperman (Cambridge, Mass.: Harvard University Press, 1983), 299–430.

22. Jeno (Yonah) Landau, *Kuntres Zikaron ba-Sefer: zikhronot ve-sipurim, meoraot ve-toladot bi-leshon Idish, peraķim le-zikhro ha-bahir shel Yoel Teitelbaum* (Brooklyn: Y. Landau, 1981), 244.

23. Shlomo Gelbman, *Sefer Retson Tsadik* (Kiryas Joel, N.Y.: Leybush Lefkovitsh, 1998), 6. See also, inter alia, 7: "The Torah was exiled from place to place and before the coming of the messiah the Torah will arrive in America and from there the Jews will go on to receive the face of the messiah."

24. Teitelbaum, *Sefer Divre Yoel: Mikhtavim*, 1:199–200.

25. See, for example, *Sefer Tsadik ka-Tamar Niflaot Maharit*, pt. 3 (Brooklyn: S. Eisner, 1985), 17. The book consists of traditions regarding Yoel Teitelbaum that were gathered by his disciples in Kiryas Joel.

26. This tradition appears in several places, including Teitelbaum, *Sefer Divre Yoel: Mikhtavim*, 1:107.

27. Teitelbaum to Moshe Gross, in *Sefer Divre Yoel: Mikhtavim*, 1:107. In his legal responsa, Yoel Teitelbaum engaged with the complicated Halakhic question whether individual Jews living in the Exile were commanded to settle in the land of Israel if it was physically possible to do so, or, alternatively, whether this was even prohibited before the *geulah* (Redemption); see, for example, *Sefer She'elot u-Teshuvot Divrei Yoel*, 1:282, 286, in which he discusses under what conditions it would be possible to leave the land of Israel if one were already there, and live elsewhere.

28. Deutsch, *Sefer Butsina Qadisha*, 2:60.

29. See, for example, Isaiah 10:20; Ezekiel 9:8; Jeremiah 23:3.

30. Gelbman, *Retson Tsadik*, 2–3.

31. Ibid., 7. See also the version that holds that Teitelbaum fasted after dreaming that he would go to America (8).

32. Jeremiah 2:2, Jewish Publication Society of America Version.

33. Gelbman, *Retson Tsadik*, 9; see also Teitelbaum, *VaYoel Moshe*, 214n109. As George Kranzler noted in *Williamsburg: A Jewish Community in Transition* (New York: Feldheim, 1961), "In the ideology of the Satmar Rebbe, spelled out in the elaborate essays of 'Vayoel Mosheh,' these [Hasidic communities] are new, intrinsically American forms of the movable 'mishkan' (the Sanctuary) and the 'Mahaneh Yisrael' (the Camp of Israel)" (271).

34. Keren-Kratz, "Rabbi Yoel Teitelbaum—the Satmar Rebbe—and the Rise of Anti-Zionism," 462, and Keren-Kratz, "Rabbi Yoel Teitelbaum—The Satmar Rebbe (1887–1979): A Biography," (PhD diss., Tel Aviv University, 2013), 226–239 (Hebrew). See also Keren-Kratz, "Is the Jewish State the Ultimate Evil or a Golden Opportunity? Ideology v. Politics in the Teachings and Actions of Rabbi Yoel Teitelbaum—the Satmar Rebbe," *Jewish Political Studies Review* 29, nos. 1–2 (2018), http://jcpa.org/article/jewish-state-the-ultimate-evil-or-golden-opportunity.

35. Abraham Gluck, *Sefer Zekher Tsadik Livrakhah* (Monroe, N.Y.: Defus ve-Hotsaat "Mazel," 2002), 1:435.

36. Ibid., 413.

37. Ibid. See also Gelbman, *Retson Tsadik*, 9, quoting the Belzer Rebber: "In the land of Israel 'every other Jew is a goy and here in America every other goy is a Jew.' "

38. Gelbman, *Retson Tsadik*, 5–6.

39. See, for example, Shoshana Kordova, "Haredization: In Israel, Gentrification Is About Religion, not Class," *Tablet*, January 7, 2011, tabletmag.com/scroll/55071/haredization.

40. Aviezer Ravitzky, *Messianism, Zionism, and Jewish Religious Radicalism* (Chicago: University of Chicago Press, 1996), 45.

41. Yoel Teitelbaum, *She'elot u-Teshuvot Divre Yoel*, 1:60. See also Deutsch, *Sefer Butsina Qadisha*, 2:111: "Our rabbi always grumbled (was bitter) concerning the great ignorance and boorishness that had taken root among the Jews in the country of America. . . . The customs of America are customs of ignorance and of course there is no need to follow such customs."

42. A Hasid of the Kalashitz Rebbe once asked Yoel Teitelbaum whether he should "join Torah Vadaath [Torah and knowledge], [and] he answered him that he should not seek Torah Vadaath but rather should only seek out 'Torah Veyira' [Torah and fear of God]. And amazingly, a few years after our rabbi, may his memory be for a blessing, came to America he established his yeshiva and Talmud Torah and he called them 'Torah Veyira' " (Gelbman, *Retson Tsadik*, 7–8).

43. Deutsch, *Sefer Butsina Qadisha*, 2:69.

44. Moshe Karona, "Williamsburg and Jewish America," *HaTsofe*, July 24, 1953 (Hebrew).

45. Yemimah Tshernovits, "Jewish Islands in New York: Williamsburg, the Mea Shearim of New York; Shatnes Laboratory and Automatic Sukkah; Fortress of Judaism in the Heart of the City," *Davar*, October 18, 1957 (Hebrew).

46. Kranzler, *Williamsburg*, 218; see also Fishman, *Sukkah Is Burning*, 43–44.

47. Steffen Krogh, "How Satmarish Is Satmar Yiddish?," in *Leket: Yiddish Studies Today*, ed. Marion Aptroot, Efrat Gal-Ed, Roland Gruschka, and Simon Neuberg (Dusseldorf: Dusseldorf University Press, 2012), 1:484: "Despite the fact that we refer to today's Satmar community as 'Hungarian' in general and 'Satmar' in particular, these designations should not tempt us to view this group as an unbroken continuation of the Hasidim who lived in the Unterland before the war." On contemporary Haredi Yiddish, including that used by Satmar and other Hungarian Hasidim in Williamsburg, see Dalit Assouline, "Haredi Yiddish in Israel and the United States," in *Languages in Jewish Communities, Past and Present*, ed. Benjamin Hary and Sarah Bunin Benor (Berlin: Walter De Gruyter, 2018). For example, according to a survey conducted in 1961, out of 860 household heads in Williamsburg, ap-

proximately 40 percent had been neither Satmar nor Sighet Hasidim in prewar Europe.

48. Phyllis Franck, "The Hasidic Poor in New York City," in *Poor Jews: An American Awakening*, ed. Naomi Levine and Martin Hochbaum (Piscataway, N.J.: Transaction, 1974), 60.

49. Jacob Leschinsky, "The Revolution in Williamsburg," *HaTsofe*, April 1, 1956 (Hebrew).

50. Kranzler, *Williamsburg*, 21.

51. Chaim Moshe Stauber, *The Satmar Rebbe* (New York: Feldheim, 2011), 153–154.

52. As excerpted in Dovid Meisels, *The Rebbe Speaks* (Lakewood, N.J.: Israel Bookshop Publications, 2012), 114.

53. Deutsch, *Sefer Butsina Qadisha*, 2:300.

54. Kranzler, *Williamsburg*, 21. In an interview conducted during this period, one local Jewish resident of Williamsburg stated why he opposed the dress of the Hasidim: "If they preferred to wear beards and cover their wives' hair, they certainly were right within the law. But as far as I and my people were concerned, I think one can be equally pious and observant without these. My father did wear a short beard, but he told us many a time that beard and *peyes* still did not make a good Jew. I also don't believe in the need for walking around with a *Bekeshe* and *Shtreimel*. They may have been proper in the old home town in Europe but it seems they have little place here in Williamsburg. They are only bound to create misunderstandings and ridicule on the part of the non-Jews."

55. Poll, *Hasidic Community of Williamsburg*, 88.

56. Ibid.

57. Yehezkel Yosef Weisshaus, *Edus Be-Yosef* (Lakewood, N.J.: Machon Lev Avos, 2008), 313. The text is in Hebrew except for Teitelbaum's response, which is in Yiddish. The literal translation of his words is "All Jews without a beard have the same face to me."

58. Ibid.

59. The town of Pupa (or Pápa) was in the Oberland region of Hungary. Most of its Jewish population was not Hasidic before World War II and followed Ashkenazi customs. Nevertheless, there were also some Hasidim, including Rabbi Yaakov Yechezkiya Greenwald, a follower of the Belzer Rebbe, who served as the rabbi of Tselem (Deutschkreutz, Austria) before arriving in Pupa, where he established a yeshiva. His son, Yosef, led a yeshiva in Satmar before moving to Pupa with many of his students in 1941. Yosef Greenwald's first wife and ten children were murdered during the Holocaust, and he was imprisoned. Following the war, Greenwald lived in Antwerp before arriving in Williamsburg, where he established many institutions in the neighborhood, including Congregation Kehilath Yakov-Pupa and, eventually, a village, Kiryas Pupa, in Westchester County, New York. As even this brief history indicates, the Haredi communities from towns throughout Greater

Hungary—Tselem, Pupa, Satmar, Sighet, and more—were linked in a variety of ways before their arrival in Williamsburg.

60. On what might be called the "Hasidification" of Williamsburg's Viener community, which was originally a non-Hasidic Haredi group in Austria whose leaders were disciples of Rabbi Avraham Shmuel Binyamin Sofer, known as the Kesav Sofer (the son of the Hasam Sofer), see Gershon Tannenbaum, "My Machberes: Vienner Kehillah Adopts *Nusach Sephard*," *Jewish Press*, May 14, 2008.

Chapter 2. Paths of Heaven

1. Simon Dumenco, "A Racial U-Turn," *New York*, July 23, 2010, https://nymag.com/news/intelligencer/topic/67288.

2. This dramatic demographic shift was paralleled in Chicago, Detroit, Philadelphia, Boston, Cleveland, and smaller cities around the United States. See Lederhendler, *New York Jews*, 81, 149–150, 154.

3. Schneerson was later joined by Rabbi Simchah Elberg and Rabbi Moshe Feinstein in his opposition to "Jewish flight." See Simchah Elberg, "Editor's Note," *Ha-Pardes* 43, no. 6 (May 1969): 5 (Hebrew); Elberg, "A Halakhic Not a Political Problem," *Ha-Pardes* 44, no. 1 (October 1969): 4 (Hebrew). On this topic, see also Avinoam Stillman, "Race and the Rabbis: The White Jew and the Segregation of the American City," *Current: A Journal of Contemporary Politics, Culture, and Jewish Affairs at Columbia University*, originally posted April 2, 2015. Our thanks to Stillman for providing us with relevant copies of *Ha-Pardes* and for insights shared during our correspondence. See also Moshe Feinstein, *Sefer Igrot Moshe* (New York: M. Feinstein, 1959–1963), *Choshen Mishpat, Helek Beyt, Siman* 22.

4. A few Lubavitchers had been in the neighborhood since the 1920s, but the sixth rebbe arrived in 1940. By 1960, there were 3,000–5,000 Hasidim, mainly Lubavitch and Bobover, around 2 percent of the total population. See Henry Goldschmidt, *Race and Religion: Among the Chosen Peoples of Crown Heights* (New Brunswick, N.J.: Rutgers University Press, 2006), 91–94.

5. Ibid., 93.

6. On the move of Bobov to Borough Park in 1968, see Edward Shapiro, *Crown Heights: Blacks, Jews, and the 1991 Brooklyn Riot* (Waltham, Mass.: Brandeis University Press, 2006), 89. On the Haredization of Borough Park, see Egon Mayer, *From Suburb to Shtetl: The Jews of Boro Park* (Philadelphia: Temple University Press, 1979).

7. Joshua Zeitz, *White Ethnic New York: Jews, Catholics, and the Shaping of Postwar Politics* (Chapel Hill: University of North Carolina Press, 2007), 153. Zeitz notes, "In the 1960s alone, the city lost a net total of 617,127 white residents and gained a net total of 702,903 black and Puerto Rican residents" (160).

8. On the Ocean Hill–Brownsville school crisis, see Zeitz, *White Ethnic New York*, 164–167.

9. On the number of people present at Schneerson's talk, see Elberg, "Editor's Note: Rabbi Menachem Mendel Schneerson of Lubavitch, 'Whether It Is Permitted to Abandon a Jewish Neighborhood and Sell One's House to a Non-Jew,' " *Ha-Parde*s 43, no. 6 (May 1969): 5 (Hebrew).

10. Menachem Mendel Schneerson, *Toras Menachem* (Brooklyn: Kehos, 2015), 56:132. For a collection of Chabad sources devoted to the topic of remaining in Crown Heights and strengthening the Lubavitcher community in the neighborhood, see *Kan Tsivah H[ashem] et ha-Brakha: Be-inyan khizuk u-visus ha-shekhuna* (Brooklyn: Khevreh Makhzike Ha-Shekhuna, 1980); see also R. Kestenbaum, "Crown Heights, the Community That Didn't Run," *Times of Israel*, October 1975, 38–41.

11. Schneerson, *Toras Menachem*, 133.

12. Ibid., 136. See also Elberg "Editor's Note," 26.

13. Schneerson, *Toras Menachem*, 138, 145. He claimed that fathers who showed such fear would have a hard time convincing their daughters to marry a *frum* (religious) man.

14. Ibid., 139.

15. Quoted in "Ha-Shanim ha-Shekhorot shel Shekhunat 'Crown Heights,' " *Chabad Info*, January 7, 2009, http://old2.ih.chabad.info/#!g=1&url=article&id= 47252 (Hebrew).

16. Lawrence Friedman, "Public Housing and the Poor: An Overview," *California Law Review* 54, no. 2 (1966): 652.

17. Nicholas Dagen Bloom and Matthew Gordon Lasner, "Public Housing Towers," in *Affordable Housing in New York: The People, Places, and Policies That Transformed a City*, ed. Nicholas Dagen Bloom and Matthew Gordon Lasner (Princeton, N.J.: Princeton University Press, 2016), 120–121.

18. Richard Rothstein, "Race and Public Housing: Revisiting the Federal Role," *Poverty and Race* 21, no. 6 (November–December 2012): 2, 15; see also Richard Rothstein, *The Color of Law: A Forgotten History of How Our Government Segregated America* (New York: Liveright, 2018).

19. Rothstein, "Race and Public Housing," 2.

20. Ibid.; see also Emily Badger, "How Section 8 Became a Racial Slur," *Washington Post*, June 15, 2105.

21. Quoted in Landmarks Preservation Commission, February 10, 2004, Designation List 348, LP-2135-A, http://s-media.nyc.gov/agencies/lpc/lp/2135A. pdf.

22. Ibid.

23. Ethan G. Sribnick, "Excluding the Poor: Public Housing in New York City," *Uncensored* 3, no. 2 (Summer 2012): 24–28, www.icphusa.org/wp-content/ uploads/2015/01/ICPH_UNCENSORED_3.2_Summer2012_Excluding-ThePoor.pdf.

24. *Brooklyn Eagle*, August 25, 1937, as cited in Landmarks Preservation Commission, February 10, 2004, Designation List 348, LP-2135.
25. Bloom and Lasner, *Affordable Housing in New York*, https://eportfolios.ma caulay.cuny.edu/botein17/files/2017/01/Public-Housing-Towers.pdf.
26. Jeanne Lowe, "The Man Who Got Things Done for New York: Robert Moses Tackles Slum Clearance," in *Cities in a Race with Time: Progress and Poverty in America's Renewing Cities*, ed. Jeanne R. Lowe (New York: Random House, 1967), 68–72; see also Samuel Zip, *Manhattan Projects: The Rise and Fall of Urban Renewal in Cold War New York* (Oxford: Oxford University Press, 2010), 17–19.
27. Harry S. Truman, "Annual Message to the Congress on the State of the Union," January 5, 1949, *The American Presidency Project*, www.presidency. ucsb.edu/documents/annual-message-the-congress-the-state-the-union-21.
28. See "Williamsburg Confidential" and "Dr. Sternberg Starts Drive for Middle-Income Housing: Names Leaders to Head Campaign for Lower Williamsburg Area," *Williamsburg News*, November 22, 1957.
29. Bloom and Lasner, *Affordable Housing in New York*, 116.
30. D. Krants, "Nyu York boyt fuftsn toyznt naye dires," *Der Tog-Morgn Zhurnal*, April 23, 1955; see also Keren-Kratz, "Rabbi Yoel Teitelbaum—The Satmar Rebbe (1887–1979)," 330.
31. Bernard Weinberger, "The Miracle of Williamsburg: How a Community Managed to Halt a Population Shift," *Jewish Observer*, April 1965, 16–17.
32. Ibid.
33. Ibid., 17.
34. Ibid.
35. Bloom and Lasner, *Affordable Housing in New York*, 120.
36. Sol Levy, "Williamsburg Confidential," *Williamsburg News*, November 22, 1957. Named after New York state senator MacNeil Mitchell and Assemblyman Alfred Lama, who sponsored the relevant legislation in 1955, the goal of the Mitchell-Lama program was to facilitate the development of affordable housing by providing private developers with financial incentives, including tax abatements, low-interest loans, government-subsidized mortgages, and a guaranteed annual return on investment. Over the years, Mitchell-Lama resulted in the construction of more than 250 buildings, with over 100,000 units, throughout New York City.
37. For use of the phrase "slum clearance" in documents related to the construction of the public housing projects in Williamsburg, see "Amendment to the Application for Financial Assistance of February 25, 1958 Low-Rent Public Housing Project By the New York City Housing Authority," Division Avenue—Roebling Street Area, Project no. NYS-101, November 24, 1958, New York City Housing Authority Papers, La Guardia and Wagner Archives, series 08, box #0085C1, FLD #11 (hereafter cited as NYCHA Papers).
38. Ibid.

39. Ibid.

40. "Public Housing to Get New Look: 'Vest-Pocket' Projects Are Planned Here—Buildings to Be Smaller, More Airy," *New York Times*, May 5, 1957. For a discussion of the projects built in this style, see Nicholas Dagen Bloom, *Public Housing That Worked: New York in the Twentieth Century* (Philadelphia: University of Pennsylvania Press, 2009), 153–154.

41. "Hearing Set on $50 Million Housing in Williamsburg," *New York Daily News*, February 12, 1958.

42. Alfred Miele, "Williamsburg in Donnybrook over Housing," *New York Daily News*, February 26, 1958.

43. Quoted in Bloom, *Public Housing That Worked*, 117.

44. Miele, "Williamsburg in Donnybrook over Housing."

45. Pincus identified himself as the spokesman for the Rabbinical Board of Williamsburg, but that designation was challenged by members of the United Synagogues and Yeshivas of Williamsburg, a sign of the emerging split within the local Orthodox leadership. On the Rabbinical Board of Williamsburg and its membership, see "Local Leaders to Pay Tribute to Popular Senator on December 11," *Williamsburg News*, December 2, 1955.

46. Moshe Sherer, "From City Hall, to Washington, to Williamsburg," *Dos yidishe vort*, March 1958, 3 (Yiddish).

47. Ibid., 3. Sherer neglected to note that some prominent supporters of the housing projects, such as Rabbi Chaim Pincus and Rabbi Bernard Weinberger, were leaders of Orthodox institutions and organizations in the neighborhood.

48. "Housing Foes Fail to Block Planners OK," *New York Daily News*, March 6, 1958. Those who viewed the low-income projects as a solution to the area's long-standing shortage of decent affordable housing celebrated the construction of the projects; as a self-described thirty-year resident of Williamsburg put it in a letter to the editor in the *Daily News* that day, "My daughter has five children and lives in a cold flat because she can't find other quarters. Why shouldn't Williamsburg have projects like any other section of the city?"

49. Bloom, *Public Housing That Worked*, 170–171.

50. "2 Groups Join Forces to War on CHA Plans," *New York Daily News*, March 7, 1958.

51. "Hit 2 Projects as Menace to Jews' Culture," *New York Daily News*, March 14, 1958.

52. See his obituary: Wolfgang Saxon, "Rabbi Pinchas M. Teitz, 87, Founder of Schools," *New York Times*, December 29, 1995.

53. "Project Sites Being Studied," *New York Daily News*, August 12, 1958.

54. Polly Kline, "City Bows to Protests, Abandons Project," *New York Daily News*, September 19, 1958. Instead of the reasons offered earlier, Abraham Newhouse now stated that his Orthodox constituency "opposes any low-income housing development in the area ... because their members are in too high

an economic bracket to qualify as tenants." Sol Levy, the publisher of the *Williamsburg News*, who had launched the campaign for middle-income housing in South Williamsburg in 1957 and then supported the city's low-income proposals, happily described the plan to build one low-income public housing project as a "big victory," and the move to transform the second project into middle-income, private co-ops as "all the better." After months of bitter struggle, it appeared that all sides were happy with the arrangement—or at least could live with it.

55. "Shtotishe hauzing prodzhekts far Vilyamsburg bashtetigt," *Der Yid*, December 26, 1958.

56. Gelbman, *Retson Tsadik*, 12.

57. Ibid.

58. Ibid., 40–41. This took place in June 1965 as Teitelbaum prepared to travel to Israel—one of four visits he made after settling in Williamsburg.

59. Ibid., 38, 50, 70.

60. In "Williamsburg Confidential," Sol Levy's weekly neighborhood gossip column in the *Williamsburg News*, April 17, 1959; see also Associated Press, "1,260 Families Flee Life Among Slums," *Akron Beacon Journal*, June 27, 1959.

61. On June 12, 1959, Levy followed up on his April column: "The Satmar [Rebbe] seriously is considering the abandonment of Williamsburg. But he is waiting. Waiting for developments regarding the proposed new housing project at Roebling and South Ninth Streets. If the Satmar is dissatisfied with the way things are going, he knows that he has the land available and would not hesitate to pick up, with his followers, and leave." Levy noted that the Satmar Rebbe "favors moving to Jersey. The Satmar's advisors are urging him to stay in Williamsburg." The solution, Levy stressed, was to develop more middle-income buildings: "Early construction of middle-income housing in the community COULD stop a planned exodus."

62. Weinberger, "Miracle of Williamsburg," 18.

63. "Exodus from Brooklyn," *Time*, June 22, 1962.

64. On Hasidic attitudes toward technology, see Nathaniel Deutsch, "The Forbidden Fork, the Cell Phone Holocaust, and Other Haredi Encounters with Technology," *Contemporary Jewry* 29 (2009): 3–19.

65. On the collapse of the deal, see Milton Honig, "Jews Ask Jersey Court's Aid in Fight on Tract," *New York Times*, September 25, 1963. Interestingly, the article mentioned that "the sect was expected to seek financial aid from the Federal Government housing program."

66. Nicole Marwell, *Bargaining for Brooklyn: Community Organizations in the Entrepreneurial City* (Chicago: University of Chicago Press, 2007), 50.

67. Bloom, *Public Housing That Worked*, 171.

68. Ibid.

69. Ibid. On Madison Jones and the NAACP, see "Branch News," *Crisis*, May 1958, 307–308. Nor were Jews in Williamsburg the only group of whites

that the NYCHA encouraged to move into its projects in this period; as Bloom noted, "Intergroup relations worked with area civic and religious groups to find diverse tenants and created brochures to promote particular projects to targeted groups" (*Public Housing That Worked*, 171).

70. Bloom, *Public Housing That Worked*, 171.
71. Ibid., 171–172.
72. Ibid., 173; see also Robert Pear, "Bias Is Admitted by New York City in Public Housing," *New York Times*, July 1, 1992.
73. Bloom, *Public Housing That Worked*, 173.
74. Ibid.
75. Ibid., 173, 175.
76. Weinberger, "Miracle of Williamsburg," 18.
77. Price, "Federal Anti-Poverty Programs," 147.
78. Ibid.
79. Ibid., 146–148; Price interviewed the official with the New York City Housing Authority in New York on August 2, 1978.
80. Interview with the authors, August 4, 2017.
81. Price, "Federal Anti-Poverty Programs," 146–148. Friedman was a community leader in Williamsburg.
82. Ibid., 149.
83. "George Swetnick, 68, Is Dead," *New York Times*, July 2, 1968.
84. As the *New York Times* obituary noted, "One of Mr. Swetnick's regular chores was arranging for Federal immigration authorities to call upon Grand Rabbi Joel Teitelbaum, leader of the world's Hasidic community. Rabbi Teitelbaum would receive his passport in the comfort of his home before embarking on a trip to Jerusalem" (ibid.).
85. Price, "Federal Anti-Poverty Programs," 144.
86. Ibid.
87. Ibid., 146–148: "There was also pressure from the politicians. Rooney, [Senator] Lentol would send notes. [Assemblyman] Cohn was a gentleman" (NYCHA official interview).
88. Ibid., 145. On crime at Jonathan Williams Plaza in the first few years after the project was completed, see NYCHA Papers, series 04, box #0067A2, FLD #11, date: 1958–75, subjects: Williams Plaza. In 1965, residents complained about a steady decrease in the number of police officers assigned to the buildings, the painting of swastikas and other acts of vandalism, the presence of drug addicts, and underage drinking (connected with a neighboring grocery story and pool hall). In 1966, Donald Schatz, general counsel of the NYCHA, acknowledged an "upsurge of muggings" outside the project, as well as the rape or sexual abuse of several girls, but asserted that "on the whole, the project does not show a rise in crime rate." In 1967, an eleven-year-old girl was "dragged from the elevator to the roof landing" of Jonathan Williams Plaza and raped, prompting a meeting with George Swetnick regarding the need for additional police protection at the project.

89. Harrison Salisbury, " 'Shook' Youngsters Spring from the Housing Jungles," *New York Times*, March 26, 1958.

90. Ben Wilensky, "Sect Plans Exodus to N.J.," *Brooklyn Eagle*, October 20, 1962.

91. "Williamsburg Crime Crisis Stirs Citizens," *Williamsburg News*, October 26, 1962.

92. Price, "Federal Anti-Poverty Programs," 146–148 (NYCHA official interview).

93. Ruben Franco, "From Welfare to Work in New York City Public Housing," *Fordham Urban Law Journal* 22, no. 4 (2011): 1200.

94. Sribnick, "Excluding the Poor," 26; see also Bloom, *Public Housing That Worked*, 176.

95. Bloom, *Public Housing That Worked*, 175.

96. Williamsburg Fair Housing Committee v. New York City Housing Authority, 76 Civ. 2125 (CHT), 1976, as cited in Price, "Federal Anti-Poverty Programs," 137.

97. Price, "Federal Anti-Poverty Programs," 143, interview with an anonymous "Puerto Rican leader," August 17, 1978.

98. For these figures, which are derived from the 1960 U.S. Census, see Weinberger, "The Negro and (Orthodox) Jew," *Jewish Observer* 5, no. 4 (September 1968): 40. On the relative population of Puerto Ricans and Hasidim in the census tracts where the housing projects were built in the 1960s, see Price, "Federal Anti-Poverty Programs," 135–136.

99. Richard Cimino, "Filling Niches and Pews in Williamsburg and Greenpoint: The Religious Ecology of Gentrification," in *Ecologies of Faith in New York City: The Evolution of Religious Institutions*, ed. Richard Cimino, Nadia Mian, and Weishan Huang (Bloomington: Indiana University Press, 2013), 61: "The 1960–1980 period also saw the establishment of inner-city social justice ministries that gained national reputations under the leadership of a younger generation of clergy-activists such as Father Brian Karvalis [*sic*] of Transfiguration Catholic Church and Rev. Richard Neuhaus of the Lutheran Church of St. John the Evangelist. Such activism was unique in Brooklyn, if not New York City."

100. On the creation of Churches United for Fair Housing in 2003, see Beck, "Knowledge Production and Emancipatory Movements," 26–28.

101. Manny Fernandez, "A Congregation Mourns Its Longtime Shepherd," *New York Times*, October 23, 2005. Stephen Price noted this change: "An examination of the baptism registers at Transfiguration Church showed that in 1956 the number of Italian and Irish surnames was about twice that of the Hispanic surnames. By 1974, virtually all the surnames were Hispanic" ("Federal Anti-Poverty Programs," 118n1).

102. *New York Sunday News*, Brooklyn section, September 16, 1962, 2, as cited in Price, "Federal Anti-Poverty Programs," 132. Price does not list the author or title of the article, and we were unable to locate them.

103. Ibid.
104. Jane Jacobs, *The Death and Life of Great American Cities* (New York: Vintage, 1961), 4.
105. WARE application for sponsorship of Williamsburg Urban Renewal Project, December 18, 1967, cited in Price, "Federal Anti-Poverty Programs," 141.
106. NYCHA Papers, series 04, box #0067A2, FLD #11, date: 1958–75, subjects: Williams Plaza.
107. See "The Passing of Former Vice Chair Blanca Cedeno," *NYCHA Now: Your NYCHA Employee Bulletin*, December 2015, http://nychanow.nyc/the-passing-of-former-vice-chair-blanca-cedeno.
108. Ibid. In a particularly powerful sign of how the gentrification of Williamsburg contributed to the outmigration of the local Puerto Rican community and its institutions, Boriqua College sold its North 6th Street campus for $31.1 million in 2018 to the developer David Dweck; see "David Dweck Buys Boriqua College's Williamsburg Buildings: Developer Plans to Construct a Mixed-Use Property on North 6th Street," *Real Deal*, May 4, 2018, https://therealdeal.com/2018/05/04/david-dweck-buys-boricua-colleges-williamsburg-buildings.
109. NYCHA Papers, series 04, box #0067A2, FLD #11, date: 1958–75, subjects: Williams Plaza.
110. Peter Kihss, "Housing Policy of City Changed: Apartments Not Being Held for Integration Purposes," *New York Times*, January 27, 1964.
111. Douglas Dales, "State Panel Asks for $165 Million in Housing Bonds," *New York Times*, January 27, 1964.
112. NYCHA Papers, series 04, box #0067A2, FLD #11, date: 1958–75, subjects: Williams Plaza.
113. Later, in 1978, when Stephen Price interviewed the person he identified only as an "official of New York City Housing Authority," that person stated, "We had no quotas at that time; we weren't trying to keep it white. The Housing Authority gave us guidelines, not quotas" ("Federal Anti-Poverty Programs," 146). This contradicted the information included in the discrimination lawsuit filed against the NYCHA in 1976, and it may reflect the official's desire to whitewash his role in the tenanting process.
114. Ibid., 123: "The Hernandez brothers, Celia Vice, and Joseph Rodriguez Erazo sought power to represent the Puerto Ricans of Williamsburg on their own. Interviews mentioned them as the key Puerto Rican leaders [in Williamsburg] during the late fifties and early sixties."
115. Milga Morales, "Acosta Vice, Celia M. (1919–1993)," in *Latinas in the United States: A Historical Encyclopedia*, ed. Vicki Ruiz and Virginia Sanchez Korrol (Bloomington: Indiana University Press, 2006), 1:31. Vice is described as "a mixture of Mother Teresa, Felisa Rincón de Gautier (the first female mayor of San Juan), and Eleanor Roosevelt."

116. Lorrin Thomas and Aldo Lauria Santiago, *Rethinking the Struggle for Puerto Rican Rights* (New York: Routledge, 2019), 80. On Cosme's work in Williamsburg, see Price, "Federal Anti-Poverty Programs," 156. A controversy later erupted around Cosme when he was appointed to an administrative position at Columbia University's Urban Center; see George Geller, "Cosme Says Low Mishandled Latin Lounge Demonstration," *Columbia Spectator* 115, no. 63 (February 19, 1971); Will Lessner, "A Dispute over 17 Staff Dismissals Embroils Columbia Puerto Rican Program," *New York Times*, August 15, 1971.

117. NYCHA Papers, series 04, box #0067A2, FLD #11, date: 1958–75, subjects: Williams Plaza.

118. Ibid.

119. The Williamsburg Community Housing Committee, whose members included, among others, Rabbi Chaim Pincus; Melmuth Steinberg, executive director of the YM & YWHA; Sol Levy; and Albert Kellet of the Williamsburg Savings Bank received permission from the housing authority to buy Independence Towers from the city ("Williamsburg Co-Op Gets Greenlight from NYCHA," *Brooklyn Daily Eagle*, April 13, 1963). By that point, the committee had already received 400 applications for the 744-unit project, which would also have Sabbath elevators. All that remained was for the New York State Division of Housing to give final approval when its members met in the next few weeks. The approval never came, however, and the NYCHA moved ahead with its plans to develop the building for low-income residents.

120. As Nicholas Dagen Bloom has shown, this shift would result in a dramatic increase in the number of public housing residents on welfare (*Public Housing That Worked*, 179–180).

Chapter 3. The Politics of Poverty

1. Daniel Patrick Moynihan, *The Negro Family: The Case for National Action* (Washington, D.C.: U.S. Department of Labor, 1965), often called the Moynihan Report.

2. For more on this group and community organizing in Bedford-Stuyvesant, see Michael Woodsworth, *Battle for Bed-Stuy: The Long War on Poverty in New York City* (Cambridge, Mass.: Harvard University Press, 2016).

3. Martin Gilens, "How the Poor Became Black: The Racialization of American Poverty in the Mass Media," in *Race and the Politics of Welfare Reform*, ed. Sanford F. Scheram, Joe Soss, and Richard C. Fording (Ann Arbor: University of Michigan Press, 2003), 101.

4. Frank Mazza and Joseph McNamara, "Bobby Plays the Field in B'klyn," *New York Daily News*, September 14, 1964.

5. Antonio De Loera-Brust, "Infographic: Revisiting R.F.K.'s Poverty Tour," *America: The Jesuit Review*, June 1, 2018, www.americamagazine.org/politics-society/2018/06/01/infographic-revisiting-rfks-poverty-tour.

6. Mike Gold, *Jews Without Money* (1930; New York: PublicAffairs, 2009), 10.

7. Naomi Levine and Martin Hochbaum, "Why Jews Get Less: A Study of Jewish Participation in the Poverty Program," in Levine and Hochbaum, *Poor Jews*, 135.

8. Naomi Levine and Martin Hochbaum, introduction to *Poor Jews*, 3: "Their absence from the rolls of the public charities, and the mistaken notion that the Jews 'are taking care of their own,' add to the general impression that there are few poor Jews, and that those who exist are being adequately cared for by the Jewish community. Nothing could be further from the truth."

9. Ibid., 2.

10. Ibid., 1.

11. Gordon Fisher, "The Development and History of the Poverty Thresholds," *Social Security Bulletin* 55, no. 4 (Winter 1992): 3–14, www.ssa.gov/policy/docs/ssb/v55n4/v55n4p3.pdf.

12. Levine and Hochbaum, "Why Jews Get Less," 141–142.

13. Ibid., 135.

14. Ibid., 137.

15. Ibid., 141.

16. Cassie Miller, "The Changing Parish: Catholics and the Urban Crisis in Twentieth-Century Brooklyn" (PhD diss., Carnegie Mellon University, 2016), 348. Miller notes, "A 1974 study found that 57.3% of eligible white persons received welfare, while 64.9% of qualified black and 74.3% of qualified Hispanic persons did so" (349). She cites David M. DeFerranti, Stephen Leeds, Joseph A. Grandfest, Valerie Leach, Peggy A. Parker, and Linda L. Prusoff, "The Welfare and Nonwelfare Poor in New York City" (Santa Monica, Calif.: RAND Corporation, 1974).

17. Levine and Hochbaum, "Why Jews Get Less," 136.

18. Ibid., 142.

19. Ibid., 141.

20. Ann Wolfe, "The Invisible Jewish Poor," in Levine and Hochbaum, *Poor Jews*, 34.

21. Ibid., p. 36.

22. Franck, "Hasidic Poor in New York City," 68.

23. See Ronald Rubin, "Brooklyn's Hasidim: The Yiddish Connection," *New York*, March 1977, 7: "Hasidim are focusing their energies not on gaining Albany or City Council posts, but on getting elected to local community boards, poverty corporations, and school-district offices. Representation on these boards assures the safety of the millions of dollars that the Lubavitcher and Satmar sects have invested in communal institutions."

24. Eleanor Norton to Mayor Lindsay, n.d., Human Rights Commission, box 53, folder 955, Lindsay Subject Files, New York City Municipal Archives [NYCMA], as cited in Miller, "Changing Parish," 351.

25. Eleanor Norton to Mayor Lindsay et al., September 15, 1972, Human Rights Commission, 1972, box 53, folder 953, Lindsay Subject Files, NYCMA, as cited in Miller, "Changing Parish," 351.

26. Miller, "Changing Parish," 351.

27. Walter A. Seymour et al. to Mayor Lindsay, March 7, 1973, Human Rights Commission, 1973, box 53, folder 955, Lindsay Subject Files, NYCMA, as cited in Miller, "Changing Parish," 352.

28. Douglas Yates, *The Ungovernable City: The Politics of Urban Problems and Policy Making* (Cambridge, Mass.: MIT Press, 1977).

29. Price, "Federal Anti-Poverty Programs," 164 (interview with Puerto Rican leader, August 5, 1978).

30. Ibid., 152 (interview with Puerto Rican leader, July 20, 1978).

31. Ibid., 206 (interview with Richard Neuhaus, August 4, 1978).

32. Steven V. Roberts, "Negro-Latin Feud Hurting Harlem: Groups Fighting for Control of Area Renewal Projects," *New York Times*, February 25, 1968.

33. Murray Schumach, "Puerto Ricans Strengthen Political Power," *New York Times*, March 27, 1971. In 1973, Herman Badillo, the first Puerto Rican elected to Congress and a future candidate for mayor of New York City, observed to the *New York Times* that in his South Bronx district, the election of antipoverty officials encouraged a " 'winner take all' situation" among local blacks and Puerto Ricans "in which the losing disadvantaged group would be frozen out of the jobs, housing and social services that the programs were designed to provide"; see Martin Tolchin, "Future Looks Bleak for the South Bronx," *New York Times*, January 18, 1973.

34. Josephine Casalena, *A Portrait of the Italian-American Community in New York City* (New York: Congress of Italian-American Organizations, January 1975), 10, 34, 50–51, cited in Miller, "Changing Parish," 347–348.

35. Diane Henry, "A Survey on Italian-Americans Finds Government Is Ignoring Their Needs," *New York Times*, February 6, 1975.

36. Judith N. DeSena, *People Power: Grass Roots Politics and Race Relations* (Lanham, Md.: University Press of America, 1999), 31–32.

37. On this phenomenon, see Dennis Deslippe, " 'We Must Bring Together a New Coalition': The Challenge of Working-Class White Ethnics to Color-Blind Conservativism in the 1970s," *International Labor and Working-Class History* 74, no. 1 (Fall 2008): 148–170.

38. Yoel Wegmeister (1837–1919) was another striking example of a Hasidic lay leader who continued the venerable tradition of *shtadlanus* while adapting the role to the changing socioeconomic circumstances of his own era—in his case, early twentieth-century Warsaw. See François Guesnet, "Joel Wegmeister," in *The YIVO Encyclopedia of Jews in Eastern Europe*, vol. 2, ed. Gershon David Hundert (New Haven, Conn.: Yale University Press, 2008), 2009.

39. Price, "Federal Anti-Poverty Programs," 157. In general, Teitelbaum adopted a quietist stance toward the U.S. government—as opposed to his highly con-

frontational relationship with Israeli authorities—while his aides-de-camp embraced a pragmatic, activist approach.

40. DeSena, *People Power,* 29–30. The Economic Opportunity Act of 1964 followed in the wake of President Johnson's call for the War on Poverty. Money was distributed via antipoverty programs. In Williamsburg, the distributor was the Williamsburg Community Corporation. According to De-Sena, Joe, a social service worker, explained: "A coalition of black and Hispanic churches [in Williamsburg] won the first community election and elected a Lutheran priest president of the Corporation. The reason we won is because the election took place in the summer, and the Hasidics weren't here. It was one of the few times we were able to defeat the Hasidics." See also Frances Fox Piven and Richard Cloward, *Poor People's Movements: Why They Succeed, How They Fail* (New York: Vintage, 1979), 270.

41. "Jews Resign from Anti-poverty Group; Charge Bias Against Hassidim," *Jewish Telegraphic Agency,* February 8, 1967, and "Williamsburg Anti-poverty Group to Consider Jewish Resignations," *Jewish Telegraphic Agency,* February 9, 1967.

42. "Valn far di anti paverti kamite in Vilyamsburg," *Der Yid,* October 13, 1967.

43. Dovid Meisels, *The Rebbe: The Extraordinary Life and Worldview of Rabbeinu Yoel Teitelbaum, the Satmar Rebbe* (Lakewood, N.J.: Israel Book Shop, 2011), 197.

44. Ibid., 239.

45. Stephen Price interviewed both Puerto Ricans and Hasidim who had participated in the early days of the poverty program and observed, "It is interesting that many Hasidim and Puerto Ricans noted the impetus generated by the civil rights movement, and that this awareness in turn strengthened their own ethnic consciousness" ("Federal Anti-Poverty Programs," 7).

46. Ari L. Goldman, "Hasidim Flexing Political Muscle," *New York Times,* October 8, 1972.

47. Meisels, *Rebbe,* 162.

48. On Yoel Teitelbaum encouraging his Hasidim to engage in work and to open businesses, see Keren-Kratz, "Rabbi Yoel Teitelbaum—The Satmar Rebbe (1887–1979)," 304.

49. Emanuel Perlmutter, "Hasidic Sect Hurt by Unemployment," *New York Times,* December 26, 1974.

50. Gerald F. Lieberman, "Brooklyn Hasidim Fighting Districting," *New York Times,* June 16, 1974.

51. Goldman, "Hasidim Flexing Political Muscle."

52. Deirdre Carmody, "Procaccino Seeks Manhattan Votes; Tours East Side and Wins Brooklyn Jews' Cheers," *New York Times,* October 1, 1969.

53. Goldman, "Hasidim Flexing Political Muscle."

54. Price, "Federal Anti-Poverty Programs," 176 (interview with Klausenburger Hasid, Brooklyn, July 11, 1978). Richmond succeeded Rooney in 1974 before being brought down several years later by a series of scandals.

55. Thomas R. Ronan, "Orthodox Leaders Act," *New York Times*, October 30, 1970.
56. Stephen Isaacs, "Hasidim Build Own Town in Heart of Brooklyn Slums," *Spokesman Review*, March 3, 1974.
57. Michael Knight, "The 1972 Campaign," *New York Times*, October 28, 1972.
58. Martin Arnold, "Rooney-Lowenstein," *New York Times*, June 21, 1972.
59. Goldman, "Hasidim Flexing Political Muscle."
60. Ron Rubin, "Brooklyn's Hasidim: The Yiddish Connection," *New York*, March 1977.
61. Ibid., 7.
62. Lieberman, "Brooklyn Hasidim Fighting Districting."
63. Jerold Podair, *The Strike That Changed New York: Blacks, Whites, and the Ocean Hill–Brownsville Crisis* (New Haven, Conn.: Yale University Press, 2002), 125–126.
64. United Jewish Organizations of Williamsburgh, Inc. v. Wilson and NAACP, 510 F.2d 512 (2d Cir. 1975), https://openjurist.org/510/f2d/512/united-jewish-organizations-of-williamsburgh-inc-v-wilson-naacp.
65. Ibid.
66. United Jewish Organizations v. Carey, 430 U.S. 144 (1977), https://supreme.justia.com/cases/federal/us/430/144.
67. Israel Rubin (not to be confused with the author of a monograph on Hasidic Williamsburg of the same name), an employee of the U.S. Department of Commerce, played a pivotal role in securing government funding for the ODA. See "Tribute to Israel Rubin" (from an obituary written by Barbara Rosenblum), Southwest Jewish Archives, University of Arizona, http://swja.arizona.edu/content/tribute-israel-rubin.
68. On the founding of the ODA, see Roy Betts and Lewis Giles, Jr., "Kestenbaum Discusses the Opportunity Development Association's Assistance in the Hasidic Community," *Minority Business Today* 4, no. 2 (May 1985): 13. *Minority Business Today* was a publication of the U.S. Department of Commerce.
69. Ibid.
70. Stewart Ain, "Hasidim Seek Advantages of Being Disadvantaged," *New York Daily News*, April 6, 1980.
71. Ibid.
72. "U.S. Rules Hasidim Not Disadvantaged as Group but Individuals May Get Aide," *Jewish Telegraphic Agency*, April 17, 1980.
73. "Rabbi Charges Needs of Orthodox Jewish Poor Overlooked in City's Anti-Poverty Program," *Jewish Telegraphic Agency*, December 20, 1971.
74. Ain, "Hasidim Seek Advantages."
75. "U.S. Rules Hasidim Not Disadvantaged."
76. On the SBA's rejection of the Hasidic petition, see "U.S. Rules Hasidim Not Disadvantaged"; see also Severo, "Reagan Grants Hasidim 'Disadvantaged' Status."

77. Chris Black and B. Jay Cooper, *Mac Baldrige: The Cowboy in Ronald Reagan's Cabinet* (Guilford, Conn.: Lyons, 2015), 182–183.

78. Severo, "Reagan Grants Hasidim 'Disadvantaged' Status."

79. Minority Business Development Agency, U.S. Department of Commerce, mbda.gov/index.php?action=faq&id=60&mode=viewfaq, accessed on November 28, 2009 (page no longer available).

80. Myron Struck, "Rights Chief Erred About Eligibility of Hasidic Jews," *Washington Post*, July 6, 1984; see also Robert Pear, "Civil Rights Head Accuses Reagan of Politicking," *New York Times*, July 3, 1984: "The chairman of the United States Commission on Civil Rights has charged that President Reagan is playing politics with civil rights. Clarence M. Pendleton Jr., the commission chairman, who was appointed by Mr. Reagan . . . expressed concern because the President had 'granted "disadvantaged" status to the Hasidic Jews, allowing them as a group to apply for Federal business assistance.' "

Chapter 4. *Chaptsem!*

The chapter epigraph comes from Roe Ethridge, "Vice Fashion: Gangs of Old New York," *Vice*, September 30, 2006, www.vice.com/en_us/article/mv9j34/fashion-v13n10.

1. Gelbman, *Retson Tsadik*, 50. For another example of the "fortress" as an image in Satmar sources, see *Sefer Mivtsar Torah ve-Yirah* (Kiryas Joel, N.Y.: Hanhalas Yeshivah Gedolah u-Mesivta Torah ve-Yirah de-Rabi mi-Satmar, 1999–2000).

2. Emily Rueb, "A Hostage Situation, Revisited," *New York Times*, September 10, 2012.

3. For the unemployment rate in Williamsburg during this period, see Cathy Lisa Schneider, *Police Power and Race Riots: Urban Unrest in Paris and New York* (Philadelphia: University of Pennsylvania Press, 2014), 68. Although Puerto Rican activists frequently complained that their community was not as united as the Hasidim, Puerto Ricans in Williamsburg made significant political strides in the 1970s. In 1971, the Puerto Rican Socialist Party (PSP) established a branch in Brooklyn that quickly became popular among residents of Williamsburg, eventually becoming what Frederick Douglass Opie has described as "the largest Progressive organization in the city and one of the best organized"; see Opie, *Upsetting the Apple Cart: Black-Latino Coalitions in New York City From Protest to Public Office* (New York: Columbia University Press, 2015), 101–102. Puerto Ricans in Williamsburg started to flex their muscles in local elections, too. In 1973, Luis Olmedo, the first chair of Los Sures, won a seat on the New York City Council, a position he held until 1984, when he was replaced by Nydia Velasquez after being convicted of conspiracy and attempted extortion charges, along with Carlos Castellanos, the Puerto Rican head of Community Board 1 in Williamsburg. And in

1981, David Santiago founded the Southside Political Action Committee to coordinate Latino political efforts in the neighborhood.

4. David N. Myers, " 'Commanded War': Three Chapters in the 'Military' History of Satmar Hasidism," *Journal of the American Academy of Religion* 81, no. 2 (June 2013): 319: "The Teitelbaums were not alone as warriors; they inhabited a Jewish milieu in Hungary rife with fierce intra-Jewish disputation and recrimination. But they were first among equals in manifesting a distinctly militaristic version of Hasidism that was directed against various circles of enmity in their midst—Gentiles, but even more so, fellow Jews of different persuasions. . . . Harsh rhetoric castigating one's enemies in books, broadsides, and synagogues was common and at times spilled over into physical violence."

5. George Vecsey, "Hasidim in Brooklyn Feuding over Israel and Neighborhood Sanctity," *New York Times*, June 1, 1977.

6. Robert D. McFadden, "Hasidic Faction Besieges Rivals in Williamsburg," *New York Times*, March 2, 1981, and Ari L. Goldman, "Guard Set for Belz Rabbi as Hasidic Tension Grows," *New York Times*, March 3, 1981.

7. See Robert A. Beauregard, *Voices of Decline: The Postwar Fate of U.S. Cities* (New York: Routledge, 2003), 168.

8. "Mourners Protest Lack of Protection by Brooklyn Police," *Sentinel*, October 25, 1962.

9. Beauregard, *Voices of Decline*, 168.

10. Samuel Schreig, "It May Be the Last Yom Tov in Once-Quiet Williamsburg," *B'nai B'rith Messenger*, September 20, 1963.

11. See also Lester Abelman, "Mug Death of Rabbi Brings Extra Police," *New York Daily News*, October 20, 1962; "Hunt Clue in Rabbi's Death," *Brooklyn Daily Eagle*, October 20, 1962.

12. See Michael Flamm, *In the Heat of the Summer: The New York Riots of 1964 and the War on Crime* (Philadelphia: University of Pennsylvania Press, 2017), 73. For coverage of the crimes at the time, see Emanuel Perlmutter, "Teacher Is Slain in Crown Heights," *New York Times*, May 31, 1964; "Violence in the City" (editorial), *New York Times*, June 1, 1964; Robert Alden, "Youth, 17, Admits Slaying 2 Women: Crown Heights Teacher Is Victim—10 Others Raped," *New York Times*, September 22, 1964.

13. Aryeh Naor, "Kishinev be-Brooklyn," *Herut*, June 1, 1964.

14. On the history and impact of the Kishinev pogroms, see Steven J. Zipperstein, *Pogrom: Kishinev and the Tilt of History* (New York: Liveright, 2008).

15. Naor seems to be referring to the widely reported attempted rape of the rabbi's wife in Crown Heights, unless he has in mind an incident that did not make it into the media.

16. Eliezer Epstein (Sender Deutsch), "Kishinev-Brooklyn," *Der Yid*, July 17, 1964.

17. Zeitz, *White Ethnic New York*, 155.

18. "Shuts far unzere lebns" (editorial), *Der Yid*, December 1, 1967.

19. Ibid.

20. "Niu Yorker yidn shturemen kegn khvalye fun mord un farbrekhn," *Der Yid*, December 1, 1967.

21. "A new genre of 'asphalt jungle' films emerged, depicting New York as the embodiment of the nation's 'urban crisis' ... During the fiscal crisis era of 1974–1976, increasingly violent, racist, B-movies took over, giving rise to the 'New York exploitation' film": Miriam Greenberg, *Branding New York: How a City in Crisis Was Sold to the World* (New York: Routledge, 2008), 156–157.

22. Martin Tolchin, "South Bronx: A Jungle Stalked by Fear, Seized by Rage," *New York Times*, January 15, 1973.

23. Stephen Isaacs, "Hasidim Build Own Town in Heart of Brooklyn Slums," *Spokesman Review*, March 3, 1974.

24. Michael Pousner, "The Gentle People Get Tough," *New York Daily News*, June 16, 1973.

25. At the beginning of the 1960s, *Commentary* hosted a debate in its pages between Martin Buber and Gershom Scholem concerning the nature of Hasidism. In the midst of this exchange, Norman Mailer began to publish, also in *Commentary*, a series of expositions on Hasidic thought. Part of a larger project that never came to fruition, these somewhat rambling pieces, which appeared from 1962 to 1963, free-associated from Buber's texts. But Mailer looked beyond Buber. Norman Podhoretz remembered: "As part of his preparation for launching the column, he wanted to see some Hasidim in the flesh. He therefore asked me to take him to the Yom Kippur eve service at the synagogue of the Lubavitch sect, which, as it happened, was located in Crown Heights, right around the corner from where he himself had grown up." Inside Chabad's headquarters, at 770 Eastern Parkway, they caught a glimpse of the Lubavitcher Rebbe and then left the service early. "Once outside," Podhoretz remembered about Mailer, "he pronounced himself delighted by how 'mean and tough' the Hasidim were. Their attitude, he said (with considerable shrewdness), was 'Out of my way motherfucker,' and he was all for it." See Norman Podhoretz, *Ex-Friends: Falling Out with Allen Ginsberg, Lionel and Diana Trilling, Lillian Hellman, Hannah Arendt, and Norman Mailer* (New York: Free Press, 1999), 205.

26. Joshua Freeman, *Working-Class New York: Life and Labor Since World War II* (New York: New Press, 2001), 223.

27. Martin Gansberg, "Williamsburg Violence Reflects Tension in the Area," *New York Times*, June 30, 1970.

28. *Der Yid*, September 19, 1969, 7, and October 10, 1969, 8–9.

29. Jewish Telegraphic Agency, "Claim JDL Was Not Invited to Protect Those in Race Clash," *Sentinel*, September 7, 1970, 5.

30. "And You Shall Expel the Wicked from Among You" (editorial), *Der Yid*, September 27, 1970, 3 (Yiddish).

31. "A Little Too Late" (editorial), *Der Yid*, January 22, 1971 (Yiddish). See also Weinberger, "Interracial Crisis," 44: "We [Orthodox Jews] are caught up in

the midst of a convulsive society where violence can erupt at any moment without notice. Danger signals are blinking all over. It is best that we reduce our visibility at such times lest we become the easiest target for all combatants." See also Israel Shenker, "Hasidic Group Marks Its 100th Year," *New York Times*, June 2, 1971: "A more deplorable and devastating approach is the one represented by the so-called Jewish Defense League which seeks to defend Jewish rights by engaging the Black militants in direct battle and confrontation."

32. Jewish Telegraphic Agency, "JDL Holds Rally in Harlem to Protest Black Panther Anti-Semitism; Clash Erupts," May 8, 1970.

33. John McGee, "Vigilante Karate: Weary of Turning the Other Cheek, the Jewish Defense League Sets a Controversial Precedent," *Black Belt*, August 1971.

34. Alex Sternberg, "Reflections of Black History by a White Jew," *BuTaeDo: Ultimate Access to World Martial Arts*, February 1, 2016, updated June 28, 2018, at https://butaedo.com/masters-speak/reflections-black-history-white-jew.

35. For more on this dynamic, see Marc Dollinger, *Black Power, Jewish Politics: Reinventing the Alliance in the 1960s* (Waltham, Mass.: Brandeis University Press, 2018).

36. Ari L. Goldman, "Young Jews Seek Dignity in Karate," *New York Times*, April 9, 1972.

37. Maurice Carroll, "Hasidic Tensions Keep Police Wary: Brooklyn Leaders Discuss Saturday's Attack on Car," *New York Times*, October 11, 1966; Jewish Telegraphic Agency, "Police Charge Riot by Synagogue Crowd in Brooklyn; One Arrested," October 10, 1966; Jewish Telegraphic Agency, "Hassidic Representative Says Williamsburg Fracas Was Not Racial," October 13, 1966;

38. "Pelea a Botellazos Entre Judíos y Puertorriqueños," *El Diario–La Prensa*, September 26, 1968.

39. "2 Charged with Harassing Police at a Purim Fete," *New York Times*, March 19, 1973.

40. As tensions rose in the late 1960s between Hasidim and Puerto Ricans in Williamsburg over issues such as street crime, competition over public housing, and access to the poverty program, physical confrontations between members of the two communities increased. In 1967, Luis Lainer, a Jew from Mexico who spoke both Spanish and Yiddish, served as a volunteer in Williamsburg for VISTA, the domestic program created to fight poverty as part of President Lyndon Johnson's Economic Opportunity Act of 1964. In an interview, Lanier recalled that he designed and distributed leaflets in Spanish and Yiddish to encourage peace between the two groups (interview by the authors, March 25, 2018).

41. See, for instance, the Yiddish-English ad that ran in *Der Yid* on September 9, 1977, for Seymour Kravet for civil court judge, which trumpeted, "Help

Make Brooklyn Safe" and " 'Jail No Bail': Keep Muggers and Killers Off the Streets and in Jail Where They Belong; Bring Back the Electric Chair." The ad promised that Kravet would "be a judge who will fight anti-Semitism in the courts."

42. "Policemen Wearing Hasidic Garb Check Attacks on Rabbis," *New York Times*, May 11, 1969; Maurice Carroll, "Police Doff Uniforms to Make Fight on Crime Costume Drama," *New York Times*, June 4, 1969.

43. Emanuel Perlmutter, "Hasidim Live in an Aura of Fear in Borough Park Area," *New York Times*, April 24, 1973; "Jews and Police Clash at Station: Hasidic Unit Irate at Attack on 2 Fellow Members," *New York Times*, April 22, 1973; "Traffic Ticket Protested by 300 Hasidic Jews," *New York Times*, February 27, 1976; George Vecsey, "Behind the Violence in Brooklyn's Borough Park," *New York Times*, December 10, 1978.

44. Pousner, "The Gentle People Get Tough."

45. "Torah Is Destroyed in Brooklyn Fire; 20 Attack Suspect," *New York Times*, December 2, 1971.

46. Mark Lieberman, "Vandalism to Keep Temple From Marking Holy Days," *New York Daily News*, September 1, 1972.

47. "Mob Attacks Driver After Fatal Mishap," *New York Times*, December 26, 1971.

48. See, for example, "Melee Follows Rites in Brooklyn Temple," *New York Times*, September 25, 1968; "Hasidic Jews in Brooklyn Seize 2 Holdup Men," *New York Times*, October 27, 1971; Andrew Malcolm, "3 Die, 3 Wounded in Shootings; One Killed in Quarrel in a Bus," *New York Times*, July 27, 1969; "A Grocery Owner in Williamsburg Slays 2 in Holdup," *New York Times*, November 7, 1971.

49. Emanuel Perlmutter, "Priest Charges Police Ignore Hasidim Assaults on Hispanics," *New York Times*, May 3, 1973.

50. Mintz, *Hasidic People*, 250.

51. Freda Stern, " 'Little UN' Vetoes Big Trouble for Teens: Williamsburg's Boys Heed Priest's Call to Peace," *New York Daily News*, June 24, 1962; "The Corinthians from Williamsburg," New York City Fighting Gangs, http://newyorkcitygangs.com/?page_id=2366.

52. Mintz, *Hasidic People*, 250.

53. Pousner, "Gentle People Get Tough."

54. Perlmutter, "Priest Charges Police Ignore Hasidim Assaults"; Retta Blaney, "Urban Contemplatives Open to the World," *National Catholic Reporter*, March 10, 2000, http://natcath.org/NCR_Online/archives2/2000a/031000/031000a.htm.

55. Michael McCardell, "Priest Feuds with Hasidic Jews, Cops," *New York Daily News*, May 3, 1973.

56. Gershon Kranzler, *Williamsburg Memories* (New York: C.I.S. Communications, 1988), 213.

57. Pousner, "Gentle People Get Tough."

58. Wolfgang Saxon, "Suspected Mugger Is Beaten by Crowd of Hasidim," *New York Times*, January 29, 1989; Ari L. Goldman, "A Mugging and a Mob Evoke Debate in Brooklyn," *New York Times*, January 30, 1989; John Mc-Quiston, "Hispanic Rally Assails Hasidim in Williamsburg," *New York Times*, October 26, 1990.

59. Deputy Mayor Judah Gribetz Files, Mayor Abraham D. Beame Collection, folder 365, box 17, NYCMA.

60. "The Brotherhood of Cops," *Wisconsin Jewish Chronicle*, November 27, 1975.

61. Chaim Moshe Stauber, "Chaptsem! Chaptsem! Viazoy?," *Der Yid*, June 14, 1974.

62. Robert McFadden, "70 Are Hurt, Including 62 Officers, as Hasidim Storm a Police Station," *New York Times*, December 3, 1978.

63. See Selwyn Raab, "New York City's Finer Are Desperate," *New York Times*, November 13, 1977.

64. "Brooklyn Youth Gangs Concentrating on Robbery," *New York Times*, August 1, 1974.

65. Marcia Chambers, "Life in City's Gangs: Some Things Have Changed, But It's Still a Dead End," *New York Times*, September 27, 1983. For the transformation of the drug trade in Williamsburg during the 1980s as heroin and cocaine gave way to crack, see Richard Curtis, "The Improbable Transformation of Neighborhoods: Crime, Violence, Drugs, and Youth in the 1990s," *Journal of Criminal Law and Criminology* 88, no. 4 (1988): 1246–1247.

66. Dennis sinneD, "A History of Gentrification: T/here in Williamsburg, Part 2: Dis/possession," *Cultural Weekly*, September 20, 2017, www.cultural-weekly.com/williamsburg-part-2-dispossession.

67. "11 from Youth Gang Arrested by Police," *New York Times*, January 9, 1978; Raab, "New York City's Finer Are Desperate"; Dena Kleiman, "Workmen Close Up Vandalized Building in Brooklyn," *New York Times*, October 29, 1977; Dena Kleinman, "Brooklyn Terror: Youth Gang Takes Over Apartment House," *New York Times*, October 26, 1977; "3 Held in Seizure of Apartment House," *New York Times*, October 27, 1977.

68. Kleinman, "Brooklyn Terror."

69. sinneD, "History of Gentrification."

70. Ethridge, "Vice Fashion."

71. On the additional police patrols that were instituted to combat burglaries of Hasidic-owned businesses on the Sabbath and holidays, see Ari Goldman, "The Talk of Williamsburg: Hasidic Enclave; A Step Back to Older Values," *New York Times*, July 7, 1986.

72. Classic NY Street Gangs: Rock the House, classicnystreetgangs.com/rockthehouse.htm.

73. Ethridge, "Vice Fashion."

74. Isaac Abraham, "Dealing with Demography," *Time*, August 7, 1989, 14.

75. "Komite in Vilyamsburg gegrindet tsu shafn private detektivn shuts," *Der Yid*, September 1, 1972; see also "Dringender oyfruf!," in the same issue.

76. Greenberg, *Branding New York*, 184.
77. Robert Curvin and Bruce Porter, *Blackout Looting! New York City, July 13, 1977* (New York: Gardner, 1979), 26–28.
78. As cited in Matthew Shaer, *Among Righteous Men: A Tale of Vigilantes and Vindication in Hasidic Crown Heights* (Hoboken, N.J.: Wiley, 2011), 45.
79. Joseph Mann, "Ft. Greene Patrolled by Youths from Area," *New York Times*, April 8, 1973. For a photo of the patrol in 1970, see Louis Ferré Sadurni, "The Rise and Fall of New York Public Housing: An Oral History," *New York Times*, July 9, 2018.
80. David Gonzalez, "Sliwa Admits Faking Crimes for Publicity," *New York Times*, November 25, 1992.
81. Yoav Gonen, "Citizens On Patrol: Hasidic Watch Group Aids Police, but Not All Feel Safe," *Block Magazine*, blockmagazine.com/features/i13v1_index.html. Criticism of the Shomrim reached a crescendo in 2013 in the wake of a vicious attack by a group of Hasidic men in Williamsburg, including several linked to the security patrol, on Taj Patterson, a gay African American student who was walking through the neighborhood on his way home to Fort Greene. The assault left Patterson with a fractured eye socket and permanently blind in one eye. Ultimately, one of the Hasidic defendants, Mayer Herskovic, was convicted of gang assault, among other charges, and sentenced to four years in prison, and several others received lighter sentences or had their cases dismissed; Colin Moynihan, "Hasidic Man Found Guilty of Gang Assault in Beating of Black Student in Brooklyn," *New York Times*, September 23, 2016.
82. Jacob Sugarman, "Watchmen: The Shomrim Who Patrol Orthodox Brooklyn," *Tablet*, May 26, 2011, tabletmag.com/jewish-news-and-politics/68298/watchmen.
83. "Ha-rav . . . Moshe Hoffman z"l nifter gevorn," *Der Yid*, February 24, 2006.
84. Although crime declined overall, physical attacks on Hasidim by African American or Latino assailants—in some cases involving anti-Semitic slurs—continued to take place in Williamsburg during this period, including a vicious assault in 2010 on a rabbi named Joel Weinberger, who suffered a broken leg, eye socket, and jaw after being knocked unconscious and stripped of his clothes and yarmulke; Rich Calder, "Jewish Hate Crime Victim Testifies After Being Beaten by Two Teens," *New York Post*, December 10, 2010.

Chapter 5. The Gentrifier and the Gentrified

1. Roslyn Bernstein and Shael Shapiro, *Illegal Living: 80 Wooster Street and the Evolution of SoHo* (Vilnius: Jonas Mekas Foundation, 2010), 35.
2. Sharon Zukin, *Loft Living: Culture and Capital in Urban Change* (Baltimore: John Hopkins University Press, 1992), 52–54.

3. Ibid., 56.
4. As cited in Tom Robbins, "In Memoriam: Luis Garden Acosta, Builder of Bridges," *City Limits*, January 15, 2019, https://citylimits.org/2019/01/15/in-memoriam-luis-garden-acosta-builder-of-bridges.
5. Ando Arike, "Kerry Smith, Legendary Right Bank Café Owner Dies at 67; Gala Memorial Planned for January," *Williamsburg Observer*, November 24, 2014, williamsburgobserver.org/2014/11/24/kerry-smith-dies-at-67.
6. Virginia Breen, "They Bank on Rich Spirit: Building Bridge of Hope Wins Couple 250G Award," *New York Daily News*, January 30, 1999; "El Puente: Bridging Communities," in *Initiatives: Promoting Social Innovation Through Participation and Community Building* 15 (Fall 1999): 10.
7. The controversy over PS 16 was a harbinger of an even more contentious—and from a legal point of view, significant—conflict in the Village of Kiryas Joel, the community in Monroe Township, in upstate New York, that Satmar Hasidim in Williamsburg succeeded in establishing in 1977 after years of frustrated efforts.
8. "Unwise Wall in Williamsburg" (editorial), *New York Times*, September 29, 1986.
9. Parents' Association of P.S. 16 v. Quinones, 803 F. 2d 1235 (2d Cir. 1986), www.leagle.com/decision/19862038803F2d1235_11829/PARENTS'%20ASS'N%20OF%20P.S.%2016%20v.%20QUINONES; quoted material at 1238.
10. Margot Hornblower, "Cultures Clash as Hasidic Jews Compete for Turf," *Washington Post*, November 9, 1986.
11. *Parents' Association*, 803 F. 2d at 1241.
12. "A brenendiker problem," *Der Yid*, September 7, 1990.
13. Avraham Friedman, "Der kamf farn ekszistents fun Vilyamsburg," n.d., National Library of Israel, Jerusalem.
14. Randy Shaw, *The Activist's Handbook: Winning Social Change in the 21st Century* (Berkeley: University of California Press, 2013), 92: "The anti-incinerator event, as Garden Acosta noted, transformed PS 16 from a 'symbol of segregation into a symbol of unity.' "
15. Ibid., 92.
16. Ibid., 84; see also 85–107.
17. For more on the art scene in Williamsburg from 1990 to 2000, see Ann Fensterstock, *Art on the Block: Tracking the New York Art World from SoHo to the Bowery, Bushwick, and Beyond* (New York: St. Martins, 2013), chap. 9.
18. Zukin, *Naked City*, 7.
19. Ibid., 39.
20. Marcus Brauchli, "Brooklyn Rents Lure Artists," *New York Times*, October 30, 1983.
21. Lisa Foderaro, "A Metamorphosis for Old Williamsburg," *New York Times*, July 19, 1987.
22. Ibid.

23. Robert Fitch, *The Assassination of New York* (London: Verso, 1993), xii.

24. Greenberg, *Branding New York*, 125; see also, J. Freeman, *Working-Class New York*, and Kim Moody, *From Welfare State to Real Estate: Regime Change in New York City, 1974 to the Present* (New York: New Press, 2007).

25. Foderaro, "Metamorphosis for Old Williamsburg."

26. Jen Carlson, "Old Bar, the Ship's Mast, Discovered Decaying in Williamsburg," *Gothamist*, February 27, 2012. http://gothamist.com/2012/02/27/photos_old_bar_discovered_decaying.php; Scout, "Inside a Williamsburg Bar That's Been Boarded Up for Nearly 19 Years: Scouting What Remains of the Ship's Mast," Scouting New York, February 27, 2012, scoutingny.com/inside-a-williamsburg-bar-thats-been-boarded-up-for-nearly-20-years-a-look-at-the-ships-mast.

27. Brad Gooch, "The New Bohemia: Portrait of an Artists' Colony in Brooklyn," *New York*, June 22, 1992.

28. Ibid., 26.

29. J. Henry Williams, letter to the editor, *New York*, July 13, 1992, 8.

30. Robert Anasi, *The Last Bohemia: Scenes from the Life of Williamsburg, Brooklyn* (New York: Farrar, Straus and Giroux, 2012), 43.

31. Ibid., 54.

32. See, for example, Christine Haughney, "Parental Lifelines, Frayed to Breaking," *New York Times*, June 7, 2009.

33. Ibid.

34. As one resident of the neighborhood put it, "By 2004 Bedford Avenue was so filled with restaurants, cafes, boutiques, record stores and bookstores, it was hard to distinguish from the East Village"; cited in Kathe Newman et al., "Gentrification and Rezoning: Williamsburg-Greenpoint," Community Development Studio, Edward J. Bloustein School of Planning and Public Policy, Rutgers University, 16, http://rwv.rutgers.edu/wp-content/uploads/2013/08/2007_SPRING_CD_Studio_Presentation_Text.pdf.

35. Ibid., 15.

36. Peter Dreier, "Reagan's Legacy: Homelessness in America," Shelterforce, May 1, 2004, https://shelterforce.org/2004/05/01/reagans-legacy-homelessness-in-america.

37. NYU Furman Center, "Focus on Gentrification," in *State of New York City's Housing and Neighborhoods in 2015*, http://furmancenter.org/files/sotc/Part_1_Gentrification_SOCin2015_9JUNE2016.pdf .

38. Ari Goldman, "A Mugging and a Mob Evoke Debate in Brooklyn," *New York Times*, January 30, 1989.

39. "A brenendiker problem."

40. Joe Sexton, "Religion and Welfare Shape Economics for the Hasidim," *New York Times*, April 21, 1997.

41. Michael Idov, "Clash of the Bearded Ones," *New York*, April 8, 2010.

42. *Brooklyn Daily Eagle*, April 8, 1943.

43. "Television Minister Sells Girdle Plant," *New York Times*, September 20, 1973.

44. Mayer Schwartz, interview by the authors, Brooklyn, December 8, 2017.

45. Itzik Mayer Schwartz, *Sefer or shivat hayamim* (Brooklyn, self-published, 2012–2013).

46. Mintz, *Hasidic People*, 326; see also Robert Eisenberg, *Boychiks in the Hood: Travels in the Hasidic Underground* (New York: HarperOne, 1996), 18–19.

47. On Brach's prominent role in the conflict, see Ari Goldman, "Schism in a Hasidic Sect Erupts in Violence," *New York Times*, April 21, 1990, and James Barron, "Sale of a Grand Rabbi's Home Is Upheld," *New York Times*, July 3, 1996. An oft-repeated misinterpretation of this action holds that the *rebbetzin* wanted Brach to be made rebbe.

48. Alex Michelini, "Bandit Gets His Back Up," *New York Daily News*, January 29, 1984.

49. George Mansfield, telephone interview by the authors, August 16, 2016.

50. The New York Psychogeographical Association, "Yuppies Can't Go Home," *Not Bored*, September 2, 1998, www.notbored.org/yuppie.html.

51. Lore Croghan, "Builders Have Lofty Plans for Edgy Williamsburg: Local Landlords Convert Commercial Spaces; Manhattan Investors Left Out," *Crain's New York Business*, May 3, 1999.

52. Idov, "Clash of the Bearded Ones."

53. Jake Mooney, "Neighborhood on the Verge?," *New York Times*, January 25, 2004.

54. Flavorwire Staff, "Utopia or Gimmick? Meet the Creative Team Behind Williamsburg's Latest Artist Housing Space," *Flavorwire*, September 22, 2009, www.flavorwire.com/39185/utopia-or-gimmick-meet-the-creative-team-behind-williamsburgs-latest-artist-housing-space.

55. Jason Sheftell, "The Artful Rental: Brooklyn's Castle Braid Opens the Door to Creativity," *New York Daily News*, April 23, 2010.

56. Mayer Schwartz, "Who Woulda Thunk!!," *ABC of ABC* (blog), November 1, 2017, https://abcofabc.wordpress.com/2017/11/01/who-woulda-thunk.

57. Aaron Short, "After Another Artists' Enclave in Williamsburg Is Sold, Tenants Live in Uncertainty," *Hyperallergic*, August 14, 2017, https://hyperallergic.com/395285/475-kent-building-sale.

58. Ben Muessig, "Bushwick Building Is One Big Art Gallery Until Tenants Move In," *Brooklyn Paper*, September 24, 2009.

59. Sara Lyons, "The Art of Gentrification, the Art in Gentrification," *Greenpoint Gazette*, August 10, 2009, http://greenpointnews.com/2009/10/08/the-art-of-gentrification-the-art-in-gentrification (page no longer available).

60. Lee Boroson, interview by the authors, Brooklyn, March 28, 2019.

61. 475Kent, www.475kent.org/about.

62. Ibid.

63. Bridget Terry, "Barge-ing into Brooklyn," *Brooklyn Rail*, February–March 2001, https://brooklynrail.org/2001/02/express/barge-ing-into-brooklyn.

64. Robin Rogers-Dillon, "Zoning Out: The Politics of North Brooklyn," *Brooklyn Rail*, October–November 2001 https://brooklynrail.org/2001/10/local/zoning-out-the-politics-of-north-brooklyn.

65. New York City's Mayor's Office, press conference, October 25, 2017, www1.nyc.gov/office-of-the-mayor/news/686-17/transcript-mayor-de-blasio-new-measures-protect-affordable-housing-loft-residents.

66. "Mayor de Blasio Announces New Measures to Protect Affordable Housing for Loft Residents," NYC: The Official Website of the City of New York, October 25, 2017, www1.nyc.gov/office-of-the-mayor/news/685-17/mayor-de-blasio-new-measures-protect-affordable-housing-loft-residents#/0.

Chapter 6. The War Against the Artists

1. That is, in the 11211 and 11206 zip codes.

2. "The Jewish Community Study of New York: 2002," UJA Federation of New York, 2000, 101: "Over the past decade, the number of people in Jewish households as a proportion of the area's total population increased from 8% to 38%."

3. Ibid., based in part on the 2000 federal census. A decade later, in 2011, the Jewish population of Williamsburg had swollen by 41 percent to 74,500 people, of which half were under the age of eighteen, the highest proportion in any Jewish community in the New York area. Significantly, the Jewish community of Williamsburg remained the poorest Jewish community in the region, with 78 percent of households reporting income of less than $50,000. Estimating the number of Hasidim from census data can be difficult; see Joshua Comenetz, "Census-Based Estimation of the Hasidic Jewish Population," *Contemporary Jewry* 26 (2006). Comenetz and others often employ the number of young Yiddish speakers to estimate the population of Hasidim in any given area. On poverty rates, see David Rubel, *South Williamsburg Workforce Development Needs and Resources Study*, prepared for United Jewish Organizations of Williamsburg, Inc., and the Consortium for Worker Education, 2004, 23–26.

4. Newman et al., "Gentrification and Rezoning," 3–4; Braden Kell, "Williamsburg Real Estate Going Through the Roof," *New York Post*, June 17, 2004: "According to a recent survey by the Real Estate Board of New York, Williamsburg average sales prices rose 19 percent in the last 12 months to $327,533, making it one of Brooklyn's fastest growing areas."

5. M. Weiss, "Yidn shraybn tsum Yid," *Der Yid*, December 11, 1998.

6. Rabbi David Niederman, telephone interview with the authors, April 15, 2008.

7. On this issue, see, for example, Ayala Fader, *Mitzvah Girls: Bringing Up the Next Generation of Hasidic Jews in Brooklyn* (Princeton, N.J.: Princeton University Press, 2009), 171–173.

8. Personal communication with the authors, September 21, 2016.

9. On the succession battles within Satmar, see Samuel Heilman, *Who Will Lead Us? The Story of Five Hasidic Dynasties in America* (Berkeley: University of California Press, 2017), 152–209.

10. Douglas Martin, "Faiga Teitelbaum, a Power Among the Satmar Hasidim," *New York Times*, June 13, 2001.

11. Rubel, *South Williamsburg Workforce Development*, 32.

12. "Mir haltn nokh bay September 10," *Der Yid*, November 7, 2003; *Der Blatt* November 7, 2003.

13. On the leaflet, see Tara Bahrampour, " 'Plague of Artists' a Battle Cry for Brooklyn Hasidim," *New York Times*, February 17, 2004.

14. "Artistn bes-hamedresh hoypt teme fargangenes khol ha moed bay drite asife fun askonim ukle koydesh in Vilyamsburg," *Der Blatt*, October 24, 2003.

15. A.S.D., "Groyser koved shemayim bay dem kinus klali fun yehidus," *Der Yid*, June 9, 1961, 4.

16. "Artistn bes-hamedresh hoypt teme fargangenes khol ha moed bay drite asife fun askonim ukle koydesh in Vilyamsburg."

17. "Problem fun 'artistn' in Vilyamsburg bahandlt bay shtormishe asifas harabonim," *Der Yid*, October 31, 2003.

18. Peter Williams, "Class Constitution Through Spatial Reconstruction? A Reevaluation of Gentrification in Australia, Britain, and the United States," in Smith and Williams, *Gentrification of the City*, 76. The image appears in many popular accounts, too, for instance, April Taylor, "Invading White Gentrifiers Call Cops on Black Residents for Walking Down Street, Knocking on Doors," Your Black World, http://yourblackworld.net/2015/10/18/invading-white-gentrifiers-call-cops-on-black-residents-for-walking-down-street-knocking-on-doors.

19. "Problem fun 'artistn' in Vilyamsburg bahandlt bay shtormishe asifas harabonim."

20. Sh. B. Margolis, "Lehatsil es Vilyamsburg miyadam," *Der Blatt*, November 21, 2003.

21. "Problem fun 'artistn' in Vilyamsburg bahandlt bay shtormishe asifas harabonim."

22. Ibid.

23. "Haredishe unternemer fun artistn proyektn droen untertsubrengen dem 'Blatt' tsulib artistn-kamf," *Der Blatt*, November 21, 2003.

24. Announcement, *Der Yid*, November 14, 2003.

25. Margolis, "Lehatsil es Vilyamsburg miyadam."

26. Ibid.

27. Ibid. On Yoel Teitelbaum's view that the desire for money may easily lead to sin, see his *Sefer mi-torato shel rabenu*, vol. 2, *Erekh mammon*, and vol. 3, *Erekh ashirut*.

28. Margolis, "Lehatsil es Vilyamsburg miyadam."

29. " 'Milkhemes artistn' kampayn," *Der Yid*, November 7, 2003.

30. *Der Yid*, November 14, 2003.

31. The property in question remained undeveloped for years as members of the community fought to keep it "Hasidic"; see Rebecca Baird-Remba, "Revealed: 176–178 Division Avenue, Williamsburg," New York YIMBY, September 25, 2015, http://newyorkyimby.com/2015/09/revealed-176-178-division-avenue-williamsburg.html.

32. "Problem fun 'artistn' in Vilyamsburg bahandlt bay shtormishe asifas harabonim."

33. Ibid.

34. " 'Milkhemes artistn' kampayn."

35. "Askonim efenen marokhe kegn geplante 'muvi studyo' nebn Vilyamsburg," *Der Blatt*, December 17, 1999.

36. Glenn Collins, "On Brooklyn Back Lot, Finally, Some Action: After Years of Talk, a Movie Studio is Being Built at the Navy Yard," *New York Times*, July 21, 2003.

37. Myers, "Commanded War," 317.

38. Ibid., 320: "The struggle to preserve purity requires constant vigilance and readiness for battle. Rabbi [Yoel] Teitelbaum inherited this martial impulse from his rabbinic ancestors, added his own stringent piety, and bequeathed it to his heirs."

39. See Board of Education of Kiryas Joel Village School District v. Grumet, 512 U.S. 687 (1994).

40. Myers, "Commanded War," 341–342.

41. As the anonymous editor of the *Kuntres milhemet hovah*, a collection published in 1995 by the anti–Kiryas Joel school district forces put it, "Our generation is an orphaned generation, the orphans of orphans, a debased generation in the full sense of the word. . . . As a result of our many sins, the principles of our faith and the pillars of our religion are being loosed and forgotten" (trans. in Myers, "Commanded War," 344).

42. Myers, "Commanded War," 344.

43. "Reklamirte artistn-mape unter frage-tsaykhn fun 'hisakhdus haaskonim ukley koydesh deviliamsburg,' " *Der Blatt*, November 28, 2003.

44. Ibid.

45. Kell, "Williamsburg Real Estate."

46. "Groystsugike aktsies geplant tsu rateven di ir ve-am be-Yisroel Vilyamsburg: asife in bes-hamedresh kahal Yetev Lev South 8th," *Der Yid*, November 7, 2003.

47. "Hunderter yidn protestirn farn 'Gretsch' bilding in Vilyamsburg," *Der Yid*, November 21, 2003.

48. "Iber toyznt yidn protestirn baym 'Gretsch' bilding in viliamsburg," *Der Yid*, November 28, 2003. The verse is Esther 4:1: "And Mordechai knew all that had happened and went out into the street."

49. "The Rabbis Speak Out: 130 Year Record of Religious Jewish Opposition to Zionism," Neturei Karta International: Jews United Against Zionism, www.

nkusa.org/historical_documents/TheRabbisSpeakOut.htm#LinkTarget_ 3072.

50. *Der Yid*, November 28, 2003, reprinting a broadside of speech by Rabbi Avrohom Chaninah Leitner.

51. Babylonian Talmud Sanhedrin 73a. Sanhedrin is a section of the Talmud that deals primarily with criminal law.

52. Translation from the Hebrew by Steven I. Weiss, *Harper's*, March 2004. On this text within the broader context of Haredi attempts to police their space in Williamsburg and elsewhere, see Samuel Heilman, *Sliding to the Right: The Contest for the Future of American Jewish Orthodoxy* (Berkeley: University of California Press, 2006), 256–257.

53. Ultimately, Hasidic protesters failed to prevent the development of the Gretsch Building, which was transformed into a luxury complex with a full-time doorman, concierge, roof deck, and other amenities. By 2012, the average list price for a unit in the building was $2,549,667, and rentals averaged $4,983 a month. The Gretsch was touted by one high-end real estate company as "the most well-sought building in Williamsburg." See "Brooklyn Penthouse with Panoramic Views," *Fresh Palace: Interior Design and Architecture*, July 10, 2012, www.freshpalace.com/2012/10/07/brooklyn-penthouse-with-panoramic-views.

54. This view was reinforced at the rally: "At the Sunday protest, Rabbi Zalman Leib Fulop declared that the growth of the local artist population was 'a bitter decree from Heaven.' Those selling real estate to the hipsters, said the rabbi, would 'never be able to leave hell.' "; Steven I. Weiss and Zackary Sholem Berger, "Hasidim v. Hipsters: Trucker Hat, Schmucker Hat; Williamsburg's Religious Jews Want the 'Hood's Arty Arrivistes to Go Away," *New York*, January 9, 2004.

55. See, for example, "Haredi Rabbis Ban Vos Iz Neias," Failed Messiah, December 22, 2010, http://failedmessiah.typepad.com/failed_messiahcom/2010/12/haredi-rabbis-ban-vos-iz-neias-news-456.html.

56. "Riziger tsibur batayligt bay 'masn rali' zuntag asara betaves baym 'gretsh' bilding," *Der Yid*, January 9, 2004.

57. Ibid.; see also a full-page ad in that issue: "Williamsburg Residents! Do you want to be able to continue living in Williamsburg? Do you want to ensure that Williamsburg will not become an *ir hanidahat* [a city that has been led astray]? Do you want your children to remain upstanding? Then participate in this rally."

58. Tara Bahrampour, " 'Plague of Artists' a Battle Cry for Brooklyn Hasidim," *New York Times*, February 17, 2004.

59. Ibid.; see also Nathaniel Deutsch, "A Plague on All Your Arthouses," *Guilt and Pleasure* 4–6 (2007).

60. Patrick Gallahue, "Heated Hasids—Protesters: We're Being Priced Out," *New York Post*, June 17, 2004.

61. Motl, interview with the authors, June 4, 2008.

62. Christopher Bonastia, *Knocking on the Door: The Federal Government's Attempt to Desegregate the Suburbs* (Princeton, N.J.: Princeton University Press, 2006), 63; see also Colin Gordon, *Mapping Decline: St. Louis and the Fate of the American City* (Philadelphia: University of Pennsylvania Press, 2008), 91; David Freund, *Colored Property: State Policy and White Politics in Suburban America* (Chicago: University of Chicago Press, 2010), 130.

63. Emma Whitford, "Is It Time for Anti-Gentrification Zones in NYC?," *Gothamist*, June 16, 2016, http://gothamist.com/2016/06/16/anti-gentrification_zone_nyc.php.

64. Adriano Espaillat, "Anti-Displacement Plan," Adriano Espaillat for Congress, www.espaillat2016.com/anti-displacement-plan (page no longer available).

65. Brooklyn Anti-Gentrification Network (BAN), https://bangentrification.org.

66. Jerome Krase and Judith DeSena, *Race, Class, and Gentrification in Brooklyn: A View from the Street* (Lanham, Md.: Lexington, 2016), 48: "Some see MTOPP [Movement to Protect the People] as antiwhite and anti-Semitic since its leader has publicly complained about the displacement of blacks by whites in general, and Jews in particular, in the context of competition for housing in Crown Heights Community District 9." Rachel Holliday noted that at a later Community Board 9 meeting, "Rabbi Eli Cohen of the Crown Heights Jewish Community Council condemned 'the rhetoric that's gone out trying to [set] one neighbor against the other, one race against another, one religion against another,' alluding to recent brochures and emails distributed by the activist group Movement to Protect the People" ("Racially Charged Shouting Match Heats Up Crown Heights Rezoning Debate," *DNAinfo*, February 5, 2015), www.dnainfo.com/new-york/20150205/crown-heights/racially-charged-shouting-match-heats-up-crown-heights-rezoning-debate.

67. Crown Heights Tenants Union pamphlet, *Brooklynian*, 2014, www.brooklynian.com/uploads/imageupload/967/7EJCDK5FRURL.jpg. According to the Crown Heights Tenants Union website, the organization began meeting in 2013 (https://crownheightstenantunion.org/about).

68. United Neighbors Organization: Fighting for Affordable Housing in Williamsburg and Greenpoint, Brooklyn, http://uno-brooklyn.blogspot.com.

69. Personal communication to authors, September 21, 2016.

Chapter 7. A Fruit Tree Grows in Brooklyn

1. The customary prohibition against cutting down fruit trees is rooted in Deuteronomy 20:19–20, in which God instructs the Israelites, "When thou shalt besiege a city a long time, in making war against it to take it, thou shalt not destroy the trees thereof by forcing an axe against them: for thou mayest

eat of them" (JPS). This puts the commandment in the Halakhic category of *bal tashchit,* or the prohibition against wanton destruction. The Talmudic discussion of this prohibition presumes that it applies also in peacetime, an interpretation later canonized by the medieval Jewish sage Maimonides. In the Babylonian Talmud Bava Kama 91b, Rabbi Chaninah states that his son died "as punishment for cutting down a fig tree before its time." The eighteenth-century German rabbi Yakov Emden ruled that while the Torah did not prohibit cutting down a fruit tree per se, doing so created a *sakana,* or "danger." Nevertheless, Emden permitted fruit trees to be dug up and moved elsewhere, a position strongly rejected by Rabbi Moses Sofer. For some rabbis, a fruit tree was said to contain the equivalent of a human soul, and thus chopping it down was akin to murder and would bring bad luck to the person who facilitated its destruction. On the attitude of Rabbi Yoel Teitelbaum toward cutting down fruit trees, see Yosef Yitzchok Lerner, *Sefer HaBayis: Jewish Law and Custom for the House and Home* (Jerusalem: Feldheim, 2001), 49n20, which quotes him as stating, "If you would listen to me—one who cares about himself will avoid this and not move the tree at all. This is what I heard from my father, that even in cases where it is technically permitted, we must be afraid of the danger that comes with cutting a tree." See also Yirmiyahu Cohen, *Read and Remember* (Brooklyn: Hamatik, 2006), 477–478.

2. Devorah Klein, "Landscaper and Tree Surgeon Lavi Needleman," *Inyan,* May 4, 2016, 44–45. An Orthodox landscaper who made a business out of removing fruit trees told the Orthodox *Inyan* magazine in a 2016 interview: "A decade ago, at a certain point when the housing market boomed, my Rav [rabbi] got so many *she'eilos* [legal inquiries] from buyers and developers about moving fruit trees that he gave a *shiur* [course] on it for three weeks. I spent a lot of time learning the *sugyos* [Talmudic passages], *halachos* [laws] and *minhagim* [customs] pertaining to fruit trees."

3. Elizabeth Harris, "Instead of Taking Down a Fruit Tree, Building Around It," *New York Times,* July 30, 2012.

4. D. W. Gibson, " 'I Put in White Tenants': The Grim, Racist (and Likely Illegal) Methods of One Brooklyn Landlord," *New York,* May 12, 2015. In her memoir, *Unorthodox: The Scandalous Rejection of My Hasidic Roots* (New York: Simon & Schuster, 2012), 44, Deborah Feldman writes about a loganberry tree in her grandparents' Williamsburg backyard: "Bubby [grandma] is worried it will prevent the sunshine from getting to her tulips, but Zeidy [grandpa] says we can't cut it down because it's a fruit tree and biblical law prohibits cutting down fruit trees. Even pruning is questionable."

5. Other scholars have produced important studies on the particular contours of Hasidic involvement in a variety of economic activities. See, for example, the pioneering work of Glenn Dynner, including *Yankel's Tavern: Jews, Liquor, and Life in the Kingdom of Poland* (New York: Oxford University Press, 2013). For a case involving Hasidim from Williamsburg, see Barak Richman,

"How Community Institutions Create Economic Advantage: Jewish Diamond Merchants in New York," *Law and Social Inquiry* 31, no. 2 (Spring 2006): 383–420.

6. Toward the end of his life, Zvi Kestenbaum became embroiled in controversy because of his relationship with the ODA; see Brad Hamilton, "$1M Handout to Ill Health 'Exec,' " *New York Post*, September 25, 2011.

7. Hugh Son, "Condo Plan Stirs Fight on Housing," *New York Daily News*, June 25, 2004.

8. Kathryn Brenzel and Mark Maurer, "Fortis of Solitude: The Long Island College Hospital Controversy Has Thrust a Mid-Sized Player That Values Its Privacy into the Limelight," *Real Deal*, November 1, 2016, https://there aldeal.com/issues_articles/the-fortis-of-solitude.

9. Roy Betts and Lewis Giles, Jr., "Kestenbaum Discusses the Opportunity Development Association's Assistance in the Hasidic Community," *Minority Business Today* 4, no. 2 (May 1985): 13. Fortis received criticism for the lack of affordable housing and "community benefits" such as parks and schools in its plan for the Long Island College Hospital site; see "As Fortis Tower Casts Shadow over Cobble Hill, NYU Langone Site Sits Idle," *Red Hook Star-Review*, February 1, 2019, star-revue.com/as-fortis-tower-casts-shadow-over-cobble-hill-nyu-langone-site-sits-idle/#sthash.teqUrL7C.dpbs.

10. Filip Stabrowski, "Inclusionary Zoning and Exclusionary Development: The Politics of 'Affordable Housing' in North Brooklyn," *International Journal of Urban and Regional Research* 39, no. 6 (2015): 1124.

11. Jake Mooney, "The New Brooklyns/Tipping Points; How Williamsburg Got Its Groove," *New York Times*, June 19, 2005.

12. "Interviu mit R. Moshe Dovid Niederman iber dem nayes 'Schaeffer proyekt,' " *Der Yid*, December 26, 2003, 59.

13. Newman et al., "Gentrification and Rezoning," 53–54. According to a press release by Mayor Bloomberg's office, "The City paid the cost for the environmental remediation and demolition at Schaefer Landing which enabled developers to set aside 40% of the total 350 units for affordable rental housing. The City allocated $2 million, New York State's Division of Housing and Community Renewal provided $36 million in tax credits and the remainder of the project's $9 million was privately financed"; "Mayor Bloomberg Announces First Affordable Housing Development in Greenpoint-Williamsburg Waterfront Area," October 7, 2005, www1.nyc.gov/office-of-the-mayor/news/385-05/mayor-bloomberg-first-affordable-housing-development-greenpoint-williamsburg#/0.

14. Newman et al., "Gentrification and Rezoning," 54.

15. Ibid.

16. Daniela Gerson, "Two Minority Communities Vying for Brooklyn Affordable Housing," *New York Sun*, November 24, 2004.

17. Ibid.

18. Ibid.

19. Broadway Triangle Community Coalition, et al. v. Michael Bloomberg, et al., 2010 N.Y. Slip Op. 31258 (N.Y. Sup. Ct. 2010), preliminary order dated May 20, 2010, 11, https://casetext.com/case/broadway-triangle-cmty-coal-v-bloomberg-1. While the city touted these figures as indicating the diversity of the building, Judge Emily Goodman of the New York State Supreme Court, who oversaw the Broadway Triangle case, had a markedly different view: "The City has cited to Schaeffer Landing, a UJO project, as an example of diversity. However, Schaeffer Landing is not a shining example since residents at Schaeffer Landing are 42% white, while the Citywide application pool, at least for NYCHA [New York City Housing Authority] housing, is overwhelmingly non-white" (17).

20. Broadway Triangle Community Coalition, et al. v. Michael Bloomberg, et al., 2010 N.Y. Slip Op. 31665 (N.Y. Sup. Ct. 2010), judge's order dated June 28, 2010, 4n2, courts.state.ny.us/Reporter/pdfs/2010/2010_31665.pdf.

21. "Bloomberg Announces First Affordable Housing Development."

22. Meredith Hoffman, "City Built Less Than 2 Percent of Affordable Units Promised to Williamsburg," *DNAinfo*, May 20, 2013, www.dnainfo.com/new-york/20130520/williamsburg/city-built-less-than-2-percent-of-affordable-units-promised-williamsburg/slideshow/388613/.

23. Miriam Greenberg, interview with the authors, October 13, 2019. On the waterfront plan, see Robert Perris and Jocelyne Chait, "Williamsburg Waterfront 197-a Plan; A Matter of Balance: Housing, Industry, Open Space," October 1998, Municipal Art Society Planning Center and the Pratt Institute Center for Community and Environmental Development, 3–7; this report is incorporated as section 2 of Community Board 1, Borough of Brooklyn, "Williamsburg Waterfront 197-A Plan: As Modified and Adopted by the City Planning Commission and the City Council," Spring 2002, www1.nyc.gov/assets/planning/download/pdf/community/197a-plans/bk1_williamsburg_197a.pdf.

24. NYC Department of City Planning, "Community-Based Planning," www1.nyc.gov/site/planning/community/community-based-planning.page.

25. Community Board 1, "Williamsburg Waterfront 197-A Plan."

26. Perris and Chait, "Williamsburg Waterfront 197-a Plan," 23.

27. Ibid., 18.

28. "197-a Plan Technical Guide," Department of City Planning, City of New York, 1997, 1, www1.nyc.gov/assets/planning/download/pdf/about/publications/197a.pdf.

29. Greenberg interview.

30. On this phenomenon, see Mark Purcell, *Recapturing Democracy: Neoliberalization and the Struggle for Alternative Urban Futures* (New York: Routledge, 2008).

31. Stabrowski, "Inclusionary Zoning and Exclusionary Development," 1121.

32. Ibid., 1126. For statistics on the number of affordable units created up to 2013, see Hoffman, "City Built Less Than 2 Percent."

33. Samuel Stein, *Capital City: Gentrification and the Real Estate State* (New York: Verso, 2019).

34. For the role of real estate development and related entrepreneurial activity in the transformation of another Orthodox Jewish neighborhood, in this case in Los Angeles, see Iddo Tavory, *Summoned: Identification* (Chicago: University of Chicago Press, 2016), especially the chapter "From Ethnic Enclave to Religious Destination," 20–41.

35. Sandy Eller, "4th Annual JCON Real Estate Summit Expected to Draw Record Crowds," *Jewish Echo*, June 24, 2019, https://jewishecho.com/community/4th-annual-jcon-real-estate-summit-expected-to-draw-record-crowds.

36. Adam Goldstein, "The Social Ecology of Speculation: Community Organization and Non-occupancy Investment in the U.S. Housing Bubble," *American Sociological Review* 83, no. 6 (2018): 1137.

37. Daniel Fridman, *Freedom from Work: Embracing Financial Self-Help in the United States and Argentina* (Stanford, Calif.: Stanford University Press, 2017), 5.

38. For example, the 2013 Pew Center Study of Jewish Americans revealed that "Haredi Jews" were just as likely as other Jews to earn over $150,000 per year. See Pew Research Center: Religion & Public Life, "A Portrait of Jewish Americans," October 1, 2013, www.pewforum.org/2013/10/01/jewish-american-beliefs-attitudes-culture-survey.

39. "The Bulletin," special advertising section, *Der Yid*, April 13–18, 2008, sec. Y, 16.

40. NYREC: New York Real Estate Course, "The Real Estate Course That Will Empower You for Success," http://nyrecourse.com.

41. Haim Handwerker, "Ha-makom hakhi magniv be-Niu York (ha-sipur ha-male)," *Haaretz*, April 2, 2014.

42. David Madden and Peter Marcuse describe a "real estate ecosystem" in New York City consisting of "thousands of small players led by a few powerful family firms" (*In Defense of Housing* [New York: Verso, 2017], 33).

43. Clement Thery, "Larry's Clique: The Informal Side of the Housing Market in Low-Income Minority Neighborhoods" (PhD diss., Columbia University, 2015), 19.

44. Ibid., 51.

45. Ibid., 387.

46. Jennifer Lee, "Subprime Crisis Festers in New York," *City Room* (blog), *New York Times*, February 11, 2008, https://cityroom.blogs.nytimes.com/2008/02/11/subprime-crisis-festers-in-new-york.

47. Gabby, "Report: Subprime Foreclosures Rampant in Brooklyn," *Brownstoner*, January 28, 2008, www.brownstoner.com/real-estate-market/report-subprime. See also Jerome Krase and Timothy Shortell, "Seeing New York City's Financial Crisis in the Vernacular Landscape," in *Cities and Crisis: New Critical Urban Theory*, ed. Kuniko Fujiwa (London: Sage, 2013), 200–202.

48. Shaun Riney, a Marcus & Milichap broker, quoted in Rey Masheyekhi, "City of Goldman: The Mysterious Developer Who's Transforming Brooklyn," *Commercial Observer*, September 13, 2017, https://commercialobserver.com/2017/09/yoel-goldman-all-year-management-brooklyn-real-estate (subscription required).

49. Mark Maurer on WNYC: "TRD Talks Hasidic Real Estate Empire on WYNC," *Real Deal*, August 26, 2016, https://therealdeal.com/2016/08/26/trd-talks-hasidic-real-estate-empire-on-wnycs-all-things-considered.

50. *Real Deal: New York Real Estate News*, https://therealdeal.com/about-us-page.

51. Greenberg, *Branding New York*, 88–93.

52. Mark Maurer, "Learning and Earning: Hasidic Brooklyn's Real Estate Machers," *Real Deal*, August 22, 2106, https://therealdeal.com/2016/08/22/learning-and-earning-hasidic-brooklyns-real-estate-machers.

53. Ibid.

54. Aaron Short, "New Effort in Williamsburg to 'Unmask' Landlords," *Brooklyn Paper*, August 25.

55. Maurer, "Learning and Earning."

56. See "Hameshet taikuni ha-atid shel ha-tsibur ha-haredi," *Behadrei Haredim*, August 15, 2013, www.bhol.co.il/news/141535; Mark Maurer, "The Rabsky Riddle," *Real Deal*, May 1, 2015, https://therealdeal.com/issues_articles/the-rabsky-riddle.

57. Maurer, "The Rabsky Riddle."

58. Cezary Podkul and Marcelo Rochabrun, "The Rent Racket: N.Y.C. Landlords Flout Rent Limits—But Still Rake in Lucrative Tax Breaks," ProPublica, November 4, 2015, www.propublica.org/article/nyc-landlords-flout-rent-limits-but-still-rake-in-lucrative-tax-breaks.

59. Ibid.

60. Mashayekhi, "City of Goldman."

61. Ibid.

62. Eddie Small, "Bondholders Accuse Yoel Goldman's All Year Management of Breaching Securities Law in Suit," *Real Deal*, January 22, 2019, https://therealdeal.com/2019/01/22/bondholders-accuse-yoel-goldmans-all-year-management-of-securities-fraud-in-suit.

63. "Toby Moscovits [*sic*] on Working in a Male-Dominated Industry," posted to YouTube by the *Real Deal*, January 9, 2018, www.youtube.com/watch?v=RlQMNqqaxdI.

64. Star Diamond Styles, "Episode 4: Toby Moskovits," April 2, 2019, www.youtube.com/watch?v=heJxJIE-Cm4.

65. The Jewish Woman Entrepreneur, "You Have an Edge: How to Leverage Your Strengths as a Woman," February 17, 2017, www.youtube.com/watch?v=XCuKvfZkMB4.

66. "About Us," Heritage Equity Partners, www.heritageequitypartners.com/about-us.

67. "Philly-Based Investor Rubenstein Partners Buys Stake in Spec Williamsburg Office Development Valued at 130 Mil," *Crain's New York Business*, December 12,

2015, www.crainsnewyork.com/article/20151224/REAL_ESTATE/151229970/philly-based-investor-rubenstein-partners-buys-stake-in-spec-williamsburg-office-development-valued-at-130-mil.

68. Erin Hudson, "Day in the Life of: Chany Rosen," *Real Deal*, June 2019, https://therealdeal.com/issues_articles/day-in-the-life-of-chany-rosen.

69. Ibid.

70. "A Day in the Life of Chany Rosen: Expediter," posted to YouTube by the *Real Deal*, June 24, 2019, www.youtube.com/watch?v=-tCn6hkSSFM.

71. See, for example, Melissa Bell, "Hillary Clinton, Audrey Tomason Go Missing in Situation Room Photo in *Di Tsaytung* Newspaper," *Washington Post*, May 9, 2011. After a media uproar, *Di Tsaytung* issued a statement on May 9, 2011, to explain its actions: "The allegations that religious Jews denigrate women or do not respect women in public office, is a malicious slander and libel. . . . In accord with our religious beliefs, we do not publish photos of women, which in no way relegates them to a lower status. . . . Because of laws of modesty, we are not allowed to publish pictures of women, and we regret if this gives an impression of disparaging to women, which is certainly never our intention. We apologize if this was seen as offensive."

72. "A Day in the Life of Chany Rosen."

73. Rosemary Ferreira, " 'Bushwick Was Mine, Bushwick es mio': Gentrification and the Emotional Displacement of Latinas," *Senior Projects*, Spring 2014 (12), 73, https://digitalcommons.bard.edu/senproj_s2014/12.

74. Adam Pincus, "Menachem Stark's Portfolio Revealed," *Real Deal*, March 1, 2014, at http://therealdeal.com/issues_articles/menachem-starks-portfolio-revealed.

75. The *Real Deal* made the much more measured observation that Stark's portfolio "certainly suggests mixed results as a landlord and real estate player"; Hiten Samtani, "Menachem Stark's Tenants, Brokers Paint Conflicting Pictures of Slain Developer," *Real Deal*, January 6, 2014, http://therealdeal.com/2014/01/06/menachem-starks-tenants-brokers-paint-conflicting-pictures-of-slain-developer.

76. Larry Celona, Jamie Schram, and Aaron Short, "Who Didn't Want Him Dead?," *New York Post*, January 5, 2014.

77. Adam Dickter, "Who Was the Real Menachem Stark?," *New York Jewish Week*, January 8, 2014, https://jewishweek.timesofisrael.com/who-was-the-real-menachem-stark.

78. Vivian Yee, "A Developer Is Mourned and Vilified in Brooklyn," *New York Times*, January 5, 2014.

79. Samtani, "Menachem Stark's Tenants."

80. Jesse Jarnow, "Why I (Sometimes) Miss Williamsburg's Infamous Murdered Slumlord," *Gothamist*, January 25, 2016, https://gothamist.com/news/why-i-sometimes-miss-williamsburgs-infamous-murdered-slumlord.

81. Telephone interview with authors November 26, 2017.

82. Email communication with the authors, October 23, 2017.

83. "Voices: Williamsburg, Esther Ungar, Married 6 Years, 3 Children," *Ami*, October 5, 2014, 172.

84. Investirer, "In di velt fun riel esteyt," *Di tsaytung*, January 29, 2010.

85. Hanoch Teller, *Soul Survivors: True Stories of Striving and Yearning* (Jerusalem: self-published, 1985), 259; Ruchoma Shain, *All for the Boss: The Life and Impact of R. Yaakov Yosef Herman* (Jerusalem: Feldheim, 1984), 338; see also Melora Koepke, "Shared Experiences," *Montreal Gazette*, June 8, 2013, and Shelly Levine, "Ask Shelly, the Real Estate Expert," *Jerusalem Post*, October 1, 2005, www.jpost.com/Cafe-Oleh/Ask-The-Expert/Ask-Shelly-the-real-estate-expert-1320.

86. Personal communication with the authors, August 16, 2019. By this point, according to the same source, *shlisl gelt* had fallen out of favor in the neighborhood, "mainly because it's a renters' market these past few years, since people started moving away from Williamsburg. Nowadays, young couples rent brand new apartments, yet they're not asked for *shlisl gelt*, because quite simply, the couples wouldn't pay it. Why should they, when there are plenty of other apartments available?"

87. S.F., "Shraybt iber di plag fun enge dires," *Der Yid*, October 16, 1998, 6, 16.

88. A.N., "Lomir zen vos zogn take di 'lendlords,' " *Der Yid*, November 6, 1998, 6, 64.

89. E. B. Solomont, "Rabsky to Offer 99 Condos in South Williamsburg for $54M," *Real Deal*, July 21, 2015, https://therealdeal.com/2015/07/21/rabsky-to-offer-99-condos-in-south-williamsburg-for-54m.

90. Lisa Riordan Seville, "Hasidic Neighborhood in South Williamsburg Is a Top Beneficiary of Section 8, but Some Question Whether Law Is Strictly Followed," *New York Daily News*, May 17, 2016, www.nydailynews.com/new-york/hasidic-neighborhood-b-klyn-top-beneficiary-section-8-article-1.2639120.

91. "Real Estate in Williamsburg," *Tachlis* 147, December 19, 2018.

92. "Historishe 'asifes harabonim' gevondn tsu hayzer aygntimer un boyers nisht khorev tsu makhn idishe Vilyamsburg!," *Der Yid*, May 15, 2015, 77.

93. "Heftiger kampeyn oystsubreyteren Vilyamsburger grenitsn in fulstn shvung," *Der Yid*, June 26, 2015.

94. On Kave Shtiebel, a Yiddish-language online forum frequented by Hasidim, a poster alluded to the same biblical phrase, but did so to convey a much more ironic and pessimistic message. The post shows an image of a family, apparently in the Middle East—perhaps even Iraq, the historical location of Abraham's hometown of Ur—with a car full of belongings, as if fleeing a war in a hurry. "Go forth from Williamsburg," the text reads, "from thy country, and from thy kindred, and from thy father's house, unto a land that I will show thee."

95. Azriel, "Di khutspe fun di rabonim dergraykht ad lev hashamayim," Kave Shtiebel, May 13, 2015, kaveshtiebel.com/viewtopic.php?f=3&t=8859&hilit. On the creation of Kave Shtiebel in 2012 and its difference from iVelt, an-

other Yiddish message forum frequented by Hasidim, see Ayala Fader, *Hidden Heretics: Jewish Doubt in the Digital Age* (Princeton, N.J.: Princeton University Press, 2020), 173–178.

Chapter 8. The Holy Corner

1. Yom Tov Ehrlich, *Oytseres hanigunim* (Jerusalem: self-published, 2003–2004), 1:4–8.
2. Mary Douglas, *In the Wilderness: The Doctrine of Defilement in the Book of Numbers* (Oxford: Oxford University Press, 2001), 60. Shortly before she passed away, in 2007, Douglas asserted, "In the extreme case, insiders are saints and outsiders shunned as sinners. A wall of virtue keeps the two apart"; Mary Douglas, "Seeing Everything in Black and White," http://proj ects.chass.utoronto.ca/semiotics/cyber/douglas2.pdf.
3. Ayala Fader, "Ultra-Orthodox Jewish Interiority, the Internet, and the Crisis of Faith," *HAU: Journal of Ethnographic Theory* 7, no. 1 (2017): 185–186. Fader writes that "in response, an emerging group of ultra-Orthodox leaders began focusing attention on *pnimiyus* (interiority)."
4. Interviews conducted between April 8 and April 30, 2008.
5. Michael Powell, "Hats On, Gloves Off," *New York*, May 8, 2006, http://nymag.com/news/cityside/16864/index3.html.
6. Mary Douglas, *Purity and Danger: An Analysis of Concepts of Pollution and Taboo* (New York: Routledge, 1966), 122–123; Mary Douglas, *Natural Symbols: Explorations in Cosmology* (London: Barrie and Rockliff, 1970), 72, 80, 172–173.
7. For early examples of Hasidic leaders attempting to regulate women's modesty, see "On Crinoline: The Memoirs of Avraham Paperna" and "Secret State Report on Tsadik Twersky's Disciples and Crinoline (1863)," in *Everyday Jewish Life in the Russian Empire: Select Documents, 1772–1914*, ed. ChaeRan Freeze and Jay Harris (Waltham, Mass.: Brandeis University Press, 2013), 303–304.
8. One of the most popular contemporary Haredi works on the subject of modesty is Pesach Eliyahu Falk, *Sefer oz ve-hadar levusha/Modesty: An Adornment for Life; Halachos and Attitudes Concerning Tznius of Dress and Conduct* (Nanuet, N.Y.: Feldheim, 1998). The 706-page book has numerous sections, including "What Torah Does for Men, Tznius Does for Women," "Ensuring That the Neckline Is in Order," "Tights (Hosiery)—Colors and Patterns," "Overdressing—Ostentatious Clothes," "Bright Red and Highly Conspicuous Colors," and many others.
9. Joseph Berger, "Out of Enclaves, a Pressure to Accommodate Traditions," *New York Times*, August 21, 2013.
10. Rabbi Yaakov Horowitz, a Haredi school principal, as quoted in Ines Novacic, " 'God's Police' Enforce Strict Modesty Code in Orthodox Jewish Brooklyn," *Irish Times*, March 5, 2013.

11. Joseph Berger, "Modesty in Ultra-Orthodox Brooklyn Is Enforced by Secret Squads," *New York Times*, January 29, 2013.

12. Feldman quoted in Allison Yarrow, "At Orthodox Sex-Abuse Trial, a Little-Known Enforcement Group Comes to Light," *Daily Beast*, December 8, 2012, updated July 14, 2017, www.thedailybeast.com/at-orthodox-sex-abuse-trial-little-known-enforcement-group-comes-to-light.

13. Berger, "Modesty in Ultra-Orthodox Brooklyn."

14. In fact, *pashkevilin* have long been one of the most important ways for Hasidic authorities to enforce communal norms in communities like Williamsburg, leading Menachem Friedman to observe, "The Haredi ghetto is thus to a large measure a 'land of announcements,'" and Samuel Heilman to label them "Orthodox Jewish calls from the walls"; see Heilman, *Sliding to the Right*, 211–295.

15. Interview with the authors, August 4, 2017.

16. Ayala Fader has demonstrated that during the same period, other "ultra-Orthodox leaders began focusing attention on *pnimiyus* (interiority)" in an "acknowledgment that unlike even a decade earlier, exterior embodied signs and practice (*khitsoynius*) could no longer cultivate an interior affective trust in God" among some members of their communities ("Ultra-Orthodox Jewish Interiority," 185–186); see also Ayala Fader, *Hidden Heretics: Jewish Doubt in the Digital Age* (Princeton, N.J.: Princeton University Press, 2020).

17. Nina Lalli, "The Hasidim Get a Food Truck," *Village Voice*, October 22, 2007. The author described patronizing the business after a concert: "Sub on Wheels is a kosher food truck catering to the Hasidic community in Williamsburg, but which welcomes us all. (Lichtenstein had never heard the term 'hipster' before, but cheerfully reported that he gets 'all types.') I discovered it after seeing some friends, the band Rainbowsssss, play their psychedelic/improvisational/experimental music the other night at Rock Star Bar. Not to get all sentimental or anything, but don't you love New York?"

18. On the controversy, see, for example, "Controversy by Hasidim over New Food Truck," *Vos Iz Neias*, October 23, 2007, www.vosizneias.com/12376/2007/10/23/williamsburg-brooklyn-ny-controversy-by.

19. "Anti-indulgence Vigilantes Continue Incidents in Williamsburg," *Vos Iz Neias*, October 12, 2008, https://vosizneias.com/2008/10/12/brooklyn-ny-anti-indulgence-vigilantes-continue-incidents-in-williamsburg%E2%80%8F.

20. "Williamsburg Hasidim Protest Chabad Beauty Salon—In Crown Heights," *Failed Messiah*, May 12, 2011, https://failedmessiah.typepad.com/failed_messiahcom/2011/05/williamsburg-hasidim-protest-chabad-beauty-salonin-crown-heights-567.html.

21. "'Williamsburg Taliban' Protest Iris Beauty Salon," CrownHeights.info, October 28, 2011, http://crownheights.info/jewish-news/38571/willamburg-taliban-protest-iris-beauty-salon.

22. Simone Weichselbaum, "Satmar Hasidic Scolds Pressure Merchants to Comply with Dress Codes, Other Standards; Force Business Owners to Choose Between Boycott or Potential Discrimination Rap," *New York Daily News*, February 21, 2013.

23. Amy Braunschweiger, "Brooklyn Space Cadets and Hasidic Jews Get Cozy in Bed-Stuy," *Village Voice*, October 19, 2004: "With slick space-age furniture and DJs that favor rock and breakbeat, Sputnik pulls in a hyped-up multicultural crowd with various sexual leanings, and occasionally hosts a rebellious group of Hasidic Jews dressed in Old Navy T-shirts." The article continued salaciously, "If you're lucky, you can see our Hasidic brother Abe perform a sexy striptease onstage by throwing off his conservative button-down and pants, ripping off his undershirt, and as a grand finale, rubbing his nipples while sporting only boxers, suspenders, and a yarmulke."

24. Sharon Udasin, "Pumping Iron for the Payes Set: In Williamsburg, Chasids and Hipsters Are Increasingly Working Out Alongside One Another," *Jewish Week*, May 17, 2010.

25. Malkah, interview by the authors, August 4, 2017.

26. David Niederman, telephone interview by the authors, April 15, 2008.

27. For the sign, see "NYC Sues Williamsburg Stores over Tznius Signs," *Vos Iz Neias*, February 16, 2013, www.vosizneias.com/124319/2013/02/16/brooklyn-ny-nyc-sues-williamsburg-stores-over-tznius-signs.

28. More recently in Israel, efforts to enforce modest dress have even crossed over into violent attacks by Haredi vigilantes on Jewish women and girls. Isabel Kershner, "Israeli Girl, 8, at Center of Tension over Religious Extremism," *New York Times*, December 27, 2011.

29. "NYC Sues Williamsburg Stores." The article stated that *Vos Iz Neias* had obtained copies of the complaints.

30. Ibid. Significantly, *Vos Iz Neias* was the subject of a boycott by Haredi (including Hasidic) leaders; see "Azharah hamurah: odot sakanat ha-veb sayt 'Vos Iz Neias,'" January 2011, Failed Messiah, failedmessiah.typepad.com/.a/6a00d83451b71f69e20148c71e6b89970c-popup (Hebrew). Among the signers was Rabbi Yekusiel Yuda Fulop, who had helped lead the war against the artists in 2003.

31. Deborah Nussbaum-Cohen, "New York City Suing Ultra-Orthodox for Posting Modesty Guidelines in Stores," *Haaretz*, February 15, 2013.

32. Ibid.

33. Jonathan Mark, "Religious Dress Codes vs. Human Rights? Non-Chasidic Support for Satmar in Modesty Fight Against City," *Jewish Week*, April 16, 2013.

34. Becket, "Our Mission," www.becketfund.org/our-mission.

35. Mark, "Religious Dress Codes."

36. Daniel Dawes, *150 Years of Obamacare* (Baltimore: Johns Hopkins University Press, 2016), 183.

37. ACLU, "Using Religion to Discriminate," www.aclu.org/issues/religious-liberty/using-religion-discriminate.

38. Joseph Berger, "No Fines for Stores Displaying a Dress Code," *New York Times*, January 21, 2014, www.nytimes.com/2014/01/22/nyregion/no-fines-for-stores-displaying-a-dress-code.html.

39. Jacob Kornbluh, "NYC Human Rights Commission Settles Lawsuit with Hasidic Store Owners over Dress Code Posters," *Yeshiva World*, January 21, 2014, www.theyeshivaworld.com/news/headlines-breaking-stories/211045/nyc-human-rights-commission-settles-lawsuit-with-hasidic-store-owners-over-dress-code-posters.html.

40. "Statement by Rabbi David Niederman Regarding 'Lee Avenue Stores' Case," *Yeshiva World*, January 21, 2014, www.theyeshivaworld.com/news/headlines-breaking-stories/211051/statement-by-rabbi-david-niederman-regarding-lee-avenue-stores-case.html.

41. Interview by authors, June 2008.

42. Philip Roth, "My Baseball Years," *New York Times*, April 2, 1973. The special bond would eventually inspire books such as *The Baseball Talmud* (Howard Megdal, 2009) and *The Baseball Haggadah* (Sharon Forman, 2015) as well as the documentary film *Jews and Baseball: An American Love Story* (dir. Peter Miller, 2010).

43. Landau, *Zikaron ba-sefer*, 49–50.

44. The Satmar Rebbe once called for a protest in Mea Shearim (a Jerusalem neighborhood) against secular women's immodest dress, but the forceful enthusiasm of his followers prompted him to call off the protest, saying that their violent response was too close to "the very characteristics of Zionism that we are protesting against."

45. Menachem Daum and Oren Rudavsky, dirs., *A Life Apart: Hasidism in America*, 1997, PBS, www.pbs.org/alifeapart/intro_93.html; see also Irwin Richman, *Borscht Belt Bungalows: Memoirs of Catskill Summers* (Philadelphia: Temple University Press, 1998), 194. On the Orthodox Bungalow Baseball League, see Steve Lipman, "Achdut on the Field," *Jewish Action*, Summer 2009, https://jewishaction.com/religion/inspiration/achdut_on_the_field, and Andrew Jacobs, "Competition So Fierce That the Yarmulkes Fly Off," *New York Times*, August 26, 2007, www.nytimes.com/2007/08/26/nyregion/26ball.html.

46. David Gonzalez, "A Storm in Williamsburg as Two Ethnic Groups Clash," *New York Times*, November 17, 1990: " 'All your problems are with two families and five or six punks,' Mr. Rodriguez [manager of a local housing project] said. 'I'm not saying that Jews and Spanish people love each other, but they tolerate each other.' "

47. Ibid.

48. NYC Parks, "Roberto Clemente Ballfield," www.nycgovparks.org/parks/roberto-clemente-ballfield/history; NYC Parks, "Jacobs Ladder Playground," www.nycgovparks.org/parks/jacobs-ladder-playground/history. See also Jason

Patch, " 'Ladies and Gentrification': New Stories, Residents, and Relationships in Neighborhood Change," in *Gender in an Urban World*, ed. Judith N. DeSena, Research in Urban Sociology 9 (Bingley, UK: JAI, 2008), 106.

49. Stormer ballplayer and Jim Sherman, interviews with the authors, June 2008.

50. All quoted material in this paragraph comes from interviews and conversations with the authors in June 2008. Itsik's response recalled an unpublished interview that Jerome Mintz conducted with a Hasid in Williamsburg in 1960: "I went to one or two baseball games in my life. But my father didn't let me go. To be very truthful I wanted to go, my father never let me go, and I went once or twice and my father didn't know and he found out, and that was the last time I went. Because I remember how he punished me. . . . Oh yes, he beat me very—I was a boy about nine—and he beat me up and that was the last time I went to a baseball game"; Henach Rosenberg, interview by Jerome Mintz, December 29, 1960, side I, 31, Papers of Jerome R. Mintz, National Anthropological Archives, Smithsonian Institution, Suitland, Maryland.

51. Mirjam Zadoff, in *Next Year in Marienbad: The Lost Worlds of Jewish Spa Culture* (Philadelphia: University of Pennsylvania Press, 2012), mentions the Satmar Rebbe, whom she incorrectly identifies as the son of the Belzer Rebbe (88).

52. NYC Parks, "Metropolitan Recreation Center," www.nycgovparks.org/parks/metropolitan-recreation-center/history.

53. Annie Bruno, "Swimming Women," *Mr. Beller's Neighborhood: New York City Stories*, March 9, 2003, http://mrbellersneighborhood.com/2003/03/swimming-women.

54. Ibid.

55. Malkah interview.

56. On whether it is Halakhically permissible for Jewish women to swim in the presence of male lifeguards, see Rabbi Moshe Feinstein, *Igrot Moshe* (New York: M. Feinstein, 1959–1963), *Even ha-Ezer, Siman*, 62. Feinstein explains that it is generally permitted, since the attention of the male lifeguard will be on preventing the women from drowning rather than on looking at their bodies. Nevertheless, he adds, "God-fearing women and, in particular, the wives of Torah scholars should be careful and avoid doing so if possible, for there is a concern that perhaps he [the male lifeguard] will cast his eyes on her and attempt to go to her house when her husband is not home and seduce or rape her. And even though this is an unlikely possibility it is worthwhile for Torah scholars to be concerned with this to the degree that it is practical."

57. Rabbi Hananya Yom Tov Lipa Deutsch published what is probably the most important collection of Halakhic responsa, or legal rulings, regarding mixed swimming: Hananya Yom Tov Lipa Deutsch, *Sefer Taharat Yom Tov*, vol. 8 (New York, 1957). After immigrating to the United States and living in Cleveland and Williamsburg, Deutsch became a passionate advocate for the building of mikvehs, or ritual baths, in his adopted country.

58. BT Eruvin 18b, BT Gittin 90b, BT Bava Batra 57; see also Bereshit Rabbah, Parsha 67, "Two things are not in a person's control: his eyes and ears."
59. Meisels, *Rebbe*, 153.
60. Ibid., 293–294.
61. Community Board No. 1, "Combined Public Hearing and Board Meeting," February 15, 2017, 8–9, www.nyc.gov/html/bkncb1/downloads/pdf/com bined_ph_bd_minutes_2_15_17; see also Gwynne Hogan, "Mayor to Consider Expanding Contentious Women-Only Hours at Met Pool," *DNAinfo*, May 17, 2017, www.dnainfo.com/new-york/20170517/williamsburg/metro politan-pool-swimmer-hasidic-swim-recreation-center-parks-department.
62. Meredith Hoffman, "Wanted: Female Lifeguard to Rescue Hasidic Swimming Sessions at City Pool," *DNAinfo*, May 14, 2013, www.dnainfo.com/ new-york/20130514/williamsburg/wanted-female-lifeguard-rescue-hasidic-swimming-sessions-at-city-pool.
63. Berger, "Out of Enclaves."
64. NYC Human Rights, New York City Commission on Human Rights, Incident Report #1033177, December 1, 2015.
65. Emily Belz, "Jumping in the Deep End," *World Magazine*, September 17, 2016, https://world.wng.org/2016/09/jumping_in_the_deep_end.
66. Community Board No. 1, "Combined Public Hearing and Board Meeting," June 14, 2016, www1.nyc.gov/html/bkncb1/downloads/pdf/meeting-min utes/Combined-Public-Hearing-Board-Meeting-Minutes-6-14-16.pdf; Community Board No. 1, "Combined Public Hearing and Board Meeting," September 14, 2016, www1.nyc.gov/html/bkncb1/downloads/pdf/meeting-minutes/Combined-Public-Hearing-Board-Meeting-Minutes-9-14-16 .pdf.
67. "Hikind Demands Special Gender Swimming Privileges at Public Pool," Kings County Politics, May 26, 2016, www.kingscountypolitics.com/hikind-demands-special-gender-swimming-public-pool.
68. Gwynne Hogan, "Women-Only Swim at Metropolitan Pool Violates Human Rights Law, City Says," *DNAinfo*, May 27, 2016, www.dnainfo.com/ new-york/20160527/williamsburg/women-only-swim-time-at-metropoli tan-pool-could-get-boot-city-says.
69. Shayna Weiss, "A Beach of Their Own: A History of the Gender Segregated Beach in Tel Aviv," *Journal of Israeli History* 35, no. 1 (2016): 46.
70. In this regard, the political strategies of Haredi Jews may be fruitfully compared with those of other religious communities whose members have navigated the tension between their sense of religious obligation and the state's commitment to rights, as Mayanthi Fernando has explored in the case of Muslim women's activism around the issue of veiling in France; see Mayanthi Fernando, *The Republic Unsettled: Muslim French and the Contradictions of Secularism* (Durham, N.C.: Duke University Press, 2014).
71. Gwynne Hogan, "End Special Treatment for Hasidic Women Swimmers at City Pool, Critics Say," *DNAinfo*, June 24, 2016, www.dnainfo.com/new-

york/20160624/williamsburg/end-special-treatment-for-hasidic-women-swimmers-at-city-pool-critics-say.

72. Karen Matthews and Rachelle Blinder, "No Men Allowed: Women-Only Pool Hours Draw Complaints in NYC," *Associated Press*, June 6, 2016, https://apnews.com/3259421f36124a34be17b68654a7bf4e.

73. Hogan, "End Special treatment."

74. Cindy Rodriguez, "Swimmers Who Don't Mind Female-Only Pool Hours at the Public Pool," WNYC, June 6, 2016, www.wnyc.org/story/public-pool-religious-accommodation-swimmers-dont-seem-mind.

75. Gwynne Hogan, "Women with 'Right Morals' Seeking to Reinstate Single-Sex Swim Hours," *DNAinfo*, September 20, 2016, www.dnainfo.com/new-york/20160920/williamsburg/bring-back-full-womens-hours-at-metropolitan-pool-swimmers-say.

76. Sarah Maslin Nir, "Pool Rules: No Running, No Eating and, Three Times a Week, No Men," *New York Times*, June 29, 2016.

77. Hogan, "Women-Only Swim."

78. Seth Lipsky, "Let My People Swim—and Damn the New York Times," *New York Post*, June 2, 2016; see also "New York Times Rails Against Single-Sex Swimming at Public Pools," *Forward*, June 5, 2016.

79. Dan Levin, "In Toronto, a Neighborhood in Despair Transforms into a Model of Inclusion," *New York Times*, February 28, 2016.

80. Yair Rosenberg, "Should There Be Different Rules for Jews and Muslims at Public Pools," *Tablet*, June 2, 2016, www.tabletmag.com/sections/news/articles/does-the-new-york-times-think-there-should-be-different-rules-for-jews-and-muslims-at-public-pools.

81. "The NYT Swims in Inflammatory Hypocrisy," Orthodox Jewish Public Affairs Council, June 2, 2016, ojpac.org/latest/the-nyt-swims-in-inflammatory-hypocrisy.

82. Gwynne Hogan, "City Changes Rules to Keep Women-Only Swim Hours at Williamsburg Pool," *DNAinfo*, July 6, 2016, www.dnainfo.com/new-york/20160706/williamsburg/parks-department-will-keep-women-only-swim-hours-at-williamsburg-pool.

83. "Himl un erd tsvishn Blumberg un Deblazio: kharedishe yidn hobn oykh mentshn rekht!," *Der Yid*, July 8, 2016.

84. Hogan, "City Changes Rules."

85. Hananya Yom Tov Lipa Deutsch, *Sefer Taharat Yom Tov*, 8:174.

86. Belz, "Jumping in the Deep End."

87. First Liberty Institute, https://firstliberty.org/about-us.

88. Eli Rosenberg, "Gender-Segregated Swimming Cut Back at 2 Public Pools Near Brooklyn Hasidic Areas," *New York Times*, July 6, 2016.

89. "Hasidic Swimming Pool Wars Rage in Brooklyn," *Forward*, September 29, 2016; "Hikind Says Metropolitan Pool in Williamsburg to Increase Hours for Women," *Yeshiva World*, January 22, 2018, www.theyeshivaworld.com/

news/headlines-breaking-stories/1454592/hikind-says-metropolitan-pool-in-williamsburg-to-increase-hours-for-women.html.

90. Community Board No. 1, "Combined Public Hearing and Board Meeting," February 15, 2017, www.nyc.gov/html/bkncb1/downloads/pdf/combined_ph_bd_minutes_2_15_17.pdf.

91. On the Borough Park meeting, see Community Board No. 1, "Combined Public Hearing and Board Meeting," December 5, 2017, www1.nyc.gov/as sets/brooklyncb1/downloads/pdf/combined_public_hearing_board_meet ing_minutes_12_5_17.pdf. See also the film *93Queen*, directed by Paula Eiselt, about a Hasidic woman from Borough Park named Rachel "Ruchie" Freier, who, during this period, created "Ezras Nashim, the first all-female ambulance corps in New York City" (www.93queen.com/about1).

Chapter 9. Two-Way Street

1. See, for example, John Stehlin, "Business Cycles: Race, Gentrification, and the Production of Bicycle Space in the San Francisco Bay Area" (PhD diss., University of California, Berkeley, 2015), 117–118: "In discourse on gentri-fication, moreover, bicycles are one of the clearest shorthands for neighbor-hood change available. The trope of the bicycle-riding (white) hipster who sips single-pour coffee in a chic cafés symbolizes of [*sic*] the current wave of gentrification."

2. Kenneth Gould and Tammy Lewis, eds., *Green Gentrification: Urban Sustain-ability and the Struggle for Environmental Justice* (New York: Routledge, 2017), 6, 125; Kenneth Gould and Tammy Lewis, "From Green Gentrifica-tion to Resilience Gentrification: An Example from Brooklyn," *City and Community* 17, no. 1 (2018): 12–15. Regarding the stretch in Williamsburg-Greenpoint, Gould and Lewis argued that the goal of the city's "green growth coalition," was "*greened gentrification* . . . a packaging of urban green-ing with luxury condo development." (*Green Gentrification*, 125).

3. Gelbman, *Retson Tsadik*, 252: "Our rabbi [Yoel Teitelbaum] decided that under no circumstances would he permit children to ride bicycles [to school] because . . . it would be impossible to monitor them and this could, God forbid, lead to an accident, and our rabbi added regarding the matter of children playing, 'take this general principle in your hands,' that every game that a child can grow up with and not abandon, one must not permit children to engage in it; only those forms of play that one grows out of are permitted to children to play during their free time." The temptation to bike evidently proved too strong, however, and in 2012, the administration of United Talmudical Academy Torah V'Yirah notified parents that their children would be expelled if they rode to school on a bicycle. For an image of the letter, see "Satmar Schools Banning Bicycles," *Vos Iz Neias*, June 10, 2012, https://vosizneias.com/2012/06/10/williamsburg-ny-satmar-schools-banning-bicycles. Even this warning was not sufficient, and

three years later, in May 2015, school administrators felt the need to issue a formal *takanah*, or ruling, forbidding the practice among students: "Unfortunately, as is already known from all of the plagues that have appeared in our day, Satan does not sleep and tests everyone with new ways of ensnaring, God forbid, in his net the holy souls of our children. . . . And it is natural that this places a terrible responsibility on us and an obligation to stand guard and struggle against the powers of impurity. . . . One of the things that has turned out to be extremely harmful for the pure education of our precious children, may they live, is the problem of 'two-wheeled bikes.' " For an image of the ban, see "Satmar Yeshiva Bans 2-Wheel Bikes," Failed Messiah, April 24, 2015, https://failedmessiah.typepad.com/failed_messiahcom/2015/04/satmar-yeshiva-bans-2-wheel-bikes-678.html; for an online discussion (in Yiddish) regarding whether Hasidim, including women, should be allowed to ride bikes in Williamsburg, see the thread "Hasidim far bayks," Kave Shtiebel, May 30, 2013, www.kaveshtiebel.com/viewtopic.php?f=24&t=3903&sid=7560fca983ea4 3ea64a2cfc22bcc7b92&start=75.

4. Lugo quoted in Perry Stein, "Why Are Bike Lanes Such Heated Symbols of Gentrification," *Washington Post*, November 12, 2015, www.washingtonpost. com/news/local/wp/2015/11/12/why-are-bike-lanes-such-heated-symbols-of-gentrification/?utm_term=.7e745be780e1.

5. See, for example, Nathan Tempey, "Williamsburg Bike Lane Battle Intensifies: 'The City Created a Mess,' " *Gothamist*, October 8, 2015, http://goth amist.com/2015/10/08/williamsburg_bike_lane_war.php.

6. Michael Bloomberg, dust-jacket blurb for Janette Sadik-Khan and Seth Solomonow, *Streetfight: Handbook for an Urban Revolution* (New York: Penguin, 2017).

7. John Cassidy, "Battle of the Bike Lanes," *New Yorker*, March 8, 2011, www. newyorker.com/news/john-cassidy/battle-of-the-bike-lanes.

8. Sadik-Khan and Solomonow, *Streetfight*, 162.

9. "Brooklyn Waterfront Greenway: A Concept Plan for Community Board 1," Fall 2008, http://bgi.wpengine.com/wp-content/uploads/Brooklyn-Green way-Plan-Greenpoint.pdf.

10. Rich Calder, "Hasid Lust Cause," *New York Post*, September 12, 2008, https://nypost.com/2008/09/12/hasid-lust-cause.

11. Ibid.

12. Robert, "Hipster Hottie Bicyclists vs. Hasids in South Williamsburg?," *Curbed New York*, September 12, 2008, https://ny.curbed.com/2008/9/12/ 10560026/hipster-hottie-bicyclists-vs-hasids-in-south-williamsburg; Jessica Pressler, "It's 'Hasids vs. Hotties' in South Williamsburg," *New York*, September 2008, http://nymag.com/intelligencer/2008/09/its_hasids_vs_hot ties_in_south.html?gtm=top&gtm=bottom.

13. Aaron Naparstek, "DOT Rolls Out Fort Greene Bike Lanes & Traffic-Calming," *Streets Blog NYC*, November 12, 2007, https://nyc.streetsblog. org/2007/11/12/dot-rolls-out-fort-greene-bike-lanes-traffic-calming.

14. John del Signore, "Will New Grand Street Bike Lane Kill Little Italy?," *Gothamist*, November 21, 2008, http://gothamist.com/2008/11/21/grand_street_bike_lane_not_so_popul.php.

15. Janette Sadik-Khan, "The Bike Wars Are Over, and the Bikes Won," *New York*, March 8, 2016, http://nymag.com/intelligencer/2016/03/bike-wars-are-over-and-the-bikes-won.html.

16. Perry Stein, "D.C. Church Says a Bike Lane Would Infringe upon Its Constitutional 'Rights of Religious Freedom,' " *Washington Post*, October 14, 2015, at www.washingtonpost.com/news/local/wp/2015/10/14/d-c-church-says-a-bike-lane-would-infringe-upon-its-constitutional-rights-of-religious-freedom/?utm_term=.7b420eb24eb7.

17. See, for example, Ben Nathan, "You Give Them 18 Minutes, They Give You the World," *5 Towns Jewish Times*, August 20, 2008, available from the Internet Archive, web.archive.org/web/20110721200810/https://www.5tjt.com/local-news/3247-you-give-them-18-minutes-they-give-you-the-world.

18. "Chasidim: Bike Lanes Not Kosher, It Brings Scantily Clad Cyclists to the Neighborhood," *Vos Iz Neias*, September 12, 2008, www.vosizneias.com/20245/2008/09/12/williamsburg-ny-chasidim-bike-lanes-not-kosher-it-brings-scantily-clad-cyclists-to-the-neighborhood. *Vos Iz Neias* was founded in 2005 by two Hasidim and two Orthodox Jews who kept their identities anonymous in order to prevent negative repercussions from Haredi leaders and others opposed to Internet use and the public airing of controversial issues within their communities. In 2010, its coverage prompted a group of prominent Haredi leaders to issue a public statement, or *kol koreh*, banning the site; see Yerachmiel Lopin, "Rabbis Issue Ban on News Site Because It Allows Some Critical Comments About Community Problems," *Frum Follies* (blog), December 22, 2010, https://frumfollies.wordpress.com/2010/12/22/ban-kol-koreh-vosizneias-vin.

19. Moshe Yida Deutsch, " 'Bayk leins' un ban linies," *Der Yid*, September 19, 2008.

20. Sadik-Khan and Solomonow, *Streetfight*, 146.

21. The growing Haredization of many non-Haredi neighborhoods in Israel and the parallel rise of groups of Haredi zealots led to an increase in violent attacks by Haredi vigilantes on Jewish women and girls whose clothing was deemed immodest, including, most notoriously, in Beit Shemesh, where an eight-year-old Orthodox girl was called a prostitute and spat on in 2011; a woman visiting Beit Shemesh was assaulted with bleach and rocks, and her car windows were broken and tires punctured; and an Orthodox woman was beaten while standing at a bus stop with her three-year-old daughter after being called a prostitute by her Haredi attacker. Isabel Kershner, "Israeli Girl, 8, at Center of Tension over Religious Extremism," *New York Times*, December 27, 2011; Oz Rosenberg, "Woman in Beit Shemesh Attacked by Ultra-Orthodox Extremists," *Haaretz*, January 25, 2012; "Ultra-Orthodox Man Attacks Beit Shemesh Woman over Length of Her Skirt," *Haaretz*, March 28, 2014.

22. "Bike Lanes Run into Opposition," *Gotham Gazette*, n.d., www.gothamga zette.com/index.php/archives/129-bike-lanes-run-into-opposition.

23. Bari Weiss, "Hasids vs. Hipsters: In Brooklyn, A Gentle Clash Over Unkosher Food and Bike Lanes," *Wall Street Journal*, April 17, 2010; Idov, "Clash of the Bearded Ones."

24. *Division Avenue*, by Miki Bone, "A Funny, Poignant and Provocative Play About Faith, Love and Bicycyles," www.divisionavenue.net/about.html; on the play, see Shulem Deen, "Williamsburg Bike Wars Provide Family Drama," *Forward*, July 22, 2013, https://forward.com/schmooze/180766/wil liamsburg-bike-wars-provide-family-drama.

25. Stehlin, "Business Cycles," 117–118.

26. The poster also noted, "The bikers here [in Williamsburg] have the moral high ground here, because they are concerned about their safety and conserving energy. The bike lane opposers just want more convenient parking, a harder issue to get behind." See "Williamsburg, NY—Hasidim Opposing Bike Lanes a No Show as 150 Cyclists with Impressive Turnout at CB1," *Vos Iz Neias*, January 14, 2009, https://vosizneias.com/2009/01/14/williamsburg-ny-hasidim-opposing-bike-lanes-a-no-show-as-150-cyclist-meet-at-cb1.

27. John del Signore, "Bike Lane Backlash: Hasidim to Block Traffic in Protest!," *Gothamist*, November 26, 2008, http://gothamist.com/2008/11/26/bike_lane_backlash_hasidim_to_block.php.

28. Ben Muessig, "Pols Back Hasids in Bike Lane Fight," *Brooklyn Paper*, December 11, 2008, www.brooklynpaper.com/stories/31/49/31_49_bm_bike_lane.html; Colin Moynihan, "New Bike Lanes Touch Off Row in Brooklyn," *New York Times*, January 3, 2009.

29. "About Times Up!," Time's Up! NYC's Direct Action Environmental Organization, https://times-up.org/about; "2008-12-15 Bicycle Clown Defend Kent Street Lane" (press release), *Time's Up!*, https://times-up.org/2008-releases/2008-12-15-bicycle-clown-defend-kent-street-lane.

30. John Del Signore, "Bunch of Clowns Rally for Kent Avenue Bike Lane," *Gothamist*, December 17, 2008, https://gothamist.com/news/bunch-of-clowns-rally-for-kent-avenue-bike-lane.

31. John del Signore, "Bike Lane Sagas: Phony Detour Sign on Kent Comes Down!," *Gothamist*, December 30, 2008. http://gothamist.com/2008/12/30/bike_lane_sagas_phony_detour_sign_0.php#photo-3.

32. Rich Calder, "Hasid Street Fight," *New York Post*, December 28, 2008.

33. John del Signore, "DIY Bedford Ave Bike Lane Fades to Black in South Williamsburg," *Gothamist*, December 11, 2009, http://gothamist.com/2009/12/11/bye_bye_bedford_bike_lane_dot_black.php; Ben Muessig, "Bike Riders Will Get Naked to Save the Bedford Ave. Lane," *Gothamist*, December 16, 2009, http://gothamist.com/2009/12/16/bike_riders_will_get_naked_to_save.php.

34. *Hasidics and Hipsters: A Battle on Bikes, Part One*, written and directed by Maria Snoek (New York: Elenchos Film, 2011), available on YouTube, www.youtube.com/watch?v=cyac9UCVDYU.

35. Sadik-Khan and Solomonow, *Streetfight*, 163–164.
36. Benjamin Sutton, "The Battle over the Bedford Avenue Bike Lane," *L Magazine*, December 8, 2009, www.thelmagazine.com/2009/12/the-battle-over-the-bedford-avenue-bike-lane: "Removing the lane, aside from looking like a cheap ploy by the city to regain the favor of the area's Hasidim voters, is a huge step backward"; Ben Fried, "DOT Wipes 14 Blocks of Bike Lane off Bedford Avenue," *Streets Blog NYC*, December 1, 2009, https://nyc.streetsblog.org/2009/12/01/dot-sandblasts-14-blocks-of-bike-lane-off-bedford-avenue; Shulem Deen, "Williamsburg Bike Wars Provide Family Drama," *Forward*, July 22, 2013. For criticism of Bloomberg, see Yossi Gestetner, "Op-Ed: Bloomberg Played Jewish Voters for Fools," *Yeshiva World*, December 7, 2009, www.theyeshivaworld.com/news/general/43051/op-ed-bloomberg-played-jewish-voters-for-fools.html.
37. Sean Patrick Farrell, "Cyclists Redraw the Lines in Brooklyn," *City Room* (blog), *New York Times*, December 8, 2009, https://cityroom.blogs.nytimes.com/2009/12/08/cyclists-redraw-the-lines-in-brooklyn; see also Christopher Glazek, "Hasids vs. Hipsters," *n+1*, February 14, 2011, https://nplusonemag.com/online-only/online-only/hasids-vs-hipsters.
38. Sadik-Khan and Solomonow, *Streetfight*, 164.
39. Nathan Schneider, "Hipsters v. Hasidim Over Brooklyn Bike Lane," *Bicycle Law*, December 28, 2009, www.bicyclelaw.com/hipsters-v-hasidim-over-brooklyn-bike-lane.
40. Kaitlin Cole, "Porn for Women, By Women: BUST's Crafty Lady Talks Smut," BUST, https://bust.com/general/8395-porn-for-women-made-by-women-busts-crafty-lady-talks-candy-rain-8395.html; Andy Campbell, "New Bedford Bike Protest Will Keep Cops Abreast," *Brooklyn Paper*, December 16, 2009, www.brooklynpaper.com/stories/32/50/32_50_ac_bedford_bike_lane_protest_update.html.
41. Schneider, "Hipsters v. Hasidim."
42. Farrell, "Cyclists Redraw the Lines"; "Brooklyn Waterfront Greenway: A Concept Plan"; John del Signore, "Bedford Bike Lane Hasn't Been Cheap," *Gothamist*, December 18, 2009, http://gothamist.com/2009/12/18/bedford_bike_lane_battle_hasnt_been.php.
43. See, for example, Glazek, "Hasids vs. Hipsters"; Nathaniel Popper, "Brooklyn's Bicycle Man Uses Two Wheels to Bring Hasids and Hipsters Together," *Forward*, August 26, 2009, https://forward.com/news/112918/brooklyn-s-bicycle-man-uses-two-wheels-to-bring; Idov, "Clash of the Bearded Ones."
44. John del Signore, "Bike Lane Battle Following Bloomberg to Copenhagen," *Gothamist*, December 10, 2009, http://gothamist.com/2009/12/10/bike_lane_battle_will_follow_bloomb.php.
45. Idov, "Clash of the Bearded Ones"; see also del Signore, "Bike Lane Battle Following Bloomberg." Regarding this purported gulf, Herzfeld declared, "The Hasids . . . actually hate the rabbis much, much, much more than I do."

The Hasids in the community are not the problem; they give me the thumbs up when I bike by, and even Hasidic women have told me they really approve what I'm doing."

46. Sharon Udasin, "Unkosher Wheels, Friendly Faces," *New York Jewish Week*, April 7, 2010, http://jewishweek.timesofisrael.com/unkosher-wheels-friendly-faces.

47. Popper, "Brooklyn's Bicycle Man."

48. Brian Ries, "Hasids and Bicyclists Debate Bedford Avenue Bike Lane," *NBC New York*, January 26, 2010, www.nbcnewyork.com/news/local/Hasids-and-Bicyclists-Debate-Bedford-Avenue-Bike-Lane-82659062.html; Ben Muessig, "Video: No Truce at Bedford Avenue Bike Lane Debate," *Gothamist*, January 26, 2010, http://gothamist.com/2010/01/26/no_truces_at_bedford_avenue_bike_la.php.

49. Ben Muessig, Mike McLaughlin, and Robert Voris, "Meet the *Other* Mayors of Brooklyn," *Brooklyn Paper*, August 27, 2009, www.brooklynpaper.com/stories/32/34/32_34_bm_other_mayors_of_ny_web.html.

50. The debate in Pete's Candy Store marked the end of the bike lane controversy in Williamsburg, but its impact continued to be felt in the neighborhood for years to come. Most importantly, in 2013 the Department of Transportation decided not to place any rental kiosks for its CitiBike bicycle-sharing program in the Hasidic enclave, in dramatic contrast with the surrounding neighborhoods. Not all of Williamsburg's Hasidim welcomed the city's decision, however, as was made clear on May 26, 2013, when a group calling itself Hasidim for Bikes, publicly announced its launch in Kave Shtiebel, www.kaveshtiebel.com/viewtopic.php?f=24&t=3903&start=75. Writing anonymously, the group's founders described themselves as "a new grassroots organization" established "after the city placed bikes in Brooklyn and left out Hasidic Williamsburg because people had informed them that we Hasidim don't want any bikes." It declared itself to be "a voice and shofar [ram's horn] for the simple masses, like you and me, who live in Hasidic neighborhoods and want to use a bike. . . . We will speak directly [to the mayor, other politicians, and the media] and leave out the *askunim* [activists], the 'middlemen' who do not listen to our needs regarding bikes." The group planned a website as well as an online presence on Twitter, Facebook, and Google, and requested small donations and help with writing and web design. On the group, see Seth Berkman, "In Hasidic Williamsburg, Not Everyone Is Against Citi Bike," *Forward*, May 31, 2013.

Chapter 10. New Williamsburg

1. Interview with the authors, July 2008.

2. JTA, "Ultra-Orthodox Jews Spread into Once-Black Brooklyn Neighborhoods," *Forward*, February 16, 2013.

3. "Heftiger kampeyn oystsubreyteren Vilyamsburger grenitsn in fulstn shvung," *Der Yid*, June 26, 2015.

4. Alison Gregor, "Bedford-Stuyvesant: Diverse and Changing," *New York Times*, July 9, 2014.

5. Kit R. Roane, "New Neighbors Pushing at the Edge: Brooklyn Hasidim Seek to Expand into a Black and Hispanic Area," *New York Times*, July 19, 1999: "Abe Stein, 51, an Orthodox Jew who has lived in Bedford-Stuyvesant for 20 years and has run a manufacturing business there for 16." Stein argued that "the unrest [about housing] was being caused by people 'who don't understand that the Hasidim are trying to live within the community.' "

6. Meisels, *Rebbe*, 394–395, 467–468. Though numerically concentrated on the north side of Flushing Avenue in Williamsburg, over the decades Hasidim continued to maintain numerous businesses (including wedding halls, matzah factories, kosher caterers) and schools in Bedford-Stuyvesant, including one of the Satmar Rebbe's preferred butchers and the Hasidic Beis Rochel school for girls; see Rabbi Hertz Frankel, *The Satmar Rebbe and His English Principal* (New York: Menucha, 2015), 44–48, 66–79, 159; James C. McKinley, "Blaze at School May Be Arson, Firefighters Say," *New York Times*, May 5, 1991; Poll, *Hasidic Community of Williamsburg*, 98, 203–204; Meisels, *Rebbe*, 404; Frankel, *Satmar Rebbe*, 66–79.

7. Douglas Martin, "About New York: First Problem Is Homelessness, 2d Is Denial," *New York Times*, September 29, 1990.

8. Interview by the authors, December 22, 2013.

9. Jay-Z, *Decoded* (New York: Spiegel and Grau, 2010), 176.

10. Kranzler, *Hasidic Williamsburg*, 26.

11. Lisa Riordan Seville, "Hasidic Neighborhood in South Williamsburg Is Top Beneficiary of Section 8, but Some Question Whether Law Is Strictly Followed," *New York Daily News*, May 17, 2016.

12. Williamsburg v. Giuliani, 223 A.D.2d 64 (N.Y. Sup. Ct. 1996), www.leagle.com/decision/1996287223AD2d64_1277/WILLIAMSBURG%20v.%20GIULIANI.

13. Joe Sexton, "New Housing Is Approved for Brooklyn," *New York Times*, June 8, 1997; see also Marwell, *Bargaining for Brooklyn*, 82.

14. Bob Liff, "W'Burg Zoning Plan Faces Test," *New York Daily News*, October 16, 1997.

15. *Der Yid*, October 15, 1997, 18.

16. Liff, "W'Burg Zoning Plan Faces Test."

17. James Bradley, "Zoning Bout," *City Limits*, March 1, 2000, https://citylimits.org/2000/03/01/zoning-bout.

18. Ibid.

19. Ibid.

20. Seville, "Hasidic Neighborhood in South Williamsburg."

21. Marwell, *Bargaining for Brooklyn*, 87.

22. Ibid.

23. Ibid., 85–87; Seville, "Hasidic Neighborhood in South Williamsburg."

24. Bradley, "Zoning Bout."
25. Ibid.
26. Seville, "Hasidic Neighborhood in South Williamsburg."
27. Frank McCourt, *Angela's Ashes* (New York: Scribner, 1996), 29.
28. Freeman, *There Goes the 'Hood*, 37–38.
29. Ibid., 35; see also Mintz, *Hasidic People*, 249.
30. L. Freeman, *There Goes the 'Hood*, 48.
31. Ibid., 40.
32. Amy Waldman, "Hasidic Pioneers Set Forth from Williamsburg to Seek Space Across a New Frontier," *New York Times*, August 10, 1997.
33. Indeed, for this reason some Hasidim refused to say the name "Satmar," for fear that they would be invoking Saint Mary and instead pronounced it "Saktmar."
34. Waldman, "Hasidic Pioneers Set Forth."
35. Ibid. Within a year of moving in, however, the honeymoon appeared to be over, and Hasidic residents circulated a petition citing numerous problems with the building, including lack of heat and hot water; Erin St. John Kelley, "Neighborhood Report: Clinton Hill; Hasidic Housing a Letdown," *New York Times*, April 12, 1998.
36. Liff, "W'Burg Zoning Plan Faces Test."
37. Roane, "New Neighbors Pushing at the Edge."
38. Ibid.
39. Stephen Witt, "Proposed Sanitation Garage Site Becomes Parking Lot for Satmar Jewish Sect," *Our Time Press*, April 24–30, 2014, 3.
40. Stephen Witt, "African-American, Hasidic Jew Relationship in Bedford-Stuyvesant Contentious: Allegations of Preferential Treatment, Sexual Misconduct and Predatory Real Estate Practices Persist," *Our Time Press*, July 25, 2013.
41. See "Hasidic House in Bed-Stuy, Repeated Target of Harassment, Vandalized by Anti-Semitic Graffiti," *Vos Iz Neias*, January 4, 2016, https://vosizneias.com/2016/01/04/brooklyn-ny-hasidic-house-in-bed-stuy-repeated-target-of-harassment-vandalized-by-anti-semitic-graffiti.
42. Janet Upadhye, "Community Board Says Yeshiva Should Move to South Williamsburg," *DNAinfo*, June 20, 2014. www.dnainfo.com/new-york/20140620/clinton-hill/clinton-hill-yeshiva-has-operated-illegally-for-20-years-local-leaders-say.
43. Katherine Eustis and David Bryan, "Brooklyn A and Bed-Stuy Community Legal Services Collaborate to Help Homeowners in Crisis," *Brooklyn Legal Services Corporation A Newsletter*, Winter 2012, 2–3, https://bka.org/wp-content/uploads/2013/02/BKANewsletterWinter2012.pdf.
44. NYU Furman Center for Real Estate and Urban Policy, cited in Maya Pope-Chappell, "Bedford-Stuyvesant: Buyers Have Upper Hand," *Wall Street Journal*, September 4, 2010.

45. "Voices: Williamsburg, Esther Ungar."

46. Chart in *Ami Magazine*, October 5, 2014.

47. MNS Real Impact Real Estate, "Brooklyn Rental Market Report," October 2014, www.mns.com/pdf/brooklyn_market_report_oct_14.pdf.

48. Stephen Jacob Smith, "Weapons of Mass Construction: Satmars' Secret to Keeping Housing Prices Low," *Observer*, March 26, 2013, http://observer. com/2013/03/weapons-of-mass-construction-satmars-secret-to-keeping-housing-prices-low.

49. Maureen Callahan, "NY's Most Loathed Architect," *New York Post*, November 6, 2011, https://nypost.com/2011/11/06/nys-most-loathed-architect.

50. "For Jewish Hasidic Yeshiva Graduates: 'The Sky Is the Limit!,' " posted to YouTube by shiezoli, June 4, 2018, www.youtube.com/watch?v=bLSY5 byoYek.

51. Moyshe Kornfeld, "Alt Vilyamsburg a shefele arum genumen mit 70 velf," *Yidishe Velt*, April 16, 2012, posted at 12:09pm, www.ivelt.com/forum/view-topic.php?t=17115. Although one commenter responded that since many *artistn* live in New Williamsburg, this may have accounted for the higher rate of Internet usage, the discussion revealed that Old and New Williamsburg had become distinct areas, with their own reputations among Hasidim.

52. "A Little Bit About Sushi K Bar," Sushi K Bar, www.sushikbar.com/about. html.

53. Gan HaTeva, www.ganhateva.com (page no longer available).

54. Natalie Rinn, "Dissent over a Clown, a Magic Show, and 'Hangouts' in Hasidic Williamsburg," *Bedford + Bowery*, June 27, 2013, http://bedfordandbow ery.com/2013/06/dissent-over-a-clown-a-magic-show-and-hangouts-in-hasidic-williamsburg.

55. See, for example, the tours of Hasidic Williamsburg led by Frieda Vizel, who grew up in the Satmar village of Kiryas Joel (Discover Hasidic Brooklyn, https://friedavizel.com). The website is home to Vizel's blog, *Posts on Contemporary Hasidic Life*, in which she provides links to her own writings on the Hasidic community, numerous photos of Hasidic Williamsburg, and other materials that, in their own right, constitute an important archive of contemporary Hasidic culture and its representation.

56. United Jewish Organizations of Williamsburg and North Brooklyn, www. unitedjewish.org.

57. Gary Schlesinger, interview by the authors, 2009. ParCare Community Health Network, "About Us," www.parcarecenter.com/our-history. ParCare explained this process on its website:

> In the 1980s many small factories located in and around New York City and other metropolitan areas were closed either due to a lack of economies of scale making them less competitive than larger production facilities or as a cost cutting measure with manufacturing being transitioned out of the country.

As a result, many areas which were commercial/industrial in nature fell on hard times with factory spaces remaining vacant and deteriorating. . . . To combat this urban decay, in the mid-1980's the New York City Department of City Planning converted much of the zoning in this area from commercial and light industrial use to residential.

A second re-zoning took place in 2005 further expanding the residential development of the area. As a result, while many areas have seen downturns in building there has been a two decades long "building boom" focusing on these formerly industrial areas.

58. Ustrikover Rebbe, interview by the authors, December 6, 2013.
59. Interview by the authors, December 22, 2013.
60. *Di Tsaytung*, May 15, 2009, 16.
61. Post by Lipa, February 19, 2016.
62. David Pollock, "Williamsburg and the Hasidic Community," 2013, Berman Jewish Databank, available at Jewish Community Relations Council of New York, www.jcrcny.org/resources/elections-demographics/jewish-demographics.
63. Hasidim cannot identify themselves as such in the federal census. Moreover, religious identity is not a category that appears on the census, nor is "Jewish" included as a distinct racial or ethnic category. Thus, to quantify the presence of Hasidim in a particular federal census tract, it is necessary to employ proxies to identify them, such as the number of people identifying themselves as "white" in an area where very few if any non-Hasidic whites reside; families with large numbers of children; or the number of Yiddish speakers (in years in which it was possible to identify oneself as such).
64. "Parshas lekhlekha in di hayntike tsaytn," *Der Blatt*, October 19, 2007.
65. Aron Friedman, telephone interview by the authors, January 8, 2008.
66. Sam Weider, telephone interview by the authors, January 8, 2008.
67. The "core" census tracts were 509, 529, 533, 535, 539, 545, and 547. Two more tracts, 525 and 549, overlapped with the South Side, which not only had a large Latino population but also a growing number of white hipsters, making it more difficult to measure accurately the Hasidic presence.
68. Census tracts 507, 531, and 537.
69. In 2010, census tracts 237 and 239 were combined to form tract 1237.
70. Badger, "How Section 8 Became a Racial Slur."
71. Cindy Rodriguez, Jenny Ye, and the WNYC Data News Team, "Section 8 Housing: Poor but Not Impoverished in Hasidic Williamsburg" (audio), WNYC, May 17, 2016, www.wnyc.org/story/section-8-part-two; Seville, "Hasidic Neighborhood in South Williamsburg."
72. "Voices: Williamsburg, Esther Ungar."
73. Badger, "How Section 8 Became a Racial Slur"; Rodriguez, Ye, and the WNYC Data News Team, "Section 8 Housing."
74. Rodriguez, Ye, and the WNYC Data News Team, "Section 8 Housing."

75. New York City Housing Authority, "Section 8 Tenants: Frequently Asked Questions," www1.nyc.gov/assets/nycha/downloads/pdf/SECTION8.TEN ANTS.FAQ.pdf: "The portion of rent you pay to the owner cannot exceed 40% of your total household income. NYCHA will conduct a rent reasonableness evaluation to determine whether the proposed rent is reasonable compared to the rent for similar unsubsidized units in the area." U.S. Department of Housing and Urban Development, "Housing Choice Vouchers Fact Sheet," www.hud.gov/program_offices/public_indian_housing/programs /hcv/about/fact_sheet: "By law, whenever a family moves to a new unit where the rent exceeds the payment standard, the family may not pay more than 40 percent of its adjusted monthly income for rent."

76. Rodriguez, Ye, and the WNYC Data News Team, "Section 8 Housing."

77. "The View from Williamsburg," *Ami*, October 5, 2014. Another article in the same edition entitled "Desperately Seeking a Place to Call Home: A Housing Market Gone Mad," showed that in some ways young Hasidim faced the same problems as the young urban professionals with whom they competed for housing: "Whereas five years ago certain neighborhoods in Boro Park and Williamsburg [i.e., New Williamsburg] were considered the 'new frontier' and prices there were still relatively affordable, those days are gone.... People are now vying to move into these communities, as they are now the 'in' places for the younger generation. And while the houses might still be cheaper than the older, established blocks, the difference isn't great, and they remain well out of reach for most people, let alone those trying to get by on a weekly paycheck."

78. Meg Kelly, "Why Is the Broadway Triangle Still Empty?," Urban Omnibus, August 15, 2012, https://urbanomnibus.net/2012/08/why-is-the-broadway-triangle-still-empty.

79. City Planning Commission, October 19 / Calendar No. 7, C 090415 HUK, www1.nyc.gov/assets/planning/download/pdf/about/cpc/090415.pdf.

80. Broadway Triangle Community Coalition, et al. v. Michael Bloomberg, et al. (N.Y. Sup. Ct. 2010), Plaintiffs' Post-Hearing Brief in Support of Motion for Preliminary Injunction, 4, www.nyclu.org/sites/default/files/Broadway% 20Triangle%20Plaintiffs%27%20Post%20Hearing%20Brief.pdf.

81. Ibid., 11.

82. Broadway Triangle Community Coalition, et al. against Michael Bloomberg, et al. (N.Y. Sup. Ct. 2011), order granting preliminary injunction, December 23, 2011, www.nyclu.org/sites/default/files/releases/Broadway_Injunction_Decision_1.4.12.pdf. See also *Broadway Triangle Community Coalition*, 2010 N.Y. Slip Op. 31258 (N.Y. Sup. Ct. 2010), preliminary order dated May 20, 2010. For reactions from the local Hispanic community to the decision, see Annie Correal, "Celebran paralización de construcción en Brooklyn," *El Diario*, January 11, 2012.

83. Liz Robbins, "Judge Cites Bias in Halting Brooklyn Development Plan," *City Room* (blog), *New York Times*, January 5, 2012, https://cityroom.blogs.nytimes.com/2012/01/05/judge-halts-plans-for-a-development-in-brooklyn.

84. Gwynne Hogan, "Massive Complex Slated for Controversial Broadway Triangle, Filings Show," *DNAinfo*, August 31, 2106, www.dnainfo.com/new-york/20160831/williamsburg/massive-complex-slated-for-controversial-broadway-triangle-filings-show.

85. Ari Feldman, "Housing War Pits Ultra-Orthodox Against Latinos in 'Last Corner' of Booming Brooklyn," *Forward*, July 7, 2017.

86. Erin Durkin, "City to Build 375 Affordable Apartments at Brooklyn's Broadway Triangle After Settling Discrimination Case," *New York Daily News*, December 4, 2017.

87. David Colon, "Activists File Suit to Overturn Pfizer Rezoning in Brooklyn," *Curbed New York*, March 20, 2018, https://ny.curbed.com/2018/3/20/17143462/brooklyn-rezoning-pfizer-broadway-triangle-lawsuit.

88. Eddie Small, "Judge Dismisses Discrimination Suit over Rabsky's Broadway Triangle Development," *Real Deal*, July 30, 2018, https://therealdeal.com/2018/07/30/judge-dismisses-discrimination-suit-over-rabskys-broadway-triangle-development.

89. Magnusson Architecture and Planning, "MAP Is Part of the Winning Proposal for the Broadway Triangle RFP" (press release), March 19, 2019, www.maparchitects.com/news/map-is-part-of-the-winning-proposal-for-the-broadway-triangle-rfp.

90. UJO of Williamsburg, March 19, 2019, 8:43 a.m., https://twitter.com/UnitedJewish/status/1108031296549388288.

Conclusion

1. "Rapidly Gentrifying Crown Heights Becoming Unaffordable," Crown-Heights.info, August 6, 2013, https://crownheights.info/crown-heights-news/396927/rapidly-gentrifying-crown-heights-becoming-unaffordable.

2. See Ezra Mendelsohn, ed., *People of the City: Jews and the Urban Challenge* (New York: Oxford University Press, 2000).

3. "Is Moving Out the Answer?," *Ami*, October 5, 2014.

4. "The Exodus . . . in Numbers," *Ami*, November 22, 2017, 24. For example, according to data provided by the New York State Education Department, between the 2015–2016 and 2016–2017 school years, the number of students enrolled in Jewish schools (most of them Hasidic) in Brooklyn rose by only 53 students (0.06 percent), whereas in Rockland County it increased by 1,132 students (4.56 percent). Nevertheless, the overall enrollment in Jewish schools in Brooklyn remained an astounding 82,534 in 2016–2017, compared with 25,971 in Rockland County. For some perspective on the relative size of the enrollment in these schools, the public school district of Buffalo, the second most populous city in New York, had 31,398 students in 2016–2017.

5. Yossi Krausz, "The Exodus: Those Left Behind," *Ami*, September 20, 2018, 120–130.

6. In this regard, it is no accident that a prominent advertisement for the real estate firm Lakewood Homebuyer accompanied the article by Krausz in *Ami* (September 20, 2018), appealing to readers "looking for a house in Lakewood, Jackson or Toms River [New Jersey]."
7. On this broader trend, see Sabrina Tavernise and Sarah Mervosh, "America's Biggest Cities Were Already Losing Their Allure. What Happens Next?," *New York Times*, April 19, 2020.
8. Joseph Berger, "Uneasy Welcome as Ultra-Orthodox Jews Extend Beyond New York," *New York Times*, August 2, 2017.
9. See, for example, Rebecca Liebson, "Uproar over Anti-Semitic Video Produced by Republicans in N.Y. County," *New York Times*, August 29, 2019.
10. Liam Stack, "'Most Visible Jews' Fear Being Targets as Anti-Semitism Rises," *New York Times*, February 17, 2020: "Jewish people were the victims in more than half of the 428 hate crimes in New York City last year, with many of the crimes committed in heavily Orthodox neighborhoods, according to the Police Department. . . . Most of the anti-Semitic incidents in New York have not been perpetrated by jihadists or far-right extremists, but by young African-American men."
11. For the most thorough examination of these attacks, see Jane Coaston, "The Conspiracy Theories Behind the Anti-Semitic Violence in New York: How Anti-Semitic Myths and Victim Blaming are Putting Orthodox Jews in New York at Risk," *Vox*, January 3, 2020, www.vox.com/2020/1/3/21039446/anti-semitism-anti-orthodox-farrakhan-conspiracy-theories-bipartisan; see also the excellent coverage by Ari Feldman, including, "Crown Heights Jews Feel 'Invisible' as Anti-Semitic Attacks Persist," *Forward*, February 5, 2019, https://forward.com/news/national/418626/anti-semitic-attack-brooklyn-hasidic-chabad; Feldman, "Six Nights of Hanukkah, Seven Anti-Semitic Incidents in New York City," *Forward*, December 27, 2019, https://forward.com/news/national/437346/anti-semitic-attacks-nyc-brooklyn.
12. Stack, "Most Visible Jews."
13. The following is only a small sample of the extensive media coverage of the miniseries: Rachel Syme, "'Unorthodox,' Reviewed: A Remarkable Young Woman's Remarkable Flight from Hasidic Williamsburg," *New Yorker*, April 9, 2020; Brigid Delaney "Unorthodox: A Thrilling Story of Rebellion and Freedom from New York to Berlin," *Guardian*, April 19, 2020; Rebecca Davison, "Twitter Goes Wild for Unorthodox Star Amit Rahav, 24, After Shooting Fame as Esty's Troubled Husband Yanky Shapiro in Netflix Series," *Daily Mail*, April 15, 2020, www.dailymail.co.uk/tvshowbiz/article-8220583/Twitter-goes-wild-Unorthodox-star-Amit-Rahav-Yanky-Shapiro.html; Morgan Smith, "The Real Life Story Behind Netflix's *Unorthodox*, About a Woman Who Flees Her Hasidic Community," *People*, April 17, 2020, https://people.com/tv/the-real-life-story-behind-netflix-unorthodox.

14. In addition to Deborah Feldman, *Unorthodox: The Scandalous Rejection of My Hasidic Roots* (New York: Simon and Schuster, 2012), some of these books include Judy Brown, *This Is Not a Love Story: A Memoir* (New York: Back Bay, 2015); Shulem Deen, *All Who Go Do Not Return: A Memoir* (New York: Graywolf, 2015); and Leah Vincent, *Cut Me Loose: Sin and Salvation After My Ultra-Orthodox Girlhood* (New York: Talese, 2014). On the phenomenon, see Tova Ross Cohen, "How Ex-Frum Memoirs Became New York Publishing's Hottest New Trend," *Tablet*, January 6, 2014, www.tabletmag.com/jewish-arts-and-culture/books/158130/ex-frum-memoirs.

15. See, for instance, the Yiddish-language feature films *Félix & Meira* (dir. Maxim Giroux, 2014) and *Menashe* (dir. Joshua Weinstein, 2017), as well as the documentary film *One of Us* (dir. Heidi Ewing and Rachel Grady, 2017), about ex-Hasidim; the directors previously made the documentary *Jesus Camp* (2006), about the evangelical movement. For a recent study of Hasidim in film, see Shaina Hammerman, *Silver Screen, Hasidic Jews: The Story of an Image* (Bloomington: Indiana University Press, 2018).

16. One striking example of this was the dramatic increase in Hasidic entrepreneurs, including many women, who conduct their businesses through Amazon; see Joseph Berger, "How Amazon Has Transformed the Hasidic Economy," *New York Times*, October 16, 2019, and Leticia Miranda, "America's Orthodox Jews Are Selling a Ton of the Products You Buy on Amazon," *BuzzFeed News*, September 4, 2019, www.buzzfeednews.com/article/leticiamiranda/amazon-orthodox-jews.

17. For example, *Der Veker* published a probing interview in English with the directors of the documentary *One of Us*, as well as interviews in Yiddish with Rachel Grady, co-director of the film, and Ari Hershkowitz, one of the film's ex-Hasidic subjects; see http://derveker.com/2018/01/25/three-of-us and *Der Veker*, February–March 2018. On the emergence of Hasidic news media in Yiddish, see Rose Waldman, "New York's Yiddish Press Is Thriving," *Tablet*, December 3, 2018, www.tabletmag.com/sections/news/articles/new-yorks-yiddish-press-is-thriving: "Perhaps nothing demonstrates the evolution of Hasidic Yiddish print as well as the relatively new publication, *Der Veker* . . . a quarterly established and run by Hasidim from different sects. . . . In their own words, the publication 'does not shy away from controversial topics and discussing challenges that the community currently faces.' Their goal is to be a platform that takes an unbiased stance. . . . Additionally, *Der Veker* encourages writing as an art form, featuring works of fiction and poetry in their pages."

18. See, for example, Frieda Vizel, "(sorta) live-tweeting watching Unorthodox," *Posts on Contemporary Hasidic Life*, March 28, 2020, https://friedavizel.com/2020/03/28/sorta-live-tweeting-watching-unorthodox; Vizel, "I Left the Satmar Hasidic Community. 'Unorthodox' Is a Grossly Inaccurate Depiction of that World," *Forward*, March 31, 2020, https://forward.com/life/442798/i-left-the-satmar-hasidic-community-unorthodox-is-a-grossly-inaccurate; Frimet

Goldberger, "Ex-Hasid: Why My Former Community Makes for Such Compelling Television," CNN.com, April 16, 2020, www.cnn.com/2020/04/16/opinions/unorthodox-shtisel-compelling-hasidim-depictions-goldberger/index.html; Naomi Seidman, "Telling the OTD Tale; or, My Scandalous Rejection of Unorthodox," *Jewish Review of Books*, May 3, 2020.

19. Liam Stack, " 'Plague on a Biblical Scale': Hasidic Families Hit Hard by Virus," *New York Times*, April 1, 2020.

20. For example, zip code 10024, roughly from 77th Street to 91st in Manhattan, had among the lowest positive rates in the city (14 percent), while zip code 11211, which includes the heart of Hasidic Williamsburg, had an infection rate more than twice as high (30.8 percent). See NYC Health, "COVID-19: Data," www1.nyc.gov/site/doh/covid/covid-19-data-testing.page.

21. Most notably, following a large Hasidic funeral procession in the neighborhood, Mayor Bill de Blasio posted a tweet criticizing what "happened in Williamsburg" as "absolutely unacceptable," followed by a second tweet a few minutes later directed to "the Jewish community, and all communities," warning that future infractions would result in "summons or even arrest . . . This is about stopping the disease and saving lives. Period"; see Mayor Bill de Blasio@NYC Mayor, April 28, 2020, 6:29pm, https://twitter.com/nyc-mayor/status/1255308172178358273?lang=en; Mayor Bill de Blasio@NYC Mayor, April 28, 2020, 6:35pm, https://twitter.com/nycmayor/status/125530 9615883063297?lang=en. De Blasio's tweets prompted a public apology from the Williamsburg synagogue that had organized the funeral, as well as criticism that the mayor was unfairly casting blame on the entire Jewish community while ignoring similar social-distancing infractions elsewhere in the city. Within Hasidic Williamsburg, many residents were frustrated at the lack of caution displayed by the funeral goers, even as some complained that the city had sent mixed messages regarding safety protocols; see, for example, "Williamsburg: Brooklyn Synagogue Apologizes for Crowd at Rabbi Funeral; De Blasio Bashed for Tweets," NBC New York, April 29, 2020 (updated April 30, 2020), www.nbcnewyork.com/news/local/mayor-de-blasio-nypd-break-up-williamsburg-streets-packed-for-brooklyn-rabbi-funeral/2394306/: "A spokesman for the Orthodox community, Isaac Abraham, claimed that the city knew about the funeral and that as many as five police precincts were involved in putting up barricades to accommodate it. Abraham says the crowd was given an hour to mourn and that there were patrols handing out masks. 'He's a lying s.o.b.,' he said. 'When you say don't kick your friend when he's down, he kicked us twice.' "

22. Liam Stack, "Hasidic Jews, Hit Hard by the Outbreak, Flock to Donate Plasma," *New York Times*, May 12, 2020.

23. Shira Hanau, "NY Ultra-Orthodox Are Acting Like They Have Herd Immunity. Could They Be Right?," Jewish Telegraphic Agency, July 8, 2020, www.jta.org/2020/07/08/health/brooklyns-hasidic-jews-are-acting-like-they-have-herd-immunity-could-they-be-right; Joseph Goldstein, "68%

Have Antibodies in This Clinic. Can a Neighborhood Beat a Next Wave?," *New York Times*, July 9, 2020; Apoorva Mandavilli, "What if 'Herd Immunity' Is Closer Than Scientists Thought?," *New York Times*, August 17, 2020. The article was accompanied by a photo of a group of Hasidic women and children standing on a Brooklyn street corner.

24. Liam Stock and Joseph Goldstein, "How a Virus Surge Among Orthodox Jews Became a Crisis for New York," *New York Times*, October 8, 2020; Ari Feldman, Avital Chizhik-Goldschmidt, and Helen Chernikoff, "In Borough Park, an Anti-Shutdown Protest Turns into a Pro-Trump Rally—and a Journalist Is Assaulted," *Forward*, October 7, 2020, https://forward.com/news/456003/heshy-tischler-borough-park-coronavirus-rules-orthodox-jews. Some of the protesters in Borough Park carried flags supporting Donald Trump's reelection. On the popularity of Trump among many Haredi voters, including Hasidim, see Nathaniel Deutsch, " 'Borough Park Was a Red State': Trump and the Haredi Vote," *Jewish Social Studies* 22, no. 3 (Spring–Summer 2017): 158–173.

25. Jerome Mintz to Margaret Mead, February 18, 1960, box 27, "Correspondence" folder, Papers of Jerome R. Mintz, National Anthropological Archives, Smithsonian Institution, Suitland, Maryland. Mintz contacted Mead because of her role in the publication of *Life Is with People: The Jewish Little-Town in Eastern Europe* (in later editions, *The Culture of the Shtetl*), which belonged to the Columbia University Research in Contemporary Cultures project, headed by Mead and Ruth Benedict.

Index

Abraham, Isaac, 130, 244, 261, 266, 267–268

Agudas Yisroel, 170, 174, 249

Aid to Families with Dependent Children, 148

All Year Management, 216, 217

Allon, Devora, 239

American Jewish Committee (AJC), 239

Anasi, Robert, 142–143

Anazagasti, Robert, 79

anti-gentrification groups, 193–195

anti-Semitism, 75, 90, 91, 95, 100, 110, 119, 121, 122, 167, 176–177, 194, 195, 221, 258–259, 301, 302, 305, 341n84, 349n66, 376n10

apocalypticism, 162, 163

Arev, Assi, 161

Arriba Juntos (Upward Together), 70–71

artistn, 164–165, 167, 169–173, 174, 192, 372n51; attitudes toward, 230–231; war against, 177–182, 196–197, 223–228

artist's colonies, 139–144

Ashkenazi, Yosef, 61

Baal Shem Tov, 4, 20–21, 150

Badillo, Herman, 332n33

Bais Yaakov school, 33, 50, 53

Baldrige, Malcolm, 96–97

baseball, 242–244, 361n50

Bautista, Jercy, 206–207

Beame, Abraham, 118, 122

Becket Fund for Religious Liberty, 240

Bedford Gardens, 274

Bedford-Stuyvesant, 66, 74–75, 79, 81, 101, 111, 118, 215, 222, 227, 235, 255, 273, 274–280, 283–286, 289, 291, 292, 299, 301, 303

Bedford-Stuyvesant Development and Service Corporation, 74

Bedford-Stuyvesant Restoration Corporation, 81

Beis Rochel school, 33, 135–136

Berger, Joseph, 233

Berkowitz, Joel, 112

Beth Sholom Congregation, 51

Bialik, Hayim Nachman, 104

bicycles and bike lanes, 255–272, 364n1, 367n26, 369n50; topless bike protest, 271–272

Binyan Dovid Yeshiva, 184

Black Panthers, 110, 111

Bloom, Nicholas Dagen, 43, 58

Bloomberg, Michael, 142, 252, 257, 268, 271

Bloomingburg, N.Y., 304

Bnei Yoel, 168